MEATHEAD

MEATHEAD

THE SCIENCE of GREAT BARBECUE and GRILLING

TEXT AND PHOTOGRAPHS BY MEATHEAD GOLDWYN

WITH GREG BLONDER, PH.D.

A Rux Martin Book

Houghton Mifflin Harcourt

Boston New York

For information about permission to reproduce selections from this book, write to trade.permissions@hmhco.com or to Permissions, Houghton Mifflin Harcourt Publishing Company, 3 Park Avenue, 19th Floor, New York, New York 10016.

www.hmhco.com

Library of Congress Cataloging-in-Publication Data
Names: Goldwyn, Meathead, author.
Title: Meathead : the science of great barbecue and grilling / text and photos by Meathead Goldwyn ; with Greg Blonder, Ph.D.
Other titles: Science of great barbecue and grilling
Description: Boston : A Rux Martin Book, Houghton Mifflin Harcourt, 2016.
Identifiers: LCCN 2015049143 (print) | LCCN 2015050718 (ebook) | ISBN 9780544018464 (hardback) | ISBN 9780544018501 (ebook)
Subjects: LCSH: Barbecuing. | BISAC: COOKING / Methods / Barbecue & Grilling. | COOKING / General. | LCGFT: Cookbooks.
Classification: LCC TX840.B3 G63 2016 (print) | LCC TX840.B3 (ebook) | DDC 641.7/6—dc23
LC record available at http://lccn.loc.gov/2015049143

Book design by Endpaper Studio
Illustrations by Lisa Kolek
Cover photo by John Boehm, jboehmphoto.com

Printed in the United States of America
DOW 10 9 8 7 6 5 4
4500607220

Additional photographs provided by Adrenaline Barbecue Company, page 89; Backwoods Smoker, Inc., page 91; Camp Chef, page 92; Flame Engineering, Inc., page 130 left; Greg Blonder, pages 271, 278; GrillGrate, pages 101 left, 107 bottom; John Boehm, pages 235, 237, 238, 239; La Caja China, page 95; Lang BBQ Smokers, page 90; Looft Industries, page 129 top; MAK Grills, page 93, page 110 top left; Maverick Housewares, page 97 top and bottom; Mo's Food Products, LLC, page 111 right; Pit Barrel Cooker, page 87 right; Primo Ceramic Grills, page 88; Smokenator, page 110 bottom right; Mary L. Tortorello, page 125; Theresa Tortorello, page 183; Weber-Stephen Products, LLC, pages 87 left, 100, 101 bottom right, 103, 128

To Lou, my wife of forty-one years, a Ph.D. microbiologist and food safety expert, who loves food and cooking as much as I do. She fearlessly eats my experiments (well, most of them), offers honest feedback (*brutally* honest), and has the patience of a pitmaster (most of the time). She is still the better cook.

CONTENTS

Foreword

This is the book barbecue nerds have been waiting for. Myth and lore abounds in the world of cooking, and nowhere more so than in the primal arena that exists when humans put open fire and meat together in the great outdoors (or suburban backyard, as the case may be). That's good news for anyone who, like me, longs to understand the science of grilling and barbecue; the thermodynamics of heat transfer under that kettle dome, the chemistry of the smoke ring, and what makes a char-grilled steak so g*&@%# delicious.

Meathead's gift lies not just in factual accuracy, but also in being able to distill complex subjects to their most essential, applicable core in a manner that is a genuine pleasure to read. You'll laugh out loud at his metaphors. A good technical writer will leave you feeling like you know more than when you started. A great one can leave you feeling like more than a passive bystander. It'll make you feel like an active participant, like you've been on a voyage of discovery for yourself. Flipping over each page to discover what lies on the next will remind you of the very first time you peeked under the cover of your grill and breathed in the alchemy that occurs between smoke and meat. You'll see conventions challenged, techniques elucidated, and myths busted, and you'll have a wildly fun time in the process.

With hundreds of pages on techniques, theory, equipment, and background science before you even get to the recipes, this is a book that is squarely aimed at cooks who don't just want a single good rack of ribs coming off their grill, but who want to understand what makes them good and how to repeat it time after time. Soak in enough of the background technique and you won't even need a recipe. You have all the tools you need to develop your own. I love to grill but I'm no barbecue guru. After reading *Meathead*, I'm gonna be pretty darned good at faking it though.

— **J. Kenji López-Alt,**
Author of *The Food Lab*

Welcome

Recipe writers hate to write about heat. They despise it. Because there aren't proper words for communicating what should be done with it. —ALTON BROWN

This is the way I think we got here: Millions of years ago a hunting party of hominids stumbled upon the charred carcass of an animal after a forest fire. The smell and taste were ethereal, and the next beast they speared went right into their campfire. And thus began the struggle to master fire, heat, smoke, and meat.

The cooked meat must have seemed miraculous to them because they knew nothing about the components of smoke; the differences between convection, conduction, and radiation; the power of infrared energy; the Maillard reaction; the conversion of collagen to gelatin; the caramelization of sugar; and the isoelectric properties of salt.

And, sadly, neither do most modern backyard cooks, who throw meals into the sacrificial pyre and are doomed to serve carbon-coated chicken wings and hockey-puck hamburgers. Many of us are cavemen in a digital age.

But barbecue and grilling are not magic. Every recipe we cook is a physics and chemistry experiment. Outdoor cooking, though, is a lot harder than indoor cooking. Very few outdoor ovens have a thermostat to control temperature (and a grill is really a crude oven), and just when you think you know how to make the perfect steak, cold air, wind, and rain embarrass you by cooling your fire and food and screwing everything up. And then there's smoke, the ephemeral spice that can go from aphrodisiac to ashtray if you don't know what you are doing.

We all have painful memories of epic failures, but they are avoidable. Understanding is the first step in mastery. This book explains the science of barbecuing and grilling in lay terms. Along the way, I use science to filter the hogwash, bust the myths, and take down the old husbands' tales and canards passed along by pitmasters whose rituals have gone largely untested since that first forest fire.

For help, I consulted several scientists, chief among them Professor Greg Blonder, Ph.D., of Boston University. A physicist, he conducted original experimental research for this book and the barbecue website I founded, AmazingRibs.com. With his input and that of others, I'll share techniques guaranteed to improve your cooking.

Three core concepts alone can elevate your food from the ordinary: two-zone set-up, reverse sear, and the use of digital thermometers. Master them and someday your children will tell their children, "Here's how Dad taught me to grill a steak." And thus you will achieve immortality.

TECHNIQUE. My motto is "Give a man a fish, and he'll probably get it stuck to his grill. Teach a man to grill, and he'll become a big fish among his family and friends." With this book, you will learn how to keep fish fillets from sticking to the grill; how to make your own rubs that taste much better and cost far less than store-bought; and how to amp up tomato sauce by grilling the tomatoes. You'll also learn that cooking time depends on the thickness of the food, not its weight; why you shouldn't soak wood for smoking; why sticking a beer can up a chicken's butt is a waste of good beer; why rubs should not have salt in them; and that you shouldn't bring cold meat to room temperature before cooking because cold meat attracts smoke better. Do you know why you should avoid making grill marks on your steaks? And that resting meat after cooking can do more harm than good?

If you are skeptical, that's all the more reason to read this book.

HARDWARE. Whether you are shopping for your first grill or your yard has enough steel to build a battleship, I think you'll find the equipment recommendations useful and at times surprising. They were compiled with the help of my associate Max Good, whose full-time job is kicking the tires of grills and smokers.

RECIPES. More than 100 recipes help you put all this knowledge to work. Of course, I have included the traditional all-American barbecue canon of pork ribs, pulled pork, beef brisket, whole hog, and chicken wings, tweaked with the latest science. I have also added creative recipes outside the box, like Japanese Happy Mouth Yakitori Ribs, Italian Suckling Porchetta, Hawaiian Huli-Huli Teriyaki Chicken, and Chocolate Chile Barbecue Sauce.

STAY IN TOUCH

If I make any new discoveries or find any errors in this book I will notify subscribers to my free email newsletter, Smoke Signals. You can subscribe on any page of Amazing Ribs.com. You can also post comments and questions there. My moderators and I usually answer queries within hours. I also post a tip every day on Twitter (@ribguy) and Facebook (facebook.com/AmazingRibs).

You can achieve greatness with these recipes, but I hope you will also create your own outstanding dishes with the techniques you learn. Remember, almost anything you can cook indoors can be cooked outdoors, only better. All it takes is the four *P*s: practice, patience, persistence, and a knowledge of key cooking principles. So come on out! The backyard gate is open. Get fired up, strap on an apron, and grab some tongs, a thermometer, and a wad of napkins.

Just one warning: There is a hazard. If you get good at this—and you will, because it is not hard—whenever there is a Little League fundraiser, a graduation, a farewell party at work, or a church picnic, someone will make a request slathered in flattery. Would you mind bringing some of your famous pulled pork or amazing ribs? Could you grill the chicken or smoke the turkey? And you will not be able to say no.

1

The SCIENCE *of* HEAT

You may have thought you left physics and chemistry behind when you left school, but if you want to cook and eat well, understanding the physics and chemistry of cooking will help immensely. Here are some foundational concepts every outdoor cook needs to know.

Foods are composed mainly of water, protein, fat, and carbohydrates, with trace amounts of minerals and other compounds. Cooking is the process of changing the chemistry of food—usually by transferring energy in the form of heat—so that the food becomes safer to eat and more digestible, and to improve its flavor, texture, juiciness, appearance, and nutrition.

When you cook outdoors, heat is transferred to food in three different ways: conduction, convection, and radiation.

Conduction heat is when your lover's body is pressed against yours.

Conduction heat is when your lover's body is pressed against yours. This is when energy gets transferred to food by direct contact with the heat source. Think of cooking a hot dog in a frying pan. Heat from the burner is transferred to the pan. The molecules in the pan vibrate and pass the heat on to the wiener where it makes contact with the pan. As the surface of the meat gets hotter, the heat transfers to the center through the moisture and fats in the meat. That's also conduction. On a grill, the grill grates transfer energy by conduction.

Convection heat is when your lover blows in your ear.

Convection heat is when your lover blows in your ear. This is when energy is carried to food by air, water, or oil. If you boil a hot dog, you are cooking with convection heat. If you cook the hot dog in your kitchen oven, where it is surrounded by hot air, that's also convection cooking. A convection oven comes equipped with a fan to speed up the natural airflow, increasing the heat transfer and cooking many foods 25 to 30 percent faster than it would cook without the fan. If you put your hot dog on one side of your grill but only heat up the other side of the grill, that, too, is convection cooking, as the natural airflow inside the grill conveys heat to the wiener.

Radiant heat is when you feel the heat of your lover's body under the covers without touching.

You know the feeling of radiant heat. Radiant heat is when you feel the heat of your lover's body under the covers without touching. It's the heat on your skin from the sun or from a space

heater. Put a hot dog on a stick and hold it to the side of a campfire, and you are cooking by radiation.

THE MAGIC OF INFRARED (IR)

Infrared (IR) radiant heat delivers more energy more quickly than convection heat. Let's make believe we have two charcoal grills side by side. On one grill, the charcoal is pushed all to the right side. The air temperature on the left side is 325°F, as the convection flow of air from the right side circulates over the left side. Let's put a big turkey on the left side. In a couple of hours it will cook perfectly and absorb a lovely smoky flavor.

On the second grill, we have charcoal spread evenly across the bottom and the air temperature on both sides is also 325°F. Let's put a turkey on this grill, too. By the time the turkey is cooked to the proper temperature, it will be blacker than a mourning hat.

The air temperature of both ovens (remember, a grill is really just another kind of oven)

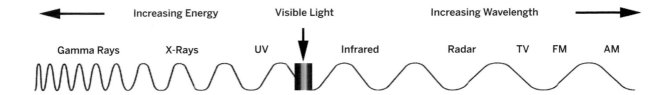

Increasing Energy · Visible Light · Increasing Wavelength

Gamma Rays · X-Rays · UV · Infrared · Radar · TV · FM · AM

was 325°F, but the IR radiant heat from below on the second grill, which can be over 1400°F, burned the bird.

Infrared waves are a part of the continuum of energy waves that surround us at all times, just up the road from visible light and down the road from radio waves.

Infrared waves pack a lot of heat energy, and they excel at creating the dark brown surfaces we crave on food. IR is the best way to deliver high heat to food. IR energy is delivered faster than convection but not as fast as conduction. In the past few years, gas grill manufacturers have added special burners that emit concentrated infrared. They are sometimes called infrared burners, IR burners, sear burners, or sizzle zones, and they are great for getting a good dark sear on steaks and crisping poultry skin. But as with the turkey, sometimes you don't want IR.

THE DIFFERENCE BETWEEN HEAT AND TEMPERATURE

Heat, in the form of energy, not temperature, cooks food. Convection, radiation, and conduction all deliver energy, but in different quantities. Fire up your grill to 225°F. Open the lid, stick your hand in the warm air, and count how long you can hold your hand in there. Most people can handle more than a minute. Place your

hand on the cooking grate. After you get back from the hospital, contemplate the fact that even though the air and the grate were both 225°F, not everything that is the same temperature transfers energy at the same rate.

That's because steel has more molecules per cubic inch than air and stores 8,000 times more energy. That's what causes grill marks.

Temperature measures the average energy of each atom, while heat is the *total energy* for all atoms. It's like money. If the average income in the United States is $50,000 per family, the total income is in the trillions.

THE IMPACT OF DISTANCE

The distance from a radiant energy source is another important factor. Energy dissipates and spreads out as it moves away from the source. In an $800 kamado grill, the charcoal may be 18 inches from the cooking surface, while on a $100 Weber Kettle, the charcoal is 4 inches away, and on a $30 hibachi, the coals may be 1 inch away. A steak on a kamado's cooking surface will not brown as well as one on a Weber or a hibachi because the coals emitting IR heat are farther away.

HOW HEAT MOVES WITHIN MEAT

When we subject food to heat, energy is transferred to the exterior of the food. Once the energy excites the molecules on the surface of the food, they then transfer heat to the molecules inside by conduction, slowly passing the energy toward the center. In other words, on a grill, hot air cooks the outside of the meat, but the outside of the meat cooks the inside.

This means that cooked meat is not uniform in temperature. The surface may register up to 212°F (evaporation of moisture keeps it from getting a lot hotter), but the temperature will gradually decrease toward the center. While a hotter, well-seared exterior surface is often desirable, the trick is to get the interior to be close to the ideal temperature from top to bottom.

This takes time, because meat is about 70 percent water, and water is a good insulator and heat absorber, especially when trapped within muscle fibers and mixed with fat, an even better insulator. Physics dictates that the meat seek equilibrium in an effort to make the temperature the same from edge to edge, and so the heat moves inward.

On a grill, hot air cooks the outside of the meat, but the outside of the meat cooks the inside.

The points and corners of the meat also cook faster because heat can attack on multiple fronts. Bones heat at a different rate than the muscle tissue in a cut of meat because they are filled with air or fat, not water. In most cases, the bones warm more slowly than the rest of the meat.

CARRYOVER COOKING

After you take food off the heat, it may continue cooking for 20 minutes or more, even at room temperature, taking a perfect medium-rare roast to medium-well and ruining it. This phenomenon is called carryover cooking.

When we remove the meat from the heat, it goes on cooking because the energy stored in the outer layers of the meat continues to move toward the center.

1. ON THE GRILL OR SMOKER. In the left image below, we see a cross-section of a beef roast cooking at 325°F in convection air,

INSIDE A T-BONE

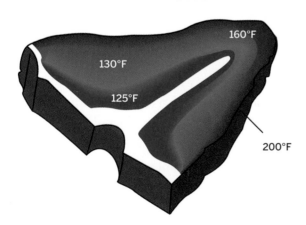

CARRYOVER COOKING

IN THE OVEN   10-MINUTE REST   20-MINUTE REST

absorbing heat from hot air on all sides. When the center hits 130°F, medium-rare, we remove it from the heat. The exterior has a nice dark brown crust and beneath it a band of brown meat, then tan, then pink, and finally a beautiful rosy cylinder.

2. 10-MINUTE REST. In the center image on page 5, the meat has been removed from the heat and rested for 10 minutes. Energy from the hot surface continues to be passed toward the center, slowly cooking the meat even though it is sitting at room temperature. The surrounding air is now cooler than the meat, so some of the heat escapes into the room and the exterior cools as energy moves away. The exterior remains dark brown and crusty on most sides, but gets soft on the bottom where it rests on the platter. The cylinder of meat in the center has now moved past medium-rare.

3. 20-MINUTE REST. In the right image on page 5, the meat has rested for 20 minutes. It has come close to an even temperature throughout, and now more heat is escaping than moving inward. The crust has cooled, the center has warmed, and the two are pretty much the same temperature, medium-well-done. Meanwhile, moisture from the inner layers has moved into the drier outer layers, softening the crust. The roast has approached equilibrium and is almost at the point at which you have to start apologizing to your guests for the overcooked meat.

HOW BOILING TEMPERATURES IMPACT COOKING

When liquid is heated, its temperature will increase until it hits the boiling point and not go any higher. So no matter how high we turn the burners under a pot of water, the water will not get hotter than 212°F (water boils at lower temperatures as you go up in altitude because the weight or "pressure" of the column of air on top of the water is lower, and it boils at slightly higher temperature if you add impurities like salt).

Steam can form at a lower temperature than 212°F, as molecules of water get hot and escape the surface of the warming water. That's why we see vapor escaping a pot of water before the water actually boils. As meat heats on a grill, some of the water on its surface escapes as steam. Even though the grill may be a lot hotter than 212°F, the meat's surface will idle along at about 212°F as water keeps steaming away.

MYTH **Plan on a 5 to 10°F carryover.**

BUSTED! There is no easy rule of thumb for calculating carryover. The thickness of the meat is a major factor in determining how much its temperature will rise in the carryover phase. Thick cuts hold more energy than thin cuts. High cooking temperatures pump more energy into the outer layer of the meat than low temperatures do, so cooking over high heat produces more carryover.

MYTH Meat needs to rest after cooking.

BUSTED! Many recipes tell you to let steaks and chops "rest" for 10 to 15 minutes—and roasts for up to 30 minutes—after cooking. We are told that if we rest meat it will be more juicy.

People who preach the importance of letting the meat rest say that if you cut into the meat when it is fresh off the heat, the juices pour out of the muscle fibers, which they think are like skinny water balloons. If you let meat rest and cool, they say, the pressure drops, the fibers relax, and fewer juices escape.

The pressure theory is a myth, says meat scientist Antonio Mata, Ph.D., because fibers are not like balloons. Water is not trapped in the fibers or the spaces between them, so the pressure equalizes quickly. And at relatively low meat temperatures, water does not expand much.

To test this theory, my colleague Professor Greg Blonder cooked two 13½-ounce ribeye steaks to 125°F. He cut one into strips immediately, rested the other for 30 minutes, and then cut it into strips. He collected the juices from the steaks and measured them. The steak that had not rested expelled about 6 teaspoons. The steak that had rested gave up 5 teaspoons—not much of a difference. Also, the meat temperature on the rested steak rose to 145°F from carryover cooking, well past medium-rare to medium-well. Naturally, the careful scientist repeated the experiment several times. Keep in mind, when we eat a steak, most of us cut into it one piece at a time; we don't slice it into strips.

And that juice isn't lost. We mop it up with the meat on our fork.

Professor Blonder then turned his attention to pork loin roasts. He cooked two large 33-ounce roasts, removing them when their internal temperature had reached 140°F. He let one sit for 3 minutes and then cut it into slices, collecting the juices released by the meat. He rested the other for 20 minutes before slicing, waited 5 minutes, collected the juices, and weighed them. The unrested meat released 3 ounces of juices, compared to 2 ounces from the rested meat, a difference of only 1 ounce.

Professor Blonder poured the 3 ounces of liquid from the unrested pork on top of the sliced meat. The meat drank up about 1 ounce of the juices, precisely the difference between the rested and unrested meat.

Resting meat has other disadvantages: making the crust or skin soft and wet, making the fat waxy, and causing overcooking. I say, serve meat hot. It will "rest" while we eat.

While the hotter molecules escape, the cooler ones are left behind, so the temperature of the meat plateaus as the surface dries out and forms a crust, or bark. At low cooking temperatures such as 225°F (the temperature I recommend for a lot of my recipes), the rate of evaporation can be so great that the meat cools as fast as it heats. In this case, the temperature of the meat in its center can get stuck—usually in the 150 to 165°F range—and remain pretty much unchanged for hours, driving the novice cook nuts. This phenomenon, called the stall, does not happen if the cooking temperature is higher, say, 325°F (another temperature I recommend frequently).

THE TWO-ZONE SETUP AND INDIRECT COOKING

Temperature control is the most important skill you can learn. That's why I recommend a two-zone setup in almost every situation. The most common grilling mistake is spreading

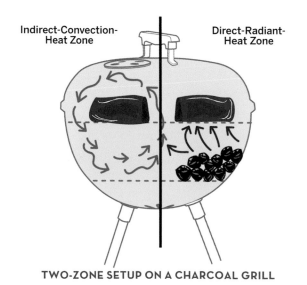

Indirect-Convection-Heat Zone   **Direct-Radiant-Heat Zone**

TWO-ZONE SETUP ON A CHARCOAL GRILL

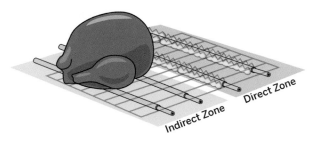

Indirect Zone   Direct Zone

coals across the bottom of the entire grill or turning on all our gas burners. That forces us to work quickly, flipping burgers and losing track of which went on first, rolling blackened hot dogs around, trying to tame flare-ups with a squirt gun, and sheepishly serving charred hockey pucks that are raw in the center.

A two-zone setup gives us better temperature control on both charcoal and gas grills. One side of the grill is hot and produces direct radiant heat, while the other side produces no heat. Food placed on that side cooks by indirect convection heat wafting over from the hot side. We'll call the hot side the direct-radiant-heat zone and the other the indirect-convection-heat zone.

USING A TWO-ZONE SETUP, WE CAN . . .

CONTROL THE HEAT. We can move food to the indirect zone, where it is bathed in gentle convection heat, to warm it slowly and evenly inside. We can also sear the heck out of it for a minute or two in the direct zone when we want a golden brown and delicious crust. That's how we win the day on the Fourth of July.

GENTLY SMOKE A BIG TURKEY in the indirect zone, evenly cooking all 18 pounds to juicy, tender perfection, and be the heroes of Thanksgiving.

SLOWLY BRING A PRIME RIB TO MEDIUM-RARE with no gray meat, get a perfectly crunchy crust, and become our mom's favorite on Mother's Day.

START CHICKENS OVER THE INDIRECT ZONE at a low temperature, cook them evenly throughout until they are almost done, then move them to the direct zone to crisp the skin, and bask in the glory at the church picnic.

MANAGE SEVERAL FOODS AT ONCE when the thickness and water content of each is significantly different, causing them to cook at different rates. Put baking potatoes in the indirect zone for an hour, add lobster for the last 20 minutes, and then, 10 minutes before dinner, sear asparagus over the direct zone for an incredible picnic on the beach.

PREVENT SWEET FOODS FROM BURNING. We can cook the most tender ribs with a sweet dry rub in the indirect zone and never burn a grain of sugar, and then move the ribs to the direct zone to caramelize the sauce to finger-licking goodness and prove to Dad you turned out all right.

WHEN TO PUT A LID ON IT

Most grills come with lids, thankfully. A lid is essential for most outdoor cooking with a few notable exceptions, chief among them searing meats. You can cook on a lidless grill, but you will be severely handicapped. It's like doing all your cooking on a stove top. On a grill, most of the heat and smoke comes from below, but much of it goes right past the food. The lid captures heat and smoke so your grill becomes a smoky oven that can cook foods with heat from all sides. In short, a lid gives you much more versatility.

You can cook on a lidless grill, but you will be severely handicapped.

As a rule of thumb, whether meat or vegetable, you want a dark, well-cooked crust and a tender, juicy center. If the food is ¾ inch thick or less, forgo the lid. If you were to close the lid, heat would attack from above and below, and the center would be done before you could get good color and flavor to both sides of the crust. For thin foods, crank up the heat, leave the lid off, and flip the meat every minute or so to prevent heat buildup on either side.

But if the food is thicker than ¾ inch, put a lid on it. The lid helps thick foods cook evenly and reduces your chances of an undercooked interior.

There is a middle ground: Sometimes you might want to wedge the lid open an inch or two to allow hot air to escape if you are having trouble getting the heat down to a target such as 225°F.

2

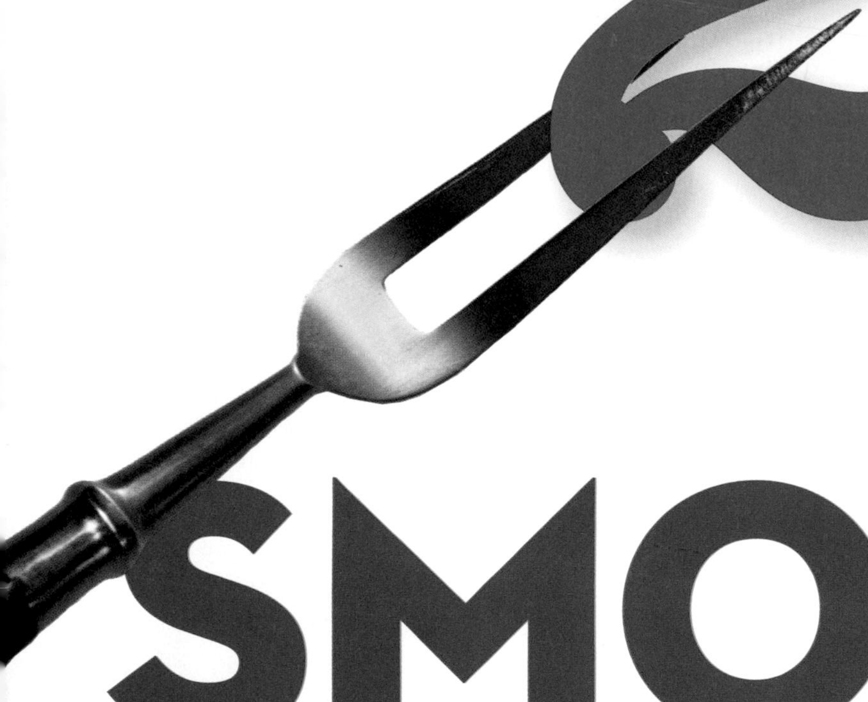

SMOKE

Smoke is the spice that is not on your spice rack. There are three sources of smoke in outdoor cooking: drippings, fuel, and wood.

Drippings of juices and fats, often laden with spices, vaporize when they hit hot surfaces, fly up, and land on the food, imparting aroma and flavor.

Fuel is the material that combusts to produce the heat. An electric grill produces no smoke or gases. A gas grill, when properly adjusted, produces water and carbon dioxide but no smoke. Charcoal is wood that has been preburned and converted to carbon. When it is just firing up it can produce a lot of billowing smoke, but when it is fully engaged and burning hot there is only a little smoke, unless the wood was not fully carbonized in the production process. Wood pellet cookers burn pure wood sawdust compressed into pellets and they produce wood smoke, more at lower combustion temperatures. Finally, there are logs, which produce the most complex and interesting aromas and flavors.

Wood smoke is the essence of barbecue. When we aren't burning logs as fuel, we can get wood smoke by throwing wood onto our grills and smokers, even if they use electricity or gas.

HOW SMOKE FLAVORS MEAT

Wood combustion starts to take place in the 500 to 600°F range and requires significant amounts of oxygen. The actual temperature depends on the type of wood, how dry it is, and other variables. Let's call the average combustion point 575°F for the sake of discussion. The heat of ignition drives water and flammable gases out of the wood, and many of them burn if there is enough oxygen. The combustion of these gases is what produces flame. If all the gases combine with the oxygen, the flame appears blue, as in a well-tuned gas grill, and there is no smoke. If the gases don't burn completely, the flame glows yellow or orange. If unburned gases escape, they cool and turn into part of the smoke.

Smoke is complicated stuff, and there are different types. Smoke from burning wood contains as many as one hundred compounds in the form of microscopic solids, including char, creosote, ash, polymers, water vapor, and phenols, as well as invisible combustion gases such as carbon monoxide, carbon dioxide, and nitrogen oxides. When these compounds come into contact with food, they can stick to the surface and flavor it. Most of the flavor comes from the combustion gases, not the particles, and the composition of the gases depends on the composition of the wood, the temperature of combustion, and the amount of available oxygen.

As smoke particles and combustion gases touch the surface of wet foods like meats, they dissolve, and some are moved just below the surface by diffusion and absorption.

Building up smoke flavor on the surface of food takes time. A thin skirt steak cooks in minutes, so it will take on less smoky flavor than a 2-inch-thick ribeye steak will. A ribeye will have a less smoky flavor than a 3-inch thick turkey breast, and a 4-inch thick beef brisket cooked low and slow for 12 hours will pick up a ton of smoke.

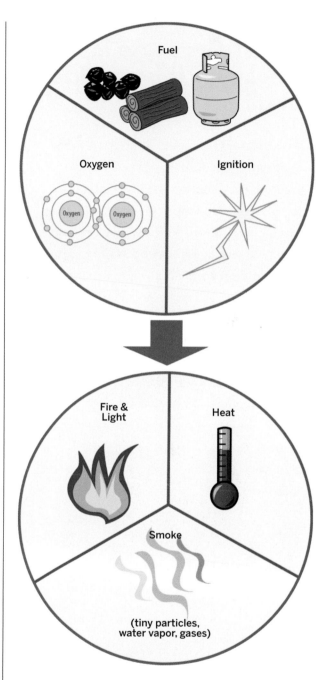

COMBUSTION INPUTS AND OUTPUTS

MYTH Creosote in smoke must be avoided at all costs.

BUSTED! Pitmasters think creosote is the boogeyman because they're confusing it with creosote from coal tar: the black stuff used to preserve telephone poles and railroad ties. Despite the similar name, coal-tar creosote is chemically distinct from wood-tar creosote.

Wood-tar creosote is always present in charcoal or wood smoke, and a few of its components—specifically guaiacol, syringol, and some phenols—are crucial contributors to smoke aroma, flavor, and color in foods. Without creosote, the meat might as well have been boiled.

Creosote is the Jekyll and Hyde of smoke cooking. On the Dr. Jekyll side, it contributes positively to the flavor and color of smoked foods and acts as a preservative (smoking meat was used for preservation before refrigeration). On the Mr. Hyde side, if the balance of chemicals in creosote shifts, it can taste bitter rather than smoky. The trick is getting the balance right.

When you smoke low and slow at temperatures like 225°F, many smokers require you to control the fire by damping the oxygen supply. This moves the fire below the ideal combustion zone, creating black smoke, soot, and bitter creosote. The best smokers combust at a high temperature to create the ideal flavor profile.

SMOKE AND FOOD

Think of smoke as a seasoning, like salt. Use too much, and you can ruin the meal.

In a smoker or grill, after combustion, the smoke rises and flows from the burn area into the cooking area. Some of it comes into contact with the food, but most goes right up the chimney and very little deposits on the food.

Around every object is a stagnant halo of air called the boundary layer. Depending on airflow and surface roughness, the boundary layer around a piece of meat might be a millimeter or two in thickness. When smoke particles approach the meat's surface, small ones follow the boundary layer. Only a few of the larger ones touch down. We've all encountered a similar phenomenon while driving: Gnats follow the airstream over the windshield, while larger insects leave sticky green splats at the point of impact.

To demonstrate the way smoke sticks to food, we did some experiments. We painted three empty beer cans white. We filled one can with ice water and left another empty, and both went into the smoker. The control sat on my desk. After 30 minutes, both cans in the cooker had smoke on the surface, but the colder can had a

Ice Water   Empty   Control

lot more. That's because cool surfaces attract smoke, a phenomenon called thermophoresis. Another factor was at play. The cold can also attracted water in the atmosphere and in the combustion gases, which condensed and ran down the can. Smoke particles stick better to wet surfaces.

Similarly, if meat is cold and wet, it will hold more smoke. As the meat warms and dries out, smoke bounces off. It's the same reason a cold mirror holds on to steam from a hot shower.

SMOKE FLAVOR IS ALMOST ALL ON THE SURFACE

Smoke particles glom on to the *surface* of foods. They may dissolve and penetrate a bit below the surface but rarely more than $\frac{1}{8}$ inch into the microscopic fissures and valleys of the meat, because their molecules are too large. Meats are especially hard to penetrate.

THE SMOKE RING

Smoked meats, like the brisket shown on page 17, often have a pink layer directly below the surface, nestled neatly under the crust. This is called the smoke ring. Alas, every year thousands of restaurant customers send back meat, especially chicken and turkey, claiming it is undercooked because it is pink. It is not undone. Smoke rings have long been emblems of authentic wood-smoked barbecue. Backyarders know they have arrived when they make their first smoke ring. Barbecue aficionados look for smoke rings to prove the meat was wood smoked.

4 SECRETS TO A SMOKE RING

No matter what cooker you use, the secrets to a great smoke ring are all related to moisture:

1. Maintain high humidity in the cooker to keep a moist surface on the meat that will attract smoke. A water pan helps.

2. Maintain a steady, low temperature of about 225°F to minimize drying on the surface of the meat.

3. Add water manually by basting or spritzing the meat. Spritzing with apple juice or vinegar is a popular method.

4. Start with cold meat. Water vapor will condense on the cold surface like it does on a beer can on a sultry July day.

MYTH The more smoke you see, the better.

BUSTED! Actually, the opposite is true. Billowing white smoke may mean there's a new pope, but the barely visible wisp of blue smoke is the holy grail to low-and-slow pitmasters.

If gas or charcoal is your fuel, start with less wood than you think is needed as you are learning your cooker. Very tight, efficient smokers like kamados will need much less wood than a gas grill that is heavily ventilated.

BUYING WOOD

The key to producing great-tasting smoke? Great wood. Hardwoods, fruitwoods, and nutwoods are the best woods for most types of cooking because they have compact cell structures and burn slowly and evenly. Steer clear of softwoods such as cypress, fir, hemlock, pine, redwood, spruce, and cedar. The wood from coniferous trees contains a lot of air and sap, which makes it burn fast, produce unpleasant flavors, and pop, crackle, and spark. Food cooked over some of these woods has been known to make people sick.

You want wood that's been properly dried. Fresh-cut wood has a lot of water in it—up to 50 percent by weight—so it produces a lot of steam as well as funky flavors and aromas during combustion. Even dried wood is rarely totally dry, with perhaps 5 to 20 percent water left, but some water is OK. Of the remaining mass, about 38 percent is cellulose (a type of carbohydrate), 38 percent is hemicelluloses (carbohydrates and sugars), 18 percent is lignin (a polymer that strengthens the wood and is responsible for most of the wood flavor and aroma), and 1 percent is minerals. The actual percentages will vary depending on how the wood was dried, the species and subspecies of the tree, its age, and the soil and climate in which it was grown. The minerals are especially important because they affect the smell and taste of the smoke.

Hardwoods, fruitwoods, and nutwoods are the best woods.

You may be able to scrounge decent wood from forests or orchards whose owners will let you gather dead trees, branches, and prunings. Just make sure you get clean wood, free of pesticides, mold, mildew, and rot, all of which could be toxic or impart off flavors to your food.

A local cabinetmaker or flooring installer will often have a wide range of scraps of kiln-dried, tight-grained chunks, chips, and sawdust. Choose hardwoods like oak, cherry, and maple. Make sure the wood is pure hardwood, untreated and unstained. If you thank your supplier with a slab of ribs now and then, you might get a lifetime supply of free wood.

The best method is to buy wood specifically intended for smoking. It is available in many forms: logs, chunks, chips, pellets, bricks, bisquettes, and sawdust.

MYTH **After an hour or two, meats stop taking on smoke.**

BUSTED! Meat does not have windows that shut as it cooks. If the surface of the meat is cold or wet, more of the smoke sticks. Usually, late in the cooking, the surface gets pretty dry, and when the coals are not producing a lot of smoke, we are fooled into thinking the meat is somehow saturated with smoke. Throw on a log for smoke and baste or spritz the meat, and the meat will start taking on smoke again. Just don't overbaste or aggressively spray, because in seconds you can wash off the smoke that took hours to build up.

MYTH A smoke ring is caused by billowing smoke.

BUSTED! You can actually make a smoke ring without smoke! Myoglobin, which is naturally reddish pink, often turns gray when heated. But some compounds can prevent myoglobin from changing color. Curing salts, which have nitrites and nitrates, make corned beef and hams permanently pink. In competitions, unscrupulous cooks have been known to sprinkle curing salts on meat to fake a smoke ring.

When smoking meats, invisible gases nitric oxide (NO) and carbon monoxide (CO) mix with wet meat juices and basting liquids and lock in the color of myoglobin. However, the dissolved gases cannot diffuse very far beyond the surface of the meat before the interior heats up. This dooms the myoglobin in the interior to its usual gray fate. As a result, pink smoke rings usually go only about $\frac{1}{8}$ to $\frac{1}{4}$ inch deep.

As the meat cooks, the surface of the meat begins to dry and less smoke sticks to the surface. That's why putting a pan of water in a smoker helps create a smoke ring by giving the gases more moisture to stick to. In fact, some smokers, called water smokers, have built-in water pans.

LOGS. Many small companies sell logs for fireplaces, usually by the cord or face cord. A cord is 128 cubic feet, or a neatly stacked pile about 4 feet high, 8 feet long, and 4 feet deep (usually cut into 2-foot lengths). A face cord is one third of a cord. You want a reputable dealer who can be trusted when he says the wood is apple, cherry, or whatever. You can buy smaller bundles in hardware stores, at campgrounds, and even in convenience stores, but you really can't be sure what is in the bundle, no matter what is on the label.

The wood should be dry, with a low percentage of bark. Wood is dried two ways: drying naturally outdoors for at least a year, or drying in an oven called a kiln. Kiln-dried wood is much more expensive. If you're buying freshly cut wood, you can dry it yourself. Try to store it off the ground (stacking it on old shipping pallets works well) and keep it under a cover that will protect it from rain and snow. The shorter the length of wood, the faster it dries. Properly stored, firewood can be kept for years.

CHUNKS. Wood chunks from golf ball to fist size are fairly easy to find in hardware stores. They burn slowly and steadily, and often a chunk or two is all that is necessary.

The quality of the meat, the spice rub, the sauce, and the temperature affect the final taste profile far more than the name on a bag of wood.

CHIPS. About the size of coins, chips are also common and easy to find in hardware stores. They burn quickly, and you may find that you need to add them frequently during the cooking

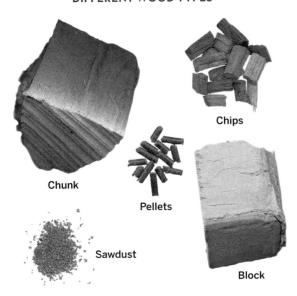

DIFFERENT WOOD TYPES

Chunk

Chips

Pellets

Sawdust

Block

cycle. They burn hot and fast, creating blue smoke (see opposite page).

PELLETS. Food-grade pellets are compressed sawdust extruded into long, pencil-thin rods that are broken into bits about ½-inch-long. They contain no binders, glue, or adhesives. When wet, they revert to sawdust immediately. Pellets can be a good concentrated source of smoke flavor on charcoal or gas grills and smokers.

Pellets for household heating should not be used for cooking because they may include pine or binders, and because the machines used to make them are lubricated with petroleum. Food-grade pellets, on the other hand, include only hardwoods, and the manufacturing equipment is lubricated with food-grade oil. They usually come in 10- to 40-pound bags.

Most pellets are made from oak, a stable-burning wood. If the label says hickory, the pellets are usually less than half hickory and the rest is oak, a fact that does not always appear on the label. These products are easy to measure and control. They burn for only about 20 minutes at 225°F, so get your meat on the cooker before adding the pellets.

BLOCKS. Similar to the pellet is the block. Wood chips and sawdust from lumber mills are compressed into blocks about 3 to 4 inches on each side. They come in a variety of flavors. I have had very good luck with them on a number of smokers.

BISQUETTES. A variation on compressed sawdust, bisquettes are designed for the Bradley Smoker. They look like small brown hockey pucks and are stacked and gravity-fed into the smoker.

SAWDUST. Sawdust burns so quickly that it's rarely used for barbecue. A few small stove-top smokers use smoldering sawdust for a light smoke flavor. You can often get sawdust from cabinetmakers.

SPECIALTY WOOD. Some manufacturers like Weber and Char-Broil sell perforated aluminum pans containing the wood flavor of your choice. Kingsford also makes a "briquet" that is not charcoal but pure wood.

WHICH WOOD?

When you are using wood as your primary fuel, which wood you choose is crucial for both heat and flavor. It's much less important when you are throwing a few chips or chunks into a pile of charcoal or onto a gas grill or pellet smoker.

For me, wood flavor can be broken down into two simple categories:

MILD. Alder, cherry, grape, maple, mulberry, oak, orange, pecan, and peach. Best for foods that are not heavily seasoned or sauced.

STRONG. Apple, walnut, hickory, mesquite, and whiskey barrel. Best for strong-flavored foods with lots of spice or sauce or for food that cooks quickly, like fish or thin cuts of meat.

If I were forced onto a desert island, I'd want three types of wood: apple chunks for steady smoke flavor, cherry chunks for a pretty reddish color on the bark of the meat, and apple chips or pellets for quick smoke during short cooks.

I cannot state this more emphatically: The quality of the meat, the spice rub, the sauce, the cooking temperature, and the meat temperature affect the final taste profile far more than the name on a bag of wood.

THE QUEST FOR BLUE SMOKE

Not all smoke is created equal. When it comes to cooking, we want thin, pale-blue smoke if possible. The smoke color depends on the particle size and how it scatters and reflects light to our eyes. Pale-blue smoke particles are the smallest. Pure white smoke consists of larger particles. Gray smoke and black smoke are produced when the fire is starving for oxygen and the smoke particles become large. Dark smoke can result in bitter, sooty food that tastes like an ashtray.

Billowing white smoke is common when you

MYTH It's important to match the wood to the meat.

BUSTED! Books and websites love to publish tables proclaiming, "Applewood goes with pork, maple with chicken, hickory with beef."

Humbug. I laugh at all the guides that attempt to describe different wood flavors. They remind me of the florid descriptions that wine critics use. Think about it. Apple might taste one way on pork but it will taste entirely different on beef or turkey.

What kind of hickory? Shagbark hickory or pignut hickory? Bark or no bark? Logs? Wood chunks? Wood cured for three years or less than a year? How much wood did you add? How hot was your fire?

Shagbark hickory logs from the Finger Lakes will taste different than barkless pignut hickory chunks from the Napa Valley.

I'll admit that mesquite is so strong it is pretty easy to taste. And on some foods, like delicate fish, wood differences are more obvious. But most of the time, the smoke flavor is lost under the flavor of the meat, rub, and sauce. And frankly, that's OK with me. Smoke should just be another instrument in the orchestra, not the soloist. Bottom line? Stop obsessing over which wood to use. Just pick one and stay with it for a while. Keep the variables to a minimum. Once you have everything else under control you can try experimenting with different woods.

just start the fire, and when the fuel needs lots of oxygen. It does not taste bad, but it is not as good as blue smoke. If you are cooking something hot and fast, like a steak, white smoke is a great way to get some smoke flavor on the food in a hurry. Otherwise, go for blue.

Sterling Ball, a champion pitmaster who owns the famous Ernie Ball guitar string company, describes the art of making blue smoke as similar to tuning a guitar: "You need control of your tools, the pit, fuel, oxygen, fire, heat, and practice." Here are some tips on how to get blue smoke.

KEEP YOUR COOKER CLEAN. Carbon buildup, soot, creosote, and sticky grease on the inside of your cooker can create greasy smoke. Often that grease is loaded with the bad kind of creosote.

USE AGED WOOD. If wood is your heat source, use aged and dried wood. Green woods have more sap, burn irregularly, and impart different flavors than aged woods.

AVOID WET WOOD. Keep the wood out of the rain. Some pitmasters will put logs on top of their smoker to evaporate excess water before adding them to the fire.

BUILD A SMALL, HOT FIRE. Low-smoldering wood creates dirty smoke, while hot fires burn off any impurities. You want to see flame coming from the wood. That means that you need a lot of oxygen. Open your exhaust vent so the hot air rising through the chimney draws in air through the intake vent. Open the chimney wide or close to it. Don't let your embers sit in ash; keep them on a grate above the bottom of the firebox. Knock ash off occasionally and, if necessary, remove the excess. If coals are choking for lack of oxygen, they will burn incompletely and can coat your food with gray soot. If that happens, get the meat out, rinse it, adjust the fire, and put the meat back on.

ALLOW THE PIT TO WARM UP. Start the fire at least an hour before the food goes on. Adjust your airflow and get the temperature, fire, and smoke stabilized. Warm the walls of the cooker. It is harder to get blue smoke in a cold environment. Warm walls will also prevent greasy buildup.

START THE FUEL ON THE SIDE. Add mostly hot coals. If you are cooking with wood, start burning it on the side and add only glowing embers. If you are using charcoal, use briquets. Lump charcoal is often not completely carbonized and can create more smoke than briquets. Remember, properly burning charcoal doesn't produce much smoke, but when you first light charcoal it produces lots of smoke. I use a chimney starter to start briquets.

USE GOOD THERMOMETERS. As with everything in barbecue, getting blue smoke is all about temperature control. Cooks who say they don't need thermometers are either seasoned old-timers who learned at the foot of a master and have been doing it for years, or they're macho knuckle draggers.

COOK ON INDIRECT HEAT. If the meat drips on the fire, water and fat will burn and make greasy, pungent smoke. These drippings can create flavor, especially for short, fast cooking, but for long, low cooking, they can create dark smoke. Keeping the meat in indirect heat means fewer flare-ups.

TRY SMALL CHIPS OR PELLETS. On some cookers chips and pellets combust and disappear quickly, but they burn hot and fast and make better-quality smoke. Chunks smolder and produce dirtier smoke.

USE YOUR SENSES. It's hard to see the color of the smoke at night, but the smell should be sweet, with meat and spice fragrances dominating. The smoke aromas should be faint and seductive.

USE THE RIGHT AMOUNT OF WOOD. The amount you need may vary according to your preferences, how tight your cooker is, the type of fuel, the thickness of the meat, and if you use chunks, chips, or pellets. Pellets are especially good for measured amounts. On a charcoal grill, start with 4 to 6 ounces of wood by weight for turkey and chicken. Use 8 ounces of wood for ribs, and no more than 16 ounces for pulled pork and brisket. Start with 2 to 4 ounces when you put on the meat and add another 2 ounces when you can no longer see smoke. On gas grills, double the amount. The proper amount depends on your cooker.

PRACTICE. Do dry runs without food in your smoker until you can anticipate when more fuel is needed. Know how to adjust the airflow, and know how to react when the smoke starts going bad.

TAKE NOTES. Weigh the wood before you add it and write down amounts and times so you can adjust it the next time you cook.

MYTH Soak wood chips and chunks for the most smoke.

BUSTED! To test whether soaking wood is effective, we weighed some wood chips and chunks on a digital scale. Then we soaked them in room-temperature water for 12 hours. Then we removed them, shook off the surface water, patted the exterior lightly with paper towels, and weighed them again to see how much water had been absorbed. Large chunks gained about 3 percent by weight and small chips about 6 percent. That's not much. Chips absorbed more because they have much more surface area than chunks.

To see just how far water penetrates into wood, we soaked three pieces of wood (a solid block of oak, a chunk of cherry, and a chip of cherry) for 24 hours in water mixed with blue food coloring. We then rinsed the surfaces, patted them dry, and photographed the exteriors. Then we cut the wood in half. As you can see in the photos to the right, the dye discolored the surface only a little and entered the interiors only where there were cracks and fissures. The rest of the wood was bone-dry.

There's another good reason not to soak your wood: If you toss dripping-wet wood onto hot coals, the water on the surface of the wood cools off the coals. The key to good outdoor cooking is to hit a target temperature and hold it there.

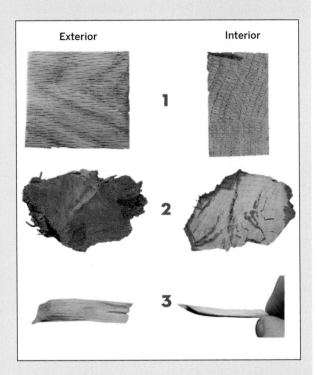

Exterior   Interior

Wet wood will not rise much above 212°F until the water steams off. Only after the water evaporates and the wood warms to the combustion point at about 575°F does it produce smoke. Most of that white stuff you see when you throw wet wood on the fire is steam.

Finally, I emailed fifteen top competition teams. Not one of them soaks their wood.

TROUBLESHOOTING CHIPS AND CHUNKS

Sometimes wood chips burst into flames. This can actually be good. With flames, you get clean combustion and blue smoke. You go through a bit more wood than when it smolders, but you get better flavor. However, the heat of the burning wood can drive your temperature too high. To prevent this, make a smoke packet by wrapping the wood in aluminum foil. Use heavy-duty foil or two or three layers of regular foil and poke holes in it. Then put the pouch on the grill as close to the heat as possible. Make several pouches in advance. When one has burned up, throw another one on. Another option is to use a small aluminum pan with holes poked in the bottom. You can even put the wood in a small cast-iron frying pan.

SMOKING WITH HERBS

I have a small herb garden, and at the end of the season, I always have a few unpicked oregano and basil bushes. I cut them above the roots and stick them in paper bags to dry. Then I crumble them and throw them on the grill after the food is on. They burn fast and add exotic aromas. I use them mostly when cooking fish and shellfish on my gas grill, since they cook quickly and don't have time to absorb slow-smoldering hardwood smoke. You can also smoke with tea leaves and spices, as is popular in China.

SMOKE BOMBS

This method is ideal for when you are cooking for a long time and getting under the grate will be tricky. This is one case when I advocate for wet wood.

Get two disposable aluminum pans. Add dry wood to both. Pour enough water in one to cover the wood and put both pans in the cooker. The dry pan will start to smoke quickly. About 15 minutes after it is all consumed, the other pan will have dried out and begun smoking.

3
SOFT-WARE

To get a handle on how cooking changes meat, it helps to know what's in it in the first place.

THE MAKEUP OF MEAT

Muscle tissue typically consists of a few basic components: water, protein, fats, and tiny amounts of carbohydrates, enzymes, vitamins, and minerals.

Animal	% Water	% Protein	% Fats	% Other
Beef	72	21	6	1
Pork	69	20	10	1
Chicken	73	21	5	1
Lamb	73	20	5	2
Cod	81	17	1	1
Salmon	64	21	14	1

These figures are averages and don't include bones. Some individual cuts will have more fat and less protein and water.

No matter how fatty or lean the cut of meat, it is constructed in the same way.

BEEF TENDERLOIN

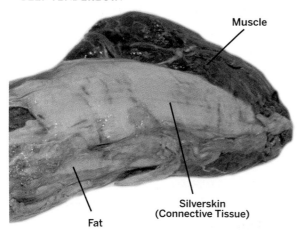

Muscle

Silverskin
(Connective Tissue)

Fat

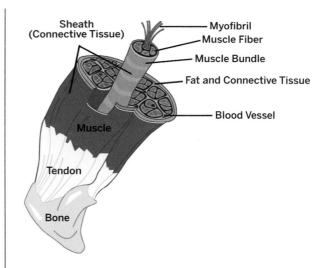

Sheath
(Connective Tissue)
Myofibril
Muscle Fiber
Muscle Bundle
Fat and Connective Tissue
Blood Vessel
Muscle
Tendon
Bone

MUSCLE CELLS. About the thickness of a human hair, muscle cells consist mostly of water and two different proteins, myosin and actin, which react differently to heat. They are surrounded by a sheath of diaphanous connective tissue that attaches the cells to one another, forming bundles called muscle fibers. Bundles of bundles are called myofibrils. As an animal ages, grows, and exercises, its muscle fibers get thicker and tougher.

CONNECTIVE TISSUES. Meat may contain several types of connective tissues, also consisting primarily of protein.

Collagen is invisibly scattered throughout the muscle, often surrounding fibers and sheaths. When you cook meat, the collagen melts and turns into the rich silky liquid known as gelatin, the same jiggly stuff that Jell-O and aspic are made from. Lean meats like pork loin and tenderloin, as well as most chicken and turkey, don't have much collagen. But tough cuts like ribs, shoulder, and brisket are loaded with it. When you are cooking these tough cuts, it's important to liquefy the collagen into gelatin, and that takes time.

A chewy, stretchy form of connective tissue, appropriately called elastin, is found in ligaments and tendons that connect muscles to each other and to bones. Silverskin, the shiny, thin sheath wrapped around muscles, is mostly elastin, and it is extremely chewy. We often call it gristle. Elastin does not break down during cooking.

FAT. This is the fuel that powers muscles. Fat is packed with calories and comes in three types. Subcutaneous fats rest beneath the skin in thick, hard layers. Intermuscular fats are layered between muscle groups, and intramuscular fats are woven among the muscle fibers themselves, adding moisture, texture, and flavor to cooked meat. Intramuscular fat is also known as marbling because it gives the meat a striated look similar to marble.

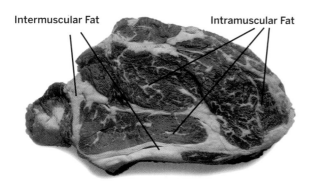

Intermuscular Fat   Intramuscular Fat

Intramuscular fat is crucial to meat texture. When cold, fat has a waxy texture, but it starts to melt at 130 to 140°F, lubricating the muscle fibers just as they are getting tougher and drier from heat. Unlike water, fat does not evaporate during cooking, but it can drip off.

Fat absorbs and stores aromatic compounds from the food in the animal's diet. As the animal ages, these flavor compounds build up in the fat. So we have a trade-off. Older animals have more flavorful meat with muscle fibers and connective tissues that are tougher. Younger animals, on the other hand, have less flavorful but more tender meat.

FLUIDS. Most of the juices in meat are myowater, water with the protein myoglobin dissolved in it. Myoglobin stores oxygen scavenged from hemoglobin in blood. Some of the myowater flows freely between fibers, and some of it is tightly bound within the cells.

SLOW-TWITCH VS FAST-TWITCH MUSCLES

Muscles need fat and oxygen for fuel. Myoglobin stores oxygen for release during heavy exertion, and in general, the more work a muscle does, the more oxygen-laden myoglobin it needs. This makes the muscle darker in color and richer in flavor. Dark meats like chicken thighs consist of slow-twitch muscles designed for steady movement and endurance. White meats like chicken breasts, on the other hand, are mostly fast-twitch muscles designed for brief bursts of energy. White meats tend to be less juicy and flavorful because the muscles are worked less and contain less myoglobin, fat, collagen, and moisture. That's why chicken breasts dry out more easily than legs and thighs. Chickens and turkeys get more exercise standing and walking, so the legs and thighs have lots of slow-twitch muscles, more pigment, more juice, more fat, and more flavor. That's why dark meat is more forgiving when cooked.

Because they fly and swim, ducks and geese get even more exercise than chickens and turkeys do and they have more dark meat. Duck breasts are deep purple, almost the same color as lamb or beef.

Modern domestic pigs raised in confinement fall somewhere in between. They don't get much exercise and have been bred to contain less intramuscular fat to become "the other white meat." But heritage pork from pastured pigs is noticeably redder, juicier, and more flavorful because of the extra exercise and the extra myoglobin the muscles get.

Beef is all pretty much loaded with myoglobin and dark red all over, so it has a deeper, richer flavor.

Fish live in a practically weightless environment, so their muscles contain very little connective tissue. The color and texture of fish vary depending on the life it leads. Small fish like rainbow trout swim with quick darting motions and have mostly fast-twitch muscles and tender, white meat. Bluefin tuna, on the other hand, swim long distances with slow, powerful tail movements, so they have firmer, darker, sometimes even red flesh. Either way, the lack of connective tissue means that fish never really gets tough when cooked, although it can dry out on the grill because there isn't much collagen to moisturize the muscle fibers.

BUYING MEAT

Lean in and I'll tell you the most important secret to getting good meat: Get to know your butcher. Knowing a good butcher is more important than knowing a good stockbroker. The head butcher is usually on duty early morning through early afternoon, and the assistant comes on for the later shift. Stop at the counter and ask for an introduction. Don't be surprised if he is a she. Get the direct phone number of the meat department. Bring her a slab of your ribs for lunch one day. Set yourself apart from the crowd.

I often hear, "I'd like to try cooking a whole brisket, but none of my local groceries carry it." Of course not. There's not enough demand. But most butchers can order whatever you want and have it there in a few days. They can also custom-grind hamburger with your favorite blend, cut steaks to the thickness you want, and get the freshest fish. If they can't or won't, find a new butcher.

Linger over the meat counter and choose carefully. Look at the thickness and evenness of the cut. If one end is thinner, that end will

MYTH **The red juice is blood.**

BUSTED! People call the pink juice from meat blood, but it is not. It is myowater. If it were blood, it would be dark, almost black, just like your blood, and would coagulate on the plate. But instead it remains pink, thin, and watery. Let's just call it "juice" from now on, OK? I'm convinced that calling it blood is why many people swear off meat and others insist their meat be cooked well-done.

overcook. Look at the exterior fat. You'll want to remove most of it, so find cuts with the least waste. Often, two packages of the same cut can have very different marbling. Look for liquid in the package. This is called purge, and it may be a sign that the meat has been frozen and thawed. This moisture and flavor cannot be replaced. Avoid packages with a lot of purge.

Remember, cool meat attracts more smoke.

Read the fine print when you shop. Meats labeled "enhanced," "flavor-enhanced," "self-basting," "basted," "pre-basted," "injected," or "marinated" can have salty fluids or flavorings injected. These additives can enhance taste and improve moisture retention when cooked, but why pay more for saltwater? You do not need additives if you prep and cook the meat properly. If you want salt, add it yourself.

TENDERNESS OF MEAT

Two major factors influence meat tenderness: the condition of the myofibrils and the condition of the connective tissues. If the myofibrils remain intact and the connective tissues remain unaltered, meat can be tough. Cooking meat slowly breaks them down and softens them. The specific muscle, the breed of the animal, what the animal was fed, its age, how it was slaughtered, how the meat was aged, and how the meat was cooked and sliced all influence tenderness as well.

MYTH Let meat come to room temperature before cooking.

BUSTED! A lot of recipes, especially those for big roasts, direct you to take the meat out of the fridge an hour or two ahead of time and let it come up to room temperature before cooking. Here's the theory: Say you want a steak to be served medium-rare, about 130°F. If your fridge is 38°F, then the meat must climb 92°F. But if the meat is at room temperature, 72°F, then it only needs to climb 58°F. It will cook faster and there will be less overcooked meat just below the surface.

But a 1½-inch-thick steak takes more than 2 hours for the center to come to room temperature. A 4½-pound pork roast 3½ inches thick takes—are you ready?—10 hours! Take your meat straight from the fridge to the cooker. It is safe, it will warm much faster in the cooker than on the kitchen counter, and remember, cool meat attracts more smoke.

ENZYME TENDERIZING

Enzymes are large molecules, mostly proteins, that act as the catalysts of the cellular world. Enzymes are largely responsible for the tenderizing of some meats as they age. You can buy powdered enzyme meat tenderizers in stores. Adolph's is the most popular brand. Its active ingredient is the enzyme papain, extracted from papayas. You can also use fresh papaya juice as a tenderizing marinade. Fresh pineapple juice also contains an effective tenderizing enzyme, bromelain. Canning and bottling render the enzymes ineffective, so you must use fresh juices.

Most enzymatic tenderizers work best in the 120 to 160°F range. They are ideal for quickly tenderizing thin cuts of meat. But on a thick cut, if you are trying to cook the meat between rare and medium, you're likely to get a mushy surface and not much internal tenderizing. Some recipes suggest poking the steak with a fork to allow enzymes to penctrate. Stabbing drives contaminants into the meat and is not a safe practice.

MECHANICAL TENDERIZING

The time-honored method of tenderizing meat is to beat it with a meat mallet. The one shown below has a flat surface on one side, which flattens the meat and breaks some of the bonds

between the connective tissues, loosening the fibers. The flip side has triangular spikes that actually cut through the fibers. Neither is recommended.

Some cooks prefer the more contemporary Jaccard tenderizer below, which has a number of very sharp stainless-steel blades that slice through the meat fibers and connective tissues. But anything that punctures the surface of the meat can push pathogens into the center. If you cook the meat above 165°F, you have nothing to fear, but if you cook to medium-rare, or pink, you could be asking for a tummy ache with a Jaccard.

POUND CHICKEN BREASTS FOR EVEN COOKING

If you cook the center of the bulge in a chicken breast to 160°F, as you must for food safety, then the tapered edges become dry and tough. The

solution is to pound the breasts flat. Now, when you cook, the heat can enter evenly on all sides.

Lay the meat in a zipper-top bag or on a sheet of plastic wrap just off center and fold the other half of the plastic over it. The plastic keeps the juices from flying around the room. Flatten the bulge with the bottom of a heavy skillet or saucepan, both of which apply more even pressure than a mallet or rolling pin. Don't haul off like you are pounding a nail. Thwack it gently and focus on the thick end. Several focused whacks work better than one vicious spanking. Take it down to about ¾ inch thick. Because it is so thin, it will cook faster.

SLICING MEAT ACROSS THE GRAIN MAKES IT MORE TENDER

Start by noting which way the grain of the fibers runs in the raw meat. In the flank steak shown at the upper right, it runs from lower left to upper right. When you slice the cooked meat, you should cut at a 90° angle across the grain from the upper left to the lower right, parallel to the black line.

In the photo below, the top slice is cut the wrong way—with the grain. It will be stringier and harder to chew. The bottom slice is cut properly, across the grain and thinly. It will be easier to chew.

Wrong

Right

JUICINESS OF MEAT

As we know, meat contains about 70 percent water, but what we perceive as juiciness is more complicated than that. So what influences juiciness?

1. Free water in the raw meat

2. Water bound with proteins

3. Water bound within the architecture of the muscles

4. Melted and softened fats, especially marbling

5. Gelatinized collagen

6. Saliva, which is activated by the sight, smell, and taste of food, as well as by seasonings, especially salt

Some meats, like pork ribs, pork butt, and beef brisket, are often smoked low and slow up to about 203°F, way past well-done and into the zone where water is supposed to disappear. Much of it does. But these cuts get their juiciness from rendered fat, melted connective tissue, and salty rubs that force you to salivate.

MYTH Searing meat seals in the juices.

BUSTED! This myth has been debunked in many labs, yet it can still be found in such improbable locations as the Ruth's Chris Steak House website: "Our USDA Prime steaks are prepared in a special 1800°F broiler to seal in the juices and lock in that delicious flavor."

Although searing browns and firms up the surface of meat, it does not weld the fibers shut and lock in the juices. As the food scientist Harold McGee says in his landmark book, *On Food and Cooking*, "The crust that forms around the surface of the meat is not waterproof, as any cook has experienced: the continuing sizzle of meat in the pan or oven or on the grill is the sound of moisture continually escaping and vaporizing."

This doesn't mean we should not sear. Searing produces browning, and as we shall see, that makes meat taste better.

WHAT YOU NEED TO KNOW ABOUT SALT

Salt is a magical rock. It is the single most important flavor enhancer. Salt is a mineral, NaCl, consisting of one ion of sodium (Na) and one ion of chloride (Cl). This tiny, water-soluble crystal suppresses the taste of bitterness, balances sweetness, and deepens and enhances flavors. Just a small amount can really improve a dish. It can also aid in moisture retention during cooking and even tenderize.

VARIETIES OF SALT

There are many types of salt, but when they are used in cooking, it is almost impossible to taste the differences.

TABLE SALT is sea salt that has usually been mined from underground salt domes. It is then dissolved in water and refined to remove

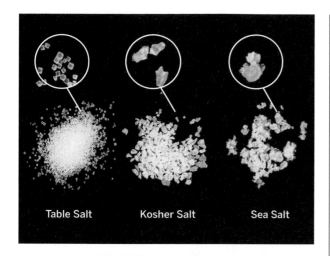

Table Salt   Kosher Salt   Sea Salt

everything except NaCl, then ground into small, uniform, cube-shaped grains. Anticaking agents are added so it flows freely from salt shakers. Some table salt also includes iodine, an additive that helps prevent iodine deficiency.

KOSHER SALT has larger, flake-shaped grains and small amounts of anticaking agents but no iodine. Many chefs prefer kosher salt because the larger grains make it easier to pinch and sprinkle. Also, it is slower to dissolve on food surfaces, making it popular as a finishing salt. Morton's and Diamond Crystal are the most popular brands, but their grain size is different. I use Morton's in my recipes to standardize results and because it is easier to find.

PICKLING SALT contains neither iodine nor anticaking additives. It dissolves well in cold water, so it is a good choice for brines.

SEA SALT, in today's marketplace, usually describes salt that has been collected from shallow ponds from which the seawater has been evaporated. All salt comes from the sea or from underground deposits that were once the sea, so technically all salt is sea salt. But sun-dried sea salt usually has minute amounts of minerals and other impurities from the sea that can give it subtle flavors and colors ranging from pink to black. The vast majority of sea salt on the market is refined in a similar fashion to table salt and contains 99.5 percent sodium chloride. Among unrefined specialty sea salts, grain size can vary significantly from producer to producer. A bag of large-grain sea salt can also include fine powder. I don't use sea salt in cooking since it is difficult to standardize quantities (see page 34). It can also be very expensive. I use sea salt only as a garnish at tableside.

SEASONED SALTS, like garlic salt and celery salt, can be found in grocery stores. I never use them in cooking because I prefer to control the amounts of these ingredients myself, as in the homemade herbed seasoned salt that I keep on my dining table.

CURING SALTS were created centuries ago, before refrigeration, to preserve meats such as bacon, hams, and corned beef. They all contain salt and nitrite, and some contain nitrate as well. These preservatives are very effective against the deadly botulism bacterium. Most curing salts are colored pink with a small amount of red dye so you don't confuse them with table salt. The most common are Prague powder #1 and Prague powder #2. Pink salts such as Himalayan rock salt should not be confused with curing salts, and pink curing salts should never be used to season food during cooking or at the table.

MEASURING DIFFERENT SALTS

A salt's grain size can make a huge difference in its volume measurement and its total sodium content, or saltiness. For example, table salt, which is fine in texture and has a cubic grain, has less air between the grains than kosher salt, which has a larger, flake-shaped grain. So if a recipe calls for 1 teaspoon Morton's Kosher Salt and you use 1 teaspoon table salt, the results will be almost twice as salty. If the recipe calls for salt by weight, such as 8 ounces, it doesn't matter which salt you use. The saltiness will be the same when measured by weight.

Here are some approximate conversions:

Morton's Table Salt	Morton's Kosher Salt
1 teaspoon	about 2 teaspoons
about ½ teaspoon	1 teaspoon
1 cup	about 8 ounces (½ pound) by weight

There are some differences among brands. Diamond Crystal Kosher Salt has a coarser grain than Morton's, so you need to use more than the Morton's. That's another reason why it is best to measure salt (as well as sugar and flour) by weight rather than volume, since a pound of table salt, a pound of kosher salt, and a pound of sea salt all contain the same amount of NaCl. If I knew that every kitchen had a good digital scale, I would list salt measurements in my recipes by weight.

BRINING

If you like your meat juicy, tender, and flavorful, salting it before you cook can improve it on all three fronts. Dry brining and wet brining both get salt into the meat, and that improves its ability to hold water and boosts flavor.

SALT AND JUICINESS

When meat cooks, a significant amount of water evaporates from the surface and some gets squeezed out from cells and connective tissues that contract under heat. Lean cuts, like chicken breasts, turkey breasts, and pork loins, can dry out easily. How do you cook these meats to proper temperatures without turning them into shoe leather? Surprisingly, salt can help.

Meat proteins are complex, long, and coiled. When sodium and chloride ions penetrate the muscles, the electrical charges alter the proteins so they can hold moisture more tenaciously. As a result, less is lost during cooking.

Researchers at *Cook's Illustrated* discovered that a chicken soaked in plain water and another soaked in wet brine each gained about 6 percent by weight. They cooked both birds as well as an unsoaked bird straight from the package. Weighed after cooking, the unsoaked chicken lost 18 percent of its original weight, while the chicken soaked in water lost 12 percent of its presoaked weight, and the brined chicken lost only 7 percent of its weight.

Lab tests conducted by Professor Blonder showed that the brine retained by the meat is concentrated near the surface. Thus, brining counteracts one of the biggest problems of grilling by helping hold moisture near the surface, which almost always dries out by the time the center is properly cooked.

SALT AND TENDERNESS

Cooking meat gently to the proper temperature can tenderize it by relaxing the proteins, a process called denaturing. Salt can also denature proteins even before the meat hits the heat. But if you add too much salt, the muscle proteins can turn tough again during cooking.

SALT AND FLAVOR

Salt actually expands our taste buds, so it acts as a flavor amplifier. It also suppresses our perception of bitterness.

HOW BRINING WORKS

To study brine penetration, Professor Blonder took a 12-inch-long section of pork loin and soaked it in a wet brine. Periodically, he lopped off a cross-section and treated it with an indicator that detects salt. Here's how far the brine penetrated:

30 minutes: $\frac{1}{10}$ inch

1 hour: $\frac{1}{4}$ inch

8 hours: $\frac{1}{2}$ inch

24 hours: $\frac{2}{3}$ inch

That's right: After 24 hours, the salt still hadn't yet traveled 1 inch into the pork. Because it has less connective tissue, chicken is more porous, and salt will penetrate farther. Fish is more porous still. But you get the picture. When you brine, the salt remains pretty close to the surface.

To see how heat impacts salt penetration, he took a pork loin and rubbed it with curing salt. Then he washed it off and cooked it at 230°F. Periodically he cut off a slice and put it on a filter paper with a chemical that reacts with the salt. When the internal temperature of the meat rose, the salt migrated farther inward, far faster than it did when simply soaking in a wet brine.

Internal temperature 100°F: about $\frac{1}{3}$ inch

125°F: $\frac{1}{2}$ inch

145°F: $\frac{3}{4}$ inch

160°F: 1 inch

Blonder's experiments also showed that even though chicken and turkey skin are more than half fat, they will absorb salt. During cooking,

MYTH **Osmosis is how salt gets into meat during brining.**

BUSTED! Cookbooks tell us that salt is pulled out of the brine and into the meat by osmosis. Osmosis is when ions and molecules pass through semipermeable membranes. Salt is a tiny two-atom molecule, and it gets into the meat primarily by diffusing through wide-open pores, sliced muscle fibers, capillaries, intracellular water, and other channels. Once within the meat, osmosis helps the salt get through cell membranes and into muscle fiber proteins.

BRINERS, BEWARE: DOUBLE-SALT JEOPARDY!

Rubs are a great way to flavor meat, and brines are a great way to add flavor and moisture. But commercial rubs often contain a lot of salt, so a salty rub on top of brined meat can make the meat unbearably saline. My advice is to make your own rub mix and leave the salt out of the blend. Most of my rub recipes do not include salt, which allows you to apply the salt and seasonings separately. Also, never brine meat that is labeled "enhanced," "flavor-enhanced," "self-basting," "basted," or "kosher" because it has already been salted during processing. Last, remember that the drippings from brined meat will taste slightly salty. If you make a gravy from drippings, be sure to taste first before adding salt. You can always add salt, but you can't take it away.

the skin releases the salt into the meat. Meats with a thick fat cap block salt penetration almost completely.

DRY BRINING VS WET BRINING

For wet brining, we submerge food in a salt-water solution of 5 to 10 percent salinity. To wet brine you need to calculate the amount of water and the amount of salt, and then you have a big container of water you need to fit in the fridge. Dry brining is simpler and equally effective.

The late chef Judy Rodgers of San Francisco's famous Zuni Café popularized the dry-brining technique, and since discovering it, I almost never wet brine anymore.

To dry brine, you simply salt the meat a few hours before cooking. How much salt? Salt tolerance is so personal that it's nearly impossible to give an exact amount. As a rule of thumb, sprinkle on about ½ teaspoon kosher salt (or ¼ teaspoon table salt) per pound of trimmed meat.

I dry brine almost all my meats, including steaks and chops, both beef and lamb, as well as many vegetables. They all benefit from the flavor boost and the water-retaining properties of salt. And dry brining helps poultry skin crisp, while wet brining softens it.

FOR STEAKS AND CHOPS

About an hour before cooking, sprinkle the salt on the meat, massage it in, and return it to the fridge. After an hour, you're ready to cook.

FOR ROASTS

Rub the salt over the entire surface area. For the best results, refrigerate the meat overnight or for a day. If the meat is tapered, like a leg of lamb, use less salt on the thin end.

FOR CHICKEN AND TURKEY

Professor Blonder's tests have proven that salt does penetrate chicken and turkey skin, so go ahead and sprinkle the salt right on the skin. It may help crisp the skin. Breasts need more salt than thighs because they are thicker. Refrigerate for at least 2 to 4 hours.

WET BRINING

Wet brining works best on fish, chicken breasts, turkey breasts, and pork loin chops: food that cooks so quickly that the absorbed moisture doesn't have time to drip out during heating. Chicken thighs, turkey thighs, and cuts of pork like ribs and shoulder are moist enough from fat that they don't need wet brines. I never wet brine red meats unless I am making a cured meat like corned beef. Wet brines can make poultry skin soggy and harder to crisp.

If you decide to wet brine, the brine should contain 5 to 10 percent salt by weight. Recipes often call for 1 cup table salt to 1 gallon water for a 7.7 percent brine by weight. If you have kosher salt, use about double the volume.

SUGAR IN THE BRINE

Sugar is a huge molecule, and it cannot penetrate more than a fraction of an inch into meat. But adding sugar to a wet brine in about the same quantity as salt does have some benefits. The sugar sticks to the meat's surface, gets into microscopic pores and cracks, and aids in browning, especially at lower temperatures.

BRINING VS PICKLING VS CURING

Pickling and curing are variations on the brining theme.

Pickling brine is more concentrated and strong enough to discourage microbial growth, thereby preserving the food. Pickling brines often include sugar, spices, and vinegar, and the brining time can last a week or more because it

may take that long for some of the larger molecules to dissolve and enter the food.

Curing brines are also highly concentrated and usually include salts with nitrites and/or nitrates, which effectively kill the bacterium that causes botulism. Corned beef, hot dogs, bacon, ham, and many sausages are cured. Curing often takes days, even weeks, and can include sugar and spice and everything nice. Curing can be done wet (with salt dissolved in water) or dry (with salt applied to the food surface). The salt content is so high that curing can dehydrate the meat.

RUBS AND SPICE BLENDS

Some meats just don't need anything more than a little salt and pepper. A great steak comes to mind, or a really fresh piece of swordfish. On the other hand, some meats like pork ribs love being rubbed with spices or swimming in sauce. As a rule of thumb, strong-tasting foods need little more than salt, while mild-tasting meats like pork, chicken breast, and turkey are blank canvases to be painted with herbs, spices, and flavorful liquids.

Dry rubs are spice blends that are rubbed onto meat before cooking. They include a wide range of flavors, such as barbecue rubs, jerk seasoning, curries, five-spice powder, chili powder, herbes de Provence, Lawry's Seasoned Salt, and Old Bay. You can buy premixed rubs, but they are easy to make yourself, and every good barbecue cook should have a signature house rub to brag about. (Steal my recipes on pages 166–173, then experiment with your own variations.)

Spices and herbs are huge molecules compared to salt and they just don't get more than a fraction of an inch past the surface. Think of salt as a treatment for the interior of the meat and spices and herbs as an exterior treatment, like a sauce.

You cannot judge a rub straight from the bottle: It tastes very different after cooking. The juices of the meat mix with the herbs and spices and they undergo chemical reactions catalyzed by the heat of the fire. You may hate rosemary, but it won't stand out among the symphony of flavors in the rub and the meat.

Find a rub recipe you like, make a big batch, and put it in a large spice shaker with a lid. If it clumps or cakes, take a tip from diner waitresses: Dry some raw rice in the oven or a pan on the stove top and add it to the jar to absorb moisture.

MYTH Massaging in the rub pierces the surface and makes the juices run out.

BUSTED! There is a reason they are called *cuts* of meat. Meat is muscle that has been cut to remove it from the bones, fat, and other muscles. It contains gazillions of muscle fibers that have been sliced open. The surface is full of microscopic ridges, valleys, pockmarks, and pores. Massaging in a rub won't hurt the meat one bit—the meat will not lose any more juice than if you were to just sprinkle it on. In fact, rubbing a rub helps get it into the meat.

INJECTING: NO WAIT, NO WASTE, MORE FLAVOR

Rubs, mops, marinades, brines, and sauces can deliver a lot of flavor to the surface of meat. But if you really want to get fats, herbs, spices, and other large molecules deep into the muscle tissue, injection is best.

You can do it at the last minute. It creates less waste. No huge containers are needed. And it doesn't create refrigerator space problems.

The secret to injecting is to go easy. A good guideline is to shoot for 1 to 2 percent of the meat's weight in salt and skip the big flavors like garlic, pepper, and herbs that mask the natural flavor of the meat. I have judged pulled pork and brisket at barbecue competitions where the meat was gushing juice, but it didn't taste like meat. It tasted like apple juice and garlic. I want pork that tastes like pork, beef that tastes like beef, and turkey that tastes like turkey.

The best injections are saltwater or stock. And you don't need much. Because meat is 70 percent water, it is already nearly saturated.

Your injection will go between the muscle fibers and bundles, not within the fibers, and any excess will squirt out.

Since injecting can push contaminants from the surface deep into the meat, I recommend it only for meats that are cooked to 160°F or higher, like chicken, turkey, pork butt, and beef brisket.

GIZMOS

There are a number of injection gizmos on the market, ranging from simple hypodermics to pumps that look like something used by the Orkin Man. For home use, I recommend a good, sturdy, meat-injector hypodermic.

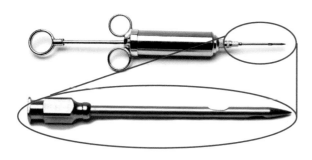

The needles for this purpose are different than normal hypodermics. They aren't open at the tip because a large opening at the tip gets clogged with meat easily. Meat injectors have holes in the sides of the needles that are less likely to clog, and the tip is a sharp point. Look for a stainless-steel one (plastic ones tend to break) with sturdy connections between the needle and the syringe body, and between the syringe and the plunger. You also want a tight gasket (preferably silicone) between the plunger

and the interior of the syringe. The needle should be easy to remove, so everything is easy to break down and clean up. It helps if the needle can be stored inside the syringe, too, and the whole hypodermic should have a capacity of at least 2 ounces. You can get a nice stainless-steel model for less than $20.

MYTH Apply the rub, then wrap the meat in plastic wrap and let it rest overnight for maximum penetration.

BUSTED! Plastic wrap does not force the large molecules into the meat like some sort of vacuum or pressure system. The plastic just gets stuck to the rub and pulls it off when the wrap is removed. Restaurant kitchens are required to cover or wrap meat so juices won't contaminate other foods like vegetables, but at home, it's not necessary if you are careful about cross-contamination.

You don't have to put on a spice rub well in advance like salt: You can apply it to the meat just before cooking. Rub the mixture right onto the bare meat or help the rub stick by first applying a little water, mustard, or ketchup. My experience is that these additions make little or no difference in the final flavor, so use whatever you want to get the rub to stick.

INGREDIENTS FOR INJECTION

Many barbecue champs use commercial products such as Butcher BBQ Original Brisket Injection, the ingredients list of which includes flavor enhancers like monosodium glutamate (MSG), hydrolyzed vegetable protein (another source of MSG), autolyzed yeast extract (more MSG), disodium inosinate, and guanylate. Butcher BBQ's blends win trophies, and I've been impressed with the product during tastings.

Marinades rarely penetrate more than ⅛ inch.

I fill my injectors with a brine that is no more than 2 percent salt by weight. It diffuses to a lower concentration within the meat, which is enough to enhance flavor and bind water, but not so much that it gives the meat a cured flavor. When I add flavor, I try not to go crazy. You can add oils, herbs, spices, sweetners, syrups, sauces, stocks, broths, colorings, pretty much anything. But be thoughtful. Do you really want your turkey to taste like Dr Pepper? If you use herbs or spices, grind them fine. Dark liquids like soy sauce or Worcestershire will turn light-colored meats like chicken or turkey an unappealing color. And don't go crazy with sweeteners. I have included some injection recipes on pages 161–162.

You can cook injected meat right away, but if you let the meat rest for an hour or more, or even overnight, the brine will disperse more evenly. Then apply your rub, and cook.

THE SECRETS AND MYTHS OF MARINADES

Marinades are simply thin liquids that foods swim in before cooking, but marinades are bathed in myth and mystery. They usually have quite a few ingredients, such as salt, oil, flavorings, and acids. The molecules of each of these ingredients are different sizes. Some are attracted to the chemicals in meats, and some are repelled by them. In a few hours, even overnight, they rarely penetrate more than ⅛ inch. This means that marinades are more effective on thin cuts of meat.

What marinades do best is find their way into cracks and crevices on the surface of meats, producing a flavorful, baked-on seasoning, much like a dry rub. You can make a marinade with ingredients like wine, fruit juices, coconut milk, soft drinks, liqueurs, and other exotic flavors you won't get from your spice rack. When the marinade dries out during cooking, it leaves behind its flavors.

The big problem with marinades is that they make the food wet. Most foods benefit from a flavorful brown crust that comes from radiant heat. When the surface is wet, it steams and doesn't brown.

GASHING HELPS MARINADES WORK

It helps to gash your food to allow the marinade flavors to sink in deeper. Cut slices into the surface or rough it up, and you'll give the marinade cracks and pits to enter. You'll also create more surface area for better browning.

MAKING A MARINADE

Once you understand how marinades really work, you can use them to your advantage.

START WITH SALT. The most important ingredient in a marinade, salt not only enhances flavors but also excels at penetrating meat. Soy sauce is a great source of salt.

GO WILD WITH FLAVORING. Typical flavorings include herbs and spices like oregano, thyme, cumin, paprika, garlic, and onion powder, and even vegetables such as onion and jalapeño. It's a good idea to add some umami, the savory, meaty flavor found in meat stocks, soy sauce, and mushrooms. It is also good to add just a little sugar to enhance surface browning.

USE ACID JUDICIOUSLY. Citrus marinades have it all: acid, sugar, flavor, and aromatics. Acids can denature proteins on the surface and make the meat mushy, so use them judiciously. I limit acid to no more than one eighth of the blend and use it primarily for flavor. Typical acids include fruit juice (such as lemon, apple, white grape, pineapple, orange, and even white or red wine); vinegar (apple cider, distilled white, sherry, balsamic, raspberry, or any flavored vinegar); cultured dairy (buttermilk and yogurt); and even sugar-free soft drinks.

MAKE IT THIN. Some recipes call for marinating in barbecue sauce. Don't do it. It's a waste of sauce because it is too thick to penetrate. And because most barbecue sauces are sweet, they can burn.

DITCH THE ALCOHOL. Marinating in wine, beer, or spirits may not be a good idea. In his

MYTH Marinades penetrate deep into meat.

BUSTED! In a series of experiments, we soaked a variety of meats and vegetables in a marinade of oil, vinegar, table salt, and green food coloring to see how deep the coloring penetrated. (Food coloring is a large molecule comparable to flavor molecules found in marinades.) Seafoods and some vegetables absorbed the coloring deeply, but for other meats, the coloring never got much past the surface.

We also soaked foods in marinades, cooked them, and carefully removed core samples from the center so as to not get juices from the surface on the samples. There was no evidence of the marinade penetrating that far.

We cut a crater in a steak and filled it with oil. After many hours, none of it had been soaked up by the meat because meat is 70 percent water, and oil and water don't mix.

award-winning *The French Laundry Cookbook*, chef Thomas Keller says, "If you're marinating anything with alcohol, cook the alcohol off first. . . . Alcohol in a marinade in effect cooks the exterior of the meat, preventing the meat from fully absorbing the flavors in the marinade. Raw alcohol itself doesn't do anything good to meat. So put your wine or spirit in a pan, add your aromatics, cook off the alcohol, let it cool, and then pour it over your meat." I agree heartily. Reduced wine brings exotic flavors to the party.

BE SAFE. All uncooked meat contains microbes and spores that thrive outside the fridge. If your marinade recipe calls for heating it, let it cool to refrigerator temperature before using, to discourage microbial growth. Always marinate in the refrigerator.

USE A NONREACTIVE CONTAINER. Acids and salts in a marinade can react with aluminum, copper, and cast iron, imparting off flavors to food. Soak in plastic, stainless steel, porcelain, or, best of all, plastic zipper-top bags. You need less marinade in a resealable bag than you do in a bowl, and there's no cleanup since you can throw it away when the marinating is finished. Squeeze or suck out the air from the bag and most surfaces of the meat will be in constant contact with the marinade.

GO NAKED. The fatty skin on chicken and turkey acts as a barrier to marinades and becomes soggy. If the skin won't get crispy, what's the point? Get rid of it. Skinless chicken will drink up more flavor.

CONSIDER CUTTING. You might want to cut larger pieces into serving sizes. Small, thin cuts of meat marinate faster.

WATCH THE TIME. Marinate fish and veggies for 30 to 60 minutes at most, depending on the thickness. An hour or two is enough for most other meats.

FLIP NOW AND THEN. Turn the meat in the bowl or turn the bag every hour or two for even marinating.

DISCARD USED MARINADES. A marinade becomes contaminated with raw meat juices. Never reuse it.

WHY I DO NOT RECOMMEND VACUUM MARINATORS

Several companies make devices into which you place the food and a marinade, and then create a vacuum. In theory, the vacuum sucks air out of the food, letting the marinade in. I don't recommend them because the vacuum can also suck in microbes from the food surface. If you don't cook the food to about 165°F, past well-done, you run the risk of a tummy ache or much worse.

INDUSTRIAL MARINADES

You have probably noticed that more and more meats in the grocery are premarinated and "enhanced," which can include injection. The advantage is that these meats make cooking dinner quick and easy. The downsides of premarinated meat are that the meat might not be the freshest, you may not want the additives and preservatives in the marinade, and the meat takes on extra weight from the marinade, so you're paying meat prices for water and flavorings.

RUB IT OR SAUCE IT

A better way to bring flavor to food than marinating is to use a spice rub. Blends of spices and herbs deliver more flavor per square inch than marinades do. Or use a sauce. Simple sauces of chopped herbs, oil, vinegar or citrus, and aromatics can be mixed up right on the cutting board. (See my recipes for Board Sauces on page 188.)

WHY WE LOVE BARK, CRUST, CARAMELIZATION, AND THE MAILLARD REACTION

When heat is applied to food, the chemicals in the food change. A lot. Heat is powerful energy. Some changes are obvious, some are subtle, and some invisible. The most important changes are the Maillard reaction and caramelization. Together they make the miracle of flavor called GBD: golden brown and delicious.

The Maillard reaction is named after French scientist Louis-Camille Maillard, who studied the browning of foods in the early 1900s. Maillard discovered that as the surfaces of foods get warm from dry heat, the compounds in meat react with one another, scores of new compounds form, and the surface begins to get

Heat + Sugars + Amino Acids = GBD
(Many different golden brown and delicious molecules)

brown and crunchy, developing a depth of flavor and texture.

The Maillard reaction begins at low temperatures but really kicks in after 300°F. As in many chemical reactions, time can be traded against temperature. Twelve hours at 225°F will brown meat nearly as deeply as 15 minutes on a hot grill, but the exact mixture of flavor compounds will differ. Good thing, too. Wouldn't it be boring if all food tasted the same, no matter how it was cooked?

Many chefs use the term caramelization to describe the browning of meats, but in most cases it is really the Maillard reaction. Caramelization is an entirely different chemical reaction, although the two can occur simultaneously and interact. The Maillard reaction involves mostly amino acids and proteins. Caramelization involves mostly sugars and other carbohydrates. It is, in fact, the reaction that creates caramel, the browning of sugar.

Grilling sweet vegetables like corn and onion deepens their flavors through caramelization. Sweet barbecue sauces develop interesting new flavors when caramelized, which is why they are hard to judge when they are tasted straight out of the bottle. But slather them on a rack of ribs and let them see a touch of heat, and the caramelized sugar changes the entire flavor profile. Honey makes a good addition to barbecue sauces because it consists mostly of fructose, which caramelizes at lower temperatures than table sugar does. But it can also burn easily, so be careful with temperatures and when substituting one type of sugar for another in tried-and-true sauce recipes.

BROWN GOOD. BLACK BAD.

The goal is to achieve a range of colors between golden amber and whiskey brown—but not black. Brown is complex lyric poetry. Black is coarse carbon. Here are some tips on how to enhance browning, as shown below in the delicious example of a smoked coulotte cut from a beef sirloin.

ADD A PINCH OF SUGAR. When making a spice rub, add a little sugar for foods that will be cooked low and slow. If you are cooking hot and fast, on the other hand, skip the sugar because

it will burn. Sugar substitutes will not aid browning.

KEEP THINGS DRY. Water can only reach 212°F, but fructose doesn't caramelize until 230°F and glucose doesn't until 320°F. For better browning, pat the food dry with paper towels before cooking. This is another reason why I am not a fan of marinades and bastes: They can prevent browning.

KEEP THINGS AT THE RIGHT TEMPERATURE. To get a good brown surface, you need one of two things: a hot direct-radiant-heat source from below, or long, low cooking times. Master your cooker. There are times when you want to quickly heat the surface of food, and there are times when you want to slowly heat the interior.

TURN FREQUENTLY. When you turn only once or twice, the heat builds up and food burns easily. But when you turn frequently, you are in a sense rotisserie cooking, letting the surface heat and brown, and then flipping it so it cools. Frequent flipping prevents burning.

GIVE 'EM SPACE. Leave plenty of space between food chunks so steam can escape, especially in a pan or on a griddle. Otherwise, the temperature will plummet and you won't get GBD.

THE FAT CAP: TO TRIM OR NOT TO TRIM

Let's say you have a hungry crowd of rowdies to feed and a big honkin' pork shoulder, beef brisket, leg of lamb, or prime rib with a thick layer of fat on top. Do you trim off the fat

cap (as shown above) or leave it on? Plenty of cooks leave it on, but that is not the best choice.

WHEN TO LEAVE ON SOME FAT

The best strategy is to remove all but a thin, ¼- to ⅛-inch layer of fat on one side only, as seen on the top of the slice of brisket shown below. I use this method for brisket, pulled pork, ham, leg of lamb, and other cuts with thick fat caps. Much of the fat will melt away, leaving a sliver behind so people can still get a taste of its flavor,

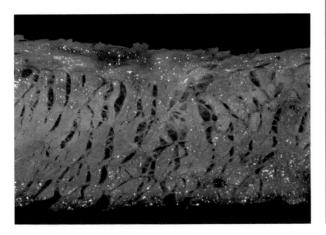

as well as the spices and herbs you lovingly blended and rubbed all over the meat.

A thin fat layer helps prevent evaporation and produces juicier meat, but it can also prevent a hard, crispy bark. If your meat sits directly above the heat in your cooker, try putting it fat cap side down to create a heat shield and protect the meat surface from drying out.

There is one exception: The coulotte, or

MYTH The fat cap will melt and make the meat juicier.

BUSTED! The subcutaneous fat cap rests between the skin and muscle of animals. It is usually white, fairly hard, and can be as much as an inch thick. Beef consultant and food scientist Dr. Antonio Mata says, "Fat will not migrate into the muscle as it is cooked. Fat is mostly oil, meat is mostly water, and oil and water don't mix." In addition, in most cases, a layer of connective tissue holding the muscle groups together forms an anatomical barrier between the muscle and the fat cap. The fat cap melts when it softens during cooking, and some of it drips onto the fire, where it vaporizes and settles back on the meat, adding flavor. But the potential danger of leaving a thick layer of fat on the outside of steaks and chops is that it can drip so heavily onto the fire that it flares up and deposits soot on the meat. Moreover, most people will trim off the fat at the dinner table, along with your carefully crafted spice rub. There goes all the flavor.

Cooked at 425°F	Cooked at 225°F
212°F – Crusty	212°F – Crusty
160°F – Dry	140°F – Moist
130°F – Juicy	130°F – Juicy

sirloin cap steak, is popular in Brazilian steak-houses partially because of the flavorful fat cap. A layer of fat is left attached and the meat is grilled on skewers above wood coals, as shown above. When served, the fat is left on and it tastes mighty nice.

WHEN TO COOK HOT AND FAST, WHEN TO COOK LOW AND SLOW, AND WHEN TO DO BOTH

In most outdoor cooking, the goal is a nice dark exterior enriched with complex flavors caused by the Maillard reaction and caramelization, along with an interior that is cooked from edge to edge as close as possible to the optimal temperature for tenderness and juiciness. This is true for both meats and vegetables. Since the heat source cooks the outside of the food, but the exterior cooks the interior, we must look at the two as separate cooking projects.

Your food is already dead. You don't have to kill it again. Chances are you cook too hot and fast. Much of the time, low and slow is better,

and more often still, a low and slow followed by hot and fast, a vital technique called reverse sear, is best of all.

WHEN TO COOK HOT AND FAST

The thinner the meat, the higher the heat. Hot and fast works for thin, skinny foods like the skirt steak pictured below, asparagus, and shrimp because they cook quickly. If you want a good dark brown sear (and you do), you need high heat to create that sear without overcooking the interior.

To cook hot and fast, you need to get the food

directly above and close to the heat source so infrared radiant heat can go to work on it. This is when you crank your grill to warp 10 and "Give her all she's got, Scotty." When cooking on high heat, you usually want the lid up, so the heat is being applied only to the bottom surface. You don't want weak reflective heat to cook the top and send heat to the center. You want all the heat from one side, and you want it pounding on the surface. Then you turn the food often, like a rotisserie, so much of the energy escapes from the top and doesn't get a chance to overcook to the center.

WHEN TO COOK LOW AND SLOW

Very thick cuts need to be cooked low and slow. Hot and fast will just carbonize the surface of thick cuts like a pork butt or beef roast before the heat gets to the center. Water is a good insulator, so heat slogs slowly through the watery interior of foods, especially meats.

Professor Blonder took two pork loin roasts about 4 inches wide and 3 inches tall and roasted one at 325°F and the other at 225°F. By the time the center of the meat hit the target temperature of 145°F, the outer layer of the one cooked at the higher temperature was a parched 170°F, while the one cooked at the lower temperature was still moist, about 160°F (see the graph at the upper right).

Lowering the temperature and closing the lid will cause less heat buildup on the exterior and give the heat time to move to the center, so more of the meat is cooked to the target temperature. Low heat is essential for tough cuts like beef brisket, pork shoulder, and ribs, which

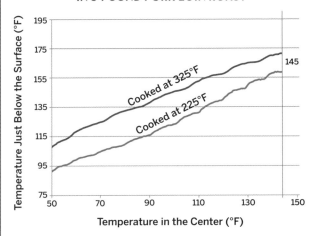

SURFACE TO CENTER TEMPERATURE DIFFERENCE IN 3-POUND PORK LOIN ROAST

have lots of connective tissue. If they are cooked long enough, to 203°F or so, magic happens. Fats melt and the tough connective tissue softens up like Homer Simpson in Marge's arms. Another benefit of cooking low and slow is that

MASTER THESE TWO TEMPERATURES

Experiment with your grill or smoker so you can stabilize the indirect zone at two vital temperatures, 225°F and 325°F, with the lid down in all kinds of weather.

At 225°F, you can roast low and slow with indirect convection heat, perfect for tough cuts like ribs.

At 325°F, you can crisp chicken and turkey skins better than at 225°F and evade the dreaded stall. Once you nail these two target temperatures, you'll be able to cook all types of food in your cooker all year round.

it gives salt time to migrate toward the center, which then seasons the meat throughout.

To cook low and slow, you need to master the single most important technique for the backyard cook: the two-zone setup (see page 8), for which you need a warm convection (indirect) zone off to the side, where warm air circulates around the food, and a hot radiant (direct) zone, where you can put food directly above the heat.

WHEN TO USE BOTH (REVERSE SEAR)

Cooking something like a 2-inch-thick steak at 225°F is problematic, because it is ideal when the interior reaches 130°F. At a cooking temperature of 225°F, you can get a beautiful even color on the interior, but you can't get a nice, dark crust on the steak.

The solution for thick steaks, chicken, and even potatoes is to combine both methods: low and slow plus hot and fast. It is called two-stage cooking, or reverse sear, and it allows you to cook both the interior and the exterior perfectly by cooking them more or less separately.

Start by setting up your grill for two-zone cooking. Try to get the indirect zone as close to 225°F as you can with the lid on. Put the meat (let's say it's a steak) on the indirect side, toss a little hardwood on the fire, and then close the lid so the meat will roast slowly in smoky convection air. Flip it once or twice, until the interior temperature is about 15°F below your target temperature. For this, you need a good instant-read digital thermometer like a Thermapen (see page 97). When your steak hits 115°F in the center (or your pork chops or pork roast reaches 130°F, or your chicken or turkey gets up to 150°F), take it

off and put it on a plate for a moment. The interior is almost done. Now it's time to work on the exterior.

Crank up the heat on the direct-heat side as hot as you can get it. If you have a charcoal grill with a height-adjustable coal bed, get the coals right below the cooking surface. You may want to dump more hot coals on the direct side of the grill. Or set up a hibachi with a thick bed of hot coals. For a gas grill, turn the burners to high or turn on your sear burner. On a pellet smoker, crank it to high and preheat a griddle or pan on the grate.

Pat one side of the meat dry with a paper towel so when you put it on the grill, evaporating water doesn't cool the surface and steam the meat. Put the meat dry side down on the hot side of the grill and leave the lid open. You don't want any heat reflecting off the lid down onto the top of the steak, roasting the interior. You want to pound one surface with energy. But

Overcooked

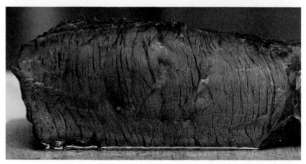

don't leave it there for long, or the heat will start to work its way to the middle. Flip it and let the surface cool. Keep flipping until the crust turns deep, dark, bourbon brown, but not black. You do not want carbonized protein or fat. You want to take the interior to about 130°F and the exterior just shy of burnt, because when you do, dazzling things happen: You have the perfect steak.

Reverse sear is the best way to get edge-to-edge even doneness on a thick steak without a thick band of battleship gray meat just under the crust.

Reverse sear works for many foods. Take chicken breasts, for example: fatty skin on one side, lean meat on the other. If you start over high heat, there's a good chance you'll blacken the skin before the inside is cooked. You could cook it skin side up, but then the meat on the bottom gets overcooked and dry, and the skin stays rubbery.

Chicken Breast Cooked Hot
Burnt Skin
165°F / Juicy
200°F / Dry

Cooked Reverse Sear
Brown Skin
165°F / Juicy
170°F / Moist

The better approach is to cook the breast in the indirect zone, with warm convection air and smoke, bring it to just under the desired internal temperature, and then move it over direct radiant heat, skin side down, to crisp it. Then you can serve tender, juicy meat and crispy skin. Check out my update of the classic Cornell Chicken recipe (page 298) to see the concept in action.

The reverse sear even works for big roasts like prime rib. Start low and slow, lid down, and finish hot and fast, lid up, and never have a 1-inch band of overcooked meat again. Even baked potatoes are best when reverse seared (page 358). In fact, many foods that are more than 1 inch thick reach perfection with two-zone, two-stage cooking.

WHAT FACTORS INFLUENCE COOKING TIME?

Many variables influence cooking time, most importantly the cooking temperature, cooking method, type of meat, thickness of the meat, weather, humidity, water pans, spritzing, and especially the accuracy of your thermometers.

COOKING TEMPERATURE. The temperature of the cooker is crucial. The hotter you cook, the sooner your food will be done. Get two good-quality digital thermometers: one for your cooker and one for your food. You couldn't cook without the built-in thermometer in your indoor oven, and you can't cook outdoors without a thermometer, either.

COOKING METHOD. Grilling directly over the flame will cook food faster than if the food sits alongside the flame. A pork butt wrapped in aluminum foil will cook much faster than an unwrapped one. Using thick, wide, cast-iron grill grates will speed cooking slightly because they absorb and conduct heat more efficiently than air does.

TYPE OF MEAT. Some foods, especially tough cuts like ribs, brisket, shoulder, and rump, get tougher at higher heat levels and tenderer at lower heat levels. Familarize yourself with which cuts of meat are tough and which are tender.

THICKNESS OF THE MEAT. Although the weight of a cut of meat is often related to its thickness, weight does not determine how long it will take to cook. Thickness determines cooking time. That's because meat is done when it reaches the desired temperature in its geographic center. Heat must travel through the meat to reach the center. The traveling time is determined by the distance from the outside of the meat to the center.

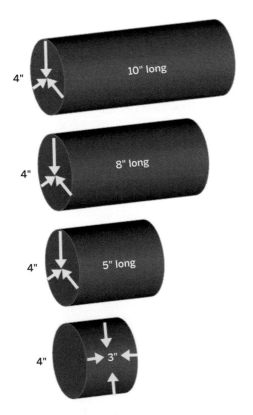

The top three take the same time to cook.
The bottom one will cook faster.

WEATHER. Another factor is the ambient air temperature outside the cooker. Cold air will cool the air coming in through the combustion air vents and cool the coals or fuel jets. Wind and rain cool the exterior of the cooker and can wreak havoc with your plans. To overcome them, you will need more charcoal or more gas. If you are not prepared for these variables, dinner will be late.

HUMIDITY. As the air around your meat warms up, moisture from the meat begins to evaporate. If you are cooking low and slow at 225°F, this evaporation can cool the meat and slow cooking for hours. If you're not ready for this temperature stall (see page 59), you better be ready to order Chinese takeout. Other things influence humidity. Cold air is usually drier than warm air, so there can be more evaporation in cold air, and on cold days, your flame has to be hotter to keep the cooker temperature up, and that can dry out the air. You can boost the humidity and reduce the meat's evaporative cooling by putting water pans inside the cooker.

A FAUX CAMBRO GIVES YOU BREATHING ROOM

There is no bigger blow to one's pride than standing in the dining room and announcing that the turkey is still not ready while your spouse's potatoes and beans give out their last gasp of steam. A faux Cambro will save your butt as well as your ribs, brisket, and turkey.

Indispensable to caterers, a Cambro is an insulated plastic box for transporting foods and maintaining temperature.

For a faux Cambro, get a beer cooler large enough to hold a big turkey or whole brisket. Make sure it is well insulated, seals tightly, and is easy to clean. Wheels are a nice feature. Buy an aluminum pan that fits inside to make cleanup easier.

Here's how to use it: If you think it will take 3 hours to smoke your turkey, then put the bird on about 4 hours before you plan to serve it. Lay a towel in the bottom of the cooler and put the disposable aluminum pan on top of the towel to catch leaks. When it is done, wrap the turkey in foil, leaving the meat thermometer probe in, then place the meat in the pan and lay a second towel on top. Close the lid, but allow the thermometer cable to hang out under the lid if possible. That's it. With this setup, I've kept meats well above 150°F for 3 hours. But beware carryover: It will continue to cook and could rise in temperature as much as 10°F.

A faux Cambro is a great way to get that smoked turkey over the river and through the woods to grandma's house on Thanksgiving or to get hot ribs to the tailgate party. A faux Cambro is almost a necessity to finish beef brisket. Holding it at a high temperature tenderizes it. The only downside is that the skin on your turkey and the bark on your brisket will soften as it sits. If that happens, you can roll the meat around on a hot grill for a few minutes just before serving to firm up the exterior.

Keep the faux Cambro clean. After each use, wash out the cooler and its components with a cleaning product containing bleach, such as Comet, or wash with soap and rinse with a dilute chlorine solution of 1 gallon water plus 1 tablespoon bleach.

FOOD TEMPERATURE GUIDE

The food temperature guide on page 53, combined with a high-quality digital thermometer, will enable you to deliver properly cooked food to the table. It shows both USDA recommended minimum temperatures and the temperatures that the pros use.

ABOUT THE MEAT TEMPERATURE GUIDE

The question of when food is cooked to a safe temperature is complicated. We should respect the USDA guide, but recognize that it is simplified for mass consumption. Temperature is just one part of the equation, time is another, the type of food is another, and the acceptable level of risk is another.

It is impossible to sterilize meat so that every

single microbe is killed and still have it remain delicious and nutritious. So we settle for pasteurizing, which means that so few pathogens are left that the chances of getting sick are minute.

The USDA has set a standard for pasteurization that is called the 7D kill rate. This means that one cell out of 10,000,000 might survive cooking. When meat is contaminated it could have just a few pathogens per gram to millions of them. For this example, let's say you have 10,000 steaks and there are 1,000 bacteria on each. A 7D kill rate means that there might be one cell surviving on only one of those 10,000 steaks.

MYTH Pink pork puts you at risk for trichinosis.

BUSTED! Once upon a time, when hogs ate garbage, it was easy to get sick from the parasite trichinosis in undercooked pork. Today trichinosis has, for all practical purposes, been eradicated in developed countries. The annual average infection rate is fewer than a dozen cases per year in the United States, and most are associated with eating undercooked wild game such as bear, not farmed pork. Modern farming and processing methods as well as public awareness of the importance of proper cooking have all but eliminated trichinosis in pork. This parasite is killed at 138°F and the USDA's new minimum recommended internal temperature for pork is 145°F. So if you're cooking bear, get it to at least 138°F, please.

But pathogens don't all just drop dead at once when the meat hits the UDSA-recommended temperature. Most pathogens start keeling over at about 130°F, and they die faster as the temperature rises. At 130°F, you can get to 7D in about 2 hours. At 140°F, pathogens die in only about 12 minutes; at 160°F, 8 seconds; and at 165°F, 7D is reached almost instantly. Carryover cooking (see page 5) continues to cook the interior when the meat comes off the heat. So if you take a turkey breast out of the oven at 155°F, it continues to kill the microbes as it rests.

Microbes are almost all on the surface of beef steaks. If you bring the surface to 165°F and the center to 145°F, you reach 7D. Burgers, in which the contaminants are mixed throughout the meat, need to get to 160°F in the center. Because of the way it is processed, the structure of the meat, and the pathogens involved, the USDA says chicken needs to be brought to 165°F. Many experts say 160°F is adequate.

Steakhouse chefs know that their expensive beef is best at medium-rare, 130°F, and if they had to cook it to 145°F, medium-well, as the USDA recommends, they would go out of business in a hurry. They also know that they would go out of business even faster if a customer died from eating one of their steaks. But if you are willing to accept a 6D kill rate as safe (10 cells left among 10,000 steaks), or even 5D (100 cells left among 10,000 steaks), you can cook steaks to a moist and tender 130°F. The risk is higher, but still pretty low. That said, the rate of contamination in ground beef and poultry is so high that you should always stick close to USDA recommendations unless you buy irradiated meat. It is all a matter of balancing risk and reward.

FOOD TEMPERATURE GUIDE

Beef, Lamb, Venison (Steaks, Chops, Roasts), Duck Breasts		USDA Minimum 145°F (63°C)
Blue, "Pittsburgh"	110–120°F (43–49°C)	Dark purple, cool, stringy, slippery, slightly juicy
Rare	120–130°F (49–54°C)	Bright purple to red, warm, tender, juicy
CHEF TEMP Medium-Rare	130–135°F (54–57°C)	Bright red, warm, tender, very juicy
Medium	135–145°F (57–63°C)	Rich pink, yielding, juicy
Medium-Well	145–155°F (63–68°C)	Tan with slight pink, firm, slightly fibrous, slightly juicy
Well-Done	155°F (68°C) or more	Tan to brown, no pink, chewy, dry
Pork, Raw Hams, Veal (Steaks, Chops, Roasts)		**USDA Minimum 145°F (63°C)**
Rare	120–130°F (49–54°C)	Pale pink center, warm, tender, slightly juicy
Medium-Rare	130–135°F (54–57°C)	Creamy pink color, tender, very juicy
CHEF TEMP Medium	130–135°F (54–57°C)	Cream color, some pink, yielding, juicy
Medium-Well	145–155°F (63–68°C)	Cream color, firm, slightly juicy
Well-Done	155°F (68°C) or more	Cream color, tough, dry
Pork Ribs, Pork Shoulders, Beef Briskets, Beef Ribs		**USDA Minimum 145°F (63°C)**
CHEF TEMP Tender, Tugs Apart	203°F (95°C)	High in fat and collagen, best cooked low and slow
Chicken, Turkey (Whole or Ground), Including Stuffing		**USDA Minimum 165°F (74°C)**
CHEF TEMP Well-Done	160°F (71°C)	Cream color white meat, pale tan dark meat
Ground Meats, Burgers, Sausages, Meat Loaf (Except Poultry)		**USDA Minimum 160°F (71°C)**
Cook these risky meats to USDA minimum and make them juicy by using a 20% fat blend		
Hams, Hot Dogs, Sausages (Precooked only)		**USDA Minimum 140°F (60°C)**
CHEF TEMP Warm	140°F (60°C) or more	Tender, juicy
Fish (Except Tuna Steaks)		**USDA Minimum 145°F (63°C)**
CHEF TEMP Medium	130–145°F (54–63°C)	Slightly translucent, flaky, tender
Tuna Steaks		**USDA Minimum 145°F (63°C)**
CHEF TEMP Rare	120–125°F (49–52°C)	Bright red
Shrimp, Lobster, Crabs, Crawfish, Scallops		**USDA & CHEF TEMP Until flesh is opaque**
Clams, Oysters, Mussels		**USDA & CHEF TEMP Until shells open**
Baked Potatoes		**CHEF TEMP 212°F (100°C)**

Other Temperature Benchmarks	
These numbers are approximate due to other variables such as the age of animal, acidity, salt content, type of heat, humidity, etc.	
34–39°F (1–4°C)	Ideal refrigerator temperature
41–130°F (5–54°C)	"Danger zone" in which many bacteria grow
95–130°F (35–54°C)	Animal fats start to soften and melt
130°F+ (54°C+)	"Kill zone" in which many bacteria begin to die
130–135°F (54–57°C)	Medium-rare, the temperature at which most meats are at optimum tenderness, flavor and juiciness
135°F (57°C)	Connective tissues begin to contract and squeeze pink juice (myoglobin and water) from within muscle fibers
150–165°F (66–74°C)	"Stall zone" when large cuts cooked at 225°F or so take hours to warm due to evaporative cooling
160–205°F (71–96°C)	Collagens melt and form gelatin, making meat succulent
160–165°F (71–74°C)	"Instant kill zone" in which most bacteria die in less than 30 seconds
212°F (100°C)	Boiling point at sea level; the boiling point declines about 2°F for every 1000 feet above sea level
225°F (107°C)	Recommended air temperature for "low and slow" cooking of tough meats high in connective tissue
310°F (154°C)	Browning of surface proteins from the Maillard reaction accelerates, forming thousands of tasty new compounds
325°F (163°C)	Recommended air temperature for cooking chicken and turkey so fat renders and skin browns and crisps
425°F (218°C)	Teflon thermometer cables can begin to melt
500–700°F (299–399°C)	Hardwood creates smoke with gases, water vapor, and microscopic particles
700–1000°F (399–538°C)	Hardwood produces flame

SERVE CHICKEN AND TURKEY AT 165°F.
I treat raw poultry like kryptonite. Researchers tell us that a significant percentage of chickens and turkeys are contaminated with salmonella. The USDA says to serve poultry at 165°F, and most chefs agree, often removing it from the heat at no lower than 160°F to allow for 5°F carryover cooking. To take the bird's temperature, push the thermometer probe through the breast at its thickest part all the way into the ribs, then back it out slowly and read the temperature along the way.

SERVE GROUND MEAT, BURGERS, AND SAUSAGE AT 160°F. Adhere closely to this USDA recommended temperature. The risk of contamination from pathogenic strains of *E. coli* is too great to mess with when it comes to undercooked ground meat. Prior to slaughter, cattle and pork are usually kept in crowded pens, and fecal matter can easily get on their hides. When the carcass is butchered, knives cutting the hide can contaminate the meat. Also, the intestines, naturally full of fecal matter, can easily be cut open by mistake and spill onto the meat, floor, knives, and gloves. A little *E. coli* on a steak is not a problem because it remains on the surface and is killed rapidly by cooking. But when meat is ground, the contamination on the surface is mixed throughout. If the center is not cooked to 160°F, pathogenic bacteria can find their way into your gut and cause discomfort, illness, or even death. That's why ground meat must be cooked to a higher temperature than whole-muscle meat. Don't screw around. Fortunately, I have a trick for making medium-rare burgers safe to eat (see page 269).

WHY CHEFS AND USDA DISAGREE ON SOME MEATS. Whole-muscle meats are a lot safer than ground meats because contamination is likely to only be on the surface and will be killed quickly when cooked. Medium-rare (130 to 135°F) is the best temperature for beef, lamb, and venison steaks, chops, and roasts, and duck breasts. Tasting panels and measuring devices agree that

---

MYTH Cook chicken until the juices run clear.

BUSTED! This is indisputably false. If you believe it, you could end up badly overcooking or undercooking your poultry.

Juices in chicken, turkey, and even pork are colored pink by the protein myoglobin. When myoglobin is cooked, its structure changes and the denatured molecules absorb light differently, so they no longer appear pink. It turns out there is no fixed temperature at which myoglobin changes color because other factors come into play. One research scientist explained to me that the acidity (pH) of the meat is a major factor. "When the muscle is high in pH (low in acid), it takes a much higher temperature to denature the myoglobin. The meat may need to be 170 to 180°F before the myoglobin in breasts is sufficiently denatured to see clear juices. The drumstick and thigh have higher levels of myoglobin, and they require an even higher internal temperature to denature it. As long as the meat reaches 165°F, it is safe to eat."

medium-rare gives the best balance of tenderness and juiciness.

SERVE FISH AT 145°F. The USDA recommends this temperature because fish are susceptible to parasites. It is easy to overcook fish, so be vigilant with the thermometer.

SERVE PRECOOKED HAM AND HOT DOGS AT 140°F. This meat is cured with salt, nitrites, and nitrates and precooked, so you are really just warming it up. No need to dry it out.

GO TO 203°F FOR PORK AND BEEF RIBS, PORK SHOULDERS, AND BEEF BRISKET. You should deliberately cook these meats up to 203°F, past well-done, in order to melt the abundant connective tissues and fats.

HOW TO GET THE PERFECT MAILLARD SEAR

How do you get perfectly even browning for maximum Maillard reactions and

MYTH Meat is safe when it is no longer pink.

BUSTED! Bottom line: Don't go by red bones or pink meat. Color is not a reliable guide in any meat. The chicken thigh with the purple bone pictured below was cooked to 180°F. It is safe to eat. Red or purple is the color of bone marrow because that's where blood is made. As birds age, more calcium is deposited on the bones, so the blood in the marrow becomes less visible. But in modern agriculture, chickens are usually sold at just 6 to 8 weeks old, before the bones have completely calcified. Purple bones can sometimes discolor the adjacent meat, so the meat appears pink even though it is safely cooked. The pink color can also happen when nitric oxide (NO) or carbon monoxide (CO) produced by the cooker lock in the pink color of myoglobin.

Ground beef can turn brown from oxidation long before the meat hits the safe temperature of 160°F. Don't go by color. Use a thermometer.

maximum flavor? Start with a piece of meat that is more than 1 inch thick. Use cheap wire grill grates to let the browning come from the direct-heat radiation of the fire. Don't let the meat sit in one place. Move it around a lot so the thin grates won't make marks, and your steak will get the maximum radiant heat and turn a nice, even mahogany color all over.

HOW BONES AFFECT THE COOKING

It is a common belief that bones make grilled and barbecued meat taste better. The truth is that the impact depends on the type of bone and on the cooking method.

Bones are complex structures, and they differ from species to species and from bone to bone on an animal. They have architectural functions, such as bearing loads and protecting organs. Here are a few other things that bones have in common and that may help you determine whether to cook your meat on or off the bone.

BONE EXTERIORS. The exteriors are walls of calcium and other minerals called compact bone. The larger the animal, the thicker the compact bone. Bone walls do not dissolve or melt during cooking. Small channels run through compact bone to carry blood to and from the marrow, but in general, the calcium is not porous, so no measurable marrow or flavor leaks out during roasting or grilling.

MARROW. Red marrow is the hard honeycomb marrow visible in ribeyes, T-bones, and porterhouses because the bones are often cut open

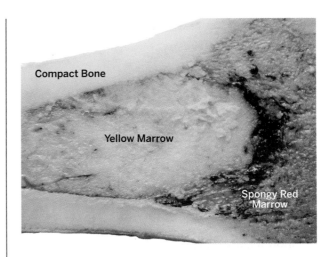

Compact Bone

Yellow Marrow

Spongy Red Marrow

by a bandsaw. It can also be seen in the ends of bones. These highly porous marrows, also called spongy marrows, are home to stem cells that produce blood. Although almost all blood is drained from muscle tissue during slaughter, some blood can remain trapped in bones. Yellow marrow is the type you find in the center of femurs and other leg bones. It is mostly delicious fat. Cowboys call it prairie butter. I call it poor man's foie gras.

CONNECTIVE TISSUE. Connective tissue surrounds the outer bone walls and anchors muscles to the bone. This sheathing remains tough no matter how long you cook it.

Collagen sheath that surrounds a beef rib

THE COOKING METHOD MATTERS. In wet-cooking methods, such as braising and slow cooking, where the meat is submerged and simmered for hours in liquid, the marrow may dissolve and can have a major impact on the flavor of the liquid and the meat. But bones contribute no significant flavor to meats in dry-cooking methods such as grilling and smoking. A tiny bit of marrow might escape the ends of the bones if they have been cut or if the bone has been sawed open lengthwise, as in T-bones and ribeyes, but the small amount of liquid in red marrow does not travel far onto or into the meat.

MYTH Grill marks are the sign of a great steak.

BUSTED! Grocery, restaurant, and grill ads show beautiful steaks and burgers with cross-hatched grill marks. Some restaurants even buy premarked chicken that they can microwave and serve. Cooking magazines and books teach readers how to get great grill marks. But those grill marks on Picture 1 (right) are merely superficial branding, unlike the deep, rich sear that delivers maximal taste and texture in Picture 2.

Only about one third of the surface is fully browned on the ribeye in Picture 1. The diamond shapes between the grill marks remain tan, well-done meat, full of unrealized potential.

When it comes to meats and many other foods, the goal is to get golden brown to dark brown color on as much of the meat's surface as possible because dark brown means hundreds of tasty compounds have been created through the Maillard reaction and caramelization (see page 43).

I'll admit that some foods do benefit from grill marks. On thin foods like shrimp, skinny chops, skirt steaks, asparagus, and bell peppers, grill marking quickly browns the exterior without overcooking the interior. But watch out that your delicious brown stripes don't turn into burnt, bitter-tasting scars.

WHAT IS THAT STUFF OOZING OUT OF MY SALMON AND BURGERS?

In salmon, the substance consists of a group of proteins called albumin. They are pushed to the surface by shrinkage, caused by heat. Brining salmon helps minimize this white ooze. It can also be wiped off with a paper towel or a brush. Another good technique is to paint the surface with a simple wash of something acidic like wine, mirin, or glaze.

According to food scientist Dr. Antonio Mata, the tan goop coming from hamburgers is protein dissolved in water, mostly myoglobin. When meat is ground, plump muscle fibers are sheared open, and as the burger begins to cook, protein and collagen shrink and squeeze out the fluids, which appear pink at first but then gel and turn tan. They are perfectly safe to eat.

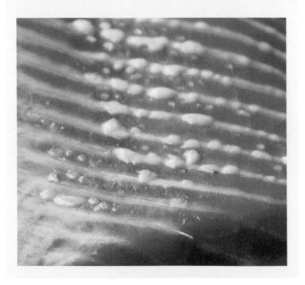

BONES CAN AFFECT HEAT TRANSMISSION.

Keep in mind that some bones, particularly those with a honeycomb-like interior, are slow to heat up because they are filled with air pockets that act like Styrofoam insulation. When the bones do get hot, they can retain heat longer than the meat because they don't cool from evaporation like muscle does. Depending on your total cooking time, meat closer to the bone can be slightly more cooked or less cooked than meat just $\frac{1}{2}$ inch away. In the case of a steak, the insulation properties of the bone can leave the meat closest to the bone 5 to 10°F cooler than the center. So if you take the steak off at 130°F, medium-rare, it may be rare along the bone.

THE BONE HELPS RETAIN MEAT JUICES.

According to Steven L. Moore, director of innovation at BRANDFormula, a food-science consultancy, in many cases bone seals the muscle, preventing it from losing meat juices as it cooks. When a muscle is deboned, there is usually a large area that is exposed and no longer sealed. Removing a chicken breast from the breastbone, for instance, drastically increases the surface area that will be directly exposed to the grill or heat, which will result in more evaporation and juice loss.

On the other hand, removing bone exposes more muscle to seasoning and browning, and seasoned brown meat is very tasty stuff. So the bone presents a trade-off between less juiciness and better browning on the meat.

As you can see, there's no right answer here. You may want to cook a rack of ribs on the bone to gelatinize all that succulent collagen, but you may want to cook a rib roast off the bone to gain more delicious browned meat. Either way, here's the best reason to leave bones in: We love chewing on them. The surfaces are often charred, and if the sheathing has softened, it can be very satisfying.

THE DREADED STALL

The Stall. The Zone. The Plateau. It has many names and has freaked out many a backyard pitmaster. You get a big hunk of meat, like a pork shoulder or a beef brisket (two of the best meats for low-and-slow smoke roasting) and put it on the smoker with dreams of succulent meat dancing in your head. You insert your fancy new digital thermometer probe, stabilize the cooker at about 225°F, and go cut the lawn. Then you take a nap.

The meat temperature rises steadily for a couple of hours but then, to your chagrin, it stops. It stalls for 4 or more hours, barely rising a notch. Sometimes it even drops a few degrees. You check the batteries in your meat thermometer. You tap on the smoker thermometer. Meanwhile, the guests are arriving, and the meat is nowhere near the 203°F mark at which it is most tender and luscious. Your mate is tapping a foot sternly, and you're pulling your hair out.

WHAT THE HECK IS HAPPENING?

Pitmasters have long believed that the stall is caused by collagen in the meat combining with water and converting to gelatin. Others speculate that the stall is caused by fat rendering (liquefying). Still others think it is caused by

protein denaturing as long-chain protein molecules break apart.

In 2010 Professor Blonder set out to determine the cause of the stall. First he did some calculations that proved that there isn't enough connective tissue to suck up all the energy necessary to prevent a large hunk of meat from increasing in temperature. He then cooked a large lump of pure fat. No stall. Next he cooked a cellulose sponge saturated with water. It climbed at about the same rate as the fat for the first hour to about 140°F, and then it put on the brakes. In fact, it even went down in temperature! When it dried out after more than 4 hours, it took off again.

He repeated his tests, tried some others, did more calculations, and the conclusion was inescapable: The barbecue stall is a simple consequence of evaporative cooling by the meat's own moisture slowly released over hours from within its pores and cells. As the temperature of cold meat rises, the evaporation rate increases until the cooling effect balances the heat input. Then it stalls, until the last drop of available moisture is gone and the surface is dry like jerky. That's the bark formation.

Nathan Myhrvold, author of *Modernist Cuisine*, put two halves of a brisket in a convection oven at about 190°F with one half wrapped in aluminum foil. The wrapped brisket did not stall. Myhrvold also concluded that the stall was caused by evaporative cooling.

The stall may begin as low as 150°F or as high as 170°F, depending on the particular piece of meat and the kind of cooker, fuel, and humidity. Generally, the higher the cooking temperature, the shorter the stall, and in some cases, as you

MYTH Flip your meat as little as possible.

BUSTED! If you flip more often when grilling at high temperatures, you get better flavor, more even color and doneness in the interior, a better, even-colored crust, and a shorter cooking time. Among the advocates of frequent flipping are Harold McGee, author of *On Food and Cooking*; J. Kenji López-Alt, managing culinary director of SeriousEats.com; Nathan Myhrvold, editor of the landmark six-book set *Modernist Cuisine*; and my colleague Professor Blonder.

Here's what McGee says: "Flip every minute. Frequent turns mean that neither side has the time either to absorb or to release large amounts of heat. The meat cooks faster, and its outer layers end up less overcooked."

approach a cooking temperature of 300°F, there may be no stall at all. Humidity is a major factor because higher humidity means less evaporative cooling. Some electric smokers are so tight and high in humidity that they may experience no stall whatsoever. However, the high humidity may also mean less bark. For tight cookers, one workaround for this problem is to skip the water pan and crank up the heat near the end to crisp the surface.

Airflow is also a major factor. The greater the airflow, the shorter the stall. For example, pellet smokers, which include a fan, create an efficient convection environment that speeds evaporation and shortens the stall.

Why doesn't the meat just stay in the stall until it is all dried out? Because much of the water in meat is bound to other molecules, like collagen, fat, and protein.

THE BENEFITS OF THE STALL

The stall has four benefits for barbecue:

1. It helps create the bark, which can be very tasty.

2. It holds the meat at a moderate temperature long enough for fats and connective tissues to liquefy, significantly improving texture, juiciness, and flavor.

3. It gives naturally occurring enzymes, always present in meat, time to tenderize.

4. It heats the meat evenly so the center and exterior are similar in temperature.

THE TEXAS CRUTCH

There are two ways to beat the stall. One is to cook at a high temperature, but this can result in tough, dry meat as proteins shrink. The other is to use the "Texas crutch": wrapping the meat in foil to tenderize and speed cooking. Practically all the top competitive barbecue teams use the crutch for brisket, ribs, and pork shoulder (butt).

The idea is to seal the meat tightly in foil, sometimes with a little water, juice, wine, or beer. The liquid mixes with the juices that drip from the meat, gently braising the meat. Braising is the same process that occurs in a slow cooker, where the meat sits partially submerged in liquid. The liquid transmits heat to the meat faster than air does, speeding the cooking, but most importantly, if the foil makes a tight seal, water cannot evaporate and cool the meat. But crutch for too long, and you will extract flavor and moisture from the meat, remove your precious rub, and seriously damage the bark, making it mushy.

Here are the basics: Use heavy-duty aluminum foil, pour 1 to 2 ounces of liquid into the foil, and crimp it tightly. Make sure that the packet will not leak and that steam will not escape. If the crutch does not hug the meat tightly, or if it leaks even a little, the meat will cool from evaporation and the cooking will slow down drastically. Insert your thermometer through the top of the foil, and crimp the foil around the probe to close the hole so the juices won't leak out.

Most competition cooks crutch ribs, pork butt, and brisket. The improvements in moisture and texture are small, but enough to make a difference when prize money is on the line. At home, I rarely crutch because I can wait and I love hard bark.

When you open the package, be careful to avoid the hot steamy air that will escape. Keep in mind that the moment you open the foil, the meat will cool rapidly and can go from 203 to 170°F in just 20 minutes. After the meat has crutched, you can take it out of the foil and return it to the cooker at 225°F for about 30 minutes to dry the surface and firm up the bark.

BASTING AND SPRITZING

Part of the ritual of working the grill is standing with the brush and periodically, like the great artists we are, painting the food with a secret liquid. This process allows us to inhale the aromas (*Ahhh, it smells sooooo good*), check on the progress (*Almost done, honey!*), look at the hypnotic flames (*Me like fire!*), and act like we know what we're doing (*I'm a grillmaster!*).

There are pros and cons to basting and spritzing.

WE ARE LENGTHENING COOKING TIME. In low-and-slow cooking, where the temperature within the cooker is less than 250°F and the meat is cooked to an internal temperature of 203°F or so, the extra moisture causes evaporative cooling on the meat's surface, which can increase the cooking time by 10 to 20 percent. For grilled steaks, burgers, and chicken, spritzing, mopping, and basting have less effect on the cooking time.

WE ARE SOFTENING THE CRUST. The danger of basting is that it can hamper browning and crust formation. For instance, the skin on chicken, turkey, and duck tastes best when dark and crispy. Painting the skin with water-based bastes, even pan drippings or butter (which has water in it), wets the skin, making it rubbery. Painting the skin with oil, however, can sometimes help browning and crisping, especially if the cooker is really hot.

WE ARE REMOVING FLAVOR. One of the problems of basting is that the process can wash off smoke, spices, and marinades. Do it too often, and you can remove a significant amount of flavor.

WE ARE ADDING FLAVOR. A thicker baste, like a Texas "mop" (page 179), can adhere to the surface, adding more flavor than will a thin mop of apple juice, beer, or wine.

WE ARE RETARDING BROWNING. Water on the surface has to steam off before the surface can brown.

WE ARE AIDING BROWNING. Mops high in sugar, such as those made with apple juice, can caramelize and help brown the surface and add new levels of complexity to the bark.

WE ARE ATTRACTING SMOKE. Smoke is attracted to and sticks better to wet surfaces. When we baste, we make the food taste smokier.

WE ARE HELPING THE SMOKE RING. By keeping the surface damp, we are allowing nitric oxide and carbon monoxide in the smoke to enter and combine with the myoglobin in the meat to create the smoke ring.

The best time to baste is after the crust forms, immediately after flipping the meat. At that point, the top surface is still hot and bubbly; the mop will mix with the juices of the meat, the

MYTH Lookin' ain't cookin'.

BUSTED! It is widely accepted wisdom, appearing in practically every barbecue book ever written, that "if you're lookin', you ain't cookin.'" The message? When you open the lid of your grill or smoker, hot air escapes, cooking slows, and each peek adds lots of time to the length of the cook. This warning is meant to caution cooks who are constantly basting their food or just admiring their handiwork. Makes sense, right? Professor Blonder tested the theory on a Weber Kettle charcoal grill and a gas grill.

On a day when the ambient temperature was in the 70s, he opened a Weber Kettle charcoal grill for 1 minute. The temperature dropped almost instantly and recovered most of the way in about 2 minutes because the metal remained hot and hot air remained trapped under the lid. But it never recovered all the way because the coals had burned down a bit. When the lid was opened for 5 minutes, the temperature bounced back fairly quickly, but again, not all the way. But most importantly, the meat was barely affected by the dip in air tempereature because the heat stored in its thermal mass was enough to continue cooking it, much like carryover. The chicken was cooking the chicken more than the air was.

He repeated the test on a gas grill. When the lid was closed after 1 minute, the air temperature recovered completely in a minute or two, because the fuel kept burning at the same rate. When the grill was opened for 5 minutes, the temperature took almost 20 minutes to recover because the metal had a chance to cool off. But again, the meat barely responded to the opening and closing.

The lesson? You can peek and you will pay only a minimal penalty. Lookin' doesn't stop the cookin'.

water will evaporate and cool the surface, and the flavor will be left behind. If you baste and flip immediately, you will merely pour off the flavorings, and you might actually retard the formation of the crust.

Remember, all uncooked meat contains potentially hazardous microbes and spores. If you use a brush you could be transferring contaminated juices from the meat to the unused baste and back, especially if it was used as a marinade. Stop basting 15 minutes before serving so any contaminated baste on the meat is exposed to enough heat to make it safe.

STRATEGIES FOR USING BARBECUE SAUCES

Here's how to get the most from barbecue sauce on different meats and different cookers.

SKIP THE SAUCE OR SERVE IT AT THE TABLE. If the meat tastes great—and it should if you've cooked it properly—you might want to skip the sauce like they do in many restaurants. A good dry rub, proper smoke flavor, and careful cooking will allow you to go commando. Or serve the sauce on the side and allow your guests to apply it if they wish.

SHOW SOME RESTRAINT! One coat is usually enough—two, max. Resist the temptation to pour sauce all over pulled pork before serving. Let the meat shine through.

SIZZLE AND CRISP THE SAUCE OVER DIRECT HEAT. Just before serving, paint on the sauce and place the meat over hot direct heat and caramelize the sugars. This changes the sauce's flavor and gives it more complexity. Stand there and watch in case the sauce begins to burn. On a smoker with an offset firebox, you may be able to sizzle on a grate over the flame in the firebox. I recommend using a preheated gas grill if you have one. Or if you have a kitchen broiler, sizzle the sauce under that for 5 to 10 minutes per side, starting with the back (non-meat) side. Another good way to crisp the sauce is to whip out your propane soldering torch or invest about $30 in a hot butane culinary torch and scorch the sauce just enough to caramelize the sugars.

PLAY IT SAFE. Pour just what you need into a cup. As with marinades and bastes, when you are done cooking, throw out any sauce left in the cup. Never save it or serve it tableside. Use fresh, uncontaminated sauce for brushing and for serving at the table.

COOKING MORE THAN ONE LARGE HUNK OF MEAT

When the whole fam-damily is coming over, you might want to cook a lot of meat at once. Let's say you want to cook three pork butts (8 pounds each) at 225°F for pulled pork. When you put several cold hunks of meat in a preheated cooker, the air temperature will drop a bit. How much depends on how much air is in there and how fast it is flowing through. In a large smoker, the drop will be barely noticeable. In a small unit, it might be 10°F or more. Once you are back at the target temperature, each piece of meat will cook independently in about the same time as if you had only one hunk in there. There might be slight variations due to humidity and impeded airflow, but they shouldn't be significant.

On the other hand, if you have those butts crammed in tight, practically touching, hot air can't flow between them and they will act like one big hunk of meat, significantly changing the cooking time. So try to keep at least 2 inches between hunks of meat.

Then there is the "heat shadow." An offset barrel smoker (see page 90) has a firebox on one side and a chimney on the other. The meat closest to the heat will cook faster, while the rest of it is in the heat shadow cast by the meat. It's a good idea to rotate the meat once or twice during cooking, so meat near the firebox doesn't overcook and meat in the heat shadow doesn't undercook.

If you have a vertical smoker, like a Weber Smokey Mountain (see page 87), there are two cooking grates. One is right above the water pan and closer to the heat source. The other is about a foot higher, below a parabolic dome. The meat on the lower rack is protected from direct heat by the water pan, and it also gets cool air and moisture from the water pan. The space between the meat and the water is small, so the airflow around it is inhibited. Meanwhile, hot air rises and goes to the exhaust vent in the dome, where some of it escapes and some of it pools. As a result, the food on the lower rack is cooler. But on the upper rack, the meat practically floats in warm currents of convection heat, and it even gets some mild radiant heat reflecting from the dome. Again, you may want to rotate the meat to compensate for hot spots. Or put the larger hunk up top.

The solution to cooking multiple big cuts of meat is simple: Start earlier than you think is necessary and monitor temperatures closely. If the meat is done earlier than expected, you can always hold it at serving temperature in your cooker, in your indoor oven, or in a faux Cambro.

COOK TODAY, SERVE TOMORROW

One of the most frequently asked questions I get goes something like this: "I got roped into serving pulled pork for fifty people at the company picnic on Sunday. I plan to cook it on Saturday at home and bring it to the park on Sunday. What's the best way to do this?"

Fresh is best. You should always try to serve food fresh from the cooker. It has hot juices, the connective tissues have melted and turned to luscious gelatin, the fat has rendered and lubricated the muscle fibers, the browned surfaces are crunchy, and the vegetables are bright and crisp. By the next day, many of the juices have evaporated or run off, much of the tenderness has been lost, the bark and other crunchy bits have become soggy, and oxidation has begun to deteriorate flavor. The reason you can smell barbecue from a block away is its volatile organic compounds, and by the next day, many of these aromatics are gone forever.

If you can't serve fresh food, you should rethink your plan. Skip the pulled pork, brisket, and ribs, and just grill up some fresh chicken, burgers, or hot dogs instead.

But there is a way to pull this off with style. Mike Wozniak is the pitmaster of QUAU, the 2010 Kansas City Barbeque Society Team of the Year. He breaks the rules and still wins—a lot. He cooked up this trick because he enters dozens of competitions every year, and he got tired of staying up all night babying his brisket and pork butt. He was kind enough to teach me his method so I could share it with you.

The reason you can smell barbecue a block away is its volatile organic compounds. By the next day, many of these compounds are gone forever.

He cooks his brisket at about 310°F for about 4 hours, taking it up to an internal temperature of about 180°F. At 310°F, there is little or no stall. He then wraps it tightly in aluminum foil, pinching off the overlaps thoroughly, and drops it into a clean, watertight trash bag, and squeezes out the air. The whole shooting match goes into a beer cooler and is then submerged under lots of ice, where it chills in a hurry. He warns that a fridge is not cold enough and the thermal mass of the warm meat will raise the fridge temperature much too high, spoiling other foods in there.

The next morning, he takes the meat out of the cooler and out of the bag, but leaves it in the foil—this is essentially the Texas crutch (see page 60)—and puts it back on the pit (you could put it in an oven because it is not going to take on smoke inside the foil) at 310°F for 3 to 4 hours until it hits 200°F. He unwraps it, saving the juices, and if they are not too salty, he uses them in his sauce. The unwrapped meat then goes back on the pit to firm the crust for no more than 30 minutes or so. Then it can be sliced, sauced, and served. Wozniak says he has even used this method and cooked the meat several days in advance, moving the chilled meat to the fridge before reheating.

The Wozniak method also works on pork butts. It's pretty convenient when you have a smoker at home but are serving at a friend's house who has only a gas grill.

I don't recommend this technique for ribs.

A CHALLENGE TO GAS GRILL MANUFACTURERS

Why don't gas grill manufacturers install thermostats? Indoor ovens have had them for about a century.

Pellet smokers have had thermostats since they first appeared in the early 1990s, and they are the hottest new category of grill, with more than a dozen manufacturers appearing in the past five years. Some come complete with programmable settings and jacks for meat probes.

The BBQ Guru, a thermostat controller for charcoal grills that controls airflow to the coals, first appeared in 2004, and there are several models and competitors on the market now.

Most replacement thermostats for an indoor oven cost less than $100 retail. Surely a major grill manufacturer could add a push-button control system just like the one in your indoor oven for a reasonable price. So what's the holdup?

Their ratio of surface area to meat is high, so they could become too dry. But if you have no choice, cook ribs for about 3 hours at 225°F, foil wrap them, chill them rapidly, and the next day warm them for 2 to 3 hours at 225°F in the foil. Remove the foil, firm the crust, add the sauce, and you're ready to rock.

FREEZING AND REHEATING LEFTOVERS

I usually cook more food than needed so I won't be embarrassed by running out. Inevitably, my guests end up fighting over the leftovers. For ribs, I plan on at least 1 to 1½ pounds per person for a meal (remember, about half the weight of a slab is bone and there is drip loss). For pulled pork and brisket, I cook about a pound per person to account for shrinkage and waste before serving. If you have leftover meat that you don't plan on eating in 3 to 4 days, here's how to freeze and reheat it later.

FREEZING. The best way to pack food for freezer (and refrigerator) storage is with a vacuum sealer (pictured top right). It sucks out oxygen, the culprit in oxidation that creates off flavors in frozen and refrigerated food. If you don't have a vacuum sealer, use a zipper-top freezer bag. Put the meat in the bag, add a little broth or stock, and then slowly lower the bag into a pot of water. The water will displace the air in the bag. You can then zip it closed. The idea is to get out as much air as possible to minimize freezer burn and oxidation. Be sure to label the bag with its contents and the date.

THAWING. Well before you plan to eat your frozen leftovers, thaw them in the refrigerator. This could take 6 to 8 hours for ribs, longer for thicker cuts.

Here's a slightly faster way to thaw meat. Fill the sink or a pot big enough to hold the meat with cold water. Put the meat in a watertight plastic zipper-top bag. Leave the bag unzipped at first, and slowly submerge it, keeping the zipper above water. The water pressure will push out all the air. Then zip it up tight. Leave it in cold water, and hold it under with a plate if necessary. Change the water every 30 minutes to make sure the meat is kept cold. Stir it occasionally to break up the envelope of cold water surrounding the meat. Allow 30 minutes per pound; a 20-pound turkey will need 10 hours.

REHEATING IN AN INDOOR OVEN. Reheat thawed meat at low temperatures so you don't dry it out. If you are going to use barbecue sauce, paint the meat all over and then wrap the meat in aluminum foil, being careful not to puncture it. Place the foil-wrapped meat on a baking pan or cookie sheet in case it leaks. Preheat the oven to about 225°F. Bake the meat on a rack in the middle of the oven until the center reaches 155°F. Ribs will take about 30 minutes. Larger cuts will take longer. If you have used sweet barbecue sauce, unwrap the meat and put it under the broiler on one side for 5 to 10 minutes, until the sauce begins to bubble. Leave the oven door open so the thermostat will not turn off the broiler. Do not walk away from the oven because sauce can go from bubbling to carbon black in minutes. Turn the meat over and broil for a few more minutes until the sauce is bubbling.

REHEATING ON A GRILL. Heat the grill to about 225°F with the lid closed and use a two-zone setup. On a gas grill, this is probably about medium. Wrap the meat in foil, and cook it in the indirect zone until the center reaches your target temperature. Unwrap and grill over the direct zone for 5 to 10 minutes on each side. Don't let the sauce burn.

REHEATING IN A MICROWAVE OVEN. For sliced meat, lay the meat in a single layer on a plate and cover with parchment paper, never foil. Don't microwave for too long, or the meat will become mushy. Microwaves can also make sauce runny. I prefer the dry heat of ovens and grills, which firms up the sauce and caramelizes the sugars. But if you must microwave, start with about 1 minute and touch the meat periodically to see if it's ready.

PULLED OR SLICED MEAT. You can freeze these in zipper-top bags or vacuum bags and reheat them in a pot of simmering water.

COOKING VEGETABLES AND FRUITS

When it comes to barbecue and grilling, most folks think of meat, but many vegetables, fruits, and seeds also taste better when grilled or smoked. Plant matter has much less protein and fat than meat, more water than most meats, and more carbohydrates. Cooking plant foods often enhances their flavors, reduces some of their bitterness, helps convert carbohydrates to sugars, caramelizes sugars, breaks down indigestible woody compounds, releases nutrients, and kills microbes.

Reverse searing is a great technique for many vegetables.

While bell peppers, asparagus, zucchini, and eggplant soften quickly over direct heat, reverse searing (see page 48) is a great technique for many vegetables. Brussels sprouts, cabbage, and cauliflower, to name just a few, are enhanced by the process. Dense and tough root vegetables like sweet potatoes and carrots can be transformed into sweet, rich treats with a slow reverse sear. Peeling, slicing, salting, and oiling will often help. Cutting root vegetables into smaller pieces like disks or chunks and cooking them on a grill topper (see page 103) speeds along the process and gives you more surface area for delicious browning. You can parboil, steam, or microwave tougher root vegetables until they begin to soften and then finish them on the grill. Serve them al dente—tender but with just a bit of crunch. Err on the side of undercooking to avoid limp vegetables.

Stems and leaves can also be grilled, albeit with more care. Cooking collapses them rapidly, and they can burn easily. Belgian endive, radicchio, and romaine lettuce all grill beautifully, especially after a splash of vinaigrette. Keep the lid up, turn them often, and keep an eye on them. A little charring is nice, but don't let them blacken too much. You can also grill sturdy vegetables such as fennel and onions.

By far our favorite plant parts, fruits are the seed-bearing organs that grow from the flower's ovaries. They tend to be laden with sugar. Tree fruits such as apples, figs, peaches, and pears are spectacular when grilled.

SMOKING AND DRYING

Tomatoes, olives, chile peppers, and other fruits and vegetables that do well in a dehydrator will also do well in a smoker. Cut them open so they can dry more easily, bring the temperature down to 225°F so the water will steam off, and then make sure you don't cook them so far that they become brittle or black. They should remain pliable. Tomatoes taste amazing when dehydrated in a smoker.

COMPETITION BARBECUE COOKING

With more than five hundred barbeque competitions a year around the nation, there is bound to be one near you. And there are more and more on TV. If you are a backyard cook just beginning to build your repertoire and skills, you have probably been thinking about emulating the techniques you see on television.

But you should absolutely *not* try to cook for your friends and family the way barbecue teams cook on TV. If you want superb food, follow my recipes precisely the first time. Then, once you have mastered the techniques and want to try something you saw on TV, attempt one trick at a time. Cooking for competitions uses a variety of gymnastic tricks and makes for generally poor-quality dining.

Here's why: Competition cooks have incredibly good equipment—huge, expensive high-tech machines like the wood burner shown below, a $15,000 trailer-mounted Jambo Pit Smoker used by Scottie Johnson of CancerSucksChicago.com. Behind him is a

$4,700 pellet cooker. (Full disclosure: AmazingRibs.com is one of his sponsors.) Chances are that not all the techniques he uses will work on your backyard smoker.

Cooking for competitions uses a variety of gymnastic tricks and generally makes for poor-quality dining.

Competition cooks also know that their entries will be one of several samples served to the judges (usually six samples at a time), and in order to win, they must really stand out. The food must be flashy. Delicacy, simplicity, subtlety, and complexity—all characteristics of great food elsewhere—get you eliminated in a competition. Instead, competition pitmasters go for big, bold, sweet flavors, knowing that most of the time the judge will take only one bite. And they may cook four racks of ribs to get just six perfect bones. Waste is a necessity in competition cooking.

In the chicken category, most pitmasters cook only thighs for competition. A typical prep involves removing the bone; peeling back the

skin; scraping off the subcutaneous fat; trimming each thigh until all are identical in shape; coating them with a sweet rub; injecting them with liquid margarine, phosphates, and MSG; folding the meat so only the skin is visible and placing the pampered thighs on top of butter in cupcake tins; and painting them with agave sugar and then a shiny, sweet, red barbecue sauce.

Trust me. Competition food is so bizarre that eating more than one or two bites becomes a chore. I have heard more than one pitmaster confide that he would never cook like this for friends or family.

Remember KISS: Keep It Simple, Students.

4
HARD-
WARE

CHARCOAL VS GAS GRILL THROWDOWN

If one thing burns brighter than the debate between Mac and PC users, it is the flame-throwing between charcoal purists and gas hotheads. Yes, there are pellet cookers, too, but this new technology is better at smoking than grilling, and electric grills aren't really grills. We'll get to those later.

CHARCOAL GRILLS: PROS

Charcoal purists are passionate, bordering on rabid. You will have to pry their charcoal from their cold, dead fingers, and they would *never, ever, no how, no way* use a gas grill.

They do have a point. A charcoal grill can lay up to a blistering 900°F on the surface of a steak, a lot hotter than standard gas grills without infrared burners. That high heat is just what you need to crisp up the surface of beef steaks and lamb chops while keeping them red or pink on the inside.

The other major advantage of charcoal is smoke, a sapid by-product of combustion. Charcoal produces a broad range of tasty flavor molecules, especially when it is first ignited. Gas fuel is a simple molecule (CH_4 for natural gas, C_3H_8 for liquid propane), and when fully combusted produces only water and carbon dioxide—no flavor. You can create smoke by adding wood to either a charcoal or a gas grill, and a lot of smoke gets produced when food drips fats and juices onto the hot surfaces below, but a brief encounter with smoke is not going to significantly change the flavor of quick-cooking foods such as hot dogs, quarter-pounders, or even skinny steaks. On thick steaks and thick cuts of chicken and turkey, smoke can make its presence known. If you use your grill for long, low-and-slow smoke roasting, you will see a noticeable difference in flavor from smoke encountering the meat. When mixed with smoke from wood chips or chunks, the combustion gases from charcoal contribute a distinctive flavor that is typical of traditional Southern barbecue. The smoke flavor produced on a propane grill is a bit more one-dimensional.

CHARCOAL GRILLS: CONS

Charcoal poses a slightly higher risk of fire, and for that reason, many apartment buildings and local fire codes ban them from balconies. Coals and sparks can escape the grill by falling through vents or from chimney starters, and you need water or a fire extinguisher handy to put them out. With a gas grill, you just turn a knob and the flame is dead.

Charcoal is dirty; it can be hard to light; it takes about 15 minutes longer to get up to temperature; it can flare up, burning the food; its heat can be difficult to gauge and regulate; it can slowly lose heat during long cooking; its temperature cannot be turned down rapidly; and it produces ash that you have to clean up and discard afterward. Charcoal grills rarely have rotisseries.

Most of these problems are easily avoided. Careful handling with gloves, shovels, and/or tongs sidesteps the mess and minimizes the fire risk. If you keep your charcoal dry and use a chimney, getting hot coals is easy. If you push the coals to one side of the grill and set up a two-zone cooking environment (see page 8), fatty meats like skin-on chicken do not drip fats on the coals and flare up; and even if there are flare-ups, a squirt gun can quell them. A removable ash tray makes cleanup a snap.

Yes, charcoal takes a bit more practice than gas, but there is little a charcoal grill cannot do once you master it. And you get to fiddle with fire!

GAS GRILLS: PROS

Gas grills offer convenience and control. Those two words alone clinch the argument for many folks. They are easy to start, heat up within 10 to 15 minutes, hold a steady temperature, and can be cranked up or cooled down rapidly. If your gas grill has two or more burners, it can easily be set up for indirect and two-zone cooking. Temperature control, which is vital to good cooking, is a lot simpler on a gas grill: Just twist the dial. If it's Tuesday, you're late getting home from work, and you need those frozen burgers ready in an hour, a gasser does the job. When you are done cooking, a gas grill is easy to clean. They're often allowed on high-rise balconies, too.

How about taste? Probably 90 percent of the world's greatest barbecue joints use gas for heat in their pits, along with wood for flavor. A similar proportion of the world's most expensive steakhouses grill their aged prime beef to perfect doneness with gas.

Barbecue joints use gas for the same reasons backyard cooks do: convenience and control. Steakhouses use gas because they want a dark

sear, and they get extremely high heat from special broilers that cook simultaneously from above and below, producing blowtorch temperatures between 800 and 1200°F.

Unfortunately, your average backyard gas grill doesn't get quite that hot. With a sear burner you might get up to 900°F or so on a small portion of the cooking surface, but most gas grills top out around 450 to 500°F. If you're buying a new one, I strongly recommend a sear burner—especially for steaks.

Although gas grills excel at holding a steady temperature, they are not perfect. A dial setting of medium may equal 300°F on a hot day; 275°F on a 70°F day; or 225°F on a cool, windy, or rainy day. But once you get to know your cooker, it is pretty easy to manage the temperature. On a three-burner grill, you might use a hot zone for meat, a medium zone for veggies, and a low zone for holding finished foods. The heat diffusers above the burners are pretty good at preventing flare-ups, too.

Cleanup is easier on gas grills because there is little ash, and drips are usually vaporized on the metal drip-protector bars, lava rocks, or ceramic rocks, sending smoke and steam back up to the food much like charcoal would. Most have grease trays that are relatively easy to empty, so the only day-to-day maintenance is scraping down the grates.

Another advantage: Gas grills usually offer a wider range of accessories. Most have rotisserie kits as an option, an add-on I highly recommend. Many come with side burners, also recommended, so you can keep sauces warm or cook side dishes. You can get night-lights, side tables, spice racks, storage drawers, bottle openers—some gas grills are even Bluetooth enabled. GrillGrates (see page 100) can be added to most gas grills, and this accessory can significantly improve the cooking characteristics of a grill by amplifying heat, preventing flare-ups, minimizing hot spots, and allowing you to smolder wood right on the grate below the food.

GAS GRILLS: CONS

Some high-end gas grills come with smoke boxes for wood chips, but most require you to make foil packets or put pans of wood under the cooking grate near the flame. For fire safety and to prevent explosions, most gas grill lids do not seal well by design, so a lot of the smoke leaks out and more wood is needed than on a tight-lidded charcoal grill.

Gas can explode if you don't handle it properly. ESPN host Hannah Storm was severely burned in 2012 when she tried to ignite her propane grill after the wind blew the flame out. Unbeknownst to her, the gas continued to course through the jets and pooled in the lower chamber because it is heavier than air. When she hit the spark button, the accumulated propane exploded in her face. Windblown flameouts happen on some grills, but it is hard to predict which ones are susceptible. Nonetheless, gas remains slightly safer than charcoal because there is little or no way for sparks or hot objects to escape a gas grill. If there is a problem, just turn off the knob on the tank.

Gas jets and venturi (air intake) valves can get clogged on a gas grill. Water can condense and block the lines on extremely cold days. Carbon and grease build up below the burners, and if you ignore it, this grease can catch fire. It is very difficult to put out such fires without a fire extinguisher rated for grease fires.

Gas grills tend to be more expensive because the mechanisms are more complex. That also makes assembly more complicated, and there are more parts that may break and need to be replaced. It is hard to tell if your tank is about to run out of gas in the middle of cooking, unlike a charcoal grill, where you can just eyeball the number of embers. As for fuel cost, it is hard to compare the two. Charcoal is often on sale, especially in spring, while propane fluctuates with petroleum prices. It is rarely on sale. Both fuels are inexpensive compared to the food.

Many gas grills don't have the important sear burners, and many sear burners are small and can only sear one or two steaks at a time. That's perfect for empty nesters, but if you're hosting a graduation party, you will want more super-hot real estate.

WHO WINS?

Imagine two slabs of center-cut ribs side by side. Both were cooked at the same temperature with Meathead's Memphis Dust (page 167) and no sauce. One was cooked with charcoal and wood chips for flavor. The other was cooked on a gas grill with exactly the same amount of wood chips by weight. In a taste test, the charcoal ribs had a deeper, smokier fireplace scent and flavor. The gas ribs had a stronger pork flavor with hints of bacon, and they were moister. Which was better? That's a matter of taste. I loved them both.

If you're just starting out and you want

no-fuss, no-muss, convenience grilling, go gas with an infrared/sear burner. If red meats and smoking are your highest priority, go charcoal. If taste is the most important factor, go charcoal.

I have many gas and charcoal grills. I cook almost all my birds, fish, veggies, pizzas, breads, and quick-cooking foods on my gas grills. I cook almost all my red meats on my charcoal grills. If you can afford it and have the space, get one of each (and a smoker, while you're at it).

Some new grills have one side for gas and the other for charcoal. It's a great idea, but most of the combos I've seen are cheaply built and compromise the advantages of both fuels.

WHAT TO LOOK FOR IN A GRILL

The database of equipment reviews on AmazingRibs.com covers about 400 grills and 250 smokers, and there are probably another 50 or so that we haven't discovered yet. The grills vary from small disposable units for picnics to huge monsters that attach to your trailer hitch and have as many wheels as a semi. Boy, do they range in price. Not long ago I saw a pricey stainless-steel job in my neighborhood hardware store that advertised "financing available"!

A good grill is an essential tool for the modern cook, not just as a backyard diversion, but as a second oven. It even comes in handy in emergencies. Just ask people how they cooked dinner after a hurricane or tornado knocked out the power. (Yes, you can use that line on your spouse when you tell her how much you *need* a new grill.)

What a grill does best is create food with well-browned flavor. Because of the high heat, it comes closer to turning out steakhouse steaks and better burgers than indoor cookers. Configured properly, a grill can even smoke low and slow just as well as a dedicated smoker.

There is no single answer to the question "What is the best grill?" because the question lacks two essential words: "for me." Before you go shopping, ask yourself what you want to cook most often. Ribs? Steaks? Two very different cooking processes are needed for those foods. Then ask how much you want to spend.

You have six fuel types to choose from—charcoal, gas, logs, wood pellets, propane, and electricity. Don't make up your mind based on what you've heard. Don't let your neighbor—the charcoal evangelist—or your coworker—the gas hothead—sway you. There's a lot of misinformation out there. Keep an open mind and check the reviews on AmazingRibs.com before you hand over your credit card. Here's what you need to know.

PRICE. What is your bottom line? As with a car, a better-equipped model is more expensive. The old reliable, very capable, versatile, and indestructible Weber Kettle charcoal grill can be had for under $100. High-end charcoal grills can go for as much as $2,000.

You can get a really nice gas grill for $400 or be the envy of the neighborhood for $800. Prices can even go up above $5,000. But keep in mind that quality does not necessarily increase with price. A lot of the $1,000 units I've used did not outperform some $400 cookers.

Quality will last. I had a Weber Genesis gas grill for fifteen years until I gave it to a nephew. He used it for five years before he gave it away and bought a new grill. It's probably still out there somewhere churning out fine dining. On the other hand, I know someone who buys a new big, shiny, stainless-steel grill from a discount store every five years because they always fall apart.

Remember to budget for thermometers. Notice I say thermometers, plural. You need a good digital grill thermometer and a good meat thermometer (see page 96).

If you are buying a propane grill, plan on buying a second propane tank as a backup. If you are going with natural gas, budget for a licensed technician (usually a heating contractor or plumber) to do the hookup.

You may also want to invest in a good protective cover for your grill. Many grills really don't need it, but some will collect water in the drip pan or cabinet unless they are covered in inclement weather. And of course, you'll need spatulas, tongs, and cleaning tools (see pages 105–113).

SIZE OF THE COOKING SURFACE. Size matters, and it relates to price. Look at the number of square inches of primary cooking surface, or the size of the main cooking grate. Some manufacturers list total cooking area, including the warming rack suspended above the primary cooking area. Yes, you can cook up there, but its distance from the flame means that food cooks differently. A removable warming rack is a nice feature, but the important measurement is the total square inches of the main cooking grate.

Area = Width x Depth

If the width is 28 inches and the depth is 14 inches, then:

Area = 28 x 14 = 392 square inches

If the cooking surface is round, the formula is

Area = pi x the radius squared

Pi can be rounded to 3.14. The radius is the diameter divided by 2, so measure the diameter (across the widest point through the center) and divide by 2. To square a number, you multiply it by itself. So the area of a 22.5-inch Weber Kettle is calculated like this:

HOW TO GET A 50 PERCENT DISCOUNT

Most hardware stores want to get rid of their grills by September. They take up too much space, and by then they're stocking Christmas trees. The end of August and early fall is the best time to get closeout bargains. By midsummer, you can also get bargains on discontinued models and floor demos. A few years ago, I bought a sweet $500 Char-Broil gasser for $250 at Lowe's. It was a display model that had a dent and was missing a couple of knobs. I found the manager, offered him half the list price, and he didn't hesitate. Sold! Char-Broil has great customer service, and they sent me the two knobs at no charge (and no, I didn't tell them I was a food writer).

Area = 3.14 x (22.5 ÷ 2) x (22.5 ÷ 2) = 397.4 square inches

Remember: You do not want to crowd a grill. You should leave at least ½ inch between foods being cooked. As a rule of thumb, allow 25 square inches for each 4-inch burger. So a Weber Kettle can handle about 15 burgers across the entire surface.

For two-zone and indirect cooking, you'll need enough space to get the food on one half of the total cooking surface. So that kettle will handle about 7 burgers. If a chicken cut into parts takes up 12 by 12 inches, or 144 square inches, then you need 288 square inches for one chicken. If you will be cooking veggies or other sides, then you need more space. You need a minimum of 72 square inches per person—about 9 by 8 inches, or the size of a dinner plate—to cook a whole meal for a person. Multiply that by 2 for two-zone cooking.

Try to determine how many people you will normally be cooking for, and don't forget the Fourth of July party. You can grill some foods in batches, but that could be really slow.

FOOTPRINT. Will it fit on your condo's balcony? (Speaking of balconies, does your building code allow grills? Check any restrictions before you whip out that credit card.) Don't forget that you need plenty of space around your cooker for ventilation and airflow, and so you don't set something on fire or melt the vinyl siding on your house. When measuring a grill's space requirements, open the lid. Sometimes it requires a foot or more of clearance behind the unit—not to mention above it.

ABOUT THAT SO-CALLED GRILL "THERMOMETER"

The most important thing a good cook needs is a reliable thermometer. Even high-end grill manufacturers install cheapo heat indicators. (I hate calling those things thermometers.) These junky dials have ruined more meals than flies on potato salad. You absolutely cannot rely on them. They are often off by 50°F or more. Most manufacturers mount the thermometer in the lid several inches above the cooking surface, useful only if you plan to eat the lid. If you have a two-zone setup with the left side hot and the right side off, the dial thermometer rests in the center where it averages the temperature of the two zones, giving you a meaningless number. Even with direct-heat cooking just below the thermometer, the air above a piece of meat exists in a heat shadow, and its temperature will be a lot cooler than the temperature on the underside of the meat that sits directly above the flame. For an accurate measurement, you need a probe clipped to the cooking surface a few inches from the food you are cooking (see page 116).

Please, buy a good digital thermometer with a probe that can be placed on the cooking surface near the food (see page 96). It will make a massive difference in your food quality and on-time delivery.

HEAD SPACE. You will want enough room to smoke a turkey in there, so make sure there are at least 12 inches of head space between the cooking grate and the inside of the lid. If there is a warming rack, it could get in the way, so it should be removable.

SMOKING. To smoke food properly, you must be able to control airflow. For example, the Weber Kettle charcoal grill does a fine job of smoking because it has excellent airflow control and a tight lid. There are some add-ons that make it even better at smoking (see page 88). Gas grills usually don't have tight lids because they need to allow combustion gases to escape during cooking and flammable gas to escape in case of a flameout. But you can still smoke on them; you just need more wood.

SAFETY. Is the grill child- and pet-safe? Are electrical parts safe from rain and snow? Is the grease pan right where the dog likes it? Do the wheels lock? Do the handles stay cool? Coiled stainless-steel handles are the best because they remain cool by dispersing heat.

GRATES. There are a wide variety of materials used for grill grates. But don't let crappy grates kill the deal. You can always buy replacements. They are not expensive. (Read more about grates on pages 100–103.)

EASY CLEANING. Personally, I don't care what the outside of my grill looks like. But cleaning the interior is a requirement. Before you buy, study the unit and ask yourself how you will clean it and if you are willing to do the work. If it's too hard to clean, you won't do it and you'll end up ruining food or starting grease fires.

MATERIALS AND DURABILITY. The best grills are made from powder- coated steel, vitreous enamel bonded to steel, cast aluminum, or high-quality stainless steel. Heavy steel holds and distributes heat better than thin steel or cast aluminum.

Paint is the least desirable coating, since it chips and peels easily. Powder coating is thick and durable. It is produced by giving a positive electrostatic charge to a polymer powder, grounding the metal of the grill, and spraying the powder on the metal. The electrical charge makes the powder stick, and it is bonded with heat.

Vitreous enamel is another excellent coating. This glasslike powder is sprayed onto the metal and melted. It is durable under heat and doesn't fade, but it can be brittle and crack if you bend or drop it, and then rust will form in the cracks. Weber Kettle grills are enamel coated.

WORKMANSHIP. Does the grill have sharp edges? Sturdy legs? How solid are the latches? How are the welds? Does it have a lot of cheap plastic parts? Will the screws rust? Do the moving parts look like they'll last?

WHEELS. If you want to move the thing after you set it up, perhaps to store it over the winter, make sure it has wheels or can be broken down easily. The wheels should be well built with sturdy welds and bolts. Are they durable rubber or cheap plastic? Are they large enough to roll smoothly on a rough or uneven surface such as pavers or grass?

WORK SURFACES AND STORAGE. Look for sturdy work surfaces and storage shelves. Will the worktable hold a turkey? Is the storage area rainproof? Will the doors withstand repeated opening and closing?

SIDE BURNERS. A side burner is not strictly necessary. They're handy for making side dishes or warming sauces, but most have trouble maintaining a low simmer, so you have to watch carefully to avoid burning. I recommend side burners, but if you're on a budget, instead of paying $200 for one that's built in, consider picking up a $25 standalone butane or propane burner, which is also portable for picnics and tailgates.

OTHER ACCESSORIES. Does it come with tools? Tool hooks? Most kamados offer deflector plates for indirect cooking, extra racks, and other add-ons, but some companies charge for them. You need them. You may also want a propane tank fuel gauge, night-lights, a cutting board, wok, steamer, drink holder, bottle openers, griddles, surround sound—there's no end to accessories.

ASSEMBLY. Grills can be tricky to assemble. And you will lose a screw. If you don't have the necessary time, tools, or skills, many merchants offer assembly services. For a fee.

MANUAL, WARRANTY, AND SUPPORT. Is there a manual? Was it translated from Chinese by a high school student? What kind of warranty and/or guarantee comes with the grill? On gassers, check the warranty on the burners. Sometimes the burner warranty is separate from the rest of the grill. Look for a 5- to 10-year warranty. Also, what is the dealer's reputation? Is there a phone number and e-mail for tech support, or are they hiding? Is the website informative? What if you need parts? How long have they been in business? Reputable companies like Weber still supply parts from models discontinued years ago.

BOTTOM LINE. Don't buy on looks. Don't buy crap, or you'll be shopping again in two or three years.

BUYING A GAS GRILL

Gas grills can be divided into two main categories: convection and infrared. In both designs, the cooking grates absorb heat and produce conduction heat where they contact the surface of the food. The dome reflects mostly convection heat. The exterior of the food absorbs heat, mostly from below, and produces conduction heat that moves to the center of the food.

Convection Gas Grill   Infrared Gas Grill

CONVECTION GRILLS. Most gassers are convection grills. They usually have burner tubes that sit below the grates upon which food sits. Gas travels through the tubes and out holes drilled in them, where it burns and generates heat. They usually have a heat diffuser over the burners to protect them from dripping grease and to distribute heat more evenly. Most use inverted V-shaped metal plates for diffusers. Stainless-steel diffusers last longer than enamel-coated. Some gas grills use lava rocks or ceramic rocks as diffusers. They eventually become saturated with grease and need replacing. Burners and the drip protectors produce a little radiant infrared heat and a lot of convection heat.

INFRARED GRILLS. These more recent designs use a highly efficient plate made of ceramic, glass, or metal above the gas burners. The plate absorbs heat and emits it as infrared radiation. Infrared grills also get hotter, often in the 500 to 700°F range—steakhouse temperatures. With infrared, there is less dry air motion, which means less moisture evaporates from the food, plus the radiant surface is usually so close to the food that dripping juices or marinades incinerate and go right back up onto the meat, adding flavor without flare-ups. Unfortunately, it is hard to get two distinct heat zones on IR grills.

LIQUID PROPANE OR NATURAL GAS. You need to choose between liquid propane and natural gas. The most popular grills burn liquid propane. Propane contains more cooking energy, about 2,500 BTUs in 1 cubic foot, than natural gas, which has about 1,000 BTUs in 1 cubic foot. But natural gas kits are designed to deliver more gas per minute than propane, so if they are set up properly, the BTU ratings should be about the same for either fuel. Most grills are set up for propane that comes in steel tanks weighing

WHAT ARE PROPANE AND NATURAL GAS?

Propane is a hydrocarbon (C_3H_8) produced from both crude oil and natural gas refining, which is compressed into a liquid state (LP). It boils, or returns to gas form, at about −44°F, so it must be stored in heavy tanks under pressure to maintain its liquid state. It turns to gas immediately after exiting the tank, so it doesn't need a carburetor to vaporize. All grills that use propane have a regulator that drops the pressure from more than 200 pounds per square inch (psi) to 0.5 to 10 psi, depending on your grill. The exact pressure in the cylinder is related to the amount of liquid in the tank and the ambient temperature, so the pressure declines on very cold days. In order to burn, propane needs to be mixed with 90 to 98 percent air, which is one reason that gas grills have so many air vents.

It burns relatively cleanly, but not as cleanly as natural gas. It is colorless and odorless, so ethyl mercaptan or other "odorants" are added to give it a foul smell, which promptly alerts us to any leaks. The odorants are destroyed by combustion. Some propane is also mixed with small amounts of butane.

Natural gas is a hydrocarbon mix that is mostly methane (CH_4). It is found deep underground, and it can be made from petroleum products. After processing to remove impurities, it also has ethyl mercaptan added, and then the gas is piped into homes for heating and cooking. It is among the cleanest of the petroleum products, meaning that when burned, it produces less carbon dioxide and carbon monoxide than other fuels.

about 20 pounds empty and holding 15 to 20 pounds of liquid propane. Some grill kits include the tank, but most do not, so plan on buying a tank filled with propane for about $40. When it is empty, you can exchange the empty for a full one for about $20 at many hardware stores, convenience stores, or gas stations. Prices really vary during the year and from place to place.

Natural gas is the more permanent option. It must be delivered to the grill by a pipeline from your house and delivered to your house by the public gas utility company. If you go with natural gas, you'll need an adapter kit and a certified contractor, usually a heating contractor or plumber, to do the installation. Some grills come with adapter kits, some manufacturers sell them as options, and some grills cannot be adapted.

The natural gas line is a hard pipe with a short, flexible connection attached, so your grill will remained fixed in a permanent location. On the plus side, natural gas comes from your house in a gaseous state, so it is more efficient in the winter than propane, which has to be converted to gas. The other advantages of natural gas are:

1. It is perhaps 20 percent of the price of propane.

2. You don't have to run to the store for refills.

3. You will never run out as long as you pay your gas bill.

If you are buying a liquid propane gas grill, check to see if it can be adapted to household natural gas and if the adapter kit is included or costs extra.

THE IGNITION SYSTEM. Gas grills need a starter to generate a spark to ignite the gas. Many ignite each individual burner when you turn the dial, and many use "crossover ignitions," in which one burner is lit and then the flame from that burner crosses over and lights the others. There are two basic ignition systems: electronic and piezo. Electronic ignition systems use batteries and they go dead. For piezo ignition, you turn a knob or press a button and a small spring-loaded hammer strikes a quartz crystal, creating voltage that produces a spark, which arcs from a wire to the burner tube. It makes a distinct clicking sound. Make sure the grill has a manual ignition hole so that if your igniter breaks, you can insert a wood match or stick lighter. Keep one or the other on hand in case the ignition fails, as it occasionally does.

WHAT ABOUT ELECTRIC GRILLS?

Electric cars are a great innovation. Electric grills? Not so much. Electric grills use a metal coil for heat. Often made from an alloy of nickel and chromium, the metal glows hot when a current is passed through it and the metal resists the flow. It works like a toaster coil and cooks like an electric frying pan. Although George Foreman, Cuisinart, Grundig, Coleman, Char-Broil, and even Weber call their electric devices "grills," there is no combustion, flame, or smoke, so I consider these devices to be large panini presses or, at best, low-temperature griddles. An inexpensive hardware store gas or charcoal cooker, if well chosen, can cook circles around any electric grill tastewise.

BURNERS. A good gas grill must have a minimum of two burners. This is essential for two-zone cooking. With three or four burners, you can have hot, medium, and low temperature zones. Most burners connect to the front and rear with knobs on the front. Others connect to the sides with knobs on the side. The best arrangement for most cooking is with the knobs on the front, so you can easily turn off one side to create an indirect cooking zone for slow roasting, and then move the food over to the direct zone for high-heat searing. You can also put food in the indirect zone for holding. The bigger the cooking surface, the more flexibility you have. Either way, you want the ability to get even heat across the entire cooking surface. If the burners are too far apart, there will be hot and cold spots. Look for high-quality stainless-steel or brass burners. Aluminum burners corrode and cast-iron burners rust.

SEAR BURNERS. Usually when a manufacturer says its grill has a "sear burner," it is referring to a small section that has an infrared radiant plate to amplify heat or a special burner that delivers extra heat. If you're in the market for a gas grill, try to get one with a sear burner so you can get better browning.

LID. A few grills, even some expensive ones, do not have lids. Without a lid, you are severely

MYTH The higher the BTU rating, the hotter the grill.

BUSTED! Grill manufacturers often tout their grills' BTUs, but the BTU rating is not indicative of the heat a grill can generate. It is derived from a calculation based on gas pressure, the size of the opening in the gas valve, and the type of gas. More BTUs indicate more fuel used, not higher heat. If you were shopping for a really fast car, the miles per gallon would not be a useful guide to how fast the car goes. It's like that.

The heat output of a grill must be calculated by BTU per square inch, or "heat flux," something that grill manufacturers never tell you. To guesstimate the flux, divide the BTU by the square inches on the primary cooking surface. Do not include warming racks. For example, a four-burner grill with a 48,000 BTU per hour rating and 500 square inches of primary cooking surface produces 96 BTUs per square inch per hour, or a heat flux of 96. A five-burner that generates 52,500 BTUs per hour with 650 square inches of grates delivers 81 BTU per square inch per hour, or a flux of 81. These examples show how, even though the bigger grill has a higher BTU rating, it actually delivers less heat to the food. Typical heat flux is about 85.

But heat flux is not a perfect measure. If the burners on one grill are a lot closer to the cooking surface than another, the closer burners will deliver more heat to the food. The distance between the burners might also create cool spots. Plus, infrared grills can generate more heat per BTU per square inch than convection grills because they are more efficient at delivering heat.

limited in the type of cooking you can do. Without it, you can't cook with convection. Some gas grills have lids made from two layers of metal with an air gap in between that helps with heat retention.

ROTISSERIE KITS. Many foods benefit from rotisserie cooking, among them turkey breasts, roasts, and, of course, whole chickens. Some high-end gas units come with a special rotisserie burner at the back above the cooking grates. This is a nice addition, but you can still cook rotisserie without it (see page 119). Some also come with a built-in rotisserie motor and attachments, but on most grills it is optional. If your grill does not offer one, buy one online. Rotisserie kits run from $100 to $200.

The typical kit comes with a spit, two forks that slip over the spear to hold the food in place, and a motor. Make sure the spit is long enough for your grill and not so long that it interferes with opening the side burner if you have one.

Be sure the kit has a sturdy motor that won't easily burn out, an on/off switch to stop the rotation so you can insert a thermometer to check doneness, and a water-resistant case in the event of rain. You will also need a utility-grade extension cord, because rotisseries rarely have a cord

long enough to be of any use. You can also get baskets that slip over the spit to hold shrimp, kebabs, or veggies. And if your grill doesn't already have a bracket on which to mount the motor, you'll need to buy one of those.

BUYING A CHARCOAL GRILL

Charcoal grills are less expensive than gas grills and produce more smoke and therefore better flavor. With the exception of gas grills that have small sear burners, charcoal burns hotter, so it is better for searing steaks. As with all things cooking, temperature control is paramount. Many of the same requirements for a gas grill apply equally to a charcoal grill, such as safety, workmanship, and cleaning.

LID. You must have a lid to capture heat, and the tighter it fits, the better.

DAMPERS. Charcoal grills need at least two dampers, an intake and an exhaust. That's how the oxygen gets in to feed the fire. Make sure the dampers fit tightly so you can accurately choke off oxygen when you want to lower the temperature.

ADJUSTABLE. Another way to control temperature is by raising and lowering the bed of charcoal. Temperature drops off as the coals drop down. Not many grills offer this feature, but I like those that do.

TWO-ZONE COOKING CAPABILITY. The most important technique an outdoor cook must learn is how to create a two-zone setup. This allows you to move the food off the flame into a cooler area where it roasts from convection and indirect heat. A good grill must have space to move the coals to one side. If your grill doesn't allow two-zone cooking, you will be handicapped. This is a problem on most round kamados.

ACCESS TO CHARCOAL. It is important to be able to easily add more charcoal or move the charcoal around. Some grills have a door. This is a very nice feature.

ASH REMOVAL. Ash is an excellent insulator, so if you don't remove it, it will absorb heat and reduce performance.

GRATES. This is a minor concern. If the grill doesn't have good grates, you can replace them. For more on what I consider good grates, see pages 100–102.

BUYING A LOG-BURNING GRILL

Almost all grills can have wood added to create smoke, but only a few are designed to burn logs as the primary fuel. In southern California, the Santa Maria–style grill is especially popular. It has an open top and a wheel-and-pulley system that lets cooks raise and lower their famous tri-tip steaks to decrease or increase heat. Santa Maria grills come in all sizes, from small backyard rigs to the one shown above right, which is used for catering.

My favorite backyard model, by Engelbrecht, has all sorts of bells and whistles and sells for $2,300 to $4,700.

In South America, grilling red meat on

SANTA MARIA GRILL

ENGELBRECHT 1000 SERIES BRATEN GRILL

a movable grate is common. Most of these wood-burners have V-shaped grates sloped forward to drain away drippings and minimize flare-ups. A company called Grillworks has several beauties that are popular with restaurants. They run from $3,300 to $14,000 and up.

There is even a small portable wood grill called Cook-Air that weighs only 17 pounds and costs only about $150. It has a blower system that gets the fuel up to 700°F in about 5 minutes. I've cooked some of the best steaks of my life on it with untreated scrap oak left over from a flooring project.

BUYING A PORTABLE GRILL

For the tailgate party, balcony, beach, backcountry hike, cattle drive, or RV trip, you need a portable grill. There are many options, from cheap throwaways to tried-and-true hibachis to pretty snazzy rigs with lids and multiple burners. Most of them have fairly limited functionality due to their size, but they operate like other grills.

When shopping for one, the same rules apply as for other grills. You need to consider price, temperature control, ease of cleanup, high heat, durability, safety, and, of course, size and weight. Many of the smaller portable units don't have lids, but a lid will increase the cooker's versatility, give you better temperature control, and help cook thicker meats without burning. Try to get enough surface area so you can create two cooking zones. Having at least two burners is ideal.

When out and about, I want convenience from a grill. A small bottle of propane will last a long time and is a lot lighter than charcoal, so my favorite portable is a lightweight gas grill. It's less messy than transporting charcoal in the trunk, too. Keep the small propane tank out of direct sunlight and don't store it in a hot car, which can exceed 120°F inside on a sunny day.

BUYING A SMOKER

Smoke is the sexy scent and inescapable difference between the Crock-Pot pulled pork served at a ballpark and the handcrafted sandwich that gets you a standing ovation in the backyard. Smoke is what makes Texans drive 150 miles just for a brisket lunch. Once, while I was marveling over a brisket sandwich at Opie's Barbecue in the middle of nowhere near Spicewood, Texas, a chopper landed out back and two guys hopped out, had lunch, and flew back to Austin.

But not any old smoke will do. Nobody wants their turkey tasting like cigarettes. As detailed in chapter 2, there is an art to getting the right-tasting smoke. It's possible to make superb smoked foods on just about any grill with a lid—even a gas grill. But adapting a grill for smoking is like adapting the family sedan for racing: The better solution is to buy a race car.

With a smoker and a little practice, you can make better food than the ribs, brisket, and pulled pork sitting in the warming oven of your local restaurant. Invest in a high-quality smoker, and you won't need to hover over your machine for 5 hours, constantly monitoring the temperature, fiddling with the vents and dampers, shoveling coals, adding wood, and spritzing your meat with moisturizers.

Most smokers have an indirect convection heat source that protects the food from searing infrared radiation. They generate smoke by burning wood. A few use wood for both heat and smoke, but most use charcoal, gas, or electricity for heat, and wood for smoke.

WHAT TO LOOK FOR IN A SMOKER

The checklist of things to look for in a smoker starts with many of the same things outlined in the checklist for grills, especially features related to construction (see page 75). When considering a purchase, check for ratings and reviews on the Internet, starting at AmazingRibs.com.

PRICE. Prices range from $100 for el cheapo charcoal smokers that don't work well, up to $10,000 and beyond for all-in-one smoker-grill combos. You usually get what you pay for. You can get a nice gas unit for under $250, a good charcoal unit for about $300, and a nifty pellet smoker starting at about $900.

WEIGHT, INSULATION, AND SEALS. The best smokers are heavy from thick steel, and some even have double walls and insulation. Thick steel absorbs heat and distributes it evenly around the cooking chamber and then radiates it back, moderating fluctuations. The better smokers have doors and dampers that close tightly, making it easier to cook on windy and rainy days. Cheap units leak heat and smoke, and that makes it hard to stabilize temperatures and manage the smokiness of your food.

DAMPERS. With wood and charcoal cookers, you control the heat by controlling the oxygen supplied to the fire. Dampers on the firebox and the chimney give you that control. Make sure they are easy to reach, operate, and seal up tight.

EVEN HEATING. Sometimes the temperature in the unit differs drastically from top to bottom or end to end, especially with offsets, where it can be 50 to 100°F hotter near the firebox. Look for tuning plates or reverse-flow construction in offsets (see page 90), and heat deflectors or water pans in drums, cabinets, and bullets.

TEMPERATURE RANGE. Most smokers are designed for low-and-slow cooking, usually under 250°F. But you need to get the Thanksgiving turkey up to about 325°F to crisp the skin. Or you may need to crank it just to get dinner done on time. Most electrics and gassers can't get that hot.

DRIP PAN. Fats and other fluids drip from the food. Sometimes it is nice to have these liquids fall onto the fire and create steam and smoke. But you may also want to capture the drippings to create a sauce, as in my Ultimate Smoked Turkey (page 307). Some smokers have a place for a pan for collecting drippings. The water pan often doubles as the drip pan.

ACCESS. With a charcoal, pellet, or wood smoker, you'll need an easy way to add chips, chunks, or pellets. You also want easy access to the food so you can move it around and check its temperature. Front-loading, cabinet-style smokers give you much easier access to the shelves than top-loading bullet-style smokers. Removable shelves make cleanup easier, and if they're adjustable, you can configure the unit to handle everything from half slabs of ribs to whole turkeys.

GRILL. Some smokers can be converted to a grill. That's a nice feature, but check to see that you can you control the heat.

VERTICAL CHARCOAL SMOKERS

Some vertical smokers are called bullets because they are usually tubes standing on end with a dome lid. Some are called Ugly Drum Smokers because they are made from steel drums. You can get cheap bullets and drums for less than $100, but they are a real pain because their air control is poor. They usually have water/drip pans between the charcoal and the food to help stabilize the heat and to add moisture to the air. These pans are also great for making gravy.

The most popular bullet smoker is the Weber Smokey Mountain (below), and I highly recommend it. The WSM comes in three sizes. The 14-inch diameter sells for about $200, the 18-inch for about $300, and the 22.5-inch is about $400. The parts can even be rearranged to use it as a grill or for sizzling on sauce at the end of a smoking session.

WEBER SMOKEY MOUNTAIN

My favorite drum is the Pit Barrel Cooker (below) for $300, including delivery to your door. It has a cooking grate, but it also has meat hooks for hanging things, and using them adds surprising capacity. Temperature management on the Pit Barrel is incredibly easy.

PIT BARREL COOKER

KAMADO, EGG, AND OTHER CERAMIC SMOKER/GRILLS

These egg-shaped cookers are sold as grill/smoker combos, but most are best thought of as smokers, not grills.

They are usually very thick and well insulated. Although they take a while to heat up, they are especially good at holding a steady temperature, even in cold winter weather. Because of this, kamados excel at smoking, roasting, and baking. They are unmatched as backyard pizza and bread ovens.

PRIMO OVAL

Easy to run in all wind and weather conditions, they use very little charcoal. Get a kamado started and bring it to temperature, and there's little need to touch it until the food is ready.

In other smokers, even expensive offsets, the airflow can cause a pork shoulder to lose 30 percent of its weight. Meats lose less water on kamados because ceramic cookers are extremely efficient, so oxygen use and airflow are relatively low.

Ceramics do have some drawbacks. The round funnel shape of most of them puts the charcoal dead center, so it is not easy to set them up in a two-zone system. Some of them come from the factory with a deflector plate that sits between the coals and the food so you can do indirect cooking (you will definitely need it for smoking), but then you have to remove it to switch to direct cooking and vice versa. When the unit is hot, this maneuver can be tricky, and it is not as quick and easy as sliding a steak from side to side as you can on a conventional grill with a two-zone setup. Because of this design limitation, it's trickier to do things like reverse sear (see page 48), a

very important technique. The Komodo Kamado and Kamado Joe both have an optional insert plate that covers the coals on one side only, creating a two-zone system. It works, but it's still not great on smaller models.

Because it is oval shaped, the Primo Oval (left) can easily be set up for two-zone cooking, and that goes a long way to making it my favorite. The XL model costs about $1,300.

Another thing to keep in mind before you buy: A lot of the necessary tools, like the deflector plate for indirect cooking, often cost extra.

THE BEST CHEAP SMOKER ANYWHERE: THE SLOW 'N SEAR

Already have a Weber Kettle grill, the most popular grill in the world? Then you should consider getting the Slow 'N Sear (opposite page). For about $80, this simple contraption, which works only on the 22.5-inch Weber, easily converts the grill into a smoker capable of making restaurant-quality smoked foods.

Invented by David Parrish, one of the moderators on AmazingRibs.com, Slow 'N Sear can be inserted into the lower half of the kettle and divides it into two distinct heat zones. Hot charcoal goes in the Slow 'N Sear, wood goes on top of the charcoal, and some water goes in the water trough. A steel plate blocks your meat from direct exposure to the heat, and the water bowl adds humidity. You can place meat on the lower (charcoal) and upper (cooking) racks, so it is possible to get eight to ten slabs of ribs smoking in the kettle at once. Put on the lid, adjust the dampers, and go drink a beer. The Slow 'N Sear pumps out aromatic smoke at just

SLOW 'N SEAR

the right low-and-slow temperature for several hours. You can cook just about anything the fancy-schmancy smokers can smoke. I've had no trouble keeping the temperature under 250°F on 100°F days.

OFFSET CHARCOAL SMOKERS

The offset smoker is one of the oldest and best designs for a smoker. Originally they were welded from oil pipes by Texas roustabouts so they could be towed to remote job sites. The fire is built in a lower side chamber, while the heat

NOT ALL STAINLESS STEEL IS CREATED EQUAL

Stainless steel is a popular choice for grills and smokers, but before you spend extra, give it some thought. What kind of stainless is it? Most manufacturers use either austenitic basic grade 304 or ferritic basic grade 430. Austenitic 304 contains more nickel in the alloy. That extra nickel makes the 304 higher in quality and cost. Ferritic 430 contains much less nickel and is not as durable, but it costs less. Most grills are made with 430. But if you want a top-of-the-line cooker, look for 304.

Either way, the biggest problem isn't the type of stainless but the thickness. Thick steel absorbs and retains heat and holds a steadier temperature, especially when you open and close the lid. Steel thickness is expressed in "gauges," usually 10 to 18. The lower the number, the thicker the steel.

Some manufacturers use heavier-gauge,

higher-quality steel on the lid only. They know a heavy lid creates a good first impression. Look at the screws, too. Sometimes they are not stainless and can rust.

All stainless shows dirt, dust, grease, and rain spots, and maintaining that beautiful shine is an ongoing task that many, including Yours Truly, cannot bear. I had a well-worn cheap grill made with 430, and it held up just fine after many years of heavy use. The exterior looked like crap because I didn't cover it. I don't care if it's dirty on the outside. It's the inside that matters.

If you have a choice between naked stainless steel, powder-coated steel, or enamel-coated steel, coated surfaces are just as rust-proof as stainless, and they are usually thicker and will retain heat better. Plus, coated steel is cheaper than stainless. Powder-coated is my first choice, enameled second, and stainless last.

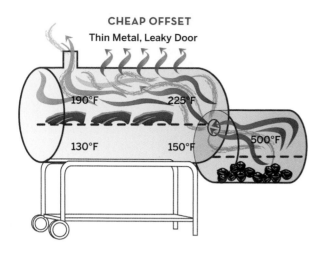

CHEAP OFFSET
Thin Metal, Leaky Door

190°F 225°F
130°F 150°F 500°F

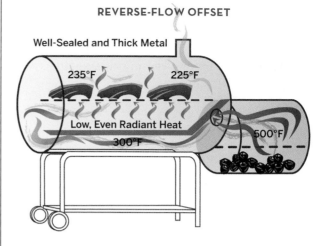

REVERSE-FLOW OFFSET
Well-Sealed and Thick Metal

235°F 225°F
Low, Even Radiant Heat
300°F 500°F

and smoke are directed horizontally into the cooking chamber. Because the fire is off to the side, you can get a really hot fire that produces blue smoke more easily than on just about any other cooker. And it looks so macho. It says, "I'm serious about barbecue."

Slow down, Mario Andretti. The cheap ones that sell for less than $500, like those from Char-Griller and Char-Broil, are a serious pain. The problem is that the end closer to the fire is usually a lot hotter than the other. Plus, only the expensive units have enough thick steel, tight-sealing doors, and venting to retain smoke and temperature properly. A few models commonly found in hardware stores are Brinkmann Pitmaster, Brinkmann Smoke 'N Pit Professional, Char-Broil Silver Smoker, Char-Broil American Gourmet, and especially the Char-Griller Smokin' Pro. Stay away from them, please.

Expensive offset smokers, on the other hand, are made from thick metal that absorbs and distributes heat more evenly end to end. Their doors and dampers are tight, so you can

fine-tune airflow and control the temperature. Some even have "reverse flow," a duct system with a thick metal plate along the bottom of the cooking chamber and the chimney on the same side as the firebox, both of which force the warm air and smoke to travel the length of the cooking

LANG OFFSET SMOKER

chamber and then across the top of the food.

Expensive offsets start at about $800 for smaller backyard models and go up to $10,000 or more for the fancy ones on trailers with attached grills, holding ovens, and other bells and whistles. Some of the best are made by Horizon, Jambo, Klose, Lang, Meadow Creek, Peoria, Pitmaker, and Yoder. My favorite backyarder is the Lang 36 with reverse flow (shown opposite, bottom), which lists for about $1,100.

CABINET-STYLE CHARCOAL SMOKERS

This design usually has two doors and opens in the front like a refrigerator. The top section is for the food, and the bottom holds the firebox and vents. That makes it very easy to refuel and add or remove food to baste and sauce it. There is often a water pan between the two sections. The better models are very tight and well insulated. I highly recommend this design. The Backwoods Smoker is the gold standard. The Backwoods Party model (right) lists for about $1,500, and the smaller Chubby is $1,300. Several newcomers include some smart innovations like a gravity charcoal feeder, but they are not cheap.

PROPANE GAS SMOKERS

If you are looking for a simple smoker on a modest budget, that is pretty close to set-it-forget-it easy, go gas. Gas-fueled smokers are almost as easy to use as electric ones. They produce a lot of clean heat. That's why large gassers are the most popular smokers in barbecue restaurants. The smoke flavor comes from

BACKWOODS SMOKER

wood chips, chunks, or pellets. Gas smokers are among the best values on the market. If your budget is very tight, I recommend them.

Most consumer units use propane and cannot be adapted to natural gas. The burner, at the bottom, is usually brass or cast aluminum, has numerous jets, and can be very durable. Above the burner is a shelf for a pan to hold the wood, and above that is a shelf for a water pan. Above that are four or more shelves for food. The bottom vents cannot be adjusted, which ensures that the gas gets enough oxygen. A chimney or damper sits at the top. You should always leave the top vent open all the way to prevent soot buildup on your meat. Sometimes the water and wood pan are combined in one unit. I don't recommend this design.

Most gas smokers are thin metal and the doors are loose, so they leak heat and smoke like a homemade submarine. That means they burn more wood chips than a tighter bullet smoker (see page 87), for instance, but the leaks don't really impact food quality, just fuel efficiency.

It is much easier to control the temperature of a gasser than a charcoal or wood-fueled smoker. They're also portable because they don't require access to electricity. And they are lightweight, although the gas tanks weigh up to 40 pounds. Plan on buying a tank, because most units don't come with it. You'll also want a spare tank to avoid running out of gas in the middle of a 12-hour cook. If the tank is low, check on it every 30 minutes or so to make sure the flame is not dead. It's a bit of a pain, especially when you're smoking a 9-pound pork butt that could take 10 hours to reach an internal temperature of 203°F. Inevitably, the flame will die at 2 a.m. If your tank is running low, hook up a fresh tank before starting a long cooking session.

The biggest drawback to these smokers is that most are too narrow to fit a full slab of ribs or a whole brisket on a shelf. You can cut the meat in half, or get creative and hang it. I have been known to use stainless-steel shower curtain hooks and hang meat from the top shelf.

One other word of caution: I love the flavor of meat from propane smokers, but it is a *tiny bit* different than the taste of meat from charcoal smokers. The combustion gases combine with

**SMOKE VAULT
GAS SMOKER**

the moisture and the wood smoke and produce a fragrance and flavor that is sometimes reminiscent of bacon. Log burners complain about this undertone, but what's wrong with a little bacon flavor?

Alas, they are not allowed in most barbecue competitions because organizers consider them too easy or untraditional. It's a silly rule because competitions allow pellet smokers, and they are so automated that you hardly need any skill to operate them.

The Camp Chef Smoke Vault 24" (above) is one of the best values on the market. It lists at $344, but it can be found for as little as $250. It's big enough to handle long slabs of ribs and whole packer briskets, and it can be hard-piped for natural gas.

PELLET SMOKER/GRILLS

Nothing beats a pellet cooker for convenience and ease of use. Truly set it and forget it. This cool, new-generation tool burns pellets made from compressed hardwood sawdust about the thickness of a pencil and about ½ inch long. A digital thermostat manages the temperature by controlling a motorized auger that feeds the pellets into a burn pot, and it also controls the air supply by regulating a fan. Of course, this means the cooker has to be plugged into a power outlet with the amperage to handle it. Flare-ups are a thing of the past with these cookers. Because combustion is so efficient, the smoke flavor is clean and understated. Cooks used to burning logs or charcoal sometimes think the food needs more smoke.

These are great smokers, but they are not very good at grilling or searing because they are really indirect-heating ovens. A few models offer direct-heat cooking, but these smokers aren't good at the task yet.

LARGE-CAPACITY, COMMERCIAL, AND TRAILER-MOUNTED RIGS FOR RESTAURANTS, CATERERS, AND COMPETITORS

Ready to start a catering biz and drag a smoker to picnics, ball games, corporate retreats, and horse shows? Fantasizing about hitting the road, getting an armful of tattoos, and doing state and county fairs? Envision yourself grabbing big prize money and trophies at the cook-offs you see on TV? You'll want a big rig on wheels. Most are high-quality offsets with the firebox separated from the cooking chamber so you can burn wood hot. Many have reverse-flow systems. Some come with a separate grill attached and/or bins for hauling wood. Prices start at $4,500, and most are north of $7,000.

All but the cheapest pellet cookers have digital thermostat control that can be incredibly precise, typically plus or minus 5°F. Beware of the cheap models that have temperature controls that say only "Low," "Medium," "High." You want one that allows you to set the temperature and walk away. My favorite is the MAK 2 Star General (above, left) that lists for $2,600. It has plenty of capacity with the upper rack, and even has a warming oven on the side. Green Mountain and others have some nice smaller models for about $800. In fact, Green Mountain has a small portable with Wi-Fi controller that lists for only $399.

ELECTRIC SMOKERS

No lighting charcoal, no checking the fuel supply every hour or so, no messy ash to clean up. Just turn it on and take a snooze. Electrics need only 2 to 4 ounces of wood to give meat a smoky flavor. And if they are well insulated, they are great for winter use. They excel at fish and things like smoked peppers, sausage, nuts, bacon, and cheese.

The bad news: I find the flavor of food cooked in electric smokers inferior to that from charcoal, gas, and pellet smokers. Remember, the heat in gas, pellet, and charcoal cookers comes from combustion, which produces gases that mix with smoke to impart a distinct flavor. That flavor is absent in electrics, where the heat comes from a glowing metal coil. Electrics also have very tiny vents, which makes them good at retaining moisture, but if you want crispy skin on a chicken or turkey or a thick, crusty bark on your pulled pork, it will be close to impossible. In addition, because the combustion temperature is too low, electrics don't usually produce a smoke ring. Even though it has no flavor, that pink layer of meat says "Southern barbecue" to the eyes.

If you already have an electric, I know you *love, love, love* it and you think I'm a flaming idiot. But I'm here to tell you, I've tested scores of smokers, and you don't know what you're missing. There is no substitute for live fire and the flavor it generates. A VW Beetle can be a delightful drive until you sit behind the wheel of

COOKSHACK ELECTRIC SMOKER

a Porsche. If you want to e-mail me and tell me what you think of me, go right ahead. Many of you already have.

On the other hand, an electric smoker is better than no smoker, especially if you're in an apartment or condo where they won't let you have gas, charcoal, or pellets. But if you are considering an electric smoker, gas smokers are almost as easy to use, make better-tasting food, and are much less expensive.

If you are shopping for an electric, Cookshack makes the best, and they start at $700 and go up to $1,900 for backyard models.

HANDHELD SMOKERS

The Smoking Gun from PolyScience has created this new category of handheld smokers. Resembling a pistol, it has a small bowl like a

THE SMOKING GUN

hash pipe in which you place sawdust, herbs, spices, tea, even hay. Light it and a small motor powered by four AA batteries draws in air through the bowl and expels smoke through a flexible hose. It's not a lot of smoke, but it can be used to add a quick undertone of smoke to sushi, butter, salads, sauces, and meringues. I use it to amp up Bloody Marys.

PIG, GOAT, AND LAMB ROASTERS

These cookers range from simple and relatively inexpensive to large and overwhelming. You can build your own, or buy one of the many clever designs on the market. Some are boxes such as the popular La Caja China (right). Called "the Cajun microwave," it encloses the meat in coffin-like box. The charcoal goes in a tray on top of the box so there is no smoke. La Caja China starts at about $340. Spitjack makes simple rotisseries that turn the meat on an open spit alongside a campfire. They can be had for as little as $460.

THINK CAREFULLY BEFORE BUYING BUILT-IN GRILLS OR SMOKERS

An outdoor kitchen with a built-in grill sure looks spiffy. But I recommend you use the space for a countertop and buy a standalone grill or smoker. Here's why. Let's say you buy a built-in gas grill that is 28 inches wide by 20 inches deep. After a few years, it gets rusty and you need to replace it. Or you don't like the sear burner and you want a more powerful one. Or you decide to go with a charcoal grill. Or you want a bigger grill.

But you are stuck with that hole and whatever you buy must fit it. Grills and smokers don't come in standard sizes like indoor ovens. Do yourself a favor. Buy standalone grills and smokers on carts. They're easier to move around, replace, sell, give away, and upgrade.

LA CAJA CHINA

EXTENSION CORDS FOR PELLET SMOKERS, ELECTRIC SMOKERS, AND ELECTRIC GRILLS

The built-in cords on outdoor cooking devices are pretty short. Household extension cords will not carry enough juice to keep your pellet smoker or electric smoker going and could become a fire hazard as they heat up trying to deliver power to the unit. Get at least a 10-amp, 12-gauge, three-pronged cord. That's more than you need, but better safe than sorry.

THE MOST IMPORTANT TOOL YOU CAN BUY: A THERMOMETER

I am often asked, "What is the single most important piece of advice you can give a barbecue cook?" My answer, without hesitation, is, "Get good digital thermometers." In 2014, *Consumer Reports* tested hundreds of chicken breasts from around the nation and found that almost all were contaminated with pathogens—about half of which were antibiotic resistant. As scary as this sounds, pathogens are destroyed and chicken is safe to eat if you cook it to 160°F or higher (see page 53). Gauging doneness is not possible without a digital thermometer. Cooking without a good digital thermometer is like driving without a speedometer, building furniture without a tape measure, or filling your tires without a pressure gauge.

Invest in good thermometers. They're inexpensive, fast, and accurate. They will pay for themselves. Nothing will improve your cooking more.

YOU NEED THREE THERMOMETERS

Temperature is paramount in cooking, and you must measure it accurately in three different places: the cooker, the food, and your refrigerator.

OVEN/GRILL/SMOKER THERMOMETER. Can you imagine cooking indoors if your oven did not have a thermometer? Then why try to cook outdoors without a good oven thermometer? (And a grill or smoker really is just an outdoor oven.) To be king of the grill, you've got to know what your cooker temperature really is. I recommend the dual probe models that combine a leave-in meat probe and an oven probe or use them both to meter different parts of the cooker or two pieces of meat. The probes are on the ends of cables, so you can snake the wires under the lid or through

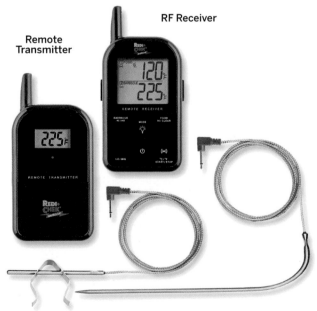

Remote Transmitter

RF Receiver

Two Probes

an access hole to the display unit. They cost $50 to $100. The Maverick ET-732 (pictured opposite) does a great job for about $60. It includes a radio frequency transmitter so you can cut the lawn or watch the game while monitoring the pit. It lets you monitor the meat's progress without having to open the lid and stab it every 15 minutes or so. It is especially helpful for big cuts like pork shoulder, hams, whole hog, pork loin, beef rib roasts, tri-tip, and turkey.

INSTANT-READ THERMOMETER. The difference between juicy chicken breasts and cardboard can be as little as 10°F. And two pork chops sitting side by side can cook at different rates. Minutes matter. I recommend that you also have an instant-read digital that can read the temperature of meat in 5 seconds or less.

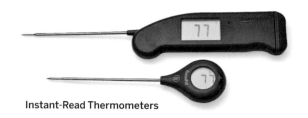

Instant-Read Thermometers

Good ones like the ThermoPop (pictured above, bottom) cost about $30, and a top-of-the-line Thermapen (top) costs about $100.

REFRIGERATOR THERMOMETER. Below 35°F, frost can form, and above 38°F, microbes grow too fast. Because fridge temperatures can vary from top to bottom, buy a thermometer that can be moved around. A liquid thermometer has enough accuracy for this task, has no batteries to die, and costs under $10.

OPTIONAL: INFRARED GUN THERMOMETER. If you want to make perfect pizza, so the top and bottom are done at the same time, you need an infrared (IR) gun thermometer. Point an IR gun at a your stone or pizza pan, and it will tell you if it is time to slide on the dough. It also is useful if you cook on a griddle or frying pan. But other than that, these toys aren't much good for anything else on the grill. (They are good for finding leaks around your windows in winter, however.)

MYTH You can tell the temperature of your grill by holding your hand over it.

BUSTED! So many "experts" say you can gauge the temperature of a grill by holding your hand over the grate and counting "one thousand one, one thousand two" until you have to pull back or your palm starts to smoke, or something ridiculous like that. Each of us reacts differently to heat, and the heat 1 inch above the grate can be significantly different than 6 inches above. Maybe an old pro who cooks 100 steaks a night can do this parlor trick, but you cannot.

Infrared Gun Thermometer

THERMOMETER SHOPPING CHECKLIST

Here is a checklist of things to look for when you go shopping for a good thermometer:

SMALL SENSOR. For a food thermometer, you want the sensitive part to be small and in the tip of the probe. A long sensor can give you misleading data because the temperature just below the surface of a piece of meat may be a lot different than the temperature in the center. Most digitals have small sensors.

SPEED TO READ. How long does it take to get a good reading? Look for 5 seconds or less.

LENGTH OF THE PROBE. A meat thermometer has to reach the middle of a big roast such as a ham or pork shoulder. A 4-inch-long probe will do the job.

ADJUSTABLE. Some thermometers can be calibrated if they slip out of kilter.

WATER RESISTANT, DURABLE, AND EASY TO CLEAN. You don't want barbecue sauce and soapy water inside the probe. Check the seal between the probe and the cable. Some cables can fail if they get crimped or smashed by the grill lid. Look for sturdy cables. Most cannot stand flame or temperatures above 450°F.

TIMERS AND ALARMS. Some digital thermometers include timers with alarms and settings for doneness. If it comes with preset doneness temperatures, many of them are wrong, so make

---

MYTH You can tell the doneness of meat by poking it and comparing the bounciness of the meat to the flesh between your thumb and forefinger.

BUSTED! As if everyone's hand has the same firmness and bounciness! Does the flesh on the hand of a 120-pound, 26-year-old woman who works out have the same resilience as that of a 250-pound, 50-year-old man who works in an office or a 70-year-old retired ditch digger? Of course not. Does a filet mignon have the same firmness and bounciness as a sirloin? Of course not. Almost all professional chefs carry a meat thermometer in their chef's coat. You should do the same.

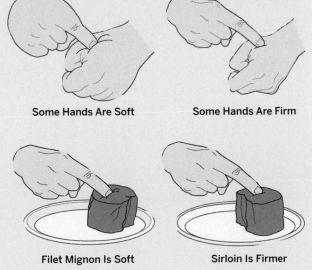

Some Hands Are Soft

Some Hands Are Firm

Filet Mignon Is Soft

Sirloin Is Firmer

sure that they are adjustable or that you can ignore them.

REMOTE READ. Some leave-in thermometers have Bluetooth, Wi-Fi, or radio frequency (RF) transmitters that can send temperature readings to a computer, smartphone, tablet, or a dedicated receiver. This allows you to watch the temperature while you are in the kitchen or even across town, record and chart cooking, set alarms, and more. I have had nothing but trouble with the Bluetooth devices, but the Wi-Fi and RF units work as advertised.

MYTH You can tell doneness by cutting into meat to check the color.

BUSTED! A lot of weekend warriors cut into their meat to check the color for doneness. The problem is that the color they see on the grill is not the color that they will see on the table. That's because myoglobin is the source of most red color. When myoglobin comes into contact with air, it changes color. When you cut into a steak, it may look perfectly done to you, but as the myoglobin absorbs oxygen, it can turn brighter red.

In the photo, we see two slices of meat from the same steak. The bottom one was exposed to air for about 10 minutes after carving. As it was exposed to the oxygen, it turned brighter red and looks to be medium-rare. The top one was sliced from just behind it, moments before the picture was taken. You can see it appears medium. In reality, both slices were medium, since I cooked them to 145°F.

The temperature at which myoglobin turns gray can range from 140 to 170°F, depending on species, slaughtering conditions, and more. In fact, under some conditions, a well-done steak can appear bright pink.

Light can deceive, too. Incandescent light is yellowish orange, fluorescent is greenish blue, and CFLs and LEDs are all over the place. Bottom line: If you really want to know when the meat is done to your liking, don't go by looks. Use a good digital thermometer.

EASE OF USE. Some new models have too many bells and whistles and are too darn confusing. Will you remember how to use all the buttons and settings? Is the readout clear? Is there a backlight for nighttime use?

WARRANTY AND CUSTOMER SERVICE. What is the warranty? Does the manufacturer have replacement parts and sell them at a reasonable price?

PRICE. Some very good units cost only $30, while all the bells and whistles might run you $200.

THE BEST GRILL GRATES

Cast-iron grill grates have mystique. They absorb and hold a lot of heat, and they brand the meat surface with that heat. But grill marks mean that only about one third of the surface has been altered by the magical Maillard reaction (see page 43). You want the radiant heat of the fire below to do the browning—not just the grates.

Grill marks come in handy for thin foods like skirt steak, asparagus, shrimp, and kabobs because they cook so quickly there isn't time to darken the whole surface. That's why my two favorite grill grates are polar opposites with completely different purposes.

THIN STAINLESS STEEL. Thin stainless-steel rods (right) are my favorites—especially on charcoal grills—because they allow more radiant heat through. Thick rods make large, dark burn marks, and they block radiant heat. Don't confuse stainless-steel grates with chrome or nickel-plated grates, which are not as long-lived.

Whether thin or thick, the real advantages of stainless are that it has the life-span of a zombie and it's easy to clean. Good stainless grates will never rust or corrode. Chrome eventually needs to replaced because you don't want rust or other oxides migrating from the grate to your food.

CAST-ALUMINUM HARD-ANODIZED GRILL-GRATES. These amazing inventions are my other fave. I recommend GrillGrates (opposite page, top left) for all gas grills and pellet smokers. Made by extruding aircraft aluminum into interlocking 5.25-inch-wide rectangles, each section is a flat plate with raised rails on which the food sits. They are available in various lengths and can be custom cut. They even have some with rounded corners for round grills. Each plate has large holes in it, so some hot air, smoke, and combustion gases can rise through, while most of the heat is trapped below and builds. As a result, the plate can get very hot, but the aluminum alloy distributes the heat evenly across the cooking surface, minimizing hot spots. The bottom of the plate, ¾ inch below

the food, becomes the main heat source, amplifying heat by 100 to 200°F in gas grills and pellet grills. The concept is similar to the infrared cooking systems on the market.

You can also throw wood chips, pellets, or sawdust into the valleys between the rails and then put food on top to impart a delicate wood smoke flavor to quick-cooking foods.

If you leave a gap between two GrillGrates panels, you can easily set up a two-zone cooking system (see page 8). I don't use these on my charcoal grill because there is usually ample heat from below, but on gas grills and pellet smokers, they can improve the surface color of foods.

ALSO RECOMMENDED

THIN PORCELAIN ENAMEL-COATED. A sturdy porcelain enamel coating is applied to a variety of metals of different weights. You often find it on rods and on upside-down U-shaped rails. I prefer thin rods, which don't block the radiant heat needed to brown the surfaces of foods.

Porcelain (top right) is easy to clean, but vigorous scrubbing and scraping can scratch it and eventually wear off the coating. Dropping these grates can also crack the surface, and then they

start to rust. However, with proper care, these grates work just fine, last for years, and are a lot cheaper than stainless. I recommend them for charcoal grills.

CHEAP CHROME OR NICKEL-PLATED WIRE GRATES. Yes, they warp under extremely high temperatures. And yes, after a year or two, they pit and the plating chips off, then they rust, and you've got to toss them. But they're so cheap that replacing them is not painful.

Their chief advantage is that they stay out of the way of radiant heat from below, leaving the surface open for real searing. If you have a Weber Kettle, I strongly recommend upgrading to Weber's Hinged Cooking Grates (below) so you can easily add more coals and wood.

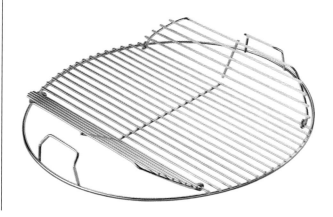

NOT RECOMMENDED

CAST IRON. Well-seasoned cast-iron frying pans and griddles are virtually nonstick, so many people believe that cast-iron grill grates (below) will be nonstick as well. They are not. Pans and griddles become nonstick because the metal is slightly porous, so oil nestles in there, then is polymerized by heat and forms a slippery surface. Cast-iron devotees call this the "seasoning" process.

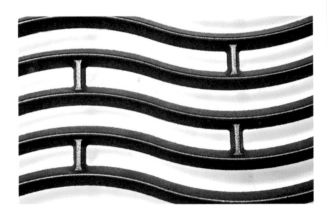

But grates get a lot hotter than most frying pans, and that heat burns off the oil or turns it to carbon. Grates also get scraped with rough abrasives, which remove any polymer that might remain. There goes your nonstick surface. Plus, many are cheaply cast, with rough, sharp edges or deep pores that grab on to food. Not only that, but the exposed iron easily rusts when stored outside in the elements, and rusty cast iron is a serious pain to clean. To handle them properly, you should serve the food, run back out, and scrape them, and after dinner, coat them with oil. They are just too thick and too much bother.

THICK ENAMELED BARS AND THICK STAINLESS-STEEL BARS. As with cast iron, these bars (below) retain and transmit a lot of heat, making bold grill marks. They are sturdy and easy to clean, but if you drop them, they can crack and rust.

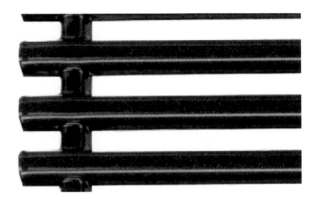

TEMPERED STEEL. Common on large barbecue pits, tempered steel grates (below) often come in diamond-shaped grids. Their main strengths are low price and light weight. On the downside, they rust, warp, and are hard to clean. They need the same maintenance regimen as cast iron.

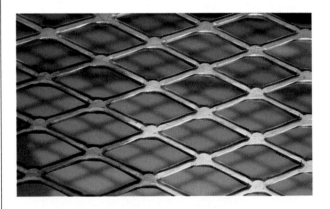

TEFLON AND NONSTICK COATINGS. Found on electric "grills" and some portable gassers, these surfaces have two things going for them: They prevent sticking and they clean easily. On the other hand, they also scratch easily, so you can't use a metal spatula, and they emit dangerous gases if they get above 450°F, a temperature you often want to reach when grilling.

GRILL TOPPERS

Grill toppers are essential for grilling all sorts of little foods like onion, peppers, and shrimp, as well as smoking things like almonds. For small chunks of meat, I'll take a grill topper over skewers any day.

Try a Frogmat (below) and you'll never go back to skewers. This inexpensive, sturdy wire mesh has a nonstick coating that is easy to clean. I use it for everything from delicate fish fillets and whole fish to onion rings and potato slices to mushrooms, bacon, and biscuits. While they're perfect for smoking and indirect cooking, they can't be heated above 400°F, but you don't have to cook fish that hot anyway. Frogmats come in a variety of sizes, even large enough for a whole hog, and you can cut them to fit. When you are done, just roll them up. A 17-by-25-inch Frogmat sells for about $25.

Another option is a grill basket. I prefer the mesh type, such as the stainless-steel Mr. Bar-B-Q Mesh Roasting Pan shown above, because the mesh lets in lots of smoke and flavor. The handles allow you to toss the food so cubed meats and veggies get evenly cooked. The pan lists for about $30.

The Weber Stainless Steel Grill Pan (below) works well, too. It has a greater surface area for browning things like salmon cakes, but still has plenty of slots for smoke to travel through. The grill pan lists for about $20.

In a pinch, you can even use the perforated top of a broiler pan.

KEEPING FOOD FROM STICKING

Food seems to have a magnetic attraction to grill grates. The best way to prevent food from bonding to metal is to pat your meat dry and then put some oil on the food rather than the metal. As you lay the oiled food down, the oil fills microscopic nooks and crannies in both the food and the grates, creating a relatively smooth, slippery surface. The cool food lowers the temperature of the grates and keeps burnt oil residue off the food. Just be sure to use oil that has a high smoke point. I use an inexpensive refined olive oil. Corn oil is good, too, as are most refined cooking oils with a smoke point around 450°F.

Keep in mind that, as the food cooks, heat causes water vapor to exit the meat where it touches the metal. That's the sizzle you hear, and it continues until the surface of the food in contact with the metal dries out, forming grill marks. Because oil and water don't mix, the steam that's created in this process lifts the meat above the oil, and eventually the food lets go. If the food is sticking when you go to turn it, try simply leaving it alone for a few minutes more. Vapor from where the meat meets the metal should eventually steam the two apart.

Sometimes, no matter what you do, food just wants to stick. Learn how to slide a thin, flexible spatula at an angle to the grates to shear off stuck food, retaining most of the browned surface.

MYTH Oil the grill grates to keep food from sticking.

BUSTED! Almost all the grill books say to roll up a paper towel, grab it with tongs, dunk it in vegetable oil, and use it to swab the grates. Grill grates, even shiny clean ones, are not really smooth but have microscopic scratches, pits, valleys, and ridges. Your food is much colder than the grates, and when the two meet, a bond forms between them. If you oil the grates when they're below the smoke point of the oil, let's say 400°F, the oil actually does coat the grate and helps the food release. But if the temperature of the grates is above the smoke point, the oil smokes and carbonizes almost instantly. The carbon and smoke don't taste good, and the dry, uneven carbon layer on the grates simply makes the sticking worse. I'm not a fan of spraying on oil, either. Many spray oils are a blend of oil and water with an emulsifier. The tiny droplets of oil can create a dangerous fireball.

CLEANING YOUR GRILL GRATES

It is vital that your food go on clean grates. Before you cook, get the grates ripping hot, close the hood, and heat the grill until the smoke subsides, about 15 minutes. After heating and before cooking, scrape the grates. I start with a scraper like CharGon (right). Then I dip a stainless-steel wire brush in water and scrub the hot grates with the wet brush, creating steam in the process. A wet towel will often work too.

Every year, there are several news stories about people eating meals with bristles hiding in them. The bristle gets stuck in their throats or digestive systems, and they spend the night in the hospital. Every so often, someone dies. Be sure to check your cooking surface for stray bristles after brushing, or give it a quick wipe with a damp cloth. Some readers tell me they run an onion or lemon half over the grates after brushing.

Periodically take the grates off the grill and lay them on a cloth on the ground. Fill a bucket with hot water and dish detergent. With a brush, scrub both sides of the grates and rinse thoroughly. For stainless grates, you can even use steel wool. You can also place the grates in a large tub, pour on boiling hot water, mix in some dish detergent, and come back the next day. The mess cleans off easily with a stainless-steel pad or a pressure washer.

Whatever you do, do not run grill grates through the dishwasher! The grease is pernicious and can coat everything inside the dishwasher, and you'll be sleeping on the couch for a long while.

Unfortunately, there is no single tool that does the job perfectly for all types of grates. Here are some recommended options. Pick the best one for your grates.

CHARGON. This solidly build metal scraper with a U-shaped tip (below) makes it easy to scrape the tops, sides, and bottoms of round grill grates with no risk of rogue bristles and the health hazard they present. It takes longer, but it does a better job. List is about $20.

STAINLESS-STEEL WELDER'S WIRE BRUSH. Designed as a paint or rust remover, these are usually found in your hardware store in the paint or plumbing department (pictured page 106, top left). The bristles don't rust if the brush is dipped in water or left out in the rain. They're

good and stiff, so they dislodge stubborn carbon deposits. They are anchored to the wooden handle well enough that I've never had a bristle pop out. The narrow ones fit between the rails of the aluminum GrillGrates well. There are a variety of options under $10.

NOT RECOMMENDED

PUMICE BLOCKS. These bricks (below) do an OK job on wire cooking grates, but they should not be used on porcelain or cast-iron grates. They work fast, but they only clean the tops. The bricks are made from ground recycled glass, and they leave a bit of dust behind, which concerns me. You will need to follow up with a wet paper towel to finish the job. Each brick will scrub only about a hundred grates before it wears out.

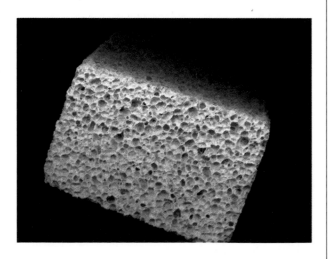

STAINLESS-STEEL SCRUB PADS ON A HANDLE. This device (above) uses a woven stainless-steel pad that does a great job of cleaning the grates—at first. When it starts to disintegrate, and it does, the woven steel can fall off onto the grill and could get into your food. You can buy replacement pads, but they are not cheap.

SCRUB AND SPRAY BRUSHES. I was impressed with these brushes (below) on paper. You get replaceable stainless-steel brush heads, and you can drip water while you scrub, creating steam. In practice, I was unimpressed. You have to fill them with water, open a small spigot, scrub, and close the spigot. And they freeze in winter. I get better results with a simple brush dipped in water.

THE FISH PROBLEM

Fish is notoriously sticky. I have several strategies.

MAYONNAISE. Coat the fish with mayo, which is about one third oil, after seasoning it. Coating fish with oil works, but mayo works better.

USE A FISH BASKET. Most of these gadgets (above) resemble two skinny tennis rackets, hinged at the top. You oil the fish, lock it between the two sides, and put the basket on the grill. Flipping is a cinch. Because the handles of the rackets are long, they might keep you from closing the lid of the grill. And, yes, sometimes the fish sticks to the basket, but usually, if you oil it well, it will release. Weber has a new handle-free design that has spring-loaded cross-members. It looks like an army cot, and, although I was never fond of my army cot, I like this a lot.

USE A GRILL TOPPER. See page 103.

START ON FOIL. Dr. Greg Blonder starts stick-prone foods like fish or ground chicken burgers on oiled aluminum foil. Then, after the meat's surface dries out a bit and the food firms up, he transfers it to the grates.

LAMSONSHARP FISH TONGS. A jumbo hybrid of tongs and spatulas (above), this is the best tool for flipping fish, burgers, and other crumbly foods. Slide one 8-inch spatula under the fish and gently clamp down with the other. They come with a lifetime warranty. I find them to be indispensable, but they are expensive, about $125.

GRATETOOL. GrillGrates (below) includes a special spatula with fingers that go into the troughs between the rails, and with them, you can easily lift fish. They come free with an order of two of their grate panels. Prices start at $40. They even make a Gratetool that has two heads like the Lamsonsharp above.

OTHER ACCESSORIES YOU REALLY NEED

Your most important cooking tools are your hands. They provide important feedback about weight, temperature, and texture, and no mechanical tool can match the dexterity of human fingers and thumbs. Wash your hands thoroughly with hot water and soap often when handling food, but don't be afraid to use this vital tool.

Your most important cooking tools are your hands.

You don't really need a lot of expensive toys. But here are a few gadgets that can help make you a better cook. Many are made by small companies and are available only online.

SUEDE WELDER'S, BARBECUE, OR FIREPLACE GLOVES. If hands are the most important cooking tools, heat-resistant gloves are the next most valuable item for the outdoor cook. Look for heavy-duty suede gloves with a cotton lining. They should be 15 inches long. Mine go almost to my elbows, and I use them to lift hot grates, push coals around, reach into the firebox to reposition logs, and lift food from deep down inside Weber Smokey Mountain smokers and ceramic egg cookers. I have even used them to pick up hot coals. They beat the heck out of oven mitts because they have fingers, making it much easier to manipulate tongs and handle grates. I have two pairs: one for lifting food, and one for all the sooty jobs. When they get dirty, I just wash my gloved hands with a bar of soap. I'm not a fan of silicone gloves. They are slippery, lack dexterity, and can melt. Good suede gloves sell for $20 to $30.

SILICONE BRUSHES. Silicone brushes load up with lots of sauce, deliver it evenly, and because they are dishwasher safe, they are easy to clean and decontaminate. There are many variations on the market: long handle, short handle, take your pick. Whatever you do, please don't buy those rustic-looking corded mops. They might look like an important tool of authentic down-home barbecue, but they are impossible to clean properly and pose a health risk. Silicone brushes sell for about $10.

BEAR PAWS. These handy plastic paws (pictured above) are designed for shredding pork, but they are also helpful for lifting large roasts and birds. I've tried all manner of gadgets for pulled pork, and these are the best. They are dishwasher safe and cost less than $15.

OXO GOOD GRIPS TONGS. OXO tongs (below) are spring-loaded, dishwasher safe, stainless steel, and feature nonslip rubber handles, scalloped ends for better gripping, a mechanism that locks them closed for storage, and a small loop for hanging. The 18-inch tongs don't have the locking mechanism, but they are very helpful if you have a deep pit. (I store them with the ends tucked into a cardboard toilet paper core.) Be forewarned, though, that the longer the tongs, the harder it is to get a good grip. They run from $20 to $30, depending on length.

STIFF METAL SPATULA. Given the choice between slotted and solid spatulas, I prefer solid, especially for pressing things down, like when you are making thin Diner Burgers (page 272) on a griddle or in a frying pan. Look for one with a sturdy handle. I like the Weber Style Professional-Grade Fish Turner (above), which sells for less than $25.

HOVERGRILL. This high-quality stainless-steel grate with legs (below) can do two good things for your cooking: It stands on top of your Weber Kettle grill's cooking grate and pretty much doubles its capacity, and it can be placed below the cooking grate and used to sear steaks, putting the meat within inches of the coals and applying maximum heat to the meat's surface. It sells for about $35.

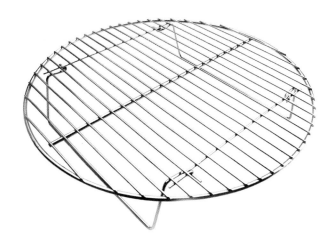

RIB HOLDER. If you have a small cooker, you probably need a rib holder. Although it is $75, the stainless-steel rib rack from MAK (above) is built to last and holds eight racks of ribs. Weber makes a good one that holds five slabs and costs about $15.

A GOOD GRILL COVER. You need a cover to keep rain, snow, wasps, birds, and other vermin out. Cheap covers last only a year or two; a good one will last five years or more. All the plastic and vinyl ones I've tried over the years have cracked and fallen apart in two to three seasons. The canvas covers also rotted in a few years. My recommendation: canvas that's laminated or impregnated with polyurethane or PVC.

BUTANE BURNER. If your grill didn't come with a side burner, buy one. Butane burners like the Coleman InstaStart butane burner (below) cost less than $40, get very hot very fast, and are good for keeping sauces warm and cooking side dishes. Butane bottles look like cans of spray paint, and you can find them in some hardware stores, outdoor stores, or Asian grocery stores.

BEWARE RIB HOLDERS

Rib holders like the one shown above are a great way to squeeze more meat into a small area, but beware potential problems. The meat is almost touching. The air between the meat in the holders will be a lot cooler than if the meat were flat on the grate and the air could surround it. That's also a lot of cold mass to heat up at the start of the cook, so expect the meat to take about an hour longer to get up to temperature. If the gap between the meat is less than 1 inch in your holders, you might need to add yet another hour to the cooking time.

CUISINART GRILLUMINATE UNIVERSAL LED GRILL LIGHT. This light (above) easily attaches to hood handles on most gas grills. Six very bright LEDs affixed to the end of a metal tube extend downward far enough to clear the bottom of the hood and deliver more light than one might expect from a compact, battery-powered device. Weather and heat resistant, it has an automatic tilt sensor switch that activates the LEDs when the hood is opened, and it illuminates a large area. It also has an adaptable clamp that can open and close down to accommodate different shaped handles, or you can slide it out of the clamp and stand it on its magnetic base. It sells for less than $20.

MO'S SMOKING POUCH. In recent years there have been perhaps a dozen new products brought on the market to hold wood and add smoke to the cooker. They work by limiting oxygen to the wood so it smolders and produces clouds of white smoke. Dense white smoke is fine, but not as good tasting as thin blue smoke (see page 19), but when you are cooking something that finishes quickly, like fish or thin steaks, you want dense smoke. This clever design (below) impresses me most. It is a pouch of fine-mesh stainless steel that holds wood chips or pellets. The air spaces in the mesh are small enough so the wood never bursts into flame. It puts out plenty of smoke, usually within a few minutes. Best of all, it smokes just by putting it on top of the cooking grate. You don't have to squeeze it down by the coals or burners. For long cooks, you will need to refill it or buy a second pouch. Refilling can be tricky since the steel gets hot and stays hot for a while. With good insulated gloves, no problem. It sells for less than $25.

GRILL PAD. A lightweight, flexible-fiber, cement pad lies under your grill and protects your deck or patio from runaway coals, spills, and grease. Grill pads come in a variety of sizes, shapes, and designs. I got mine with a Florida Gator logo, for my alma mater.

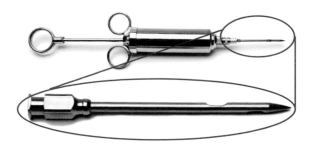

BUTTERBALL 2-OUNCE STAINLESS MARI-NADE INJECTOR. This heavy, stainless-steel injector (shown above) holds 2 ounces of fluid and has a 2¼-inch-long needle with two staggered holes on the sides. It's a great all-purpose injector and the one I use most. It works for thick meats like turkey breasts as well as thin cuts like thin pork chops. There is a comfortable three-hole finger grip and a removable lid to make cleaning easy. The silicone gasket provides a good seal. There are many models in the $20 range.

GALVANIZED ASH CAN. When my fire cools down, I dump my ash into a 5-gallon metal ash

can and discard it. Depending on size, they sell for $20 to $40.

DIGITAL KITCHEN SCALE. I don't know how I lived without a good, accurate digital kitchen scale for so many years. It is indispensible. Take salt, for example: 1 cup of table salt has almost twice as much salinity as 1 cup of Morton's kosher salt because kosher salt has more air space between the grains. But 1 pound of any salt contains exactly the same amount of sodium chloride. Without a scale, making a brine requires a calculator. Packed brown sugar measures differently in volume than loose brown sugar, but weights are constant. All the best bakers use weights for flour, not volumetric measures.

My favorite scale is the OXO Good Grips Stainless Food Scale with Pull-Out Display (above), which sells for about $50. It accurately weighs food up to 11 pounds and down to fractions of an ounce. Push a button and it converts to metric. Put the bowl on the scale, slide out the display so it's not obscured by the bowl, push a button, and it zeros out so the bowl's weight is not included in the measurement. The top also comes off for easy cleaning. It will significantly improve your cooking.

KITCHEN SHEARS. You need good stiff scissors for cutting a chicken apart. Regular scissors won't do the job. Get sturdy stainless blades that come apart at the hinge so they can go in the dishwasher to clean every nook and cranny. Try the OXO Good Grips Professional Poultry Shears (below).

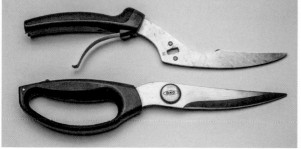

GARLIC PRESS. When a recipe calls for garlic to be crushed, minced, or pressed, I use a garlic press. A good garlic press releases more oils and flavors than a knife does, and pressed garlic coats the food more evenly. Get a press that is sturdily built, easy to grip, easy to clean, and has a large hopper to hold big cloves. I have a well-used Trudeau Garlic Press that sells for about $25, and I recommend it.

USER'S GUIDE
KEEP A COOKING DIARY

Take notes! Whenever you cook, keep a diary, at least until your methods are instinctive. There are so many variables to master. You should be making notes on the meat, its grade, its weight, where you bought it, how you prepared it, what rubs and sauce you used, the cooker temperature, the ambient air temperature, the wood you used, when you added the wood, and how much. Take a few photos with your camera phone. Below is the diary I use. You can download a PDF or an Excel version at http://amazingribs .com/tips_and_technique/cooking_log.html.

USING THERMOMETERS

THERMOMETER CALIBRATION

You should check a thermometer's accuracy soon after you buy it, then once every year, and again if you drop it. Here's how.

BOILING WATER. Bring a pot with at least 3 inches of water to a boil and insert the probe in the center, away from the metal. It should read about 212°F. Notice the key word *about*. The exact reading can vary slightly with air pressure and altitude. Remember that the boiling point of water goes down about 2°F for every increase of 1,000 feet in altitude. In Denver, it is about 203°F.

MEATHEAD'S COOKINGLOG Date _____ Cooker _____

Notes (meat source, expiration date, price, weight, fresh/frozen, injection, brine, rub, mop)
_____
_____
_____
_____

Time	Cooker Target Temp	Cooker Actual Temp	Meat Temp	Ambient Temp, Weather	Action taken: Vents, wood, fuel, water, mop, turn, etc.

Finishing and serving (seasoning, sauce, accompaniments) _____

Finished product (aroma, bark, color, smokering, texture, tenderness, moistness, smokiness, flavor)
_____
_____

Next time: _____

1/24/09   For more great barbecue info visit http://amazingribs.com

---

ICE WATER. Fill a tall glass with ice cubes (not crushed ice), add cold water, and let it sit for a few minutes. Insert the probe among the ice cubes (not below them) and stir gently, making sure the tip is not touching the ice. The temperature below the ice can be several degrees above 32°F and the temperature of the ice itself can be below 32°F. (The ice-water test does not vary with altitude.)

HOW TO SEASON A NEW GRILL OR SMOKER

The cooking chamber of a new grill or smoker often contains dust, grease, oil, metal shavings, or cardboard scraps from the manufacturing and shipping process. Break in a new cooker by wiping down all surfaces with soap and water and rinsing thoroughly. Fire it up, toss in about 8 ounces of wood chips or chunks, and get the cooker as hot as you can for about 30 minutes with all the vents open. This removes all traces of contaminants and lays down a thin layer of carbon on the walls.

CALIBRATING YOUR GRILL OR SMOKER WITH DRY RUNS

Some of the saddest requests we get on AmazingRibs.com are from naïfs who purchased a brand-new grill Saturday and are cooking steaks for twenty, including their in-laws, on Sunday. Instead of cooking tips, they should really be asking for divorce advice. Before you invite the gang over, calibrate your cooker with dry runs. No food needed. You need to practice getting the indirect side of your grill to 225°F and 325°F, and you need to know what warp 10 (maximum heat) is on the direct side. Almost all my recipes call for one of these three temperatures. Figure out how much charcoal you need or what dial settings get you there. Take notes.

The goal is to give you a feel for how your cooker responds to you, and most important, how to hit target temperatures in recipes in all kind of weather. See below for gas grill instructions. To calibrate a charcoal grill, see page 133.

USING YOUR GAS GRILL
HOW TO CALIBRATE A GAS GRILL

You need to know how to hit your marks: 225°F, 325°F, and warp 10 (maximum heat) in the indirect zone, and you need to know how to get there quickly and easily in all kinds of weather. To gain mastery of your tool you need to fire up your cooker without food, make adjustments that will change the temperature, and take notes in a cooking diary.

You are doing experimental research here, so it is important to apply a vital rule of the scientific method: Change only one variable at a time, and you will learn something factual. Playing with both vents at once, for example, is like trying to control the speed of your car by using both the gas pedal and the brake at the same time.

Controlling temperature on a gas grill or a smoker seems simple: Just turn the knobs. Alas, knobs on gas grills don't tell you the temperature, so you need to figure that out when you calibrate the grill.

WHERE TO STICK IT

You want to measure the temperature of your cooker where the food is. But a bubble of cold air surrounds the food at first, so keep the thermometer probe just above the cooking surface, about 2 inches away from the food. Some thermometers come with a handy clip, but if yours doesn't, use a ball of foil to hold it in place. Just make sure the tip, where the sensitive parts are, protrudes from the foil.

PROBE PLACEMENT

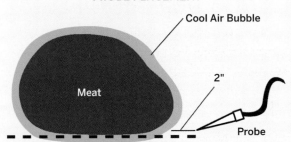

One problem with a lot of grills is that you have to thread thermometer cables under lids, down chimneys, or through vents, and then find a way to attach the probe to the grates without letting the tip touch metal. The lids often crimp or cut the cables, and you're never quite sure where the tip of the probe is, and if it is touching meat or metal. Then you forget about it, lift the lid, and your thermometer goes flying into the neighbor's yard. One solution is to drill a hole just above or below the cooking grate and insert the probe through the hole. Make the hole just a bit larger than the probe, and don't worry if it leaks a little. That small amount of leakage won't hurt anything. If you wish, look for silicone grommets at your hardware store. Not all probes are the same diameter, but $3/16$ inch should work for most. Make sure you route the cable away from direct flame or super-hot grill grates because most cables will melt if exposed to temperatures greater than 450°F.

When measuring the temperature of the meat, test in more than one location, because the composition of the flesh, the rivers of fat, and the bone can fool you. Insert the probe in the center of the side until it almost comes out the other side. To get a reading of the cross-section you just created, pull it back slowly and read the temperatures as you go.

Always ignite the grill with the hood open. Gas can build up under the hood and when you hit the ignition, the lid can blow open. Or worse. Turn one burner on high and leave the others off. Put a thermometer probe above the hot burner, close the lid, and start timing. When the temperature stabilizes, write down the temperature and how long it took to get there. Then move the thermometer probe above the cold burner furthest away, and record the temperature there. If you have three or more burners, add one burner at a time and take measurements at different dial settings. Keep fiddling until you figure out how to get to 225°F and 325°F on the indirect side. Measure the temperature on the upper grate, too.

Now check for hotspots. You'll need a loaf of white bread. On a piece of paper, draw the cooking surface of your grill, roughly to scale. Divide it into quadrants by drawing a line down the middle of both sides. Turn all burners to medium, close the lid, and let the temperature stabilize. After about 15 minutes, place the bread on the grill in a grid, with 1 or 2 inches between each slice. Move quickly or have someone help you. Close the lid for a few minutes.

Then peek at the bread. When they are toasted, quickly flip the bread. You will see that your grill has some hotspots. Mark them on your drawing or just take a picture and print it for future reference. Finish toasting the bread, make some sausage gravy, and chow down.

COOKING ON A GAS GRILL

Turning the knobs might not change the actual temperature the way you'd think. Fortunately, you have another tool with which to control temperature. On better grills, you have more than one burner, and that allows you to turn at least one burner off and one burner on, which should help you get to your target temperature. Here's how to set up a gas grill for two-zone cooking.

If you have a grill with only one burner, or you have more meat than will fit in the indirect zone of your grill, put a water pan beneath the meat. The water will absorb heat and minimize temperature fluctuations. If you keep the cooker temperature at 225°F, the water should not boil

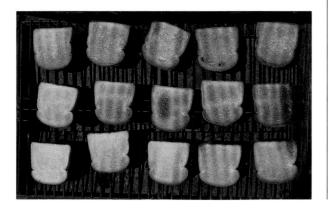

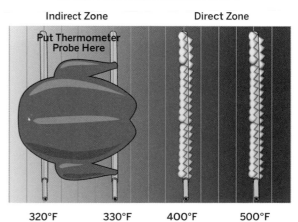

INDIRECT ZONE AVERAGES 325°F

Indirect Zone — Direct Zone

Put Thermometer Probe Here

320°F   330°F   400°F   500°F

because the surface area will allow evaporation that will cool the water, keeping it below 212°F. If the water is boiling, you are running hot. Turn it down.

Here are the two primary methods for using water pans on a gas grill:

WATER PANS UNDER THE GRATES. Get two disposable aluminum roasting pans that together are, ideally, just about the same size as the interior of your gas grill. They should have 2- to 3-inch-high sides. The pans will get smoke stains on them, so do not use your best roasting pans. Remove your grill's grates and put the pans on top of the flavor bars, lava rocks, or other heat diffuser. Do not put the pans right on top of the burner tubes. Fill the pans to within 1 inch of their rims with hot water. For smoke, put a pan of wood chips or pellets as close to the flame as possible.

Then place the grates over the water pans and put a thermometer probe on top of the grates just over the water near the meat. Experiment to get the temperature called for in the recipe.

This could take 30 minutes or more with all that water to heat. Adjust the flame up or

down, and if you need more heat, fire up another burner. Take notes.

WATER PANS ON TOP OF THE GRATES. If you cannot put pans under your grates, you can put them on top and use wire baking racks or the grates from your indoor oven on top of the pans. Try to keep at least 2 inches between the meat and the water's surface, otherwise the bottom of the food will be heated by the water temperature, which will be closer to 160°F than 225°F.

ROTISSERIE AND SPIT GRILLING

If you love the rotisserie chickens from the grocery store, you really need to start cooking them on your grill. You will be surprised at how much better they taste when they aren't left to dehydrate for hours under heat lamps and when they pick up a little smoke.

When you grill the normal way, it is easy to overcook one side of the food. Rotisserie cooking rotates the food at a steady, slow speed on a spit, ensuring that it cooks evenly on all sides. With continuous rotation, all of the food's surfaces are exposed to infrared heat that promotes browning. Those surfaces see the heat and then rotate away into a heat shadow, allowing a small amount of the absorbed energy to escape while some of it continues to penetrate the food. Meanwhile, the interior slowly and gently roasts. I recommend rotisserie cooking with the hood open because it slows down the cooking and prevents the exterior layer from building up too much heat and drying out or burning.

As with other forms of cooking, the meat rises in temperature as it heats and juices are squeezed to the surface. On a rotisserie, many of the juices tend to roll around the surface of the meat, basting it, cooling it, and keeping it moist instead of rolling off. Some water still evaporates and drips, of course, leaving behind protein, sugars, fat, and flavor, and creating a great crust, or bark.

When spit-roasting a whole chicken, the wings and drumsticks must not be allowed to flop around or they could burn or even fall off. Place the forks carefully and you won't need to tie the wings and drumsticks to the rest of the bird.

Some people fear that the metal spear will carry heat to the center of a piece of meat and overcook the roast, but the metal spit inside doesn't get any hotter than the meat itself, except for a fraction of an inch at the ends.

Check the distance from the spit to the cooking grates. You might need to remove the cooking grates when cooking with the rotisserie so that the meat doesn't drag on the grates. If you have a rear rotisserie burner, you'll also want to put a drip pan under the meat and fill it with potatoes or other veggies that will roast and collect the essence of meat that drips from the rotisserie. Put a little water in the pan so the

drippings don't burn. With enough drippings, you can make a delicious gravy for the meat and/or sides.

If you have several chickens on and space is tight, you can run the spear through the sides of the birds. There is no law that says you have to run the spear up their butts. One last warning: The exposed part of that spear is a red-hot poker. You must wear insulated gloves when removing it from the grill and removing the bird from the spear.

If you don't have a rotisserie burner, it is best to use indirect heat. On a four- or three-burner unit, turn off the center burners and use indirect heat from the two end burners. If you have only one or two burners, use them both and cover them with a drip pan large enough to block the direct heat from the meat. Keep the pan partially filled with hot water and check it regularly. You will get some steam condensing on your food, which will cool it and slow the cooking. As the meat approaches its target temperature, remove the pan and get some dry heat on the surface to firm up the crust or crisp the skin.

TROUBLESHOOTING AND CLEANING YOUR GAS GRILL

Most gas grills use some sort of heat diffuser between the burners and the cooking grates. Sauce and grease can remain on them and the grates. Before you cook a meal, heat the grill all the way to carbonize this gunk. If you skip this step, there can be a lot of greasy soot on your meal. Even with preheating, drippings can cake up on the deflectors, insulating them and reducing their heat output. It helps to pull out the deflectors and scrape them now and then. They take the brunt of the heat and are pretty inexpensive, so replace them when they become warped or corroded. Enamel-coated deflectors corrode with time and need to be replaced, so if there is a stainless-steel replacement, get it. It will last longer.

Inspect lava rocks and ceramic briquets periodically, spreading them around so they are evenly distributed. They are very porous and absorb grease, but when the grease heats up, it usually turns to carbon. Ceramics and lava rocks can often be flipped, but when all sides are full of carbon or loaded with grease, they will need to be replaced.

If you are using water to clean, remove electrical parts like igniters or cover them with plastic wrap and tape. Some new grills have glass or ceramic infrared burners. They need to be handled very carefully. Read the manual.

To clean the inside bottom of the cooking chamber, remove the heat diffusers over the burners and anything else that is easy to remove; scrape below and between the burners with a putty knife.

Clean the louvers that allow exhaust to escape, if only to make sure they are unblocked. These louvers provide draft through the cooking chamber, which pulls oxygen into the combustion system so you get optimum flame.

HOW GAS SYSTEMS WORK AND HOW TO TROUBLESHOOT THEM

Gas grills have a system for regulating the flow of fuel from a pipeline or tank, mixing it with

oxygen, igniting it, and turning the flow up or down to adjust the temperature. A number of things can go wrong with the process, although they rarely do. You need to maintain the system to keep it efficient and operating at optimum heat, and to make sure it is safe.

Before you do anything, make sure the gas supply is disconnected and the valve is closed.

In order to function properly, the propane tank or natural gas pipe must be connected properly. Keep in mind that for safety, the threaded connection works in reverse of the usual "righty tighty, lefty loosey" rule. Gas connections tighten when you turn them to the left. There is often a flexible hose connecting the gas to the grill, and somewhere along the line there is a flying saucer–shaped regulator (above). Look for cracks, cuts, or kinks in the hose. If there is anything suspicious, replace it. Wipe the threads with a cotton cloth or towel on all sides before mating them. The regulator has a small hole on the top. Make sure it is not clogged. To protect it, turn it so the hole is facing downward.

If you smell or suspect a leak, mix up some soapy water and, with a brush or cloth, paint it on the tubes. Open the tank or pipeline valve

and look for bubbles. If you find leaks, turn off the gas immediately and call the manufacturer or a licensed technician experienced in working with gas systems.

On the other end, the hose will probably connect to a brass pipe that carries the fuel to the valves, one for each burner. That connection needs to be tight. The valves are controlled by knobs. Each knob must turn easily. If a valve is acting up, you can remove the knob and look around, but you should not risk breaking it. Contact the manufacturer for instructions on replacing it.

There is usually a short brass pipe coming from the valves. It floats inside the venturi, the adjustable air intake valve shown in blue in the illustration below. It functions like a carburetor, and it is where air and gas mix. Make sure the pipe is centered in the venturi and there are no obstructions like leaves, spiderwebs, or wasps' nests.

The venturi connects to the burners. They are usually stainless steel, brass, or aluminum pipes with small holes or jets. Inspect the tubes and the gas jets to make sure there are

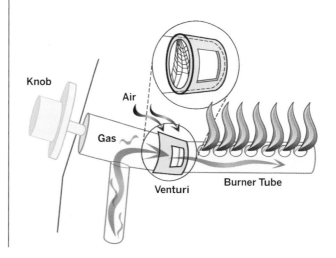

HOW TO TELL WHEN THE GAS TANK IS LOW

There are a number of gauges that attach to the hose near the tank, but I am not impressed. I do like the Grill Gauge (pictured below). It is not much different than the type of scales fishermen use to weigh their catch. Hoist your tank, and the gauge gives you a pretty good guesstimate of how much propane is left. I take mine along when I exchange empty tanks for full ones. You'd be surprised how many are sold underfilled. Regardless, you should always keep a backup tank on hand. You back up your computer, don't you? It is no fun running out of gas in the middle of cooking.

Here's another trick: Take a quart of warm water and pour it slowly over the side of the tank. It will warm the thin metal where the tank is empty, while the metal in contact with the liquid propane remains cold. Run your hand down the side to locate the liquid level.

no obstructions. If there are cracks, replace the tubes. If they are clogged anywhere, straighten a paper clip and poke it through the gas jet holes to unclog them. You can even shoot water through the tubes to clear them out.

The factory typically tunes the proper mix, but occasionally it needs adjustment. Loosen the venturi's set screw, fire up the grill, and rotate the venturi until the flame coming out the burner tube appears blue with little or no orange at the tip. Do this at night so you can clearly see the color of the flame.

Gas

MODIFYING THE GAS FLOW TO GET LOW HEAT

Some gas grill owners find it hard to dial the temperature down to 225°F for low-and-slow cooking. Fiddling with the gas supply system, as some writers suggest doing, can create an explosion or fire, resulting in death and the destruction of your home. I strongly recommend that you hire a professional if you wish to modify your grill's factory setup. Your local LP gas company will be glad to help for a fee. Frankly, if your grill is running too hot, I recommend that you try to cool it with water pans (see page 118), by leaving the lid slightly ajar, or just by learning to cook at the higher temperatures. Better still, buy a dedicated smoker designed to cook at 225°F (see pages 86–94).

TROUBLESHOOTING IGNITION

If you can't ignite the grill, it is usually either an ignition system problem or a gas supply problem. If the igniter does not work, and yours is battery operated, check the batteries. Locate the spark generator, typically a stiff wire, where the spark jumps to the burner. Make sure the spark generator is located properly, usually about $\frac{1}{8}$ inch in front of a gas jet. If there is no spark, clean the igniter and check all the wiring to make sure it is connected properly and the spark generator is not touching metal. If it still doesn't work, you should be able to light the burner with a long match, a long-handled butane lighter, or a match held with tongs. If you need a new igniter, most manufacturers sell replacements.

If the igniter works and the grill still won't fire up, the tank may be misbehaving. Some

MYTH **The best way to clean the grates on a gas grill is to cover them with foil, turn up the heat, and close the lid. This will carbonize the grease and make it easier to remove.**

BUSTED! This method blocks ventilation and could cause a dangerous buildup of gases. It forces hot air out through the knob holes and can melt plastic knobs and flexible hoses. It can also crack ceramic and warp metal.

BE CAREFUL OF EXTREMES

Mind your propane in extreme weather. The regulator on a propane tank can jam or become contaminated with condensed water on very cold days. In the north, where temperatures can get well below zero, the gas pressure drops too low for the regulator to operate properly. As a result, some gas grills have problems in very cold weather, especially if the tank is not full. At 32°F, there is still plenty of pressure to run the grill, but at −30°F, you will have an issue.

On really hot days, the tank's safety valve can also vent propane out of the tank. If you are bringing home a full tank on a hot day, don't put the tank in your trunk because it can vent gas into the trunk and explode. Always carry propane tanks in an open truck bed or in the back seat of your car with the windows open. And don't store them in your house or attached garage.

propane tanks contain a safety device that slows the flow of gas if it thinks it's moving too fast. It can be wrong. To outsmart it, turn the tank valve off and disconnect the tank. Open the grill lid. Turn the knobs on the grill to high for 1 minute to bleed off any gas in the pipes and then close them. Reconnect the fuel tank and turn on the valve slowly. It should light now.

If the problem persists, you may have a regulator problem. They occasionally stick and you won't get enough gas flow. To keep your regulator from sticking, when you are done cooking, make sure that you turn off the control knobs on the grill first, then turn off the tank valve. The next time you want to cook, open the tank valve slowly. If it still doesn't work, buy a new regulator or try your spare tank.

USING YOUR CHARCOAL GRILL

Charcoal is lightweight and cheap, and packs more potential energy per ounce than raw wood. It burns more steadily and gives better heat control than wood, and although it produces less smoke, by adding small amounts of wood, you can still get great smoke flavor.

Consisting mostly of pure carbon, also called char, charcoal is made by burning wood in a low-oxygen environment. The process, known as pyrolysis, can take days and burns off volatile compounds such as water, methane, hydrogen, and tar. Burning takes place in large concrete or steel silos and stops before the wood turns to ash. The process leaves black lumps and powder, about 25 percent of the original weight. When ignited, the carbon in charcoal combines with oxygen and forms carbon dioxide, carbon monoxide, water, other gases, and significant quantities of energy in the form of light and heat.

BRIQUETS OR LUMP?

This is a debate that can end in gunplay. Let's see if we can settle the argument without the author being shot.

Charcoal briquets   Lump charcoal

ABOUT CHARCOAL BRIQUETS

Kingsford is by far the largest producer of charoal briquets. Briquets begin as scrap sawdust and chips from mixed woods from timber mills. The company says that it doesn't use whole trees. The company claims that its suppliers' mills don't treat lumber with chemicals to make it weather- and insect-proof, so there is no chance that those chemicals will be in their product. Kingsford's quality-control staff says they inspect the raw material to make sure there is not too much softwood.

The sawdust arrives by truck, and a bulldozer pushes it into a conveyor that separates large chunks and foreign matter like rocks. Another conveyor moves it to a huge rotating barrel for tumble-drying, which takes the moisture from about 50 percent down to about 35 percent. Then the sawdust goes into special ovens called retorts. With little air in the retort, the wood burns down to char, and comes out at about 25 percent of the weight that went in. It is then crushed.

Kingsford's standard blue bag of Sure Fire charcoal is mixed with small amounts of anthracite coal (almost pure carbon), mineral charcoal (a form of charcoal found in coal mines), starch, sodium nitrate, limestone, and borax. The slurry is then molded into distinctive pillow-shaped briquets with the K-shaped

CHECK THE WEATHER

Weather plays an important role in hitting your target temperatures. The sun baking on your cooker will make it warmer, reducing your need for fuel. But on a cold day, cold air coming in through the intake vents will cool the coals or gas jets, and you will need more fuel to get to your target temperature. Wind, rain, and snow can also cool the exterior of your cooker, increasing your need for fuel. For more consistent performance, try to protect your cooker from the elements. Some cooks build plywood boxes as weather shields. You can line it with foil or metal and hinge it at the corners so you can collapse it and store it.

Maintaining a steady temperature depends a lot on the ability of your cooker to retain heat. A Weber Kettle is thin metal and has much less heat-retention capacity than a Big Green Egg, which is made from thick ceramic. Get to know your cooker and how it responds to the weather.

Wind can blow so viciously across the top of the chimney of a charcoal or wood-burning pit that it can suck out hot air, creating a bellows effect in the firebox, kicking the temperature up 50°F and altering the smoke flavor. It can also suck in so much cold air that it cools off the cooking chamber. Wind can also blow out

a flame on a gas grill and, if you're not paying attention, it might sit there, flamed out but still pumping gas into the cooking chamber for an hour. Hit the igniter and you could spend the night in the burn unit.

Never roll your cooker into the garage to cook on a windy day or push it up against the side of your house. Love barbecue, but love your family more.

channels that promote airflow during the burn.

The additives act as binders, improve ignition, promote steady burning, reduce air pollution, and make manufacturing more efficient. Some cooks complain about the additives, but I don't see anything scary in them. All of these components can be found in nature. Some folks say they can taste the additives in their food. I can't, and in a previous career, I was a professional wine taster.

Self-igniting Match-Light charcoal, which has mineral spirits added to promote ignition, is a different story. Kingsford and government regulators say it is safe if you follow the instructions, but I can smell the hydrocarbons and fear they can taint the food. I don't use the stuff.

In 2008, Kingsford introduced Competition Briquets in a brown bag. The company says they are made with only char, starch as a binder, and a bit of borax to help it release from the manufacturing presses. My friend John Dawson of PatioDaddioBBQ.com did a comparison test of regular blue-bag Kingsford and Kingsford Competition. He showed that the Competition briquets ignite slightly faster, burn slightly hotter, and produce less ash, with a burn time that is about the same as that of ordinary briquets. Sensitive palates say Competition tastes better. The problem is they cost almost twice as much as the blue bag.

There are other good charcoals out there. I like Royal Oak and Duraflame Real Hardwood Briquets. Wicked Good 100% All Natural Hardwood briquets are made from just char and starch. They are not widely available.

ABOUT HARDWOOD LUMP CHARCOAL

Hardwood lump charcoal is made from scrap wood from sawmills and manufacturers of flooring, furniture, and building materials. Branches, twigs, blocks, trim, and other chunks are carbonized, resulting in lumps that are irregular in size, often looking like limbs and lumber.

Lump's big advantage is that it burns thoroughly and leaves little ash because there are no binders or other additives. Also, the bags are lighter and easier to handle because the lumps are lighter and shaped irregularly, so there is more air in the bag.

Often, lump charcoal is not thoroughly carbonized. Some of the larger chunks frequently have cellulose, lignin, and other wood components left in them, and when they burn, they

MYTH Lump charcoal burns hotter than briquets.

BUSTED! The folks at *Cook's Illustrated* took two typical charcoal chimneys and filled one with lump charcoal and one with briquets. They fitted two identical grills with seven digital thermometer probes each, and learned that by volume, not weight (volume being how most of us measure charcoal, especially if we use a chimney), the two burned at about the same temperature for about 30 minutes, but after that, the briquets held heat longer and the lump turned to ash faster. They repeated the test eleven times, with the same results.

give off smoke and flavor. This can be a pleasant addition to your food, but it isn't controllable. You don't know from one meal to the next what you're getting. Top pitmasters prefer to burn charcoal and then add the wood of their choice to produce the quantity and quality of smoke they want.

Lump is harder to find than briquets, more expensive, and burns out more quickly so you need to add more during long cooking sessions. It does not coat with ash as briquets do, so it's hard to tell when it's burning at peak temperature. It varies in BTUs per pound; it varies in wood type from bag to bag; and it varies in flavor from bag to bag.

If you use lump, you'll often find charcoal dust and small crumbs in the bottom of the bag. Discard them. If you pour them in your grill, they can clog the air spaces between the coals, constrict airflow, and choke back your fire by as much as 50°F. Remember, oxygen is just as important as charcoal.

Finally, it is not uncommon to find rocks, metal pieces, and other foreign objects from the lumber operations where the wood is gathered.

I am also concerned that some of the wood used to make lump charcoal could contain wood preservatives such as creosote, chrome, copper, pesticides, fungicides, and arsenic (now illegal but found in plenty of scrap from building demolitions).

Bottom line: It's inconsistent. For this reason, few of the top competition teams use lump.

You'll find more than seventy-five brands of lump charcoal out there, including everything from hickory, mesquite, and cherry to coconut shell and tamarind. For definitive ratings and reviews of lump charcoal, visit Doug Hanthorn's website, NakedWhiz.com.

SO WHICH IS BEST?

As a cook, you need control and consistency. You get that from briquets, not from lump. There are about 16 Kingsford briquets in a quart, and 64 in a gallon. A Weber chimney holds about 5 quarts, or about 80 briquets. That's a constant quantity of energy. There are many variables in outdoor cooking, and having a steady, reliable heat source is a big plus.

Harry Soo of Slap Yo' Daddy BBQ, one of the top ten competition teams, once told me, "I buy whatever briquets are on sale." Mike Wozniak, of QUAU, winner of scores of barbecue championships, says, "I cook on whatever brand the competition sponsor is giving away for free. Charcoal is for heat, not flavor."

Pick one brand of briquet, learn it, and stick with it for at least a year until you have all the other variables under control.

SETTING UP A CHARCOAL GRILL

THE WORST WAY TO START A CHARCOAL FIRE

Please don't use starter fluid, mineral spirits, gasoline, or kerosene to start a charcoal fire. They soak into the coals and emit a stink that can be smelled at the other end of your neighborhood, and the fumes can get into your food.

Let's not even talk about how many sleeves have caught fire while trying to light coals with lighter fluid and a cigarette lighter. If your fire doesn't get off to a roaring start, *please, please, please* don't squirt it with lighter fluid unless you want to see what the inside of the hospital's burn unit looks like.

Here are some starting techniques that work. Remember that there are really two fuels here, charcoal and oxygen, so make sure all the vents are open wide when you try to light the coals.

THE BEST WAY TO START A CHARCOAL FIRE

THE CHARCOAL CHIMNEY. With a chimney, there is no chemical aftertaste and no solvent smell in the air, and it's a lot cheaper and safer than using lighter fluid. A chimney is a tube with an upper compartment and a lower compartment. First you stuff newspaper into the bottom compartment and add charcoal to the top compartment, then you light the paper. After about 5 minutes, grab the handle and give the chimney a shake, so the unlit coals from above land on top of the lit coals on the bottom. That's

about it. In another 10 minutes or so, the coals will be white and ready.

Best of all, a charcoal chimney is like a measuring cup with a fixed amount of fuel (see page 127) that will generate a known quantity of heat. With practice, you learn how many more briquets to add on cold days, and how many fewer on hot days.

Some folks drizzle cooking oil on the newspaper to make it burn longer, but I've never found this necessary. Because hot newspaper ash likes to float away and become a fire hazard, I prefer to use a Weber Firestarter, small cubes of paraffin under the chimney (opposite page, top left). You can even make your own firestarters by wadding up half a page of newspaper, dunking it in melted paraffin or candle wax, and letting it dry. Just light the newspaper and it will burn long enough to start the charcoal. The small wad of ash remaining is too heavy to drift off and

start a forest fire. If you have a gas grill with a side burner, just turn on the burner and put the chimney on top. No fuss, no muss.

Another cool thing about the chimney: You can cook on it! It makes a hotter wok fire than anything in your kitchen. Just plunk your wok on top and start stir-frying. You can also put a grate on it and grill thin foods right on top of the chimney, a technique I call the afterburner method (see page 247).

One note of caution: Make sure you place the hot chimney on something heatproof after you dump out the coals—and keep it well away from children and pets. The list price is about $20.

OTHER WAYS TO LIGHT IT

LOOFTLIGHTER. This (pictured top right) is a real boy toy. It is a hair dryer–blast furnace hybrid. Just make a pile of coals, place the red-hot tip of the Looftlighter against the coals, and within 20 seconds you'll see sparks flying. Pull back a few inches, and in about a minute or two you have a ball of hot coals. Stir, and in about 15 minutes, you're in biz. Looftlighter is

an excellent way to start a chain of coals for the fuse method described on page 132. On the minus side, you need an outlet, you don't want to use it in the rain, you have to stir the coals, and you have to be careful where you place it when it is hot. It lists at about $75.

THE ELECTRIC STARTER. This is an electric coil similar to the coils on a hotplate (below). Pour a pile of charcoal in your grill, jam the starter into it, and plug it in. As the coals ignite, remove the coil, and mix the unlit and lit coals together with a fireplace shovel. When you are done, make sure you place the hot coil on something that is not flammable until it cools.

It's an OK firestarter, but you need access to an outlet, and you don't want to be using it in the rain. Unlike the Looftlighter, however, you can

walk away while it is doing its thing. List prices start at about $15.

PROPANE TORCH. Then there's the real flame-thrower. Connect it to a propane tank, hit the spark, and whoosh! Within a few minutes, you can get a whole bag of charcoal glowing, and that makes it popular on the competition circuit. Unlike gasoline or lighter fluid, propane is flavorless and odorless when it burns. It is also good for burning weeds from the cracks in your patio and flushing out enemy woodchucks. This is the kind of tool Carl Spackler would love. The Red Dragon Torch is shown below. List price is about $100.

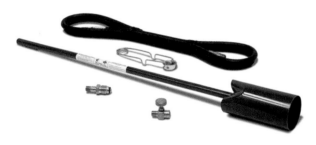

CONTROLLING TEMPERATURE ON CHARCOAL AND WOOD-BURNING GRILLS AND SMOKERS

You have two primary ways to control temperature: fuel and air. Most charcoal and wood grills and smokers have two air controls.

THE INTAKE DAMPER (top right) is near the charcoal or wood, and its job is to provide them with oxygen. The intake damper is the carburetor of your cooker. Close it off and you starve the fire, and it will burn out even if the exhaust damper is open. Open it all the way and the

temperature rises. On most grills and pits, you can control temperature mainly by controlling the intake damper.

THE EXHAUST DAMPER (AKA FLUE, VENT, OR CHIMNEY) has two jobs: allow the combustion gases, heat, and smoke to escape and create suction that pulls oxygen in through the intake damper. The exhaust damper (shown below)

needs to be at least partially open at all times in order to do both jobs.

If the temperature starts to get away from you, choke the fire by closing the intake damper. It is more important than the exhaust damper. But don't expect an instant response. It can take 10 minutes for you to see real movement in the thermometer.

If the temperature drops too low, open the dampers wider. You may need to knock some ash off the coals with a stick or remove ash to keep it from blocking the airflow. If the temperature is still too low, add more coals.

If it is running too hot, and you have already closed the intakes, you can crack the lid. In the picture above, the hot coals are pushed all the way to the left and the meat all the way to the right. The lid is partially off, so hot air from the coals will flow over the meat and out. I have also been known to remove the lid altogether and put a metal pan over the food as a makeshift lid on a hot day when the fire is running hot (as shown at right).

Adjusting the quantity of charcoal also controls the temperature. That's why a chimney and briquets work so well together. With practice, you'll learn how many coals a full chimney, half chimney, and so on gets you to your target temperature. Each coal is a bundle of energy. Add more, and you add energy.

After you've been cooking a while, the coals will start to die, and you will need to add more. Get a feel for what happens when they ebb, and add fully lit coals from the chimney starter as soon as you see the temperature sliding down. You can add unlit coals, but they will belch smoke, and they take some time to get up to temperature. You will need to experiment to learn how many to add and when. The problem is that an hour later, you have to add more. This means you have to watch the thermometer like a bachelor at a beauty pageant. Every cooker design is different, so master your tool by practicing.

For long cooks, there are other ways to stablilize the temperature.

THE MINION METHOD. Jim Minion, a caterer, invented this technique for his Weber Smokey Mountain smoker. It involves pouring lit coals on top of the unlit coals at the start of cooking. The hot coals above gradually ignite the unlit coals below as the old coals die out. It works remarkably well and can keep your cooker chugging along at the same temperature for hours, although it does produce some white smoke.

The exact amount of lit and unlit coals varies from device to device and from season to season.

THE FUSE METHOD. For this technique, the coals are laid out in a line, and hot coals are added to the end of the line. The coals ignite like a slow-motion fuse, burning from one end to the other, producing a steady supply of heat for hours. Above is a U-shaped fuse made with bricks.

WHEN YOU NEED REALLY HIGH HEAT

To get a dark sear on a wet surface like a steak or burger, raise the bottom grate by placing bricks under it and use lots of hot coals. That

MYTH Caveman steaks are the best.

BUSTED! Here's how this parlor trick works: Once you get your coals down to glowing embers, fan them to blow away any loose ash. Some people use a hair dryer. Take a steak, pat it really dry, and lay the meat right on the coals. Every time I've tried it, small amounts of ash and even whole coals have stuck to the surface, and there have been seriously scorched dry spots. Here's a better idea: Place a wire rack 1 or 2 inches above the coals. That prevents scorching, dry spots, and ash, while still giving you heat intensity. Live in the Stone Age if you wish, but I'm here to tell you, things are better in the Iron Age.

puts the heat source about 2 inches below the food grate. When you add hot coals, they will be just 1 inch below the meat. Perfect for searing!

CALIBRATING CHARCOAL GRILLS

Now it is time to practice. Let's do some dry runs with a good thermometer, but without food.

When coals are fully lit and covered in gray ash, they are at peak temperature. From there, they slowly lose heat as they are consumed by combustion. It will take about 15 minutes for them to ash over, so don't dump the coals into the grill until 20 minutes after you have lit them. Repeat these steps exactly for each test.

To set the grill up for two-zone, or indirect, cooking, dump one chimney of lit coals on one half the grill and none on the other half. Open all dampers all the way. Put the thermometer probe just above the grate in the middle of the indirect zone. Measure the distance from the edge where you placed the probe and write it down so you can put it in the exact same location on repeat tests. Put the lid on. On a Weber Kettle, place the exhaust damper over the indirect side. Wait for the temperature to stabilize by watching the thermometer; it should take about 5 minutes on a simple metal grill, longer on a kamado.

Now try to control the heat by controlling the oxygen reaching the coals. That means controlling the intake damper only; leave the exhaust damper open all the way. Make a note of how long it takes to stabilize. Now try to get to 325°F, then 225°F.

Move the probe to the center of the direct side, right over the coals, put the lid on, and take a reading when the temperature stabilizes. Make sure you are using a thermometer that can withstand high heat. It can get to 600°F or more on the hot side. Write down the reading.

Then let it die. Clean it out, fire it up again, and try to go right to 225°F. If you can, you are dialed in!

CLEANUP AFTER GRILLING

My favorite method of putting out a charcoal fire is to suffocate it by closing all the vents and depriving it of oxygen. It can take an hour or more for the coals to die, but they will go out—as long as your cooker is reasonably airtight. The unburned coals can be used again.

You can extinguish a charcoal fire by dousing it with water, but beware, steam will come rushing up and can scald you. Plus, the hot water and ash will drain out the bottom of your grill and onto your sandals, which could put you in a wheelchair. Wet ashes can also form a concrete-like crust that will corrode your firebox. If you have a ceramic grill, never use water to douse the fire; the rapid temperature change and steam created in the ceramic might crack it.

When the coals are thoroughly dead and dry, any partially burned ones can be shaken to slough off excess ash, dried in the sun, and then used again. But it can take days for coals to thoroughly dry, so if you plan on using the grill soon, don't douse them with water.

After grilling, empty the bottom of your grill and discard the ashes. Don't leave it in there for next time. Ash is a great insulator, and it reduces the amount of heat bouncing off the bottom of the cooker. Too much ash can choke off oxygen or be stirred up and coat your food.

SMOKING

Having a smoker opens up brave new worlds of cooking, but you don't need a dedicated smoker to make quality smoked meats and vegetables. Most grills can be adapted to the task. That said, it is usually easier to control temperature with a good smoker. Most smoking in my recipes is done at 225°F, and a few at 325°F. Let's look at how to smoke.

SMOKING ON A CHARCOAL GRILL

There's no secret to smoking on a grill. Just use a two-zone setup, keep the heat on the indirect side low, place the food on the indirect side, and place wood on the hot coals. Start by pouring about 1 cup of dry hardwood, fruitwood, or nut-wood on the heat source until it smokes, and resist the temptation to add more wood until

you've tasted the food and learn how much smoke flavor your grill creates and how much you like. You'll need to experiment with where you place the wood and if you wrap it in foil or put it in some other container.

Every grill design is different, but here's how to set up the world's most popular charcoal grill, the Weber Kettle for smoking. If you don't have one, you can easily adapt these concepts to your grill.

Weber manuals tell you to put coals on both sides and the food in the center (pictured below), but there is a better way that gives you more indirect cooking area and won't singe the edges of the meat. Push all the coals to one side, and add a water pan or two if possible.

> ### MYTH The parabolic shape of the Weber Kettle acts like a heat reflector.
>
> **BUSTED!** Salesmen love to say this. But the vast majority of the heat in a kettle grill radiates directly from the surface of the glowing coals. Some heat may reflect from the sides, but very little reflects off the curved bottom of the bowl. Any heat that hits the bottom of the kettle just bounces back into the coals. So the parabolic shape of the kettle is no more efficient than a square box.

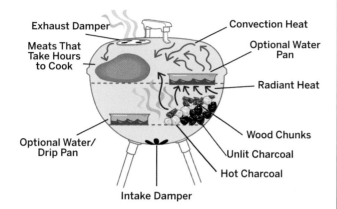

If space allows, place a pan of hot water directly *above* the coals and another under the food as shown above. Fill the pans with hot water so the coals don't expend energy just heating up the water.

Position the grate with one of the handles over the coals. There's a gap under the handle that makes adding more coal and wood chips easy. Weber sells a grate with hinges (see page 101) to make adding coals even easier, and I recommend it.

SMOKING ON A GAS GRILL

For smoke flavor on a gas grill, use hardwood chunks, chips, or pellets. On cookers with inverted V-shaped burner covers (flavor bars), you can often just put a big chunk of wood in the gap between them. You can also put chips or pellets in a foil pouch and poke holes in the foil. Place the pouch under the cooking grate, as close to the flame as possible. If the wood won't smoke because the burners are not hot enough, put the wood onto a burner and turn

DON'T WORRY IF YOUR WOOD BURSTS INTO FLAME

Readers often write that they are not getting enough smoke because their wood bursts into flame, so they soak their wood or buy fancy gadgets that limit oxygen, hoping their wood will smolder longer and produce lots of smoke.

Stop worrying and stop soaking (see page 22). Remember that the best-tasting smoke, blue smoke, is barely visible, and it happens when wood burns hot and fast. If your wood burns up in a hurry, just add more wood. When you are cooking something quickly like a flattened chicken breast and you need a lot of smoke in a hurry, then reach for a smoldering device like Mo's Smoking Pouch (see page 111) or make a foil packet.

it on high until the wood smokes, then dial it back. Or try starting the wood with a lighter to get it going. Another trick is to place two charcoal briquets on the heat diffuser above the burners. The charcoal will ignite but won't be hot enough to significantly change the oven temperature. Put the wood chunks on the hot charcoal and the wood should start smoking within a few minutes.

When you see smoke and the temperature is stable, put the meat on the rack in the indirect zone. You will be amazed at the rich, complex flavors you can get with this simple technique on a gas grill.

SMOKING ON A WEBER SMOKEY MOUNTAIN OR OTHER BULLET SMOKER

The Weber Smokey Mountain is an old design that still is among the best and easiest to use. It certainly is the best-selling smoker. Here are some tips to get the most out of it and its imitators.

If you can, buy a second bottom grate and lay it on top of the one that came with your smoker so the bars are perpendicular to each other, creating a checkerboard pattern. This will prevent coals and wood from falling through.

There are several charcoal configurations that work better than lighting the coals all at once (as is recommended by Weber) because they hold a steady 225°F temperature for much longer. With the Minion Method (page 131), you pour unlit coals in the basket and pour lit coals on top.

TEMPERATURE GRADIENTS IN A WEBER SMOKEY MOUNTAIN

If you use a good digital thermometer, you will notice that the dial thermometer in the dome of your Weber Smokey Mountain is not accurate. You'll also see that the dome temperature is hotter than the top grate, and the top grate is hotter than the bottom grate. By how much? On a nice summer day in the 70s, in the shade with no wind, the dome will be about 10 to 15°F hotter than the top grate, which will be 10 to 15°F hotter than the bottom grate. Your mileage may vary.

With the Soo's Donut Method, you hollow out the center of the charcoal, making a ring, and pour hot coals into the center. With the Fuse (page 132), you line up the coals and light one end (it works best on the larger unit).

Put together the rest of the smoker, positioning the door so it is easily accessible. Line the water pan with heavy-duty aluminum foil to make cleanup easier. Insert the water pan and fill it with boiling water to within 1 inch of the top. Place the cooking grates in position.

Leave the top vent open all the way at first. Resist the temptation to close it. Regulate the temperature with just the bottom vents. The top vent is needed to create a draft, sucking in fresh air for combustion. If you must, you can close the top vent up to halfway, but no more. Start with the bottom vents open about halfway, more on cold days. When the temperature gets up to about 200°F—and it will get there quickly on a hot day—throttle back the bottom vents to about one third open and keep fiddling with them until you stabilize at 225 to 250°F. Regulating temperature may be a bit trickier on a new unit because it is shiny inside. They can run a bit hot, especially the larger unit. Once it has been broken in and the interior has a dull carbon coat, it will run cooler. When the temperature has stabilized at 225 to 250°F, you can open the side door and drop in some wood on top of the coals. For recipes that call for 325°F, use more lit coals and open the vents to bring up the temperature.

New Weber Smokey Mountains come with a hole drilled in the side for a thermometer probe, but you may want several, so go ahead and drill. Don't worry, small holes won't hurt anything and you can always stuff a screw in them to prevent

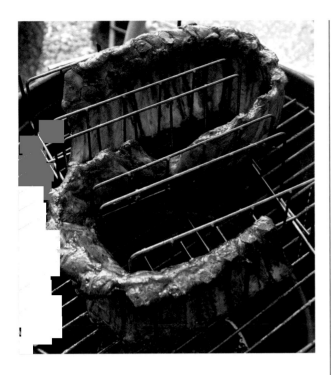

leaking smoke. If you don't want to drill holes, thread thermometer cables through a top vent hole. Place an oven thermometer probe near the meat. Insert a leave-in meat thermometer probe into the center of large cuts and add the meat. If you can fit it all on one grate, use only the top grate and remove the lower grate to keep it from getting greasy. If you need to use both grates, put the faster-cooking food on top so it is easier to remove. If I want food on both grates to finish together, I rotate the top and bottom grates. The top grate is usually warmer than the bottom one because it sits above the water pan. Placing a pan of beans on the lower grate for catching drips is always a good idea (see page 361).

One of the problems with the 18.5-inch bullet smokers is that they have 15.5-inch grates. Many slabs of ribs, especially St. Louis–cut ribs, just don't fit. But you don't have to cut them in half. The picture at left shows how to get two full

slabs on a single cooking grate: Use rib racks and bend the slabs to fit. If you do this on both the upper and the lower grates, you can get four slabs on a Weber Smokey Mountain. Another technique is to roll the slab in a circle and run a long skewer through the spot where the ends overlap. This method works fine and keeps the ends from burning.

After the smoke stops, you can gradually add more wood if you know that the meat needs it. There's always the risk of oversmoking, so until you really know your machine, don't add any more.

Every hour, check to make sure the water pan has not dried out. When it gets low, carefully add hot water.

Keep an eye on the meat temperature and when it is done, remove it and serve. Then close all the vents to smother the coals and preserve them for the next cook.

When storing a Weber Smokey Mountain, clean it thoroughly, leave the vents open, and take the door off so it will not get moldy inside. Remove all the ash, which can attract moisture and set up like concrete. Put a good cover over the unit, and make sure the cover drops low enough to keep rain out of the lower seam.

SMOKING ON KAMADOS, EGGS, AND CERAMIC SMOKERS

Because kamados are so well insulated, they take a while to absorb heat and stabilize, and once they are hot, they are very slow to cool. If you overshoot your target temperature, it may take a while to get it back to where you want it. Sterling Ball of BigPoppaSmokers.com says, "It's like stopping a semi. You've got to brake early."

If you need to add coals while you are cooking, some models require you to remove the food, the cooking grates, and the deflector plate, which is a pain. But most ceramics are so efficient that you will not need to add fuel even during long cooking.

Some kamado manufacturers recommend that you use lump charcoal instead of briquets. They argue that briquets produce more ash than lump does and that the ash can block airflow. However, there can be a lot of dust in a bag of lump charcoal as well, and that can also hamper airflow. If you're worried about ash, some briquets—such as Kingsford Competition Charcoal—produce less than others. I prefer briquets for numerous reasons (see page 124).

When you are done cooking, close the dampers. The coals will extinguish quickly, and you can reuse them. Ceramic interiors are more or less self-cleaning. They do not need to be scrubbed. In fact, wire brushes can damage the surfaces. You only need to scrape the cooking grates and brush the ash out of the bottom.

WARNING: Kamados and eggs are susceptible to a very dangerous phenomenon: flashback. These cookers are nearly airtight except at the intake and exhaust, and the coals can get starved for oxygen at low temperatures or during shutdown. When you open the lid, oxygen rushes in, and poof: say goodbye to your eyebrows. To prevent flashback fireballs, "burp" the cooker by slowly opening the top damper a bit and waiting a minute. Open the lid slowly and stand to the side rather than the front. Always wear fire-resistant gloves, the longer the better.

SMOKING ON A GAS SMOKER

Owners of gas smokers often complain about cheap construction, and when you look at the price tag, there's no argument. Here's how to improve the performance of a cheap gas smoker.

NEVER CLOSE THE UPPER VENTS. You need airflow and you need smoke to escape. I know it seems wasteful, but you don't want to trap stale cooling smoke in the chamber with your dinner.

TURN DOWN THE HEAT. Most of the models I have worked with run hot—in the 250 to 275°F range on the lowest setting. Most meats will smoke fine at that temperature, but I prefer 225°F. To drive down the temperature a bit, try using ice in the water pan or leaving the door slightly ajar. This wastes fuel but will do the job.

INCREASE THE WATER SUPPLY. Using a larger water pan than the one that comes with most units helps stabilize the temperature.

DON'T FIDDLE WITH THE GAS FLOW. The Internet has several schemes for throttling back the gas flow to lower the temperature. They are risky. You don't want an explosion.

USE RIB HOLDERS. Buy at least two rib holders in order to pack in enough meat to feed all the people who will come sniffin' around.

SMOKING ON PELLET SMOKERS

Pellet cookers usually have an auger or another feed mechanism that pushes the pellets into a burn pot, typically a bit larger than the size of a beer can ripped in half. An igniter rod sits in the bottom of the burn pot, and when you turn on the unit, it glows like the element on an electric stove. The auger slowly turns, pushing pellets into the burn pot. As the pellets ignite, a fan feeds them oxygen, and the igniter shuts off. It might draw 300 watts an hour while the igniter rod is on in the first few minutes, then drop down to drawing only 50 watts an hour, less than a standard lightbulb, for the duration of the cooking session.

On the better models, a temperature probe in the cooking area tells the controller the temperature, and if it is below the target, the controller feeds more pellets and blows more air. As with any thermostatically controlled oven, even your indoor oven, the thermostat in a pellet smoker cycles heat on or off as needed. Set it for 225°F, and it cycles on until it hits about 230°F, then it cycles off until the temperature drops to 220°F, then it cycles back on until the temperature comes back up to 230°F, so the average is 225°F.

The small burn pot is covered with a large deflector plate that absorbs the heat and spreads it out below the cooking surfaces. It functions a lot like your indoor stove. The burn pot is small, so there is often a hot spot directly above it. Some units have an optional perforated section above the burn pot that allows you to put meat over direct flame, but the ones I've tested still do not sear very well. But this is new technology, so I'm sure they will solve the problem in the near future. Until then, there are two good ways to

get an edge-to-edge sear with a pellet smoker: 1) While the meat is cooking, preheat a cast-iron pan or griddle, then turn up the heat and sear the meat directly on the pan, and 2) keep a charcoal grill handy. Even a small hibachi will give you enough infrared heat to get a beautiful sear on a thick steak.

You need to keep the deflector plate clean since it sits right below the food. If you leave sauce and grease on there, it can smolder and deposit soot on your food. Carbon buildup will also diminish its heat transmission. Cleaning it can be a real pain. If you wrap the deflector plate with foil before use and dispose of it after cooking, this problem will never arise.

After 6 or so hours of cooking, you need to vacuum out any ash from the burn cup and the firebox and you're good to go for the next cook. Don't worry, the ash won't mess up your shop vac because there is no grease in the burn cup.

Cooking pellets look like rabbit chow, with the diameter and length of a couple of pencil erasers set end to end. Most are made from oak blended with different hardwoods, each of

which imparts a distinctive flavor to the meat. Hickory, maple, alder, apple, cherry, hazelnut, peach, mesquite, and pure oak are among the flavors available. They are all natural, with no petroleum, fillers, chemicals, or glues, and if pellets get wet, they turn back into a pile of soggy sawdust. Be sure to buy cooking pellets, not heater pellets, which can contain softwoods such as pine, treated lumber, and other chemical contaminants that make their smoke potentially hazardous for food. BBQr's Delight is my preferred brand.

According to Bruce Bjorkman of MAK, maker of my favorite pellet smokers, his cookers use about ½ pound of pellets per hour when set on "Smoke" (about 175°F). At 450°F, the unit's high temperature, a MAK burns about 2.3 pounds per hour on a nice summer day. On average, that's comparable to other pellet smokers.

Some owners say the flavor of the smoke is too mild for them. That's because the wood burns so hot and efficiently. If you want a deeper smoke flavor, use hickory or mesquite pellets, start with cold meat, set the grill to about 200°F for the first hour when it is less efficient and produces more smoke, and then keep the meat moist by lightly painting or misting it with water.

ADD A WATER PAN OR TWO

One trick for both grills and smokers at any temperature is to use a water pan, which goes over the heat source. The difference between a drip pan and a water pan is that a drip pan goes under the food, while a water pan goes over the heat source.

Vertical smokers like the Weber Smokey Mountain often come with a pan. A water pan has many important functions:

1. The water in the pan absorbs heat and never rises above 212°F, helping to keep the cooking-chamber temperature down.

2. A water pan blocks direct flame, so you can cook with indirect heat.

3. Water vapor mixes with combustion gases to improve flavor.

4. Water vapor condenses on the meat and makes it "sticky," encouraging more smoke to adhere.

5. Condensation wets meat and cools it, which slows cooking. This allows more time for connective tissues and fats to melt.

6. Water adds a small amount of humidity to the atmosphere in the cooker and helps keep food from drying out. This effect varies significantly depending on the design of the cooker.

7. Higher humidity in the oven can also help with the development of the smoke ring (see page 15).

Fill water pans with hot water. Cold water will cool your cooker and should only be used if your grill is running hot and you need to cool it down. Fill the pan to just below the lip so you don't have to keep opening the lid to refill. Put it above the hottest place in your cooker so more water will evaporate.

On a charcoal grill, put the coals on one side and put a water/drip pan on the other. Put the

top rack on, put the meat on the top rack above the water/drip pan, and put another water pan on the rack above the coals (shown above).

WHAT GOES IN THE WATER PAN?

Pitmasters argue over this. Some like to put beer, wine, apple juice, onions, spices, and herbs in water pans. Some folks like to put sand, dirt, gravel, or terra-cotta in the water pan. But there's a reason it is called a *water* pan.

Drink the beer. Drink the wine. Drink the juice. Put the spices on the meat. Just use hot water in the water pan.

Many of the compounds in these other liquids will not evaporate, and even if they do, they have no impact on the flavor of the meat. You may be able to smell them, but the number of flavor molecules in beer, wine, or juice are so few that even if they were deposited on the surface of the food, they would be spread so thinly you would never notice them. The flavors of the spice rub you put on the surface of the meat, the smoke, and the sauce you use are much stronger and will mask any molecules of apple juice or whatever else is in the pan that might end up on the meat. And that goes for drip pans, too. Their job

is to collect drippings, not to vaporize flavors.

Many cooks like to put sand or gravel in their water pans. Solids do nothing for the humidity or the flavor. They may help stabilize temperature fluctuations a little, but they will not keep the temperature down like water does. And although water will never go over 212°F, sand and other solids will heat up to whatever the oven temperature is.

To further increase evaporation, fill the pan with those red lava rocks sold at garden stores, and then add the water. Don't cover the rocks. They are very porous, so they act like wicks, and the large surface area pumps more moisture into the air.

If you line a water pan with foil, cleanup will be a lot easier. When you are done, you will have a pan full of smoky water and possibly fat. Let it cool and the fat should solidify. If it's taking too long, throw in some ice cubes. Then it is easy to peel off the fat and discard it. I discard the liquid in old bottles or flush it down the toilet (be prepared to clean the toilet after). If you are using charcoal, you could mix the drippings with ash and throw them out with the trash.

DRIP PANS

A drip pan is different. The purpose of a drip pan is to collect the flavorful juices that come off the meat for use in a sauce or stock. The gas grill shown on page 142 is set up with a drip pan under the meat and it is filled with goodies to make a flavorful stock for gravy. To the left is a small pan with wood chips for smoke. It is resting on a hot burner so the chips will smolder.

If loaded with water, a drip pan can also absorb heat from the fire below, reduce the grill temperature, moderate temperature fluctuations, prevent flare-ups, and add humidity to the cooking chamber. My Ultimate Smoked Turkey recipe (page 307) is a good example of how to use a drip pan. When you're done, you have a smoked turkey stock that becomes the base for the most incredible gravy.

Keep an eye on your drip pan so it doesn't dry out and burn all your precious gravy. Keep adding steaming hot water so the liquid is always at least an inch or two deep.

CLEANING THE EXTERIOR OF YOUR GRILL OR SMOKER

Never use steel wool or metal brushes on a grill or smoker. Use a scrub sponge, warm water, and dish soap. For stubborn stains, try vinegar or diluted ammonia. To remove water spots, try club soda. On stainless, make sure the surface is cool, not hot, and follow the grain. Stainless-steel cleaning solutions do a pretty good job of restoring the luster.

Do not paint the interior where food goes or any surfaces where heat might vaporize the paint. If you need to paint the exterior of a rusted grill or smoker, Professor Blonder recommends Rust-Oleum High Heat Primer, Northline High Temperature Paint, or Cerakote Ceramic Coatings. Brush the exterior with a wire brush, sand, wipe clean with mineral spirits, let dry, and then lay down a light layer of paint. Let it dry thoroughly, and then paint another light layer. Let dry overnight. Be sure to run the grill for an hour or two before using it with food to allow any volatile organic compounds to escape.

CLEANING THE INTERIOR OF THE COOKING CHAMBER

Before each cooking session, clean the grates thoroughly (see page 105) and do a little light cleanup to keep your grill or smoker performing optimally, prevent off flavors, and prolong your cooker's life. Then, at least once a year give your device a more thorough cleaning (two or three times a year if you use it a lot), and clean it if you store it for winter. Check your grill's manual for any special instructions. If you can't find it, many manuals are available for download on manufacturer websites.

CLEAN OUT THE ASH. Ash holds moisture and reduces heat, and the combination can chemically attack steel. To make a scoop for removing cold ashes, cut up a plastic half-gallon milk jug and like the one shown opposite. You can also use a fireplace shovel. Needless to say, do not remove ashes while they are hot, and always put ashes into a metal can. Gray embers hiding in ash can remain hot for far longer than you'd think.

CHARCOAL GRATES. On charcoal grills and smokers, check the lower coal grate for corrosion. If it is warped, don't try to straighten it out. It will probably crack. As long as it is not preventing airflow underneath, you can keep using it. Replacements are easy to find.

OFFSET SMOKERS. Grease can pool in the bottom of the smoke chamber of an offset smoker. To prevent messy cleanup, line the bottom chamber with foil before cooking. It is easiest to peel out the foil while the chamber is still warm, but not when it is hot.

GREASE PANS. Grill manufacturers have different strategies for dealing with drippings and grease. If yours has a grease pan or collector, check it before cooking. It can overflow or catch fire. If there is a grease chute, make sure it is cleaned, too.

CERAMIC SMOKERS. Do not wet the interior of ceramic smokers. Follow the manufacturer's instructions.

MOVING PARTS. Check, clean, and lube any moving parts like vents and chimneys.

PELLET GRILLS AND SMOKERS. Because of their electronics, water is the enemy of pellet smokers, so keep your hose and pressure washer

FIGHTING MOLD

It's shocking when you rip the cover off your cooker in the spring to discover the interior covered in white fuzz. Mold loves moisture and grease. Weber Smokey Mountain owners are especially vulnerable to this jolt. To help prevent it, use your cooker often! When you are done cooking, add fresh coals, crank it, and burn off that food and grease residue. Every now and then—especially if you don't plan to use the cooker for a while—scrape grease off the interior with a plastic putty knife. Store your cooker with the vents open and in a dry place so moist air is not trapped inside. On the Weber Smokey Mountain, remove the side door. If mold invades your cooker, here's what to do.

1. Discard any charcoal, lava rocks, ceramic briquets, or other porous materials.

2. When it is cool, scrape and scrub everything in sight with a wire brush or a pressure washer. Remove parts and scrape or pressure wash them.

3. Wash everything down with soapy water. Then rinse thoroughly.

4. Finally, fire it up one last time to burn off any mold, grease, and soap residue. Now you're ready to cook.

To remove mold from a ceramic cooker, do not use chlorine or solvents, do not power-wash, and do not use a metal scraper or a wire brush on the ceramic parts. With ceramics, heat is your only tool to burn off the mold and residue.

MYTH A thick black seasoning is needed inside a smoker or grill.

BUSTED! The "seasoning" on the inside of a smoker is carbon, grease, and creosote. I don't worry about a thin coat of carbon, but the flaky schmutz, called "scale," is carbon that can drop off and land on your food. Scrape it off and vacuum it up. When you clean, work on a surface you don't mind getting dirty. I use a plastic disposable drop cloth like the ones painters use. The best cooks clean the interior of their cookers regularly. You wouldn't eat in a restaurant where the ovens were all greasy and dirty, would you?

far, far away. Plus, the pellets are made from sawdust, and they will turn into a slurry if they get wet and will then harden like concrete.

Pellets burn very efficiently, so they produce very little ash. A shop vac or handheld vac is all you need, with an occasional scrape of the inside of the lid. (Note that if you use a shop vac, the exhaust on the machine will smell like smoke forever.) Check the vents for creosote blockage. Wipe the tip of the thermometer probe and remove carbon buildup. Keep the deflector plate beneath the food clean. Grease buildup could catch fire.

SMOKING WITH LOGS

The next time you hear a charcoal snob say gas grills are for wimps, the proper rejoinder is, "Charcoal is for wimps. Real pitmasters cook with logs."

If you have mastered smoke roasting with charcoal you may be ready to smoke with logs. Fun and flavor await the patient and practiced outdoor cook.

Direct-heat pits are still used extensively in restaurants throughout Texas and Chicago, and I've seen them scattered around the nation in Alabama, Memphis, Kansas City, southern California, and elsewhere. In Texas, the "pulley pit" (opposite page, top) is common. It is a large brick box with a steel cooking grate below a heavy metal lid that is hinged at the back. This weighty cover is tied to a rope that goes through a pulley hanging from the ceiling and is tied to a counterweight to help the pitmaster hoist it open.

In Chicago, the "aquarium pit" (middle) is still in use. It is similar to the pulley pit, but the top is enclosed by thick tempered glass that rises from the bricks and connects to the chimney, making it look like a giant aquarium.

If you want to smoke with logs, the modern way to go is with a high-quality offset smoker

(see page 90). Modern units like Johnny Trigg's Jambo (bottom) have two chambers, one for the food and the other for the fire. They are heavy metal and airtight. The cheap offsets in hardware stores are not suited for "stick burning."

GRILLING WITH WOOD

Some of the best food I've ever eaten was cooked over a campfire. The incredible aroma is reason enough to go back to your Stone Age roots and connect with your inner caveman. Wood smoke's seductive aroma makes marinades, brines, spice blends, rubs, and sauces seem like a waste of time and money.

You can grill with wood over a campfire, over a fire pit, or even on a charcoal grill. But wood can be tricky and takes practice. It requires total involvement and all the senses, which also makes it one of the most fun and rewarding cooking and entertaining methods.

CAMPFIRE AND FIRE PIT COOKING

Check with your local fire department before building a campfire in your backyard. There may be an ordinance against it. Check with the neighbors, too. If you raise a stink, they might raise a stink, and neighborly relations are as important to the outdoor cook as good meat. Invite your neighbor over occasionally to cement goodwill.

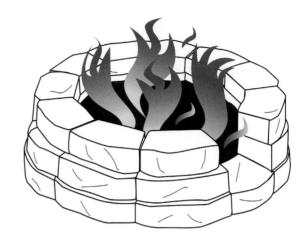

CAMPFIRE. Try to place your fire behind a windbreak such as a fire-resistant building, hill, or stand of trees. Find a spot away from flammable buildings, tents, shrubs, and overhanging branches. Dig a hole 6 to 12 inches deep to contain the coals. Keep the dirt handy so you can smother the fire when you are done. It's a good idea to enclose the fire pit with big stones, bricks, cinder blocks, or something on which you can place a cooking grate. Rocks reflect heat into the fire, and they keep you and your guests warm. But don't use wet rocks from the bank of a creek. They can be waterlogged, and when they heat up, they might explode. Never leave a campfire unattended. Keep a bucket of water or dirt handy to douse your fire when you are done or just in case things get out of control.

If you can, make one side of the rock ring higher than the other so part of the grate is higher and further from the coals. That helps you moderate temperature. Leave one side of the fire pit open so you can reach under the grate with a rake or shovel to rearrange the logs and embers when necessary.

FIRE PIT. You can build a permanent fire pit in your backyard quickly and cheaply with bricks, cinder blocks, flat slate, or, as shown above, concrete garden-wall blocks. They may split over time, but they are cheap. Firebricks will last longer. You can also buy a cooking grate to go over the top.

FIRE RING. Used in many campgrounds, a steel fire ring encloses the fire and acts as a windbreak as shown below.

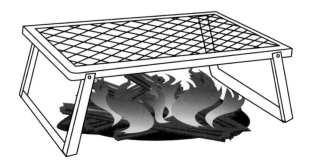

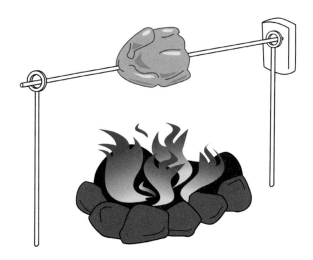

COLLAPSIBLE GRATE. You can use the cooking grate from almost any grill, but manufacturers sell campfire grill grates with folding legs designed specifically for this purpose.

CAMPFIRE TRIPOD. My favorite tool is the campfire tripod, with three legs and a cooking grate that hovers above the fire on three chains. You can even skip the grate and hang a cast-iron pot or even a haunch or bird on the chain.

SPIT. You can even buy a campfire spit. Some have battery-powered rotisserie motors, or you can crank them yourself.

HOVERING GRILL. Another nice design is a simple pipe that you drive into the ground. The grate slips over the pipe, and it can be raised, lowered, or moved to the side.

BUILDING YOUR FIRE

Lay fuel out in a two-zone setup. This is especially important for a wood fire because you often need to get the food into a safe zone to avoid burning it. Make sure you have plenty of real estate to move food out of the way of hungry flames.

Getting the fire going is like accelerating a car with a manual transmission. To get into first gear, you need tinder; to get into second gear, you need kindling; and finally, you need firewood to cruise along in third and fourth gear. Ideal tinder is small, pencil-thick dry sticks, pine needles, pinecones, or bark. Kindling is finger-thick sticks and twigs. If you prefer, you can use charcoal instead of kindling. As for firewood, use only dry hardwood, fruitwood, or nutwood logs about the size of your forearm or a little larger. Wet wood and softwoods like pine sputter and put out acrid smoke, which can ruin your meal.

The two best methods to build the fire are the teepee method and the log cabin method. For the teepee, start by piling tinder, build a teepee of kindling around the tinder, and then build a teepee of firewood around the kindling. For the log cabin (right), lay 2 logs parallel to each other, and lay two more on top perpendicular to

the first layer. Repeat 3 logs high. In the center, make a pile of tinder, then a pile of kindling on top of the tinder.

If you wish, you can drizzle an ounce or two of cooking oil on the tinder and kindling. Light the fire with long wooden matches or a long-necked butane lighter. You can also use a stick as a match by wetting the end with cooking oil and lighting it.

There are two important things to remember about cooking over a wood fire: Too much heat or too much smoke is bad. A few gentle flames licking the food are OK, but a roaring fire and belching smoke will quickly ruin dinner. The first trick is to start the fire and let it burn down a bit before the food goes on. You want a bed of glowing embers, ideally about 1 inch thick.

Wood burns out quickly. If you are just doing a couple of burgers or steaks, you won't need to add more. But if you are cooking anything thicker, like a spatchcocked turkey or butterflied leg of lamb, you'll need to add wood. You can toss a log or two on as needed, usually off to the side to allow it to burn down to embers.

MYTH **The best tinder is dry leaves or newspaper.**

BUSTED! Dry leaves and newspaper can produce fly ash, big floating hot flakes that can easily land on your food or set the forest or your house on fire.

Keep a close eye on the food. Wood fires put out some serious infrared radiation, and fats dripping on hot embers can create an inferno in a hurry. Be prepared to move the food around. Have a safe zone. Don't let the food get too close to the heat. If the fire is too hot, rake away some embers or raise the cooking surface. If it is too cold, add embers or lower the grate. Getting the hang of it takes practice, but when you do, you'll beam with pride. If this is your first time, cook meat under 1 inch thick. You don't want a 1½-inch-thick USDA Prime ribeye to come out tasting like a cheap cigar. Once you know how to tame a wood fire, try thicker cuts.

Pick up a pair of long-handled tongs and well-insulated welder's gloves (see page 108) for turning the food and moving embers around. As primal and basic as cooking with wood may seem, you still need a good digital food thermometer.

I like to keep a squirt gun on hand to beat back flare-ups. If you use one, beware that they can kick up ash, so it's a good idea to move the food away before you pull the trigger.

When you're done cooking, douse the coals with water (stand back: steam can burn you just as badly as flame), cover them with dirt, and discard any dirt or ash that has drippings still on it to discourage wildlife from coming round.

WOOD GRILLING ON GRILLS

As with a campfire, build a fire with tinder, kindling, and firewood, and let it burn down to embers. Once you have embers, you can move them around to create your classic two-zone setup. As the embers wane, toss small chunks onto the coals. Cook just like you would with charcoal, but watch out—it can get hot in there!

SMOKING WITH WOOD ONLY

The procedure goes more or less like this: Start with a chimney's worth of hot charcoal in the firebox. Throw on 3 well-dried logs, each about the diameter of a beer can. Open all dampers and doors and let the dark black smoke pour out as the logs heat up and ignite.

After about 30 minutes, as the flames rise in the firebox, as the smoke color turns white, and as the metal body heats up, you can close the cooking chamber and firebox doors and start the process of stabilizing the temperature. It takes 30 to 60 minutes, longer in cold weather, to get the unit up to temperature and load the metal body with heat. Some cooks like to spray the inside of the cooking chamber with water at this stage to create steam and loosen any grease that may remain from the last cooking session, but it is far better to steam clean after cooking than before.

Begin adjusting the firebox damper until the flames are smaller and your logs have turned black, cracked, and have begun glowing. You still want to see yellow flames. Then start playing with the chimney damper and try to get the temperature in the center of the cooking chamber to about 275°F. Smoking with logs usually needs to be done at a higher temperature than smoking with charcoal, gas, or pellets, because wood needs to burn at a higher temperature in order to create clean smoke.

Don't close the exhaust damper too much, or you will produce meat that is too smoky, pungent, and bitter. The color of the smoke will tell you how clean your fire is.

Once the smoker is at temperature, throw on your meat. Until you are experienced with your machine, check the temperature every 15 minutes or so. As the logs burn down, continue adjusting the airflow with dampers and add a new log every 45 minutes, or when you see the temperature start to dip. If your firebox is insulated, you may be able to add wood less often. Clean out excess ash to keep it from blocking airflow to the wood.

When you are finished cooking, spray everything with water and let it steam. Scrub it down with a wire brush and drain away all grease. Don't use soap.

BURN BOXES

To fire their wood pits, pitmasters often use a mega charcoal chimney called a "burn box." The burn box shown here is simply a 55-gallon drum. Logs are dropped into it, and they rest on rebar that has been inserted near the bottom. The glowing embers fall through the bars, are removed from an opening cut in the side, and are then shoveled into the pit.

ROASTING WHOLE ANIMALS

As festive as it makes us feel, roasting whole animals, from hogs to fish, is not a great way to cook. The problem is that different parts are different thicknesses and cook at different rates, so you inevitably end up with some meat overcooked or undercooked. Break the animal down, and you can cook each part to optimum doneness. Why overcook the turkey drumsticks while waiting for the breasts to be done? Why destroy a hog's loins, best at 135 to 145°F, while waiting for the shoulders to hit 203°F? And pity the poor tenderloins!

If you cannot be dissuaded and still want to roast a whole hog, lamb, or goat, you can fit small animals onto some horizontal smokers and grills. Or you can buy rigs specially designed for the job. For more, see my recipes for Whole Hog (page 222), Suckling Porchetta (page 235), and Ultimate Smoked Turkey (page 307).

GRIDDLING AND PAN ROASTING WITH STEEL, WOOD, AND SALT BLOCKS

The griddle, or *plancha*, as it is called in Europe, goes back to the primitive technique of heating a flat rock in a campfire and putting the meat on the hot rock. Today most griddling is done on a steel flattop, but you can also buy ceramic pizza stones, slate slabs, salt blocks, metal plates, basalt slabs, marble slabs, paella pans, and wood planks on which to griddle. In most cases, this method is very much like cooking in a frying pan without the sides and handle. In fact, there's no reason why you can't just use an oven-safe skillet. You can still get that outdoorsy taste with a griddle if you use smoke on your grill.

The great advantage to griddling is that cooking is fast and you get an unmatched dark sear because you are cooking by conduction, the most efficient heating method. Griddling lets you achieve a perfect sear on a piece of meat even when using a cooker, such as a pellet smoker, which doesn't have the horsepower to darken the meat all over with direct infrared radiation. Get

the griddle or pan blistering hot, add a little oil to prevent sticking, and sear the meat right on the metal. It should take only 2 to 3 minutes per side. You can preheat the pan indoors, on your grill's side burner, or right on the grill grates. This is also a good application for reverse searing (see page 48). You start low and slow, with a little smoke, on whatever grill or smoker you have, and then sear the outside in a hot pan or griddle. It improves on the classic restaurant technique of pan roasting by adding a little smoke.

TIPS FOR GRIDDLING SUCCESS

1. To check the temperature of the griddle, use an infrared laser gun thermometer (see page 97). Just point the gun at the surface and pull the trigger, and the gun will tell you if you've hit that 400 to 500°F temperature necessary for proper searing.

2. To lubricate the griddle, don't use spray oil because it has additives that get gummy. Use a cooking oil with a high smoke point, such as corn or canola.

3. After you add the food, close the lid to get some heat to the top of the food.

4. When you flip the food, move it to a different part of the griddle because the wet food will have slightly cooled the surface just below it.

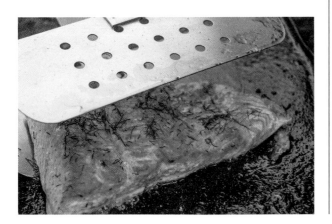

GRIDDLE SURFACES

CAST IRON

When shopping for a cast-iron griddle (right), you'll find most have one side that is corrugated to give you "grill" marks and one side that is flat. You want the flat side with a lip. A lip keeps the oil from running off into the flames below and creating a firestorm. Avoid griddles with a moat along the edge. All the oil will run into that moat, and you want it to stay on the griddle surface. For that reason, you also want to make sure that your grill is level and your griddle is not warped.

COWBOY AND CHUCK-WAGON COOKING

There is a whole subculture of cowboys and cowboy wannabes devoted to recreating chuck-wagon cooking. Chuck wagons were the original RVs and meals-on-wheels rolled into one, and they accompanied cattle drives up the Chisholm Trail from Texas to Kansas and on to the slaughter-houses in Chicago. These modern culinary historians are experts at campfire cooking and take it to another level with an array of cast-iron pots, pans, griddles, and Dutch ovens.

The chunk-wagon cook's tool set starts with a cast-iron Dutch oven, 10-quart capacity or more, for about $50. Camp Chef models have a slit on the rim for thermometer probes. These cast-iron warhorses also come in handy around the house. Who needs those pricey Le Creuset French ovens? These Dutch ovens are perfect for whole chickens or slow braising in the oven or on the grill. You can even sit them on top of coals and shovel more coals on top of the lid, which is flat with a raised rim. With Dutch ovens, you can cook classic chili, baked beans, cornbread, casseroles, and even cobblers. Some even include a perforated aluminum basket for steaming, frying, or boiling. Do you like fried chicken? I thought so. But you don't make it, do you? Because it spatters all over your stove, it smells greasy, and sets off smoke alarms. Do your fried chicken in a Dutch oven on your grill. No fuss, no muss. And it makes real old-fashioned Southern fried chicken.

Cast-iron griddles, pots, and pans will rust in a hurry if left outside or if not lightly coated with oil after use. As you use the pan, the metal absorbs more oil and the heat creates a polymer that can prevent sticking. When handled properly, cast iron becomes practically nonstick.

Most new cast iron comes pre-seasoned at the foundry; that is to say it has been coated with oil that has been baked on to help make it nonstick. If you need to season a cast-iron griddle, start by washing it with warm soapy water to remove any grease or metal from the manufacturing process. You can hit it with steel wool if it is rusty. Pat it dry completely with paper towels. Put it in a 300°F oven for about 30 minutes to dry it thoroughly and open the pores. Then coat it on all sides with a light layer of cooking oil, spreading it around with a paper towel and wiping off all but a very thin layer. Put the pan back in the oven and put some foil or a pan underneath to catch any drips. Crank the oven all the way up. Bake it for 1 hour and then remove it from the oven and let it cool. Repeat the procedure at least two more times. When you're done, allow the griddle to cool and store it in a dry location. It now has a polymer coat almost as good as Teflon. But it is fragile, and it can be scraped off if handled roughly.

As for cleaning, it's best to just wipe the pan with warm water and paper towels. No scrubbing, no soap. For tough stuck-on bits, pour a little cold water onto a hot griddle to create some steam, then gently scrape the bits with a wooden paddle. Don't scrape with a metal spatula or you'll scrape off the polymer. When you are done cleaning, give it a light coat of oil with a paper towel.

If my griddle is really badly gunked up, I put it in the sink, fill the sink with hot water, and squirt in some dish soap so the surfactants in the soap can loosen the grease. I let it soak for an hour or so. Then I drain the water and make an abrasive slurry of salt and water and liberally apply elbow grease with a scrub sponge. I can see the cast-iron experts retching out there, but it works just fine, and sometimes after griddling a batch of fish, a simple wipe just won't do the trick.

STAINLESS STEEL

Stainless griddles with lips perform exceptionally well on the grill, and stainless is the preferred surface for many burger joints. I found one by Chef King in a restaurant supply store. It sears beautifully, but it can scorch and it is hard to clean.

CAST ALUMINUM

Cast aluminum is another excellent griddle surface. Mine has a gravelly texture that holds the oil well. It transfers heat quickly and cools rapidly when removed from the grill.

WOOD PLANKS

Planking is a variation of an old salmon-cooking technique said to have been developed by Native Americans in the northwest and Canada. I am not a fan.

To use one, begin by soaking a ¼-inch-thick plank of wood in water for an hour or so. The most popular planks are untreated red cedar (not cedar house shingles, which are generally

not food grade). Get the grill hot and place the plank on the grill. Some cooks leave the plank there to preheat. Place the food, most commonly salmon, on the plank. By the time the food goes on, most of the water on the underside of the plank has evaporated and the wood will begin to smoke.

As heat and smoke rise from below the plank, a low-pressure area is created above the food, so the smoke is pulled over the top like the air over an airplane wing. Some of the smoke lands on the food, but very little. And since wood is full of air and is not a very good heat conductor, there is no searing or browning of the food surface that contacts the wood.

The best part of planking is the presentation. It looks impressive when you present your guests with a slab of charred wood on which rests a perfectly cooked side of salmon, its juices gently dribbling down the edges. But from a taste standpoint? There's not much benefit. There's almost no wood taste and there's no searing. The cedar doesn't really flavor the fish, and if it did, it wouldn't get past the skin, which most people won't eat because it hasn't crisped like it would on a metal griddle. Another drawback to planking is the cost. When you are done, you must discard the expensive plank, which is

badly burned on one side and full of fish juices on the other.

SALT BLOCKS

You can even buy thick slabs of pink Himalayan salt blocks on which to griddle your food (shown opposite). They sear meats and veggies beautifully, season food automatically, and make an awesome table presentation.

Pink Himalayan salt blocks are actually mined in Pakistan, not the Himalayas (it's a long story). They are most definitely not the same as pink curing salt used for curing bacon and corned beef (see my discussion of salt on page 32). When you cook on one, the moisture in the food dissolves some of the salt, which then penetrates the food, creating a delicate balanced saltiness that you can't get from other methods. In the mouth, the salt seems to be more evenly distributed than when you sprinkle individual salt crystals on the food.

Here's my favorite thing to do with a salt block: Heat it slowly on the grill to about 500°F, bring it to the dinner table, and let guests sear ½-inch-thick slices of flank steak on it.

To prevent cracking, the block must be warmed in stages, on low heat, then medium, then high, in 15-minute increments. It can take 45 minutes to get the block up to searing temperatures of 450 to 500°F. To check the temperature, use an infrared gun thermometer.

The surface is surprisingly nonstick, so there is no need to oil it for meats. Whatever you do, do not put marinated or brined meats on your salt block. The water seeps down in, turns to

steam, and cracks your block. Brined meats will come out too salty. Leave at least ¼ inch between slices and turn the food with metal (not plastic) tongs or spatulas after it has seared on one side. Getting the proper thickness and doneness takes a little practice, especially since the salt block is constantly declining in temperature on the table.

To clean a salt block, skip the soap. Just use warm water and a stainless steel scrubbing pad.

Dry the block with paper towels and put it on a rack so air can circulate all around until it is thoroughly dry. You'll get a dozen or more uses from a single block before it starts to crack and disintegrate. The heat and salinity make salt slabs very unfriendly to pathogens.

Himalayan salt blocks sear meats and veggies beautifully, season food automatically, and make an awesome table presentation.

Some blocks are higher in quality than others, so order cooking-grade salt blocks from a specialist like SaltStoneChef.com or AtTheMeadow.com. Make sure they are at least 1½ inches thick. The 8-x-8-x-2-inch slabs cost about $50 and last for at least a dozen uses if handled properly.

5
BRINES, RUBS, and SAUCES

ABOUT MY RECIPES

A nation's cuisine is at the core of its culture, and barbecue is as central to America's heritage as jazz—the fact that 80 percent of U.S. households own an outdoor grill or smoker is proof. The recipes in this book include all the barbecue and grilling classics, the dishes every grill jockey wants to master, the essential "barbecue canon" woven into our culture.

But I'm a contemporary, creative cook with food science on my mind and a digital thermometer in my hand, so I have often tweaked the classics to fit modern methods, equipment, groceries, and diets. I am also a minimalist: I like the natural flavors of most foods, with minimal seasoning and sauce. Turkey does not need to be injected with garlic and chipotle. Most steaks are at their best with only salt and pepper and a little smoke. I am also a tinkerer, so you will find recipes in here that you probably never thought of as backyard recipes, like Sweet and Sour Pork Tenderloin (page 212). Just about anything you cook indoors can be cooked even better outdoors.

Chef Ryan Udvett, my test kitchen director and a Le Cordon Bleu–trained chef, helps me test all our recipes on several different grills and smokers, but it would be impossible for us to give specific directions for every fuel—charcoal, gas, logs, and wood pellets—and for all the devices that use them. But if you understand the concepts in chapters 1 through 4, you will know what to do on your cooker. It just takes four *P*s: practice, patience, and persistence, and a knowledge of key cooking principles in this book.

ABOUT MY INGREDIENTS

A good rule of thumb: Buy quality ingredients, come up with a simple plan, and get out of the way. Unless otherwise specified:

BUTTER is unsalted.

CHILI POWDER is American or Mexican chili powder, medium heat, not ground hot chiles as in some other countries.

EGGS are large.

GARLIC SALT cannot be substituted for garlic powder.

MILK is whole.

FLOUR is all-purpose.

PAPRIKA is "sweet" or mild Hungarian or Spanish. It is not hot as it is in many other countries.

PRODUCE is medium size.

SALT is Morton Coarse Kosher.

SUGAR is granulated white.

GARLIC, ONIONS, CARROTS, AND FRESH GINGER are peeled.

ABOUT MY METHODS

Preparation times include all the washing, measuring, chopping, and peeling.

I have not specified how much wood you will need for smoking because the strength and flavor of wood depends on many variables, not the least of which are the nature of your cooker and your preferences. Go easy at first. A meal is never ruined by too little smoke. I strongly recommend that you use the same wood and fuel for a year until you have all the other variables under control. Measure wood and keep records with a cooking diary (see page 114).

Try to **follow my recipes closely the first time**, with no substitutions or improvisation. Then, on your second go-round, you can customize and riff on them. Although it may seem logical to swap honey for molasses, their chemistry is very different, and the outcome can be disappointing.

If you change a recipe, it is a good idea to **change only one thing at a time** in case something goes wrong.

For most recipes on a grill, I recommend two-zone cooking (see page 8), even if most of the cooking is over direct heat. The cooler indirect-heat zone is your safe zone for when pieces finish early or if they are cooking too fast. Whenever cooking over indirect heat, I always specify an air temperature, usually 225°F or 325°F. That's because it is easy to measure temperature on the indirect side. But over direct radiant heat, I usually do not specify the temperature beause most cooking thermometers cannot go high enough. Moreover, the direct radiant heat is usually only being used to brown the surface, and the food isn't there for long. You will know when it is ready by looking at it.

Unless otherwise noted, almost all the recipes in this book require you to cook with the lid down and to sear with the lid up.

MISE EN PLACE

French chefs say *mise en place* (pronounced "MEEZ-ahn-plahss"). Boy Scouts say, "Be prepared." Nothing will improve your cooking more than putting "everything in its place."

READ THE ENTIRE RECIPE. In the same way athletes visualize the game, do a mental walk-through before you start. Photocopy recipes so you can take them into the kitchen and scribble on them.

Pay close attention to the way a recipe is worded. There is a big difference between "½ cup fresh basil, chopped" and "½ cup chopped fresh basil": In the first instance, the basil is measured and then chopped, and in the second, the basil is chopped and then measured.

CLEAR OFF YOUR WORK AREA. Get all the unnecessary stuff out of the way and wash your work surfaces.

GET YOUR HARDWARE TOGETHER. That means fuel, knives, bowls, pans, paper towels, thermometers, etc.

GET YOUR "SOFTWARE" TOGETHER. Wash, measure, and chop your ingredients.

PREHEAT. Heat the cooker, clean the grates, and then close the lid. We want the metal in the grill to absorb heat so when you lift the lid and then close it, the inside temperature bounces right back. Kamados need at least 30 to 60 minutes to preheat properly.

BRINES, MARINADES, RUBS, SPICE BLENDS, PASTES, AND INJECTIONS

DRY BRINES

The idea behind dry brining, which simply means sprinkling salt on the meat in advance, is to enhance the water-holding power of the proteins and amp up flavor by driving salt deep into the meat. In most cases I prefer dry brining to wet brining. You'll need ½ teaspoon kosher salt for 1 pound of trimmed food.

Pinch the salt between your thumb and forefinger and hold it about 8 inches above the meat, as shown below, right (sprinkling the salt from 8 inches allows it to cover a wider swath than if you held it closer). Apply the salt lightly on the thin parts of the meat and lower your hand to sprinkle more on the thick parts. After salting, put the meat on a wire rack in a pan. You do not need to wrap it in plastic. If you are dry brining poultry, you actually want airflow around the meat to help dry the skin.

SPRINKLING SALT

4" Away

8" Away

THE SIMPLE BLONDER WET BRINE (6.3% SALINITY)

Like dry-brining, wet brining enhances water-holding and amps up flavor by submerging the food in salt water. Wet brines take up a lot of space, waste a lot of salt, and don't work better than dry brines in most cases. But I sometimes wet brine pork loin, chicken breasts, and turkey breasts because the process does suck in just a tiny bit of water and these lean cuts need all the help they can get.

In general, you want a wet brine in the 6 percent salinity range. The total wet brine should weigh at least two to three times the weight of the meat so there is enough salt to do the job. This means that if you have 1 pound of meat you should make 2 to 3 pounds of brine. A pound of water is about 2 cups. So you need 4 to 6 cups of wet brine per pound of meat.

Your container needs to be food grade and large enough to hold the meat and the brine with the meat submerged. It cannot be made of aluminum, copper, or cast iron, all of which can react with the salt. Brining bags or large zipper-top bags work fine. If you brine in a bag, periodically grab the bag and squish things around, flipping the meat so the brine can get at it from all sides. Place the bag in a pan in case of leaks.

The thing to keep in mind when making a wet brine is that there are different types of salt—table salt, kosher salt, pickling salt, sea salt—and they all occupy different volumes. But a pound of any salt contains the same amount of sodium chloride (NaCl). When you are making a brine, go by weight and you'll never go wrong. If you don't have a scale (and you should), use Professor Blonder's easy method to determine how much salt to use, regardless of the type of salt, based on Archimedes's principle of displacement.

MAKES *1¼ gallons, enough for 5 pounds of meat*
TAKES *20 minutes*

- 1 cup plus 1 gallon cold water
- ½ pound salt (any type)

1. Pour 1 cup of the water into a 2-cup measuring cup. Add salt until the water reaches the 1½-cup measuring line. This will be about ½ pound of salt by weight.

2. Stir until the salt dissolves. Dump this slurry into a large container with the remaining 1 gallon cold water, and you have a 6.3 percent brine.

3. Submerge the meat in the brine and chill. Move chickens and other birds around to force any air bubbles from the cavity. Keep the brine below 38°F (in the refrigerator). When it is time to cook, remove the meat, flavor as desired, and cook.

BASIC BRINERADE

As we discussed on page 41, marinades are primarily a surface treatment, since they do not penetrate much more than ⅛ inch (the exceptions being seafood and some vegetables). But if you are soaking meat in a marinade, you might as well add salt and get the benefits of a brine by making a *brinerade*. This is my standard recipe for brinerade. Use it on pork, chicken, and even zucchini or eggplant.

HOW LONG TO BRINE?

Meat should be wet brined or dry brined in the refrigerator. How long depends on how thick it is.

Thickness	Time
½ inch	½ to 1 hour
1 inch	1 to 2 hours
2 inches	4 to 6 hours
3 inches	12 to 16 hours

MAKES *2 cups, enough for 1 pound of meat*
TAKES *15 minutes*

- 1½ cups water
- ¼ cup red wine vinegar
- ¼ cup inexpensive balsamic vinegar
- 4 large garlic cloves, minced or pressed
- ¼ cup kosher salt
- 1 tablespoon dried basil
- 1 tablespoon dried oregano
- 1 tablespoon sugar
- 1 teaspoon freshly ground black pepper
- ½ teaspoon white miso paste (optional)

Put all the ingredients in a large zipper-top bag and shake vigorously. Use right away or refrigerate until needed, up to a week. Add the meat and follow the specific recipe or the chart above for brining times.

BRINES FOR INJECTION

Injections are the best way to get salt and flavor deep into the meat. You can simply inject a brine, or add sugar, spices, herbs, or even oils. But go easy. Injected ingredients can

overwhelm the meat's natural flavor. For information on injectors, see page 112.

MAKES *about 1 quart, enough to inject about 30 pounds of meat or poultry*

TAKES *10 minutes to make, 5 minutes to inject*

PORK BRINE INJECTION

   2 tablespoons kosher salt

   1 tablespoon sugar

   1 tablespoon Worcestershire sauce

   2 tablespoons rice vinegar

   1 cup apple juice or low-sodium pork, chicken,
      or beef stock

   3 cups water

BEEF OR VENISON BRINE INJECTION

   2 tablespoons kosher salt

   1 tablespoon sugar

   2 teaspoons Worcestershire sauce

   4 cups water or low-sodium beef stock, or a
      mix of both

CHICKEN OR TURKEY BRINE INJECTION

   2 tablespoons kosher salt

   1 tablespoon sugar

   4 cups water or low-sodium chicken stock, or
      a mix of both

   ½ teaspoon white miso paste (optional)

1. Mix the ingredients for the brine in a large bottle or jar. Shake vigorously until the salt and sugar have dissolved.

2. Insert a marinade injection needle into the container of brine and fill the syringe. Insert the needle into the meat and push it toward the center. Press the plunger slowly and ease the needle out, injecting as you go.

3. Insert the needle in intervals about 1½ inches apart. Inject about 2 tablespoons of fluid per pound of meat. You want to avoid pockets of liquid. A little liquid will naturally follow the needle out of the puncture hole, but if it comes spurting out, apply less pressure.

4. You can cook injected meat right away or let the meat rest for an hour or even overnight. The injection will disperse a bit with time. (Discard any brine remaining in the syringe, which will be contaminated by the needle.) You can store unused brine in the refrigerator or freezer for months.

LUBING TURKEY BREASTS

Most grocery-store turkey has been injected with a salt solution at the factory and its label will say so. Even so, the breasts are so lean that the addition of fat can really help. You can goose up the richness by injecting oil into the breasts. Yes, that's how Butterball got its name (the company no longer uses real butter).

Even after you have injected a brine, you can go back and then inject a small amount of oil. You can't mix the oil with the brine since it just floats to the top. Canola oil or another neutral-flavored oil like corn oil is a good choice. Olive oil can be strong flavored. Melted butter hardens when it comes in contact with the cold meat, so it is not a good choice.

You can shoot up the turkey the day before or at the last minute before cooking. It won't make a big difference. I usually inject only the turkey breasts because dark meat is moister and more forgiving than white meat, but you can give the dark meat a shot or two if you wish.

MAKES *enough for one 12-pound turkey*
TAKES *20 minutes*

> **4 tablespoons neutral-flavored cooking oil, such as corn or canola**

Pour the oil into a narrow container like a test tube so you can get the needle deep into the oil. Inject every inch or so as described on the opposite page. If there is any oil left, add it to the gravy. It has been contaminated by the needle, so do not save it for another use.

RUBS AND BLENDS OF HERBS AND SPICES

A great ribeye steak or a fillet of fresh fish needs nothing more than a little salt and perhaps some ground pepper. But when used judiciously, herbs and spices can enhance, not mask, the taste of the ingredient you are seasoning.

Spices are made from dried seeds, berries, fruits, bark, and roots. They are usually sold as seeds, granules, or powders. Seeds usually need to be cracked or crushed to release their goodness.

Most culinary herbs are green leaves and stems. The taste of fresh herbs is significantly different from that of their dried counterparts. Fresh herbs are about 80 percent water, so the flavor of most dried herbs is more concentrated than fresh. Some herbs change more than others when dried. Dried rosemary is a lot like fresh rosemary, but dried dill bears no resemblance to fresh. **My rule of thumb is 2 parts fresh herbs = 1 part dried (approximately).** Some say 3 to 1. It depends heavily on how fine the herbs have been crushed and how fresh they are. Swapping fresh for dried can have a major impact on the recipe. Try to use what the recipe calls for, at least the first time you make it.

When herbs like oregano and basil are dried, they are usually crushed, which allows fragrance and flavor to oxidize and flee. After a year, they can lose most of their oomph. Other herbs, like rosemary and bay leaf, are usually not crushed when dried, and thus retain more of their volatile oils (the things that give them scent and flavor).

Of course you can crush or powder them if you wish. I use powdered bay leaves in some of my rubs because they pack a bigger wallop than crushed. It's hard to find powdered bay leaf in stores, so I crush whole leaves in my hands and then take them for a spin in my coffee grinder or blender.

The flavors in herbs and spices are generally locked in and need to be crushed, dissolved, and heated to be at their best. Sometimes they are dissolved in our saliva, but during cooking, heat, moisture, and fats from the food help a rub explode into a flavorful coating.

It is common to start cooking a sauce by warming oil in a pan, adding onions and stirring until they wilt, then adding garlic and dried herbs and cooking for about a minute to extract their oils, a process called blooming. There is another benefit to this process: Testing has found that many raw spices and herbs contain pathogens, especially salmonella, because they grow outdoors, where they are exposed to birds, rodents, flies, and other critters. Cooking, even for a minute, can be enough to destroy bacteria.

Rubs do not penetrate more than 1/8 inch.

Dried spices and herbs are often added at the beginning of cooking so they can absorb water and give up flavor, while fresh spices and herbs are usually added a minute or two before serving, to preserve their freshness. Chopping fresh herbs helps them release their flavors more easily.

For black pepper, it is always better to grind your own with a pepper mill as you need it. If you use ground pepper on steaks or other things you are grilling hot, grind your pepper and sift it through a mesh strainer. Save the powder for something else, like your homemade barbecue sauce, and use the big chunks on the steak. Sprinkle them on and press them in with your hands.

When a recipe calls for a particular herb or spice, you really should try to get it. But in a pinch, here are some good substitutions.

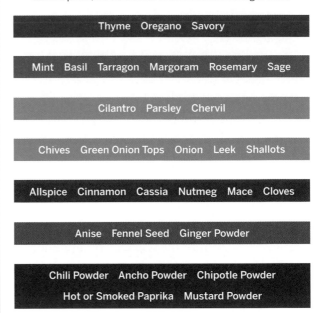

Thyme   Oregano   Savory

Mint   Basil   Tarragon   Margoram   Rosemary   Sage

Cilantro   Parsley   Chervil

Chives   Green Onion Tops   Onion   Leek   Shallots

Allspice   Cinnamon   Cassia   Nutmeg   Mace   Cloves

Anise   Fennel Seed   Ginger Powder

Chili Powder   Ancho Powder   Chipotle Powder
Hot or Smoked Paprika   Mustard Powder

THE SCIENCE OF RUBS AND SPICE BLENDS

Every good barbecue cook should have signature house rubs to brag on. Just steal my recipes. Keep in mind that a rub tastes very different after cooking. The juices of the meat mix with the herbs and spices, and they undergo chemical reactions catalyzed by the heat.

I keep jars of all of these rub recipes on hand at all times. You don't want to have to scramble and make a batch every time you need it. Store rubs in tightly sealed bottles in a dark place. They will slowly decline in quality but should be fine for up to a year. If a rub clumps after being stored for a while, chop it up, or spread it on a baking sheet and put it in a 225°F oven (no hotter, or it might burn) for 15 minutes to drive off moisture. Dry some rice in the oven or in a pan and add it to the jar to absorb moisture, too.

Remember, rubs are a surface treatment. They do not penetrate more than ⅛ inch. To use a rub, lightly coat the food with water to help the rub stick (I just wet my hands and pat the food's surface) and then sprinkle liberally with the rub—even if you are a conservative—not so much that you completely coat the meat. Then rub it in. Work it into the cracks and pores. And you don't have to let it sit overnight. It just won't go very far. You can cook soon after applying it.

Salts, rubs, and sauces are like oil, antifreeze, and gas. They all go into the engine, but don't mix them!

THE THREE S'S OF A GOOD RUB

A good rub is like a good orchestra; it has a range of instruments to play all the notes in harmony. They are:

SUGAR. Sweetness is a flavor enhancer, helps browning, and is essential for crust formation. You only need a little to have a big impact.

SAVORY. Savory flavors come from amino acids called glutamates, green herbs, some spices, garlic, and other flavorings. They add richness, depth, and complexity.

SPICY. Hot chile pepper sensations, often called spicy flavors, are often included in rubs because they add excitement. Black pepper is another common source of spicy, as are ginger, horseradish, and mustard powder. Go easy.

NO SALT IN RUBS

Salt penetrates deep into the center of the meat, so the amount you apply should depend on the weight of the meat. Spices and herbs are large molecules and sit on the surface, so they should be added in proportion to the surface area.

You need more salt on rib roast than a ribeye steak, and more on a ribeye steak than on the thinner skirt steak. But the quantity of spices and herbs is about the same per square inch. Applying the salt, spices, herbs, and sauce separalely is like controlling the gas pedal, brake, and clutch. Work them in harmony, but separately. There are other good reasons to keep salt out of your rubs:

1. You do not need any salt at all on cured meats like ham, bacon, or corned beef, but you might want a rub.

2. Nowadays almost all turkeys and many other meats are injected with a salt solution at the processor. If the bird has been salted at the plant, you don't want salt in your rub.

3. Some people are on salt-restricted diets.

4. Leaving salt out of the mix also gives you room to add a finishing salt just before serving. A sprinkle of large-grain salt on a steak as soon as it comes off the grill gives it real pop. If you plan on using a finishing salt, you can cut back on the salt before cooking without reducing the herbs and spices.

MUSTARD OR OIL UNDER THE RUB?

Most spices and herbs dissolve better in water than in oil. You can put a rub right on bare meat, or you can help it stick by moistening the meat with a little water, a slathering of mustard or ketchup, or some cooking oil.

My experience is that they make little difference in the final outcome. So here's my typical routine: I dry brine well in advance, then I wet the surface lightly with water and apply the rub perhaps 30 minutes before cooking. Finally, just before cooking, I add a light coating of oil to help prevent the meat from sticking to the grill.

DALMATIAN RUB

This is easily the simplest recipe in the world. In Texas, where beef is king, the standard basic rub is simply salt and pepper in roughly equal amounts. Dalmatian. Get it?

MAKES *1 cup*
TAKES *about 2 minutes*

½ cup kosher salt
½ cup freshly ground black pepper

Blend the salt and pepper together. That's all there is to it!

BIG BAD BEEF RUB

Beef brisket and barbecued beef ribs can handle, and benefit from, a more potent mix than Dalmatian Rub. This rub creates a rich, flavorful, crunchy crust, called bark.

Beef rub is different than pork rub. Pork loves sweetness, but beef does not, so the small amount of sugar in this rub is there only to help with bark formation. Black pepper, on the other hand, works great with beef. This rub brings complexity with different flavors and different levels of heat. If you can find dried ancho chile, go with it. It has a nice raisin-y character. Either chipotle or cayenne can give you a kiss of heat, but chipotle has better flavor.

MAKES *about ½ cup*
TAKES *about 10 minutes*

3 tablespoons coarsely ground black pepper

1 tablespoon sugar

1 tablespoon onion powder

2 teaspoons dry mustard

2 teaspoons garlic powder

2 teaspoons chili powder or ground ancho chile (see headnote)

1 teaspoon ground chipotle or cayenne chiles

Mix the ingredients together in a bowl.

2 tablespoons freshly ground black pepper

2 teaspoons dried rosemary leaves, crushed in a mortar and pestle or blender

2 teaspoons dried thyme or oregano

1 teaspoon garlic powder

1 teaspoon onion powder

1 teaspoon paprika

1/2 teaspoon chipotle powder

Mix all the ingredients together in a bowl.

MRS. O'LEARY'S COW CRUST

This rub is specially formulated for beef roasts and named for the cow falsely accused of starting the Great Chicago Fire in 1871. She may not have started it, but she was roasted—sadly without a good rub.

MAKES *4 tablespoons, enough for 10 to 12 pounds trimmed beef*

TAKES *about 10 minutes*

MEATHEAD'S MEMPHIS DUST

Although this recipe is formulated for pork, I've used it with success in sausage blends, on smoked salmon, on celery stuffed with cream cheese, on the rims of Bloody Mary glasses, and even in popcorn. It is designed to add flavor and color and form the proper crust when cooked at low temperatures.

MAKES *about 3 cups*

TAKES *15 minutes*

¾ cup packed dark brown sugar

¾ cup granulated sugar

½ cup paprika

¼ cup garlic powder

2 tablespoons freshly ground black pepper

2 tablespoons ground ginger

2 tablespoons onion powder

2 teaspoons crushed dried rosemary

Mix all the ingredients together in a bowl. If the sugar is lumpy, crumble it by hand or against the side of the bowl with a fork.

SIMON & GARFUNKEL RUB

Parsley, sage, rosemary, and thyme make a pretty good song as well as an all-purpose rub for pork, turkey, and chicken. I also sprinkle it on sautéed veggies, scrambled eggs, grilled potatoes, the outside of baked potatoes, grilled asparagus—you name it.

MAKES *about ¼ cup*

TAKES *10 minutes*

2 tablespoons crushed dried sage

1 tablespoon crushed dried parsley

1 tablespoon crushed dried rosemary

1 tablespoon crushed dried thyme

1 tablespoon crushed dried oregano

1 tablespoon crushed dried basil

1 tablespoon crushed bay leaf

1 tablespoon freshly ground black pepper

1 tablespoon sugar

Put everything in a blender or food processor and pulse for a few seconds until you have a coarse powder.

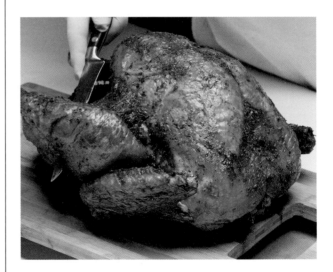

1 tablespoon paprika

1 teaspoon ground bay leaves

10 garlic cloves, minced or pressed

Mix everything together in a bowl. Since it contains fresh garlic, store in the refrigerator for up to 1 week.

MARIETTA'S FISH RUB

M arietta Sims was my sous chef for several years, and she perfected this herb blend for fish. I use it on a wide variety of fish, and it works wonderfully.

MAKES *a bit less than ½ cup*

TAKES *5 minutes*

1 tablespoon dried chives

1 tablespoon dried tarragon

1 tablespoon dried parsley

1 tablespoon dried chervil

1 tablespoon freshly ground green peppercorns (see Notes, page 170)

1 tablespoon dried lemon zest (see Notes)

1 teaspoon garlic powder

DOLLY'S LAMB RUB

R osemary and garlic are the classic seasonings for lamb and mutton, with good reason. Forget the mint jelly. Lamb is very much like beef, a hearty red meat. You wouldn't put mint jelly on roast beef, would you? Now, if you want to chop up a bit of *fresh* mint and toss it in the rub, go for it.

Dolly the lamb was the first cloned mammal, an amazing achievement, so I named my lamb rub after her because it makes your lamb taste amazing.

MAKES *about ⅓ cup, enough for a 6-pound leg of lamb or lamb shoulder*

TAKES *about 10 minutes*

2 tablespoons dried rosemary leaves, broken up or crushed a bit by hand

1 tablespoon whole mustard seeds

1 tablespoon freshly ground black pepper

Crush all the ingredients with a mortar and pestle or in a bowl with a wooden spoon so they are about the same size but not powdered. Mix.

NOTES: If you can't find green peppercorns, substitute black. The taste is significantly different, but it works. Do try to find green ones.

Some stores sell dried lemon zest, but it is easy to make. Just scrape off the thin colored layer of the lemon, leaving behind the bitter white pith. Lay it in a bowl or plate for a day or so and it should dry out nicely.

CAJUN SEASONING

Cajun seasoning is the flavor of bayou country in southern Louisiana. This rub is our interpretation and a fine way to wake up chicken, a boring pork chop, or even fish. It can be used for blackened meats or in jambalaya or gumbo. I use it to make andouille sausage.

MAKES *⅓ cup*

TAKES *15 minutes*

- ½ teaspoon celery seeds
- ½ teaspoon caraway seeds
- 4 bay leaves
- 1½ teaspoons crushed dried rosemary leaves
- ½ teaspoon crushed dried oregano
- 1½ teaspoons crushed red pepper flakes
- 1½ teaspoons freshly ground black pepper
- 4 teaspoons paprika
- 2 teaspoons ground ancho chile
- 1 teaspoon garlic powder
- 1 teaspoon onion powder
- 1 teaspoon sugar
- ½ teaspoon dry mustard
- ⅛ teaspoon ground mace
- ⅛ teaspoon ground allspice

Put the celery seeds, caraway seeds, bay leaves, rosemary, oregano, and red pepper flakes in a spice grinder or blender and pulse until finely ground. Transfer to a bowl and add the remaining ingredients. Mix.

CITRUS SALT AND PEPPER

I use this seasoned salt on fish before cooking or as a finishing salt tableside. It also works in some pastas, like carbonara. But remember, it contains salt, so don't double salt by brining and then seasoning with this mixture.

MAKES *¼ cup*

TAKES *3 to 4 hours*

1 medium lemon

1 medium lime

1 tablespoon whole black peppercorns

2 tablespoons kosher salt

1. Preheat a grill on the lowest possible setting and position a grill topper (see page 103) over indirect heat. Cut the lemon and lime into thin slices and remove the seeds. Place the citrus slices on the grill topper, close the lid, and allow the citrus to dehydrate completely. This could take from 1 to 3 hours, depending on the air temperature and airflow. (You can do this in your indoor oven if you wish, I won't tell on you.) Remove from the grill and cool.

2. In a blender or food processor, mix the peppercorns and dried citrus and pulse until everything is pulverized. Stir in the salt but don't pulverize it.

COWBOY JAVA RUB

Legend has it that cowboys on the trail would rub their steaks with coffee grounds for added flavor. It works!

MAKES *about 2 ½ tablespoons, enough for about 6 ribeye steaks*

TAKES *about 2 minutes*

1 tablespoon brown sugar

1 tablespoon ground coffee

¼ teaspoon ground cinnamon

1 teaspoon crushed black peppercorns

Mix all the ingredients together in a bowl.

SMOKED GARLIC POWDER OR ONION POWDER

Smoked onion and garlic can add a taste of the outdoors to your indoor cooking. They are great for rubs, sauces, dips, spreads, oils, compound butters, flavored mayonnaise, and more. The procedure is pretty much the same for onion and garlic.

MAKES *¼ cup*

TAKES *1 to 2 hours smoking time, plus 4 to 8 hours to dry*

>   **4 whole heads garlic**
>   or
>   **2 large onions**

1. Prep. For garlic, break the heads into individual cloves, cut off the roots, and peel them. For onion, cut off the ends, peel, cut into quarters, and break the quarters into slices.

2. Fire up. Set the smoker to 225°F or set up your grill for smoking in a two-zone configuration.

3. Cook. Put the garlic cloves or onion slices on a grill topper (see page 103) or a sheet pan on the indirect-heat side to keep them from committing suicide by jumping into the fire. Keep the smoke rolling for 1 to 2 hours.

4. Remove the garlic cloves or onion slices and let them cool. Cut the pieces in half and place them in a pan in the indoor oven on the lowest setting for 2 to 4 hours, or until dry. If you have a dehydrator, use it.

5. Pulse the dehydrated garlic or onion in a blender, food processor, or spice grinder until no large pieces remain.

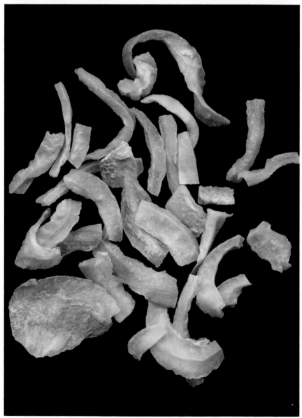

BUTCHER BLOCK SEASONING

Apply this blend liberally to steaks, pork chops, chicken, or seafood before grilling, at the time you would dry brine. Use about ¾ teaspoon per pound of meat. It also makes a great finishing salt for meats, as well as for soups, salads, and baked potatoes. You can even try it on popcorn to kick up your next movie night. It really shines on steaks.

MAKES *¼ cup*

TAKES *about 10 minutes*

3 tablespoons Citrus Salt and Pepper (page 170)
1 teaspoon Smoked Onion Powder (opposite)
1 teaspoon Smoked Garlic Powder (opposite)

Mix together all the ingredients. Say thank you to Chef Ryan Udette, who created this.

SAUCING STRATEGIES

Some sauces are great right from the bottle, but most benefit from cooking on food. Juices and heat can alter the molecules and their flavors. At temperatures above 320°F, some sugars will begin to caramelize, creating a more complex flavor than plain sugar. A sweet sauce can get gummy or even burn, so apply it at the end of cooking, just long enough to heat it and cook it without burning it. Don't oversauce. One or two coats should be all you need.

If you are cooking low and slow, add the sauce about 30 minutes before removing the meat. For the final sizzle, put the meat right over direct radiant heat and cook for about 5 minutes on each side. If you're cooking on a smoker, you might need to crank up your grill or move the meat indoors under the broiler. Stand there and watch like a cat eyeing a bird so the sauce does not burn. It can go from red to black faster than a clean hog can go from pink to brown. Incineration is not the only hazard with this technique. If you have perfectly cooked ribs, sizzling the sauce can result in overcooking the meat.

All undercooked meat can contain microbes and spores and is therefore potentially hazardous. Pour only as much sauce as you need into a cup or bowl and dip in your brush or spoon. When you are done, throw out the extra sauce in the cup. Boiling it may not properly kill spores. Use only fresh, uncontaminated sauce for serving at the table.

BARBECUE SAUCES

To most Americans, barbecue sauce is red and sweet and smoky and lives near the ketchup at the grocery store. We who eat lunch in back of a rickety shack under a shade tree know that barbecue sauce comes in a rainbow of colors and flavors. Most of these are tied to their areas of origin and their ethnic roots.

Barbecue sauce is alchemy. Standing over the pot, adding a dash of this, a pinch of that, adjusting and tasting makes you feel like a wizard. To be a real grillmaster, you must have a signature barbecue sauce in a jelly jar so that when your guests ask, "What brand of sauce is that?" you can plunk a hand-labeled bottle on the table. When they beg you for the recipe, you can then tell them, "It's a secret" and mumble the old saw that ends "but then I'd have to kill you."

Here are eleven distinct, classic American barbecue sauce types. The following pages have recipes for all of them. If you feel ambitious, serve your guests a choice of several of these sauces.

KANSAS CITY RED

Based on tomato paste or ketchup, it is typically sweet, often laced with molasses or brown sugar, thick, and by far the most popular type of barbecue sauce.

SOUTH CAROLINA MUSTARD SAUCE

Sweet, tart, and yellow.

EAST CAROLINA MOP SAUCE

The Low Country may be the home of the oldest sauce in the nation. The original was probably just vinegar with a pow of hot chile peppers and black pepper, and many pitmasters use only those ingredients to this day.

LEXINGTON DIP

Similar to East Carolina, but with some tomato added and a hint of sweetness.

TEXAS MOP SAUCE

In the Republic of Texas, where beef is king, sweet sauces were rare until recently. The original was a thin brown sauce, almost a gravy, which works both as a mop during the cook and as a finishing sauce. It features sweet and hot peppers, cumin, and often beef drippings.

ALABAMA WHITE SAUCE

Invented for smoked chicken at Big Bob Gibson Bar-B-Q, a north Alabama restaurant, this mayonnaise-based sauce is so popular in the state that many restaurants now have a version.

KENTUCKY BLACK SAUCE

In western Kentucky, where sheep were once a big thing, pitmasters still baste their mutton with a thin blend of vinegar and Worcestershire.

HAWAIIAN HULI-HULI SAUCE

A variation on teriyaki, this sweet, thin, soy-based marinade/baste/sauce can be found wherever you see smoke rising in Hawaii, other than in the volcanoes.

FLAVORED AND FRUIT SAUCES

Creative cooks have found countless ways to take the classic Kansas City style and amp it up with everything from fruits to whiskeys to hot sauces.

SWEET GLAZES

These tend to be sugar-forward and shiny enough that a thin layer is all you need.

TARTAR SAUCE

Smoked fish was the continent's first barbecue, and since this sauce has been around longer than memory, I include it for historical honesty.

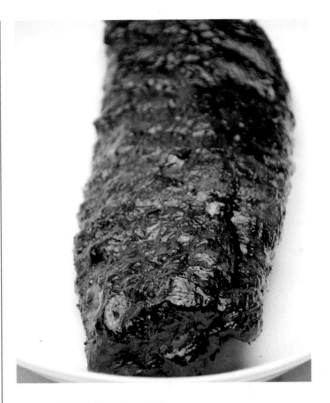

KC CLASSIC

The original Kansas City–style sauces were vinegary, hot, and not sweet, similar to Arthur Bryant's Original Barbeque Sauce, first made in the 1970s. In the past fifty years, a contemporary style has emerged, the prototype of which has been KC Masterpiece—tomato-based and sweet, often laced with molasses and liquid smoke. Even Arthur Bryant's now has a sweet sauce. The style has spread coast to coast and nowadays, when you say "barbecue sauce," most people think of this KC style.

The best KC sauces are brass bands with multiple layers of flavor from multiple sources of sweetness (brown sugar, molasses, honey, and onion); multiple sources of tartness (vinegar, lemon juice, hot sauce, and steak sauce);

multiple sources of heat (chili powder, black pepper, mustard, and hot sauce); and other flavorings such as Worcestershire and garlic. Because they are thick and tomato-y, they sit on top of the meat, not penetrating very far. That's the idea behind my recipe. Try it and you'll never use the bottled stuff again.

MAKES *6 cups*

TAKES *about 45 minutes*

- 2 tablespoons chili powder
- 1½ teaspoons kosher salt
- 1 teaspoon freshly ground black pepper
- 2 cups ketchup
- 1 cup packed dark brown sugar
- ½ cup yellow ballpark-style mustard
- ½ cup apple cider vinegar
- ⅓ cup Worcestershire sauce
- ¼ cup lemon juice
- ¼ cup steak sauce (see Notes)
- ¼ cup dark molasses
- ¼ cup honey
- 1 teaspoon hot sauce
- 3 tablespoons vegetable oil
- 1 medium onion, finely chopped
- 4 garlic cloves, minced or pressed

1. Prep. In a small bowl, mix the chili powder, salt, and pepper. In a large bowl, mix the ketchup, brown sugar, mustard, vinegar, Worcestershire, lemon juice, steak sauce, molasses, honey, and hot sauce.

2. Cook. In a large saucepan, heat the oil over medium heat. Add the onion and sauté until limp

HOW LONG CAN YOU KEEP A BARBECUE SAUCE?

We don't want any microbes setting up housekeeping in our sauces, and we want the flavors to remain bright and fresh. Commercial barbecue sauces usually have preservatives so they can keep in the fridge in a bottle with a tight lid for many months, even a year or more. My recipes have no added preservatives.

The good news is that vinegar, salt, sugars, some spices, and other common ingredients have antimicrobial and preservative properties, so they tend to help sauce stay fresh tasting and safe from microbes for months. As long as you keep your sauce refrigerated, you should have little risk of foodborne illness. Just make sure that when you are done making the sauce, you put it in a very clean glass bottle with a tight-

fitting lid. I use Ball canning jars and lids and run them through my dishwasher, but jelly jars and bottles from other condiments work fine as long as they are ultra clean and have tight lids. Another good strategy is to pour the sauce into a clean bottle while it is still boiling hot. The heat can help kill any stray microbes from the air.

Oxygen and heat are the natural enemies of freshness, so don't let bottles of sauce sit out on the dining table for long, and certainly don't keep them on the shelf next to the grill.

Store-bought herbs and spices are often steam treated or irradiated to kill microbes, but fresh herbs and spices can be contaminated just by airflow or birds or critters, so they pose a small risk. That's why most of my sauces call for dried herbs and spices.

and translucent, about 5 minutes. Add the garlic and cook for 1 minute more. Add the chili powder mixture and stir for about 2 minutes to allow the flavors to bloom. Add the ketchup mixture and stir. Simmer the sauce, uncovered, for 15 minutes to thicken it a bit.

3. Taste and adjust the seasonings, adding a little of whatever you think it needs. The sauce may taste a bit vinegary at first, but that will be less obvious when you use it. Remember, it is going on meat and will be cooked once again, which will alter its flavor profile. Strain it if you don't want the chunks of onion and garlic. I like leaving them in because they give the sauce a rustic, homemade texture.

4. You can use the sauce immediately, but I think it's better when aged overnight.

NOTES: There are many different brands of steak sauce, and they all have different flavor profiles, but what you want here is the meaty, savory depth they call umami in all of them, so use whatever you have on hand.

Secret optional ingredients: Add 2 tablespoons tamarind paste. This exotic ingredient has a sweet, citrusy flavor and really brightens a sauce. If you can't find it in an Indian or Asian grocery store, order some online. If you want a smoky flavor, add ½ teaspoon liquid smoke. But if you are cooking outdoors you shouldn't need it.

COLUMBIA GOLD: A SOUTH CAROLINA MUSTARD SAUCE

An outsider wandering into a Charleston, South Carolina, barbecue joint is likely to be jolted when served a pulled pork sammie with a yellow sauce. In a swath of mid-South Carolina, from around Columbia to the coast around Charleston, barbecue sauce is yellow, not red, a by-product of the region's German heritage (in Germany, pork and mustard are a common combination).

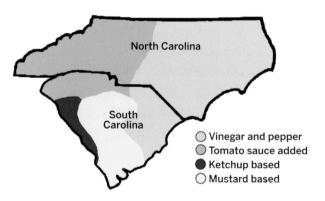

The taste profile is similar to conventional red barbecue sauce, sweet-tart, but the base flavor is mustard, not ketchup, and the sweetness is cane sugar, not molasses. It works! In fact, I prefer it to red sauce on pulled pork. I also use it on hot dogs or brats or anywhere I might use bottled mustard. Here's a quick and easy typical South Carolina mustard sauce.

MAKES *about 3 cups*

TAKES *30 minutes*

2 teaspoons dried rosemary

1 teaspoon celery seeds

2 teaspoons chicken bouillon granules
   or 1 chicken bouillon cube, crushed

¾ cup sugar

1 tablespoon dry mustard

2 teaspoons onion powder

2 teaspoons garlic powder

1½ teaspoons kosher salt

1 teaspoon freshly ground black pepper

2 cups yellow ballpark-style mustard

⅔ cup apple cider vinegar

3 tablespoons tomato paste or ketchup

½ teaspoon Tabasco Chipotle Sauce or your
   favorite hot sauce

1. Prep. Crush the rosemary and celery seeds in a mortar and pestle or in a blender or coffee grinder. Transfer to a bowl, add the remaining ingredients, and mix thoroughly.

2. Cook. Pour the mixture into a saucepan and bring to a simmer. Cook for 5 minutes. Taste and adjust the seasoning as you wish. Storing it overnight in the fridge helps meld the flavors.

EAST CAROLINA MOP SAUCE

Ribs and pulled pork are rich, and the best way to balance the silky, fatty meat is with acid. Along the coasts of North and South Carolina, in East Carolina or the Low Country, as the locals call it, they figured this out a long time ago. They developed a simple vinegar-based

sauce—probably the oldest barbecue sauce in the nation. The original was probably just vinegar with hot peppers and black pepper, and some pitmasters use only those ingredients to this day.

Low Country vinegar sauce is used on naked meat without a rub, and it does double duty as both a mop and a sauce. A mop is brushed on the meat while it cooks to cool it and flavor it. Because it is so thin, it penetrates as the meat dehydrates during cooking.

The best sauces are made with distilled white vinegar, not apple cider vinegar. I tried my recipe with both, and I like the distilled better. If you want to use cider, feel free. For people like me who love vinegar and a bit of heat, this simple sauce is all you need on chopped or pulled pork. Many of you will find it a bit severe, but it is really worth a try.

MAKES *about 1½ cups*

TAKES *about 30 minutes*

1½ cups distilled white vinegar

2 tablespoons sugar (granulated white, light
   brown, or dark brown sugar)

2 tablespoons kosher salt

2 teaspoons crushed red pepper flakes

2 teaspoons finely ground black pepper

1 teaspoon hot sauce (see Note)

Pour all the ingredients into a jar with a tight-fitting lid; shake well. Refrigerate for at least 12 hours (a week is better) to allow the flavors to meld.

NOTE: Texas Pete Hot Sauce is big in North Carolina. I usually use Tabasco Chipotle Sauce. And if you want something more interesting than run-of-the-mill red pepper flakes, use crushed chipotles.

LEXINGTON DIP: THE WEST CAROLINA BARBECUE SAUCE

Inland from the coast in North and South Carolina, in the western parts, the area known as Piedmont or Hill Country, or the Foothills, the people call the sauce "dip," and they apply it to their favorite cut, pork shoulder. Small amounts of tomato, usually ketchup, and sugar, are added to the simple vinegary East Carolina Mop Sauce (opposite). The result is still thin and penetrating, unlike thick Kansas City sauce, so it can be used as a mop during cooking, and as a sauce at the table.

The debate over whether ketchup belongs in barbecue sauce has caused many a shouting match and even stirred a raucous debate in the North Carolina legislature. Some recipes omit the sugar, but I think it rounds out the flavor. Using apple juice also veers from the standard, but it adds depth. I stole the idea from my favorite North Carolina sauce, George's, made in Nashville, North Carolina, for many decades.

MAKES *about 1½ cups*

TAKES *about 30 minutes*

1 cup distilled white vinegar (see Note)

¼ cup ketchup

¼ cup apple juice

3 tablespoons light brown sugar

1 tablespoon kosher salt

1 teaspoon hot sauce

1 teaspoon crushed red pepper flakes

1 teaspoon freshly ground black pepper

Whisk together all the ingredients and refrigerate for at least 3 hours to allow the flavors to meld. Overnight is better.

NOTE: I prefer apple cider vinegar in many of my sauces because it has more flavor, but in this recipe, I prefer distilled.

TEXAS MOP SAUCE

Texas barbecue includes many meats, but beef brisket is king. A huge dark mass of cooked beef breast, brisket is usually sliced about ¼ inch thick across the grain and served

on brown butcher paper without sauces or forks. Now that's minimalist.

Old-timey Texans take their brisket naked. They don't cotton to sloppy, sticky, ketchup-based sauces like they make way up north in Kansas City. That's because steers don't need sugar any more than they need wolves. Some pit stops have given in to public demand and now serve sauces. Some serve gloppy red sauces, but only a few serve the original.

The old-fashioned Texas sauces are used as mops during the cook because in Texas, commercial pits often cook the meat 2 to 3 feet directly above coals. They can run hot, and they are opened often to add and remove meat. A mop splashed on the meat during cooking replenishes moisture and cools the meat.

These mop sauces feature local flavors: chili powder, ground ancho chile, hot sauce, cumin, beer, onion, beef drippings, and sometimes even coffee grounds. Thin as this sauce is, it adds a richness and depth to the meat because it doesn't just sit on the surface, it penetrates. Pitmasters make up a batch and use it on everything: brisket, beef ribs, pork ribs, pulled pork, chicken, mutton, goat, and sausage (which they call hot guts).

Here's a very tasty sauce formula inspired by the sauce at legendary Cooper's Old Time Pit Bar-B-Que in Llano, Texas. Customers come up and point at the meat they want; if they want sauce, the meat is dunked in the bucket, flavoring both. Trimmings are also tossed in the bucket. So if you go to Cooper's, tell the pitmaster to dip it—don't wait until you get to the table, where there is bottled sauce.

MAKES *about 5 cups*

TAKES *about 30 minutes*

- 1 tablespoon paprika
- 2 teaspoons freshly ground black pepper
- 2 teaspoons chili powder
- 1 teaspoon ground cumin
- 1 tablespoon butter or rendered beef fat
- 1 medium onion, finely chopped
- 4 garlic cloves, minced or pressed

1 green bell pepper, seeded and chopped

2 cups beef, veal, or chicken stock

1 cup Lone Star beer or any other lager

¼ cup ketchup

¼ cup apple cider vinegar

3 tablespoons Worcestershire sauce

3 tablespoons steak sauce

2 tablespoons brown sugar

2 teaspoons hot sauce

1. Mix the paprika, black pepper, chili powder, and cumin in a small bowl.

2. In a 2-quart saucepan, melt the butter over medium heat. Add the onion and gently cook until translucent.

3. Add the garlic, bell pepper, and the spice mixture and stir. Cook for 2 minutes to extract the flavors.

4. Add the remaining ingredients and stir until well blended. Simmer over medium heat for 15 minutes. Drink any beer left in the can. Taste the sauce and adjust as needed. Divide it in half and use half to mop the meat when cooking. Use the remainder to splash on the meat when you serve it.

ALABAMA WHITE SAUCE

Big Bob Gibson Bar-B-Q, in upstate Decatur, Alabama, has been a popular hangout since 1925. In the past decade, the place has achieved national fame on the coattails of the acclaim slathered on Chef Chris Lilly and his Big Bob Gibson Bar-B-Q competition team.

That's Chris in the red shirt (top right) with his father-in-law, Don McLemore, co-owner of Big Bob Gibson and son-in-law of Big Bob himself. Below is pitmaster Ken Hess.

Their team has won practically every major competition on the circuit. Big Bob's red sauce has been named "Best on the Planet" at the American Royal Open in Kansas City, but their signature white barbecue sauce for chicken is their most famous because it was once unique (it now has several imitators).

This is not what most folks think of when you say barbecue sauce. It is white, first of all. And it is not sweet. I don't care for it on pork or beef, but it's very nice on chicken. It's an American classic, and worth a try if you love barbecued chicken. At Big Bob's, the cooks dip chicken in a vat of the stuff as Hess is doing, but at home you can just paint it on.

MAKES *1 ½ cups, enough for 2 large chickens or 3 Cornish game hens*

TAKES *10 minutes*

- ¾ cup mayonnaise
- ⅓ cup apple cider vinegar
- ¼ cup lemon juice
- ¼ cup apple juice
- 1 tablespoon garlic powder
- 1 tablespoon prepared horseradish (in vinegar or creamy)
- 1 tablespoon coarsely ground black pepper
- 1 teaspoon dry mustard
- ½ teaspoon kosher salt
- ½ teaspoon cayenne pepper

Whisk together all the ingredients in a large bowl. Transfer to a jar with a tight-fitting lid and refrigerate, covered, for at least 2 hours to allow the flavors to meld. Use for Big Bob Gibson's Chicken in 'Bama White Sauce (page 301).

SUNLITE KENTUCKY BLACK SAUCE FOR LAMB AND MUTTON

This sauce is indigenous to a small area of western Kentucky around Owensboro, just west of Louisville. It's a fascinating blend of mostly vinegar and Worcestershire sauce, and it is designed to go with the specialty of the region, slow-smoked mutton.

Once upon a time, in the 1800s, Kentucky was the largest lamb-producing state. It has now fallen to number thirty-four. But the tradition of slow-smoked mutton lives on in dozens of barbecue joints and church socials. The cuts of choice are shoulder and rear leg.

Sweet sauce would be all wrong. This thin, tart sauce cuts the rich taste of lamb fat, which is more intensely flavored than beef, pork, or chicken. The sauce is used as a baste because it is thin and penetrates the dried meat surface. It is also used as a finishing sauce.

Some places, like the Moonlite Bar-B-Q Inn, the most famous of all the western Kentucky barbecue joints, have two slightly different recipes, one for basting and one for serving. So I set about trying to reverse-engineer them and create one sauce that does both.

MAKES *3 cups*

TAKES *25 minutes*

- 2 cups water
- ½ cup Worcestershire sauce
- ½ cup distilled white vinegar
- 7 tablespoons brown sugar
- 2 teaspoons kosher salt
- 1¼ teaspoons lemon juice
- ½ teaspoon freshly ground white pepper
- ¼ teaspoon ground allspice
- ¼ teaspoon onion powder
- ¼ teaspoon garlic powder

Mix all the ingredients in a small saucepan and simmer for 10 minutes. Separate a portion of the sauce to use as a mop for slow-smoked mutton or lamb shoulder while it is cooking. Serve the other portion of the sauce as a dipping sauce on the side.

HAWAIIAN HULI-HULI TERIYAKI SAUCE AND MARINADE

In 1955 Ernest Morgado cooked up a big batch of chicken for a farmer's group. It had been marinated in his version of the classic Japanese teriyaki sauce and painted with the sauce on the grill. It was such a hit that he built a business around it.

Rather than turn scores of chicken pieces one by one when he was catering an event, he

sandwiched the meat between two mesh grates and, with the help of an assistant, flipped the whole contraption. When it was time to turn, he would shout *"Huli!"*—Hawaiian for "turn"—to his assistant, who would shout *"Huli!"* back, grab the handles on the other side of the grates, and turn the chicken over.

In 1986 Morgado started bottling the gingery soy-based sauce, then trademarked the name, and aggressively began protecting his brand by threatening lawsuits against other cooks using the name. But the flavor had momentum and, despite his best efforts, the name became generic. Now there are scores of huli-huli stands under shade trees, in parking lots, and at fund-raisers. Drive around Oahu—if you see smoke rising and smell something sweet, it is likely huli-huli chicken. It is said that the locals keep napkins in their glove compartment just in case.

Huli-huli sauce was originally a teriyaki sauce, which in Japan is a simple blend of soy sauce, mirin (a sweet rice wine), and a little sugar reduced to a glaze. But nowadays there are scores of variations on the theme. I use it whenever a recipe calls for teriyaki sauce. (See page 299 for my Hawaiian Huli-Huli Teriyaki Chicken recipe.)

MAKES *about 3 cups, enough for 2 whole chickens*

TAKES *30 minutes*

- 1 cup pineapple juice
- 1 cup low-sodium chicken broth, white wine, sherry, or water
- ¼ cup soy sauce
- ¼ cup ketchup or red barbecue sauce
- ¼ cup rice vinegar, lemon juice, or lime juice
- ¼ cup packed dark brown sugar
- ¼ cup finely grated fresh ginger
- 2 tablespoons Worcestershire sauce
- 2 teaspoons Sriracha sauce (see Note)
- 1 teaspoon toasted sesame oil
- 4 garlic cloves, minced or pressed

Mix all the ingredients together in a medium saucepan and simmer gently for about 10 minutes. Use the sauce right away or store in a tightly closed container in the refrigerator for months.

NOTE: Sriracha is a garlicky, hot chile sauce. It is widely available, but feel free to use whatever kind of hot pepper sauce you have around. The small quantity called for here does not make the sauce very hot.

TARTAR SAUCE

Smoked mullet and grilled fish are the classic barbecue dishes of Florida, and that is probably where Native Americans gave birth to barbecue in what is now the United States.

Sauce tartare, as it was originally called in France, has been around a long time. It is in the same family as aioli (garlicky mayo), or remoulade (mayo, herbs, capers, cornichons, and anchovies), and all oil-and-egg-based sauces. Tartar sauce is classic as a finishing sauce, but you can also slather it on the fish before you grill.

MAKES *about ½ cup*

TAKES *about 15 minutes*

- ½ cup mayonnaise
- 1 tablespoon chopped green onions, white parts only
- 1 tablespoon chopped green onions, green parts only
- 1 tablespoon chopped sweet pickles
- 1 tablespoon lemon juice
- 2 teaspoons finely chopped drained capers
- 1 teaspoon dried tarragon or 1½ teaspoons fresh, chopped
- ½ teaspoon whole-grain or coarse-ground mustard
- A few drops of hot sauce, optional
- Kosher salt and freshly ground black pepper

Mix everything but the salt and pepper in a bowl. Season to taste with salt and pepper. Let it sit in the fridge for a couple of hours. It will keep for at least a week.

NOTES: There is plenty of room to play with this recipe, but I think tarragon is essential because it really complements fish. If you wish, use lime juice, vinegar, or pickle juice instead of lemon juice. If you don't like capers, you can substitute cornichons, or just forget about either one. Finely minced celery is a nice addition. You can use sweet pickle relish in place of the sweet pickles. Dijon-style mustard can be swapped in for the whole-grain mustard. Skip the hot sauce if you like, or add more, or use red pepper flakes or chipotle powder to contribute the heat.

CHOCOLATE CHILE BARBECUE SAUCE

This concoction clearly has nothing whatsoever to do with Southern barbecue sauce traditions, but it has a lot to do with modern American cuisine: novel combinations that sound shocking, but somehow work. This sauce has the classic taste profile of all the most popular barbecue sauces—sweet, tart, and slightly spicy—but with a wonderful twist: the seductive

taste of chocolate balanced with the mild bite of smoked chile peppers.

I love it on pork ribs and meat loaf. If you put it on pork ribs, skip the herb and spice rubs. Paint it on your ribs just before they are done. Then, for a festive touch, grate some orange zest on top.

MAKES *a generous 2 cups*

TAKES *45 minutes*

¾ cup sugar

½ cup water

¾ cup rice vinegar

½ cup tomato paste

¼ cup orange juice

2 tablespoons unsweetened cocoa powder (see Note)

1 tablespoon Worcestershire sauce

½ teaspoon pure vanilla extract

½ teaspoon kosher salt

⅛ teaspoon chipotle chile powder

In a saucepan, combine the sugar and water and bring to a simmer over low heat. Simmer until the sugar has dissolved, then add the remaining ingredients, stir well, and simmer for 30 minutes more.

NOTE: I use Hershey's Natural Unsweetened Cocoa.

GRAND MARNIER GLAZE

Sweet glazes work well on salty foods like hams, and they are popular in the South, where everyone has a recipe for a glaze made from Coca-Cola. Although this recipe uses only a small amount of the regal orange liqueur, its taste shines through. I especially like this glaze on cured ham, grilled turkey breast, and, of course, duck à l'orange.

MAKES *a generous 2 cups*

TAKES *45 minutes*

- 1½ cups fresh orange juice
- 1 cup sugar
- 6 tablespoons Grand Marnier liqueur (see Note)
- ¼ cup honey
- ¼ cup orange marmalade
- 1 tablespoon Dijon mustard
- ½ teaspoon fresh thyme leaves
- ⅛ teaspoon kosher salt
- ⅛ teaspoon freshly ground black pepper

Combine all the ingredients in a medium saucepan and bring to a simmer for about 5 minutes, then pass the sauce through a strainer. Return the strained mixture to the saucepan and bring to a very low boil. Cook until the sauce has reduced by about one third. Paint it on ham and other meats at the end of the cook.

NOTE: If your budget is tight, you can use another orange liqueur such as Cointreau or triple sec.

CASCABEL MOLE, INSPIRED BY CHEF RICK BAYLESS

Chef Rick Bayless is a James Beard Award winner and one of the most highly regarded chefs in the world for the food at his Chicago restaurants, Topolobampo, Frontera Grill, and Xoco. He has mined Mexico for its finest recipes and ingredients and applied his well-honed sensibilities.

In 2014 my wife and I saw Chef Bayless's play *Cascabel*, produced by Chicago's Lookingglass Theatre and created in collaboration with Heidi Stillman and Tony Hernandez. *Cascabel* is the romantic story of a lovelorn cook played by Bayless himself. Like a great Bayless meal, there is a convergence of disparate ingredients: drama, dance, acrobatics, comedy, and romance. Best of all, the audience got to eat a meal like the one he prepared on stage, and it is every bit as superlative as the play. The main dish was a slice of beef tenderloin with the best *mole* I have ever tasted. It works beautifully with grilled chicken or a thick pork chop, and I serve them with brown rice so I have something to soak up extra sauce.

MAKES *8 servings*

TAKES *1 hour*

- ½ onion
- 3 (8-inch) corn tortillas
- 4½ ounces whole dried ancho chiles
- 2 ounces whole dried cascabel chiles
- 5 tablespoons sesame seeds
- ¼ cup raw slivered almonds
- ¼ cup lard or vegetable oil
- 6 garlic cloves, coarsely chopped
- 1 (1-inch) cinnamon stick
- 1 teaspoon dried oregano
- ½ teaspoon freshly ground black pepper
- ½ teaspoon ground cloves
- 4 cups beef or chicken stock
- 2 ounces unsweetened dark chocolate, chopped or shaved
- ¼ cup honey
- 1 tablespoon sugar
- Juice of 1 lime
- 1½ teaspoons kosher salt
- 8 pieces of chicken, pork chops, or steaks
- 8 servings of rice

1. Slice the onion into 3 thick rings. Grill them over medium-high direct heat with the lid up until they char a little on both sides. Set aside.

2. Grill the tortillas until they start to brown, turning them every 5 seconds to prevent burning. Set aside.

3. Heat a 3-quart pot on the stove top over medium-high heat. Stem and seed the chiles and break them into large, flat pieces. Lay them in the pot skin side down and as they warm, gently press them flat against the hot metal to toast and release their oils. Do not let them burn. The moment you see smoke, flip them and get them outta there.

4. Put the sesame seeds in the pot and toast them over medium heat until they get faint golden splotches. Set aside ¼ cup of the seeds for the sauce and reserve the remaining 2 tablespoons for garnish.

5. Add the almonds to the pot. When they get golden spots, remove them, too. Add the lard to the pot and when it is hot, throw in the onion, chiles, ¼ cup sesame seeds, the almonds, garlic, cinnamon stick, oregano, black pepper, and cloves. Let the mixture sizzle for about 1 minute and then add the stock, chocolate, honey, and sugar. Tear up the tortillas into small chunks and add them. Bring to a simmer and cook for about 30 minutes.

6. Remove the pot and let the sauce cool a bit. Working in batches of about 1 cup, puree the sauce in a blender or food processor until smooth. Wipe out the pot in which you cooked the sauce. Pour the sauce through a medium-mesh strainer back into the pot. Add the lime juice and salt.

7. Return the sauce to a simmer and cook at a very low boil until it is thick. Stir and scrape the bottom every 5 minutes or so to make sure it doesn't burn or stick. Taste and adjust the seasonings, adding more salt or sugar if needed. Add water until you get it to the desired thickness (it should be similar to bottled spaghetti sauce).

8. While it is simmering, salt and pepper the meat, then lightly oil it, and grill. Make 8 servings of rice to accompany.

9. Spoon some sauce onto each of eight plates and place a scoop of rice and a piece of meat on top.

NOTE: Anchos are dried poblano chiles and are essential here; there is no substitute. They have a uniquely rich prune, raisin, and chocolate character and very low heat. Cascabels have a bit more heat, and are often hard to find. Guajillo chiles are close to cascabels in flavor and are more common.

BURGER GLOP

Here's my favorite hamburger sauce. I've been known to use it on both burgers and fries. It's got a mild kick. I keep the condiments simple and let the beef shine through. Most folks put their sauces on top of the patty, but I spread the liquid stuff on the bottom so it can soak into the bun, coat the meat, mix with the juices that drip down, and anchor the patty in place. You can vary the ingredients to your taste or doctor them with other ingredients.

MAKES *about 1 ¼ cups*

TAKES *about 5 minutes, if you take a nap during the process*

- ½ cup mayonnaise
- ½ cup Kansas City–style barbecue sauce or ketchup
- 3 tablespoons yellow mustard
- 1 tablespoon Tabasco Chipotle Sauce
- ¼ teaspoon kosher salt
- ¼ teaspoon garlic powder

Whisk everything together in a bowl until smooth. Refrigerate the sauce in a tightly lidded container for 1 to 2 months.

BOARD SAUCES

Green sauces that use fresh herbs and oil are nothing new. They include pesto, chermoula, chimichurri, and gremolata. They're not hard to make, but chef Adam Perry Lang had an idea so simple and original that I slapped my forehead for not thinking of it myself.

In his book *Charred and Scruffed*, he takes a handful of fresh herbs and throws them on a cutting board, then he pours some olive oil on them, minces them together, lays meat snatched from a hot grill on the mixture, carves the meat, and tosses the cut meat in with the board sauce, which is enriched by the meat juices. The board sauce keeps the meat moist and brings it delicate new flavors. You might think the herbs would overwhelm the meat but you would be wrong. They maintain their proportional place in the background.

Don't make board sauces ahead of time because, when mixed with other ingredients, the oil is friendly to the botulism microbe, even in the fridge.

MAKES *about ½ cup, enough for 2 pounds of meat*
TAKES *30 minutes*

5 large fresh sage leaves
2 tablespoons fresh thyme leaves
1 garlic clove
½ fresh red jalapeño, stemmed and seeded
¼ teaspoon coarsely ground black pepper
6 tablespoons high-quality extra-virgin olive oil
Salt (optional)

While the meat is cooking, coarsely chop the sage, thyme, garlic, and jalapeño and put them in a coffee cup. Add the black pepper. Drizzle the oil into the cup. When ready to use, pour the herb-and-oil mix onto a cutting board or platter. Carve the meat and let the juices run! Roll the meat in the sauce so everything gets a light coating.

CHIMICHURRI SAUCE

There are numerous variations on this simple, classic, no-cook green sauce for beef from Argentina, but the foundation is usually the same: olive oil, garlic, fresh parsley, and salt. This version, created by Chef Ryan Udvett, my test kitchen director, adds brightness and lift to the rich flavors of beef. Use it on darkly seared flank steak, tri-tip, and beef subs. It even works on smoked brisket.

Grill the meat and spoon a small amount of sauce over the top or on the side when you serve it. Not too much—it is strong, and we don't want to cover that great steak taste. People can always add more if they want.

MAKES *enough for 8 to 12 servings of steak*
TAKES *20 minutes*

½ cup olive oil
⅓ cup distilled white vinegar
1 cup finely chopped fresh flat-leaf parsley leaves
1 cup finely chopped fresh cilantro leaves
¼ teaspoon kosher salt
¼ teaspoon freshly ground black pepper
3 garlic cloves, minced or pressed
2 dried chiles de árbol

Combine all the ingredients in a food processor or blender. Pulse until the green parts are small bits, scraping down the bowl as needed. You don't have to make this sauce homogeneous, chunks are OK. Use the sauce right away or store it in the refrigerator for a day or two. Its bright green color will fade slightly, but the goodness will remain.

PESTO

In Genova, Italy, where fragrant fields of basil grow abundantly, the aromatic herb leaves were originally made into a paste using a mortar and pestle, hence the name. Today we use a food processor or blender. Pesto is one of the world's great sauces, and making it is quick and easy.

The quality of the ingredients in this recipe is crucial. Fresh basil is essential. High-quality extra-virgin olive oil is essential. Good Parmigiano-Reggiano cheese, not "parmesan" from the green paper tube, is also essential.

You know pesto as a superb sauce for pasta, but it is far more versatile. Add a tablespoon or two to any tomato sauce to bring it extra life, try it on potatoes, spread it on toast and top with fresh tomatoes for an August lunch, or slather it on my Pesto-Crusted Pork Loin Roast (page 215).

MAKES *a bit more than 1 cup, and that's a lot*

TAKES *15 minutes*

> 3 cups firmly packed fresh basil leaves (see Notes)
> ½ cup pine nuts (see Notes)
> ½ cup grated Parmigiano-Reggiano cheese
> 6 kalamata olives, pitted (see Notes)
> 3 large garlic cloves, coarsely chopped
> ½ teaspoon ground black pepper
> ¼ teaspoon table salt
> ⅔ cup extra-virgin olive oil

Dump all the ingredients except the oil into a blender or food processor and let 'er rip until everything is chopped fine, but not smooth. With the blender on low, slowly drizzle in the oil until, presto, pesto, you have a paste. The fragrance is heavenly. It can be kept in an airtight jar in the fridge for a week before it starts to brown. If you need to keep it longer, top it with olive oil as a seal. Or freeze it. It freezes very well.

NOTES: Substitute a little Thai basil or mint for some of the basil to add depth and complexity, but don't use a lot (up to ½ cup).

Pine nuts have become obscenely expensive in recent years—especially the good ones from Italy. Inexpensive pine nuts from Asia can taste metallic and bitter. Feel free to substitute green pistachios, sunflower seeds, unsalted cashews, or blanched skinless almonds for the pine nuts if you wish.

Yes, I know olives rarely appear in pesto recipes, and certainly not in authentic Genovese pesto. Just try it.

ROASTED RED PEPPER AND GARLIC COULIS

A coulis is a thick pureed vegetable sauce. This one is lovely served as a dipping sauce for both grilled meats and potatoes. Mix it into your next risotto.

JAPANESE HAPPY MOUTH YAKITORI SAUCE

MAKES *about 1 ½ cups*

TAKES *about 25 minutes*

- 2 roasted red peppers, coarsely chopped
- 7 roasted garlic cloves, peeled
- 6 tablespoons extra-virgin olive oil
- 2 tablespoons lemon juice
- ¾ teaspoon kosher salt
- ½ teaspoon freshly ground black pepper

In a food processor or blender, whir all the ingredients together until smooth. Use right away or cover and refrigerate for up to 1 week.

Years ago my wife was invited to deliver a scientific paper at a conference in Japan. I came along and registered for the "wives" tours and learned flower arranging and tea service, visited a silk factory, and ate marvelous morsels.

One evening my wife and I went to a baseball game to watch the Ham Fighters play the Carp. From a vendor with a steaming box strapped around his neck, I bought two bamboo skewers of hot grilled meat. One had bite-size chicken livers and the other had squid, both shiny with a dark, chestnut-colored sauce.

The next day I learned the dish was called yakitori, and we went to one of the many *yakitori-ya*, small afterwork hangouts where skewers of meat are grilled over charcoal and coated with this wondrous sauce. I asked a waitress if she could tell me what the sauce was. She replied, "Happy mouth." So I took lots of notes and when I got home, I set about researching and reverse-engineering it.

Yakitori, I learned, is a thick, rich teriyaki-like glaze, a soy-based elixir laced with ginger and garlic. In addition to being terrific on chicken livers and squid, it's great on salmon, chicken, turkey, chunks of pork, and many veggies, especially onions. First, grill the meat, then paint on the glaze and cook it for a minute or two more over medium heat, but beware—it will burn if you don't keep turning the skewers.

Try my recipe for Happy Mouth Yakitori Ribs (page 210) the next time you have the gang over to watch a ball game.

- ½ cup soy sauce, preferably low sodium
- ½ cup sake or dry white wine
- ½ cup orange juice
- ¼ cup sugar
- ¼ cup grated fresh ginger, and any liquid exuded during grating (see Note)
- 3 tablespoons honey
- 2 tablespoons toasted sesame oil
- 1 tablespoon hot sauce, or to taste
- 5 garlic cloves, crushed
- 1½ teaspoons cornstarch

1. In a 2-quart nonreactive saucepan, mix all the ingredients except the cornstarch and gently simmer over medium-low heat for about 30 minutes.

2. Strain the sauce through a fine-mesh sieve into another saucepan. By now, the chunky stuff has given its all and it's time to discard it like letters from ex-lovers. With a ladle or spoon, gently press the mush left in the sieve to release all those good juices. Taste the sauce and adjust the honey or hot sauce if you wish. Put the saucepan back on a burner over medium-low heat.

3. Put the cornstarch in a coffee cup and add 2 tablespoons of cold water. With a fork, whisk the mixture until the cornstarch has dissolved. Before it has a chance to separate, dump the cornstarch slurry into the sauce. The sauce will get milky, thicken considerably, and start burbling like lava when it warms up. Simmer for 10 to 15 minutes, or until it's as thick as motor oil and has clarified a bit. Now paint it on everything except the kitchen walls.

NOTE: To get enough ginger, begin with one fat ginger finger, perhaps the size of a your thumb. Grate it on a Microplane or the small holes of a box grater.

GREEK LADOLEMONO FOR SEAFOOD

Ladolemono is a classic Greek sauce of two parts high-quality extra-virgin olive oil, something Greece excels at, to one part fresh lemon juice, which Greece also excels at, whisked together with salt and pepper. If you wish, you can spark it up with an herb. Drizzle it on grilled seafood like a simple grilled fish, lobster, shrimp, or calamari (page 334).

MAKES *½ cup, enough for 2 to 4 servings of seafood*
TAKES *10 minutes*

- ¼ cup high-quality extra-virgin olive oil
- 2 tablespoons fresh lemon juice
- 2 teaspoons finely chopped fresh oregano (see Note)
- ¼ teaspoon kosher salt
- ¼ teaspoon coarsely ground black pepper

Combine all the ingredients in a jar with a lid and shake thoroughly. Shake again just before using.

NOTE: If you use dried oregano, halve the quantity. This is also good with fresh parsley, basil, or fennel.

GRILLED MARINARA SAUCE

The traditional Italian marinara is made entirely in a pan or pot. Guess where I start mine? Grilling the ingredients really revs up the flavors and complexity.

You can pour this sauce over pasta or use it on pizza, in grilled eggplant Parm, or on just about anything except ice cream. If you use it on pasta, a drizzle of really good fresh extra-virgin olive oil on top gives it a nice boost. Or real Italian Parmigiano-Reggiano cheese. Or a heaping teaspoon of pesto, or ¼ cup cream, or 2 tablespoons fresh chèvre cheese, or meatballs, or Italian sausage, or . . .

MAKES *about 4 cups*

TAKES *about 90 minutes*

> 2 pounds ripe meaty tomatoes, halved
> Inexpensive olive oil
> 1 small onion, halved
> 1 carrot, peeled
> 1 celery stalk, leaves removed
> 2 garlic cloves
> 1 bay leaf
> 1 teaspoon kosher salt
> ¼ teaspoon freshly ground black pepper
> ¼ teaspoon dried thyme (see Notes)
> ¼ teaspoon dried basil (see Notes)
> ¼ teaspoon dried oregano (see Notes)
> Red wine (optional)
> Sugar (optional)

1. Preheat the grill to medium-hot, and when it is ready, clean the grates thoroughly. (Clean grates are very important for this recipe.) Get some smoke started.

2. Paint the cut sides of the tomatoes lightly with oil. Put the tomatoes on the grates over direct heat, cut sides down, and cook for 5 to 10 minutes with the lid down, or until they start to get some dark grill marks. Roll them over and grill the skin side. Don't worry if they blacken a bit on the skin side; you're going to remove the skins. While the tomatoes are cooking, put the onion, carrot, and celery on the grill and roll them around until they are well marked and limp. Remove everything from the grill and let cool.

3. When cool enough to handle, slip the skins from the tomatoes and set them aside. Finely chop the onion, carrot, and celery. In a 2-quart pot or large frying pan, warm 2 tablespoons olive oil over medium heat. Add the garlic, bay leaf, salt, pepper, thyme, basil, and oregano and cook for about 10 minutes, stirring occasionally to prevent sticking. If the food sticks, deglaze the pan with a splash of red wine or water and scrape the pan with a wooden spoon.

4. Add the tomatoes to the pan, turn the heat to medium-low, and simmer, uncovered, for about 1 hour, stirring occasionally. If the sauce gets too thick, add some water.

5. Remove the bay leaf, and whup the sauce up in a blender or food processor or use a stick blender.

Taste, and adjust the seasonings. If the sauce is too acidic, add up to 2 teaspoons sugar to balance it.

NOTES: You can use fresh herbs if you wish. Double the quantity for each.

While the whole shebang is in the pan, amp it up a notch with a pinch of red pepper flakes or chipotle powder. If you have some pesto, add a teaspoon.

BACON AND ONION JAM

This sauce is sweet, salty, smoky, and savory. You'll want it on all your burgers and sandwiches. Try it on thick grill-toasted Italian bread with a fried egg on top. I have tried this using different vinegars, cocoa or dark chocolate, allspice, other types of vinegar, honey, Worcestershire, chipotles in adobo, and raisins. They all work. The recipe here is my go-to for simplicity and balance.

MAKES *2 cups*

TAKES *2½ hours*

1 pound bacon
2 onions, thinly sliced
4 garlic cloves, minced or pressed
¼ cup inexpensive balsamic vinegar
¼ cup pure maple syrup, any grade
3 tablespoons packed brown sugar
½ teaspoon dried thyme or rosemary
¼ teaspoon freshly ground black pepper
Splash of hot sauce (optional)

1. Cut the bacon into ¼- to ½-inch slices and cook in a frying pan over medium heat until it gets a bit curly and golden, but is not fully cooked and firm. If necessary, cook it in two batches. Brown bits will likely stick to the bottom of the pan. Scrape them loose with a spatula. Remove the fried bacon with a slotted spoon and let it drain on paper towels on top of newspaper.

2. Pour off all but 2 tablespoons of the bacon fat, trying to leave behind the brown bits on the bottom of the pan. (Save the fat for frying broccoli or other veggies, but don't pour hot fat into a plastic tub or it may melt.) Add the onion and cook until translucent, but not browned. Add the garlic and cook for 1 to 2 minutes. Add 1 cup water, the vinegar, syrup, sugar, thyme, black pepper, and bacon and stir. Reduce the heat to low and simmer until the sauce is a thick, gloppy, jammy, sweet, luscious goo, 1 to 2 hours. Turn off the heat and let the sauce cool.

3. Taste and add more sugar or a splash of hot pepper sauce, or both, if you wish. Spoon it into a bottle, screw on the lid, and refrigerate. Serve at room temperature or warm.

D.C. MUMBO SAUCE

Washington, D.C., is the nation's most international city. Much of the population comes and goes with the political tides. As a result, there aren't many indigenous dishes, but there is one concoction the locals proudly claim as their own: mumbo sauce.

Theresa Vargas, in a July 2011 article in the *Washington Post*, wrote, "For many D.C. natives, the sauce that captures the flavor of home is called *mumbo*. Few can tell you how it's made or where it originated, but they know this: If you grew up in one of the mostly African-American areas of the city, you've likely known the taste your entire life. If you didn't, you probably have no idea what it is."

Mumbo sauce, which is also called mambo sauce, mombo sauce, mumba sauce, mumble sauce, and even mummbah sauce, is different from joint to joint. It ranges in color from orange to red, is thinner than the typical red barbecue sauce, and tastes more like Chinese sweet-and-sour sauce. In fact, it can be used for just this purpose. Mumbo sauce is most popular on chicken wings, but it works on just about anything deep-fried. That may sound odd, but remember, in the Deep South, fried chicken and fish are often served with honey.

Since there is no official recipe, I've created one inspired by the best examples I've tasted in the D.C. area. Try it on fried chicken, fish, shrimp, or egg rolls. I use it on Sweet and Sour Pork Tenderloin (page 212). As unorthodox as it may sound, it's pretty good on barbecued ribs and pulled pork, too.

MAKES *2⅔ cups*

TAKES *less than an hour, even if the kids are in your hair*

- 1 cup sugar
- 1 cup distilled white vinegar
- 1 cup pineapple juice
- ½ cup (4 ounces) tomato paste
- 4 teaspoons soy sauce
- 1 teaspoon ground ginger
- ¼ teaspoon hot sauce, or more if you wish

Mix all the ingredients together in a saucepan and whisk to break up the clumps of tomato paste and ginger. Simmer over low heat for about 20 minutes to marry the flavors and thicken it a bit. Do not let the sauce boil. Taste and adjust the seasonings to your preferences. When it is time to serve, you can drizzle it on the food, serve it in a bowl for dipping, or both. Mumbo sauce can be refrigerated for months.

NOTE: You may be tempted to use apple cider vinegar or something with more flavor, but resist. Plain old distilled vinegar is the right call.

6

PORK

PERFECT PULLED PORK

With smoke woven through shards of succulent meat, potent bits of spiced bark mixed in, and a gentle splash of tangy barbecue sauce, pulled pork is the most versatile and practically foolproof low-and-slow smoked meat, perfect for feeding large crowds. It is cheap. And you can do it on practically any grill with a lid.

Pork shoulder is laced with fat and connective tissue. The cooking process, which can take 8 to 12 hours or more, is the quintessence of Southern barbecue. You set up a lawn chair and sip a cup of coffee as you put the meat on in the wee hours. As the sun gets high, you switch to cool, refreshing beer. As dusk approaches, the fat melts and the connective tissue dissolves into gelatin, your guests begin to arrive, and you switch to bourbon.

MAKES *3 pounds pork, enough for 8 to 12 generous sandwiches*

TAKES *25 minutes to trim and salt the meat; 12 to 24 hours to let the salt penetrate (optional; see Butt Basics, page 200); 8 to 12 hours cooking time at 225°F; 20 minutes pulling time, if you do it with your fingers (ouch!), 10 minutes with Bear Paws (see page 109)*

- 1 pork butt (about 5 pounds)
- ½ teaspoon kosher salt per pound of meat (2½ teaspoons for 5 pounds)
- ⅓ cup Meathead's Memphis Dust (page 167)
- 12 kaiser rolls or hamburger buns
- 1 cup barbecue sauce (use your favorite—I'm partial to South Carolina Mustard sauces like the one on page 177)

1. Prep. The day before serving, trim all but ⅛ inch of the fat from the exterior of the meat. If it has flaps hanging out, you might need to tie it with butcher's twine. Don't worry if it doesn't look fancy. Rinse the meat to remove any bone shards from butchering. Dry it and salt it, using ½ teaspoon per pound of meat. It's best to let it rest in the fridge overnight.

2. Just before cooking, lightly moisten all surfaces of the meat with water. This will help the rub adhere and also help it dissolve to aid bark formation. Now cover your butt (ahem) generously with Meathead's Memphis Dust.

3. Insert a leave-in digital meat thermometer if you have one, positioning the tip right in the center of the meat. Make sure it is not within 1 inch of the bone.

4. Fire up. Get your smoker up to 225°F or set up the grill for two-zone cooking and shoot for about 225°F on the indirect side.

5. Cook. Put the meat right on the grate, not in a pan. Put about 4 ounces of wood on the fire and make your sauce, slaw, and beans. Watch the game. Then cut the lawn. Wash the windows. Read a book. You've got plenty of time.

Check the cooker every hour or so to make sure the fuel is sufficient and the temperature is holding at 225 to 250°F. This cut is forgiving, so if it goes up to 300°F, don't worry, but try to keep it under 250°F. Add about 4 ounces fresh wood every 30 minutes for the first 2 hours for a total of 1 pound. No need to add more.

When the meat hits about 150°F, you can expect the stall (see page 59). The exact temperature will depend on a number of variables, but if you are cooking under 300°F, the meat will stall. During cooking, moisture is constantly evaporating from the surface of the meat, and it cools the meat like sweat on a marathon runner. The cooling effect of the evaporation just about equals the heating of the meat.

Now you have a choice. You can let it take its time. The surface will dry out, making your bark, and when the pork reaches about 170°F, collagens, which are part of the connective tissues, begin to melt and turn to gelatin. That's magic, baby. The meat gets much more tender and juicy when this happens. Or you can power through the stall by tightly wrapping the meat in foil, a process called the Texas crutch (see page 60), so moisture cannot evaporate and cool the meat. This can cut as much as 4 hours off your cooking time. The meat will be just as moist and tender

but the crutch will make the bark softer. Your choice. Me? I rarely crutch.

When it hits 195°F, it may be ready, but I recommend you wait until the pork hits 203°F. If there is a bone (see page 200), use a glove or paper towel to protect your fingers and wiggle it. It should be loose enough to pull out. The exterior should be dark brown. Some rubs and cookers will make the meat look black like a meteorite, but it is not burned and it won't taste burned. There may be glistening bits of melted fat on the surface. On a gas cooker, it may look shiny pink. Don't add sauce while it is on the cooker. That comes after you pull it.

6. When the pork is finally ready, go ahead and take a taste. You should notice a thick, flavorful crust with the telltale smoke ring directly beneath it.

7. If you are more than an hour from mealtime, you can leave the meat on the cooker with the heat off or put it in the indoor oven at about about 170°F and hold it there. If you are more than 2 hours from mealtime, wrap it in foil to keep it from drying out and hold it at 170°F. If you are taking the meat to a party, wrap it in foil and put it in a faux Cambro (see page 50).

On the following page, the bone has been removed from the butt after cooking. The elbow joint is at the top, the humerus is in the center, and the shoulder

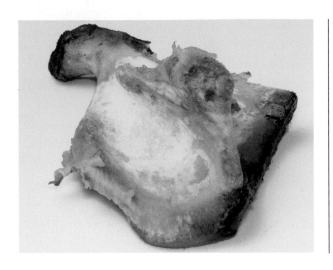

blade is in the foreground. If the meat is properly cooked, this bone should pull out easily with two fingers and have almost no meat stuck to it, just like this one.

8. About 30 minutes before sitting down for dinner, put the meat in a large pan to catch the drippings. Now pull the clod apart with Bear Paws (see opposite page) or use gloved hands or forks. If you wish, you can slice it or chop it like they do in North Carolina, but I think you lose less moisture when pulling it apart by hand since the meat separates into bundles of muscle fibers, which is why it is called pulled pork.

BUTT BASICS

HOW MUCH MEAT WILL YOU NEED?
There is significant shrinkage during cooking and waste in the form of bone and globs of fat that you discard when pulling. Count on about 30 percent loss—if there is less, you'll have leftovers. I usually buy 1 pound per person and look forward to leftovers. It freezes beautifully.

SKIP THE MARINADE, INJECTIONS, AND BRINES
Some folks like to inject butt with an internal marinade. If you are in a competition, you should consider injections to get an edge, but the improvement is small. When I'm cooking at home, I don't bother. Dry brining works, and if you can get salt on a day in advance, it will penetrate deep. Then use a good rub, and let the smoke flavor it and the internal fat and collagen moisturize it.

COOKING TIME
The determining factor in cooking time for all meats is its thickness, so smaller butts will cook faster because they are skinnier. Surprisingly, if you are cooking a whole shoulder with the butt and the picnic combined, it will not take much longer than a butt alone, since the added weight isn't thickness but length.

The meat is at its maximum tenderness and juiciness when it hits about 203°F. If the roast is not ready on time, don't panic. You can crank up the heat if you are running behind. Butt can handle it. The bark might get a bit dry and there might be a little more shrinkage than usual, but it will still be delicious. If you kick the temperature up to about 275°F, you can cut the cooking time by 2 to 4 hours.

If it is time to serve and the butt is still not at the ideal internal temperature, just slice the meat. Don't pull it because it won't shred easily. Slices of smoked pork butt are wonderful.

Discard any big chunks of fat. Try not to eat all the flavorful crusty bits when you are doing the pulling, and instead distribute them evenly throughout. Make sure you save any flavorful drippings.

9. Serve. The classic pulled pork sammich is my favorite way to serve it. Mound it high on a nice bun. Top it with a small amount of your favorite sauce. KC Classic (page 175) sweet red sauce is always popular, but pulled pork is where the East Carolina Mop Sauce (page 178) really shines. Or try Lexington Dip (page 179). I also love the mustard sauces like Columbia Gold (page 177).

I like my pulled pork with chopped raw onion mixed in. My wife likes hers with grilled onion on top. Sometimes we chop up raw apple and mix it in, too. Occasionally I slice the roast rather than pull it and douse it with a classic Texas sauce (page 179), which is thin and more like a gravy. It lets the meat flavor come through without masking it. I know folks who like to garnish pulled pork with sliced tomato, pickle chips, and a raw onion slice. In South Carolina and other places in the South, people like to mound it on a bun with slaw (use my Classic Deli Slaw, page 364).

For big parties away from home, I smoke 3 or more butts, pull them, and then put them in a big pan. I add about ½ cup sauce per 5 pounds meat, and about 1 tablespoon butter per pound to keep it moist. I carry it to the party in a faux Cambro (see page 50). When I get to the party, I heat it in a slow cooker and serve the sauce on the side.

LEFTOVER PULLED PORK

Plan on making more pulled pork than you need. There's nothing like tossing a frozen brick of pulled pork into the microwave on a Tuesday night after working late and chowing down on a big juicy sandwich that will wash all the stress away.

Mix in a bit of barbecue sauce with the leftovers, and freeze measured meal-size portions in zipper-top bags. (The sauce prevents freezer burn.) The best methods for reheating are to slowly warm the pork in the bag in simmering water or remove the pork from the bag, put it in a bowl, and microwave it.

There are myriad uses for leftover pulled pork. Try it in tacos, enchiladas, nachos, scrambled eggs, egg muffins, BBQ eggs Benedict, jalapeño poppers, dirty rice, bistro salad, Brunswick stew, BBQ spaghetti, ravioli, hash, sausages, mac and cheese pie, grilled cheese sandwiches, rangoons, egg rolls, or on a baked potato (see page 202).

REALLY LOADED POTATO CANOES

It seems as though almost all the hip gastro-pubs serve some sort of "loaded" potato skins, but usually they are not really very loaded. My potato canoes, on the other hand, are not only loaded with enough of the good stuff to capsize them, but one of them can even make a meal.

MAKES *4 servings*

TAKES *about 2 hours*

> 2 large russet potatoes
> 2 tablespoons vegetable oil
> 3 tablespoons sour cream
> ½ pound Perfect Pulled Pork (page 198)
> 2 ounces shredded cheddar or another melting cheese
> ¼ cup sliced green onions

1. Prep. Wash and scrub the potatoes.

2. Fire up. Set up the grill for two-zone cooking and get it to 325°F in the indirect zone.

3. Cook. Wrap the potatoes in foil and bake to an internal temperature of at least 210°F. Depending on how thick the potatoes are, this can take 1 hour 15 minutes to 1 hour 40 minutes. Now normally you don't want to cook potatoes in foil because the skin won't crisp, but in this case we will have a chance to correct this problem.

4. Unwrap the potatoes and let them cool until you can handle them, about 10 minutes. Slice them in half lengthwise and use a spoon to scoop out the center of each half, leaving about ¼ inch of potato flesh all the way around. Set the scoopings aside and freeze them for use in potato soup, mashed potatoes, or potato pancakes.

5. Brush the potatoes inside and out with oil and arrange them, scooped sides down, on the grill over direct heat until the flesh is toasty golden. Flip them skin down and grill until the bottom gets dark but not burned, about 5 minutes.

6. Spread about 1 teaspoon of the sour cream in each hollowed-out potato. Divide the pork evenly among them and top with about 1 tablespoon of the shredded cheese. Slide the potatoes back onto the grill on the indirect side until the cheese melts.

7. Serve. Top each with another spoonful of cold sour cream and sprinkle generously with chopped green onions.

PORK RIBS: THE HOLY GRAIL

Pork ribs are the holy grail, the recipe that all backyarders want to master. Here's how.

The ribs that win championships are a mélange of flavors: a complex spice rub, roast porcine richness, silky mouthfeel, firm bark, springy texture, succulent juiciness, and tangy sweet sauce, all underpinned by elegant hardwood smoke. Their scent clings to your fingers for hours.

With this recipe, you will make ribs good enough to bring home a trophy in a cook-off. In fact, many of my readers have done exactly that.

Below the sauce, the surface of the meat should have a crusty bark, a little crunchy and a little chewy. The meat in the center should be tender, yet still retain resistance when you bite into it, like a steak. It should pull off the bone cleanly and with little effort, leaving behind bare bone, but it should not fall off the bone. If it does, chances are it has been boiled or steamed, and that robs the meat of the natural pork essence.

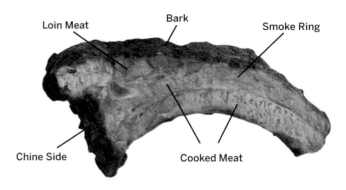

ANATOMY OF A BABY BACK

Loin Meat

Bark

Smoke Ring

Chine Side

Cooked Meat

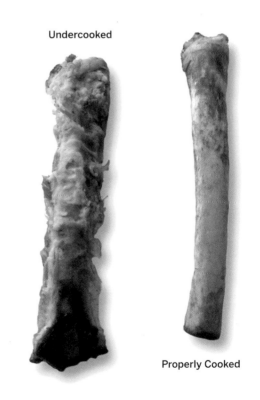

Undercooked

Properly Cooked

THE DIFFERENT CUTS OF RIBS

Pigs have 14 rib bones. They are attached to the spine and are usually divided into four popular cuts: back ribs, spareribs, center-cut ribs, and rib tips.

BACK RIBS (AKA BABY BACK RIBS, BABY BACKS, LOIN BACK RIBS, LOIN RIBS, CANADIAN BACK RIBS)

Connected to the backbone, nestled beneath the loin muscle, baby backs are the most tender and lean ribs. They are sometimes called "babies" because they are shorter than spareribs. A typical full slab has 11 to 13 bones. The slab is tapered at one end, with the shortest bones only about 3 inches and the longest about 6 inches. They are usually curved like a hockey stick at the end where they meet the spine. Depending on how the butcher removes the loin meat that is on the humped side of the bones, some can have up to ½ inch of delicate, lean loin meat on the top of the bones. There is usually more meat on top of the bones than between them—about 2 pounds per slab, about half of which is bone. Hungry adults can eat a whole slab of baby backs.

When you shop, try to buy slabs without shiners, bones showing through on top. You want a layer of meat on top of the bones.

SPARERIBS (AKA SPARES, SIDE RIBS)

Nobody knows for sure how they got the name, but spareribs are not extras, leftovers, or an inferior cut. Nor are they so named because the meat is scant. Spares are excellent tasting, usually richer and more flavorful than baby backs because they are fattier and have more connective tissue. A slab should have at least 11 bones, and there is usually more bone than meat in a slab of spares, with more meat between the bones than on top of them.

Spares are cut from the ends of baby backs, farther down the side of the hog; they run all the way down to the breastbone. Look at a slab of spareribs and you will notice that along one edge, the ends of bones are showing and

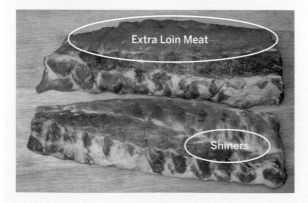

Extra Loin Meat

Shiners

you can see marrow. This is where they were cut from the baby backs. The other end, with no bones sticking out, is from the chest. It is a flap of meat, small bones, cartilage, and gristle called rib tips.

A rack of spareribs generally runs 3 pounds or more and can usually feed two people.

Spareribs are a little less expensive per pound than back ribs because they have more bone and because demand for baby backs has grown significantly since the Chili's restaurant chain began promoting them with a catchy jingle.

CENTER-CUT RIBS (AKA ST. LOUIS-CUT, SLC, BARBECUE CUT, KANSAS CITY CUT)

Take a slab of spareribs, lop off the gristly rib tips, trim the loose meat from the edge, and what remains is a flat rectangular slab that goes by several names. If your butcher doesn't know what St. Louis–cut or center-cut means, ask for spareribs with the tips removed. Then again, you may want to remove them yourself and cook them, too. A standard 2-pound slab can serve two people or one really hungry big man. These are the cut I like best.

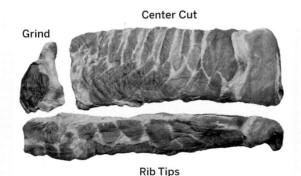

Grind

Center Cut

Rib Tips

RIB TIPS (AKA BRISKET, COSTAL CARTILAGES, BREAKS)

Rib tips are strips that have been cut from the lower ends of the spareribs when making center-cut ribs. They typically run 8 to 12 inches long and 1 to 3 inches wide. Eating rib tips takes a bit more gnawing than other cuts because they are chewy, and the small tubes of cartilage in them go every which way. In some regions, tips are a delicacy and preferred over other cuts, while in other regions, nobody wants them. When served, they are usually chopped with a cleaver into chunks about 2 inches square. Two full strips trimmed from a slab of spares will serve a normal person.

COUNTRY-STYLE RIBS

Country-style ribs are not really ribs at all but pork chops (see page 213).

LAST-MEAL RIBS

This recipe needed a name when I first published it on AmazingRibs.com, and Doug and Trudy Calvin of Palm Springs, California, provided it. Doug wrote, "I fixed ribs yesterday by following your recipe. My girlfriend made me promise that, for her last meal on this planet, I would fix the same ribs."

MAKES *2 servings*

TAKES *15 minutes for trimming, about 2 hours for dry brining, about 5 minutes for rubbing; cooking time is 5 to 6 hours for spareribs or center-cut ribs, 3 to 4 hours for back ribs; if you use rib holders so they are crammed close to each other, add another hour*

> 1 slab center-cut pork ribs (11 to 13 bones)
> Kosher salt
> ¼ cup Meathead's Memphis Dust (page 167)
> 1 cup barbecue sauce (optional)

1. Prep. Remove the membrane (see page 208). Rinse the ribs in cool water to remove any bone bits from butchering. Salt the meat, using ½ teaspoon per pound. If time permits, get the salt on 1 to 2 hours before cooking.

2. Sprinkle the Meathead's Memphis Dust right on the meat, or help it stick by first moistening the meat with a little water or a slather of mustard, ketchup, or cooking oil. Sprinkle enough rub to coat all surfaces but not so much that the meat doesn't show through—about 2 tablespoons per side, depending on the size of the slab. Rub it in.

3. Fire up. Set up the grill for two-zone smoking or fire up the smoker and preheat to about 225°F.

4. Cook. Add 4 ounces of wood, add the meat, and close the lid. When the smoke dwindles after 20 to 30 minutes, add a little more wood. That's it. Leave the slab meat side up. There is no need to flip it. If

you have more than one slab on the grill, halfway through cooking, move the ribs that are closest to the fire away from the heat, and the slabs that are farthest from the fire closer to it.

5. This is one of the few meats for which using a digital instant-read thermometer is not very helpful. The bones and the thin meat make it hard to get an accurate reading. Instead, use the bend test to see if they are ready. Pick up the slab with tongs in the center and bounce it gently. If the surface cracks, the ribs are ready.

Bend Test

6. Now it is sauce time. Or not. Taste them without. Sauceless ribs, with rub only, are a thing in Memphis, Tennessee. It shows you have confidence in the meat. But let's be honest: A glistening coat of sweet and tart sauce is mighty nice. But not too much. Here's a rule of thumb: A full slab of spareribs with the tips

still on will need at least ¾ cup of a thick sauce for both sides, a slab of St. Louis–cut ribs will need ½ cup, and a slab of baby back ribs will need ⅓ cup. But don't forget that you will want to have another ½ cup or so in a bowl on the table for folks who want more.

7. Finally, sizzle the sauce by heating the sauced ribs on a hot grill or under the indoor broiler for just a few minutes. This caramelizes the sugars and alters the chemistry for the better. Watch the sauce very carefully because it can go from caramelized to carbonized in a hurry.

8. Serve. Be ready to take a bow when the applause swells from the audience.

60-MINUTE RIBS
DREAMLAND STYLE

I went to Dreamland in Tuscaloosa, Alabama, with a chip on my shoulder. I had heard about how they cook their ribs, and it sounded all wrong. I had a couple of barbecue mavens with me so I would have validation of my inevitable disdain: Dave Raymond, creator of Sweet Baby Ray's Barbecue Sauce and restaurants, and

Barry Sorkin, the man who makes my favorite barbecue in Chicago at Smoque BBQ.

Dreamland has been around since 1958, and not much has changed. Even on a bright summer day, it is dark, worn, creaky, and smoke stained. Straight to the back is the aged brick grill, right on the edge of the dining room.

When John "Big Daddy" Bishop opened the first Dreamland, he cooked his whole sparerib slabs hot and fast 30 to 36 inches above burning logs. That's direct heat—all wrong. Well, I'm here to tell you that those ribs were all right with Sweet Baby Ray, Barry, and me.

HOW TO SKIN AND TRIM RIBS

Turn the slab to the bone side. On center-cut and spareribs there is a flap of thick meat from the diaphragm that most chefs remove. I slice it off, toss it in the smoker, and munch on it a few hours into cooking. Cook's bonus!

If the butcher has not removed the shiny silvery membrane on the concave bone side, you should do so. It can get rubbery. In addition, removing it helps the layer of fat under the membrane melt and drain.

Insert a butter knife or, as this cook is doing, an ice pick, between the membrane and the meat at one end. Work your fingers around under it to loosen it, so you can get a grip on it. Gently begin peeling it off, trying not to rip it. I like to use a paper towel to help me grip the slippery thing.

If the slab is irregular at the ends or too long to fit on the smoker, trim off a bone or two. Cook these loose bones with the slab. They'll be done in a couple of hours, so you can grab them before the rest of the ribs are done. Another cook's bonus!

Because they cook in an hour or two, they are very different from low-and-slow ribs that can take up to 6 hours, like my Last-Meal Ribs (page 206). First of all, there's the flavor. Before the sauce is applied, there's some charring on the surface. It still tastes like pork, but there is a distinct overtone of a hot grilled steak, and it is a luscious surprise. It comes by its special personality from the radiant heat, the hot metal grates the meat rests on, the wood embers, and the drippings that hit those embers and are vaporized and borne back up to light on the meat. Part of the secret is that the logs have been mostly

reduced to embers, so they put out little smoke, but every now and then, the pitmaster throws another log on the fire and it belches smoke.

The other big difference is one you would expect: texture. These ribs have some chew. Now, mind you, they are not tough, they just chew more like a strip steak than most other Southern-style ribs.

You can make Dreamland-style ribs at home. The trick is in the grill setup. You will need a charcoal or wood-burning grill, and you need a way to get the meat at least 24 inches above the coals. A bullet smoker like the Weber Smokey Mountain is perfect for the job. Just remove the water pan and cook on the top grate. Or you can simply make a campfire and suspend a grate above it. You will also need a long-handled pair of tongs because the cooker will discharge smoke every time you toss on the wood.

MAKES *2 servings*

TAKES *2 hours*

> 1 rack spareribs or center-cut ribs
> 1 teaspoon kosher salt
> 1 teaspoon coarsely ground black pepper
> ¾ cup barbecue sauce

1. Prep. Skin and trim the ribs (see opposite page) and rinse off any bone chips. Sprinkle with the salt and pepper 1 to 3 hours before cooking. Press the seasoning into the meat so that it doesn't fall off during cooking.

2. Fire up. Fire up a good bed of charcoal or embers 2 coals deep and wait until they are covered with white ash. Throw on some wood. If you have logs, use some that are about one third the size of a baseball bat. If you have chunks, 4 fist-size chunks should do the job. Chips or pellets will quickly burn, so I don't recommend using them here.

3. Cook. Put the meat on the grill, lid off, and turn it every 5 to 10 minutes, watching to make sure it browns but does not burn. Add more wood every 30 minutes or so. After 1 hour or so, depending on your setup, it should start getting bronze in color. At this point, stop adding wood.

4. Serve. When the slab passes the bend test (see page 206), leave the ribs on the grill for a little longer, meat side down, until the fatty spots verge on blackening. If you're not sure they're ready, cut off a bone and taste. Paint a coating of sauce over the ribs, and you're ready to roll with the tide.

HAPPY MOUTH YAKITORI RIBS

Ribs are not traditional in Japanese yakitori restaurants, where chicken on skewers is popular, but the sauce is wonderful on them. Here's how I do yakitori ribs.

MAKES *2 servings*

TAKES *20 minutes to prep, and about 90 minutes to cook*

- 1 slab baby back ribs
- ½ cup Japanese Happy Mouth Yakitori Sauce (page 191)
- 2 green onions, thinly sliced, for garnish

1. Prep. Skin and trim the slab (see page 208). Cut the slab into individual bones, trying to leave the same amount of meat on all sides of all the bones.

2. Fire up. Get your smoker up to 225°F or set up the grill for two-zone cooking and shoot for about 225°F on the indirect side.

3. Cook. Put the ribs over indirect heat. Put the lid on and resist the temptation to add wood. (Smoke

flavor clashes with the sauce.) They cook a lot faster when cut into individual bones than when cooked as a slab. After about 1½ hours, insert a fork and twist it. If it twists easily, the ribs are done. (The meat is too thin to get an accurate reading with a thermometer.) Paint both sides of the ribs with sauce or dip them in the sauce and put them back on the grill in the indirect zone for about 15 minutes to bake it on. One coat should be enough.

4. Serve. Just before serving, sprinkle the ribs with the green onions as a garnish. If anyone reaches for a knife and fork, throw him out.

NOTE: If you like the high heat of wasabi, put a dab on your plate and dip the meat into the paste.

KERMIT'S SECOND-FAVORITE PORK CHOPS

Kermit the Frog's first love is Miss Piggy, but the last time we went out for drinks, he told me he liked thick pork chops. Could this be why they broke up? Pork chops are best when cut thick, at least 1 inch; thin chops are easy to overcook. You can ask your butcher to cut the chops thicker than those on display.

This is one of the rare occasions when I prefer a wet brine, because a bit of water is drawn into the meat, and this lean cut needs all the water it can get. I recommend you cook low and slow with indirect heat at about 225°F. Low and slow is especially important for shoulder chops, which have a lot more connective tissue.

MAKES *2 servings*

TAKES *about 5 minutes to prepare, 2 hours to wet brine, and 45 to 60 minutes to cook*

- 2 pork chops, at least 1 inch thick
- 2 cups The Simple Blonder Wet Brine (page 160)
- 2 teaspoons Meathead's Memphis Dust (page 167)
- ½ cup Columbia Gold (page 177; see Note)

1. Prep. If you have loin chops, there might be a band of fat around the perimeter. Beneath the fat is a thin layer of connective tissue called silverskin. You need to trim off the fat and silverskin because as it cooks, it shrinks and causes the meat to form a cup.

2. Pour the brine into a 1-gallon zipper-top bag or nonreactive bowl. Add the chops and refrigerate for 2 hours.

DON'T STUFF THE CHOP

I don't recommend that you stuff pork chops. Stuffed chops are made by cutting a slit into a thick chop, working a knife around to create a pocket, and stuffing filling in the pocket. By the time the center of the stuffing is warm enough to kill bacteria, the meat, which is now really two thin chops sandwiching the stuffing, is overcooked. If you must stuff a chop, pre-cook the stuffing so you can get the meat off the heat sooner, and cook the chops at 225°F and no hotter.

3. Season the chops with Meathead's Memphis Dust just before cooking.

4. Fire up. Set up the grill for two-zone cooking and shoot for about 225°F on the indirect side.

5. Cook. Toss in some wood and cook on indirect heat with the lid down. When the meat hits about 125°F, paint one side of the chops with the sauce. Move them to direct heat, sauce down, paint the second side, and leave the lid open. After 3 minutes, flip the chops and cook for 3 minutes longer. You've got to be careful here: The sauce will blacken unless the chops are watched carefully. They are ready to remove from the heat when the centers reach 135 to 140°F. You may see a little pale pink in the meat. When there is still a hint of pink, it is at peak tenderness and juiciness. Don't worry about trichinosis. It is never found in modern USDA-inspected pork. For all practical purposes, it is extinct.

NOTE: You can use your favorite barbecue sauce instead of the Columbia Gold, but I've tried them all and this mustard-based sauce is by far my favorite.

PORK TENDEROIN WITH COWBOY JAVA RUB

Tenderloin is a small tube of muscle, at most 2 inches in diameter, that is the most tender on the hog. It is not the same as the loin, although many people confuse them. The tenderloins lie inside the rib cage, while the loin lies on top of the rib cage. A single tenderloin is a meal for four, and a whole loin can feed twenty. But beware: Nowadays packers have been putting two tenderloins in a plastic bag so they look like one big thick tube. Then you open the bag, and surprise!

Because it is tender and juicy, you can cook it over high heat in order to brown the exterior. There is a skinny end and it will cook faster. If you have somebody who won't eat slightly pink pork, then you're all set.

This recipe is especially good grilled over wood.

MAKES *4 servings*

TAKES *30 to 45 minutes*

> 1 pork tenderloin (about 2 pounds)
> 1 teaspoon kosher salt
> Cowboy Java Rub (page 171)

1. Prep. Trim the surface fat and silverskin from the tenderloin. Sprinkle with salt and dry brine the tenderloin in the refrigerator for an hour or two.

2. Moisten the meat and liberally apply the Java Rub. Pat firmly to help it adhere.

3. Fire up and cook. Grill the tenderloin over a hot fire, lid up, until an instant-read thermometer registers no more than 135 to 140°F, about 30 minutes, depending on your grill. Slice the tenderloin into ¼-inch-thick disks and serve.

SWEET AND SOUR PORK TENDERLOIN

You will be amazed at how good this riff on the deep-fried Chinese classic is when cooked on the grill, and you will be delighted by how easy it is. By grilling, you get wonderful pork flavor, and the meat remains tender and

TYPES OF PORK CHOPS

There are several types of pork chops you need to know about. They are all easy to overcook and ruin, so be sure to use a thermometer and cook to 135 to 140°F. They respond well to wet brining followed by a reverse sear (see page 48).

BONE-IN LOIN CHOP (AKA RIBEYE)

This comes from the loin muscle that runs along the backbone (*longissimus dorsi*). The meat is very lean. This is the "other white meat" you've heard of, mild and tender because the loin muscle does not get a lot of work. It is usually about 4 inches in diameter, with a curved rib bone attached to the other side.

BONELESS LOIN CHOP

This is the same cut as above, but the rib bone has been removed. Like a chicken breast, it is lean and tender. Sometimes it is slit along the side and folded open like a book, making a butterflied loin chop.

T-BONE OR PORTERHOUSE

Cut from behind the rib cage, this T-shaped bone has a large hunk of loin meat on one side, and on the other side of the bone is a smaller round section of the tenderloin.

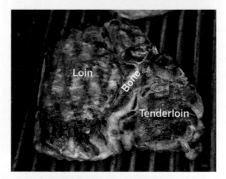

COUNTRY-STYLE RIBS (AKA COUNTRY RIBS, BLADE STEAKS, BLADE CHOPS)

Country-style ribs are really pork chops, not ribs, more meaty and less marbled than real ribs, and should be cooked like chops, not ribs. They are cut from the front end of the baby backs near the shoulder. A tray of country-style ribs in the grocery store might contain a rib or two, but more than likely there will be a section of shoulder blade. Because they vary in size and thickness, they are hard to cook to an even doneness. They often contain large chunks of fat and gristle.

moist. Grilling fresh pineapple to caramelize the surface makes it infinitely more interesting than just tossing in canned pineapple and warming it. Oh, and unlike the fried stuff, leftovers are good straight from the fridge in the wee hours.

MAKES *4 servings*

TAKES *1 hour*

- 1 pork tenderloin (about 2 pounds; see Notes)
- Kosher salt
- 1 large onion, halved through the equator
- 1 large red, orange, or green bell pepper, stemmed, seeded, and halved
- 3 round, ½-inch-thick slices fresh pineapple
- Vegetable oil
- 4 servings of rice
- ¼ cup unsalted cashews
- ½ cup D.C. Mumbo Sauce (page 195)
- 2 tablespoons chopped fresh chives, for garnish (optional)
- 2 tablespoons chopped green onions, for garnish (optional)

1. Prep. Trim off any excess fat and silverskin from the pork. Slice the tenderloin in half lengthwise. Salt the meat and dry brine in the refrigerator for an hour or two before cooking.

2. Coat the onion, bell pepper, and pineapple with a thin layer of oil so they won't stick.

3. Start the rice on the stove top and cook according to instructions on the package.

4. Put the cashews in a dry frying pan without oil and, over medium heat, toast them until they start to get brown spots.

5. Fire up. Set up a grill with two zones and get the indirect zone to about 325°F.

6. Cook. Start grilling the onion, pineapple, and bell pepper over the hot part of the grill with the lid closed. Keep a close watch so nothing burns. Turn the food during grilling and take the pieces off when they are limp and grill-marked.

7. Put the meat on the direct-heat side and cook with the lid open. While the pork is cooking, chop the grilled veggies and pineapple into bite-size chunks. Put them in a pot or metal bowl on the indirect part of the grill to stay warm. Warm the sauce on the side.

8. Remove the meat when it hits 140°F and slice it in half again. Bundle the quarters and slice across them to make ½-inch chunks. Add the meat to the pot with the chopped veggies and pineapple and stir everything together.

9. Serve. Place a scoop of rice on each plate, top with the meat, pineapple, and peppers, and drizzle the warm sauce over everything. Garnish with the optional chives and green onions. Add the toasted cashews right before serving so the nuts don't get soggy.

NOTES: I strongly recommend that you resist the temptation to use another cut of pork. You can, however, substitute chicken or shrimp. If you are making this with chicken, the internal temperature must be 160°F. If you use shrimp, pull them off the grill as soon as they turn pink and the centers are opaque.

If you want a little heat, add a poblano chile to the cooked veggies or garnish with a finely chopped jalapeño or two.

PESTO-CRUSTED PORK LOIN ROAST

Pork loin is the "prime rib" of the hog, the same muscle that runs through the ribeye. When people talk about eating high off the hog, this is the cut they mean. The problem with pork loin is that it is so lean that if you let your guard down and overcook it the tiniest bit, you get cottonmouth. It is also a relatively bland meat, so it can use a little pick-me-up. I like to inject it with a brine and coat it with an oil-based rub, in this case, pesto, which we make and freeze every August. The oil helps reduce evaporation slightly and adds a small amount of fat. Then I wrap it with parchment paper, which is porous and lets a little smoke through (do not use wax paper), and tie it with kitchen string.

MAKES *8 servings*

TAKES *3¼ hours to make the injection and to rest the meat after injecting, and about 1 hour to cook*

- 6 pounds center-cut pork loin
- ⅓ cup Pork Brine Injection (page 162)
- ½ cup Pesto (page 189)
- 3 tablespoons high-quality olive oil
- ¾ cup Smoked Bone Broth (optional; page 220)

1. Prep. About 3 hours before cooking, trim off all fat and silverskin and inject the meat with the brine. Insert the needle into the top of one end, and walk your way from end to end, inserting the needle as deep as you can before pushing the plunger down. Gradually pull the needle out to distribute the brine as evenly as possible. Gently massage the meat to work the fluid around inside the meat. Some may squirt out. Refrigerate for 3 hours.

2. Mix the pesto with the oil and slather it all over the meat. (The pesto already has oil in it, but it is easier to apply and sticks better with a little extra.)

3. Wrap the meat in a single layer of parchment paper and tie it closed with butcher's twine.

4. Fire up. Get your smoker up to 225°F or set up the grill for two-zone cooking and shoot for about 225°F on the indirect side. Add wood for smoke. You want heavy white smoke so that some will get through the parchment paper wrapper.

5. Cook. Place the meat on the indirect side and smoke it until an instant-read thermometer inserted into the center registers 135 to 140°F.

6. Serve. Cut the twine, unwrap the pork carefully, and cut it into ½-inch-thick slices to serve. If you have some Smoked Bone Broth in the freezer, you have the perfect gravy. You don't need to do anything to it, just heat it and drizzle it over the meat, or mix in a little pesto if you like.

STUFFED PORK LOIN ROAST

Another way to combat the propensity of loin to dry out is to stuff it. You can use a wide range of stuffings, from classic bread stuffing to herbs and spices to dried fruits, and beyond. Because the stuffing layer is thinner than in a stuffed pork chop, the meat won't overcook.

You can also make a sauce for this but it shouldn't be necessary. I like to make a piccata-style sauce, something not too sweet, or simply a little Smoked Bone Broth (page 220).

MAKES *12 servings*

TAKES *45 minutes preparation time, 2 hours cooking time*

> 1 (6-pound) fresh bone-in center-cut pork loin roast
>
> 1½ tablespoons kosher salt
>
> 1 pound your favorite bread stuffing (see Notes)
>
> ½ cup dried cranberries (see Notes)
>
> 2 tablespoons Simon & Garfunkel Rub (page 168)
>
> Vegetable oil

1. Prep. Trim off all surface fat and silverskin from the pork. Sprinkle the meat with salt and rub it in. Let it sit in the fridge for 3 hours or so.

2. Make the stuffing.

3. Insert a long, sharp knife into the meat about ¾ inch up the side of the meat. Work the knife along at the same height, unrolling the meat until you have a long ¾-inch slab of loin, as shown below.

4. Place the stuffing on the cut portion of the meat and sprinkle with the dried cranberries. Try to level it from edge to edge, front to back. In the picture (opposite, bottom) the pork has been spread with pesto stuffing.

5. Roll the top of the meat over the stuffing and into a log shape. Tie the roast with butcher's twine every inch or so. Coat the rolled and tied meat with the rub.

6. Fire up. Get your smoker up to 225°F or set up the grill for two-zone cooking and shoot for about 225°F on the indirect side.

7. Cook. Lightly oil the meat and add the meat and the wood for smoking at the same time. Go easy on the wood. You only want a hint of smoke. Roast for about 2 hours, until the meat registers 135 to 140°F—the exact cooking time will depend on how thick it is, what is in the stuffing, and how steady you can keep the temperature. Plan on 30 minutes per inch of thickness at the widest part.

8. Serve. Remove the roast from the grill and slice it into ½-inch-thick pieces.

NOTES: Make the bread stuffing extra moist. Prepare extra, so you can cook and serve some on the side. You can substitute raisins or dried cherries for the cranberries if you prefer. Sometimes I soak the cranberries in rum and microwave them for about 30 seconds to speed the soaking. (I then drink the rum that has not been absorbed.) Occasionally I make a stuffing of whatever dried fruits I have on hand and mix in some chopped walnuts or pecans, some melted butter, and some sweet red wine.

WET-CURED HAM

By far the most popular hams in the United States are wet-cured hams, most of which have been injected with a cure and then precooked. The cure usually has salt, sugar, and spices, as well as sodium nitrite and sodium nitrate, and the cooking often includes smoking. This was a method developed for preserving large hunks of meat like hog rumps long before refrigeration was invented.

Wet-cured hams are pinkish purple in color from the preservatives, often have a sweet glaze baked on, and are frequently put on a lathe where a blade can spiral-cut them. This makes carving them a snap. They usually come in shrink-wrap, and if it says "cooked" on the package, you could eat it cold right out of the bag. But cured hams are better served warm, with a sweet glaze to counterbalance the saltiness from the brine.

Standard cooking technique on the package and in all the cookbooks says to heat it at 325°F until it reaches 140°F. But that is a recipe for dry meat. If you take a little care, you can really step up the flavor on the grill (and it works better on a grill than a smoker). In fact, the same method works fine indoors.

First, try to find a ham that has been trimmed properly. You don't want skin or a thick fat layer. Nobody will eat them, and they don't add moisture or any flavor to the meat (see page 45). You can use the glaze that is packed in with the ham, but I chuck it and make my own instead.

If you play it right, there will be leftovers, and that means sandwiches with South Carolina Mustard Sauce (page 177), fritattas, Hoppin' John beans, eggs Benedict, Hawaiian pizza, ham salad, egg McMuffins, and a bone for split pea soup.

MAKES *8 servings*

TAKES *10 minutes to prep, 15 to 20 minutes per pound to cook (timing will vary depending on the thickness of the ham)*

- 1 cup Grand Marnier Glaze (page 185)
- 1 cup chicken broth
- 1 (8-pound) precooked bone-in wet-cured ham

1. Prep. In a small saucepan, combine ¼ cup of the Grand Marnier Glaze with the chicken broth to make the mop. Whisk over medium heat until the glaze has dissolved. Refrigerate the mop and the remaining glaze. The glaze and the mop can be made days in advance.

2. If the skin has not been removed from the ham, remove it. Trim off almost all the fat, leaving no more than ⅛ inch. If there is a glaze already on the meat, rinse it off. This glaze is better (I guarantee there is no Grand Marnier in store-bought). If the ham is spiral-sliced, let some water get into the sliced areas to help mitigate moisture loss.

3. Fire up. Set up the grill for two-zone cooking and shoot for about 225°F on the indirect side or get your smoker up to 225°F. This method works best on a grill because you'll need direct heat at the end.

4. Cook. Place the meat in the smoker or on the indirect side of the grill, cut side down. Add a handful or two of wood for smoke. You do not need much since the meat has been smoked once already. Close the lid and smoke-roast for about 30 minutes. Tear off about 5 feet of aluminum foil (if you have heavy-duty foil, that's better). Fold it in half to make it about 2½ feet in length.

5. Put the ham, cut side down, on the foil, making sure you don't puncture the foil with the bone. Pour ½ cup of the mop over the meat and seal it in the foil, making it look like a giant candy kiss. Tightly crimp the seams. You don't want the mop to leak. This technique helps the ham cook faster by generating a little steam, which transfers energy faster. Put the wrapped ham back over indirect heat at about 225°F. If you have a leave-in meat thermometer, insert it now through the foil into the fat end, not so low that the mop will leak; the tip should be about 1 inch away from the bone.

6. When the meat hits about 125°F, open the foil and paint on some of the remaining mop. Leave the foil open to catch drips. Close the lid and roast for about 10 minutes and mop again. Keep mopping every 10 minutes. This cools the meat so it warms more slowly and sets a base for the glaze to come.

7. While the mop is setting, get out the remaining glaze and warm it on the hot side of the grill, the grill's side burner, or indoors on the stove top. Lift the ham out of the foil and pour any drippings into the saucepan with the glaze.

8. Remove the thermometer and move the ham to the hot side of the grill, laying it on a curved side. Paint it with the glaze. Leave the lid open and stand right there, making sure the glaze does not burn. Don't walk away, even to get a beer.

9. Let the glaze sizzle, but not blacken. You are just trying to caramelize the sugars and develop more flavor. After 3 to 4 minutes, roll the ham a bit and keep rolling it every 3 to 4 minutes until all sides have sizzled except the flat side. By now the temperature should have risen to 135 to 140°F. Go ahead and check if you want, but trust me, it's there.

10. Serve. Blend together any leftover mop and glaze to make a sauce, thin it with water or more chicken stock to sauce consistency, put it in a pot, bring it to a boil, and immediately turn it off. Pour the sauce into a gravy boat and move the ham to a cutting board, bare side down. Carve it by slicing in from the sides toward the bone in the center of the top. Then slice down along the bone to release the slices. Serve and spoon a little sauce over the meat.

GRAND MARNIER– GLAZED HAM STEALS

Talk about your quick-and-dirty yet glamorous Tuesday night dinner! Ham steaks are precooked, so all you need to do is heat them to 135 to 140°F, hit them with a sweet glaze to balance the saltiness, and serve in 20 minutes.

MAKES *2 servings*

TAKES *20 minutes*

> 2 precooked ham steaks
> ⅓ cup Grand Marnier Glaze (page 185)

1. Fire up. Preheat the grill on medium, direct heat.

2. Cook. Place the ham steaks on the grill until they get some grill marks. Flip and paint the cooked sides with the glaze. Flip the ham steaks and paint again. Flip, paint, flip, paint, and serve when they hit 135°F.

SMOKED BONE BROTH

Nothing is more satisfying on a chilly day than a cup of rich homemade soup made with bone broth. Soups and stocks are easy to make, and they use things you might otherwise discard, such as bones, onion skins, celery leaves, and mushroom stems. Homemade broth is so much better than store-bought. The secret is in the bones. The marrow is full of collagen and flavor. When your homemade broth chills, the collagen turns it into a gel. The canned stuff doesn't. It's just flavored water.

This mother recipe improves on the classic technique of roasting the bones by smoke-roasting them. It calls for pork bones, but you can just as easily make it with beef bones or chicken bones. Next time you're at the grocery, just ask the butcher for 5 pounds of bones. You might get them for free.

When you are done, you can store the broth in the refrigerator for 2 weeks, or freeze it for 6 months. I like to freeze it in an ice cube tray,

and then put the frozen cubes of broth in a zipper-top bag. Whenever I want to enrich a sauce or rice or couscous, I grab a handful of cubes.

MAKES *2 quarts*

TAKES *5 to 6 hours*

    5 pounds pork bones (see Note)
    4 carrots, peeled
    3 onions, chopped into chunks, skins and all
    2 celery stalks, plus leaves
    3 garlic cloves
    4 button mushrooms, coarsely chopped, stems and all
    1 teaspoon kosher salt
    1 tablespoon freshly ground black pepper
    2 teaspoons sugar
    2 tablespoons grated fresh ginger (optional)

1. Fire up. Start by firing up your smoker to 325°F or set up your grill to 325°F on the indirect side. Add wood and get some white smoke rolling.

2. Cook. Toss the bones, carrots, onions, celery, and garlic onto a sheet pan. Put the pan in the smoke for about 1 hour. Roll the ingredients around during roasting so that the bones and veggies brown on all sides.

3. After an hour, the bones should be nice and brown and the veggies limp. Transfer them to a large stockpot and add 1½ gallons water. Bring to a boil and then immediately reduce the heat to a simmer. Add the rest of the ingredients. Simmer for 4 to 5 hours, or until the liquid has reduced by half. Strain the broth into a bowl and discard the solids.

4. Use a gravy separator or a large flat spoon to discard the fat from the surface. Taste the broth and adjust the seasonings. In fact, don't just taste it, pour yourself a steaming mug. Or make the next recipe. Or freeze it in an ice cube tray so you can use it later.

NOTE: Much of the flavor here comes from the bone marrow. If your butcher can cut the bones into 3- to 4-inch chunks and the heavy femurs lengthwise, more of the good stuff will get into the broth.

MOMOFUKU-INSPIRED RAMEN BOWL

David Chang is a celebrity chef with a deep interest in food science. He started with Momofuku Noodle Bar, featuring fresh ramen. The restaurant became all the rage in New York City and rapidly expanded into an empire with outposts from Toronto to Sydney.

You may think of ramen as dehydrated noodles in a packet with some sort of mysterious flavor powder eaten in dormitories. But in Asia, ramen means fresh noodles, rich stocks, herbs, and meats. You can prepare the broth and meats for this recipe days in advance.

MAKES *4 large bowls*

TAKES *8 hours*

> 3 pounds trimmed pork shoulder
> ¾ pound pork belly in a whole solid slab, not sliced (see Notes)
> 2 teaspoons kosher salt, plus more for broth
> 2 teaspoons freshly ground black pepper
> 2 teaspoons garlic powder
> 2 teaspoons onion powder
> 2 quarts Smoked Bone Broth (page 220)
> 6 large button mushrooms, sliced
> 1 pound fresh or dried ramen noodles (see Notes)
> 4 large pasteurized eggs (see Notes)
> 4 green onions, thinly sliced

> 4 (4-inch-square) pieces nori (see Notes)
> 4 radishes, thinly sliced
> 1 jalapeño, thinly sliced
> ½ cup chopped fresh cilantro

1. Prep. Trim any excess fat from the pork shoulder and cut it into fist-size chunks. Leave the belly whole. Sprinkle both the chunks and the belly with the salt, black pepper, garlic powder, and onion powder.

2. Fire up. Set up your grill or smoker for smoking and shoot for 225°F. Add wood for smoke.

3. Cook. Put all the pork in the smoker and place a pan with 1 inch of water beneath the meat to catch the drippings. Cook the shoulder to an internal temperature of 203°F, 4 to 6 hours. The belly will be done by then. Remove the meat from the smoker.

4. Taste the drippings from the smoked meats. If they are too thin, boil them down to a nice rich consistency. Heat the broth to a simmer and add the drippings and the mushrooms.

5. From here on you want to move quickly so ingredients don't get too cold. Shred the pork shoulder with

Bear Paws (see page 109) or forks. Slice the pork belly into ¼-inch-thick squares. Set aside.

6. Fill a 1-gallon pot with water and bring to a boil. Add 3 or 4 pinches of salt and drop the ramen into the water (discard the seasoning packet if it came with one). Cook just until tender. You do not want to cook the noodles all the way through because they will continue cooking when you move them to the broth. Drain them and hold them in a bowl until needed.

7. While the noodles are cooking, start another pot of water boiling. It must be wide and deep enough to hold four coffee cups or ramekins. Lightly coat the cups or ramekins with cooking oil. Crack each egg into one of the cups and lower it into the pot. It only takes about 5 to 6 minutes for the eggs to cook, depending on the thickness of the cups. They are done when the top of the yolk gets a bit milky.

8. Serve. Now build the bowls. Start by dividing the noodles evenly among four large bowls, preferably wide and shallow. Ladle 1½ to 2 cups of the broth over the noodles in each bowl to cover. Put 3 or 4 tablespoons of shredded pork in each bowl, piling it near one outside edge. Spoon a pile of green onions next to the pork and then lay 2 slices of pork belly near the onions. Put a square of nori near the edge of the bowl and scatter radish slices over the soup. Sprinkle on some jalapeño and cilantro. Finish with a poached egg in the center. Serve the bowls with a spoon for slurping all the goodness and some chopsticks for picking up the noodles and meat.

NOTES: You will probably need to order the pork belly from your grocery store's butcher since she or he probably doesn't keep it in stock.

You don't have to settle for dried ramen. Sun Noodles makes excellent fresh ramen noodles that are sold in some Whole Foods Markets and many Asian food stores. They are far superior to dried.

If you want runny yolks, you should always use pasteurized eggs.

Nori is dried seaweed and it comes in paper-thin sheets. You can buy it at Asian groceries or online.

WHOLE HOG PIG PICKIN'

Practically every society has celebrations and ceremonies surrounding the sharing of a whole beast, and for many, hog is the beast of choice. Before you commit to cooking a whole pig, keep this in mind: It is a lot of work and it is not the best way to cook pork (see page 150).

When it comes to whole hog, there is no place on earth that takes it as seriously as the folks in the eastern parts of North and South Carolina, the Low Country. Many joints feature a "Pig Pickin'," a sumptuous buffet featuring a whole hog on display. You just sidle up to the counter and pluck off whatever you want with tongs. When lunch is over, there is nothing left but bones. Even the skin is gone, because when the hog is cooked the way I describe below, fabulously crisp "cracklins" become an essential part of the feast.

MAKES *This recipe is for a 75-pound hog that has been gutted (dressed). Allowing for shrinkage, trimming excess fat, skin, and bones, it will yield about 35 pounds of edible pork, enough to make about 70 pulled pork sandwiches.*

TAKES *Normally I tell readers to cook most foods at 225°F and to learn how to peg their cookers at that temperature, but if you don't crank the temperature up to 250°F or so, a hog can take forever. That's the temperature recommended by Mike Mills of 17th Street BBQ in Murphysboro, Illinois, and since he has a room full of trophies for his whole hog, you can trust him on that. The cooking time depends on the thickness of the meat, not the weight, but since the thickness is related to the weight, you should go by the weight of the whole hog. Plan on these times, and if Piggy is ready early, you can safely shut down the heat on the pit and hold it there for an hour or two. Just remember, the pig is in control, not you.*

Dressed Weight	Approximate Cooking Time
40 pounds	3.5 hours
75 pounds	9 hours
100 pounds	12 hours
125 pounds	15 hours
150 pounds	18 hours
175 pounds	21 hours
200 pounds	24 hours

SPECIAL TOOLS

1 hog pit and stretcher (see pages 231–234)

1 large empty cooler or refrigerator

1 table, at least 5 feet long

4 plastic tablecloths

2 rolls of paper towels

1 hammer

1 sharp clean hatchet

1 Sawzall (optional, but very helpful)

1 sharp, flexible filleting knife

1 food-grade injector

1 disposable razor or butane lighter

1 digital meat thermometer

1 digital pit thermometer

10 (14-pound) bags charcoal briquets

1 stack newspapers

1 wheelbarrow or grill to start the coals in

1 long-handled shovel

2 pounds hardwood chunks

1 pair heat-resistant gloves

1 watering can filled with water

1 set Bear Paws (see page 109) or large forks for pulling the meat

1 roll heavy-duty aluminum foil

1 sauce brush

Tongs and other serving utensils

Platters

1 bucket of beer

2 lawn chairs

Tunes

1 assistant/pig sitter to help flip the hog and take shifts sitting by the pit through the entire cook in case something goes awry (if you leave it unattended, there will be a grease fire)

1 (75-pound) hog (see page 224)

3 cups kosher salt

1 gallon Pork Brine Injection (page 162)

1 cup Meathead's Memphis Dust (page 167)

2 quarts of your favorite barbecue sauce, preferably homemade, or a selection of three, so people can pick their fave: Columbia Gold (page 177), Lexington Dip (page 179), and/or KC Classic (page 175)

2 cherries or grapes, to replace the eyes

70 buns

20 pounds coleslaw

20 pounds potato salad

ORDERING THE HOG

Many local butchers, even some grocery stores, will special-order a hog for you. If not, find a wholesale meat packer or, best of all, a local farmer who will deliver it fresh and dressed to order. Maybe even a heritage breed. Contact your supplier at least 2 weeks in advance.

A dressed hog has had the belly slit open, the organs and hair removed, and usually the eyelids cut off. In some states, the law dictates that the head be removed. Dressed, it is about 70 percent of its live weight. Keep the dressed weight under 100 pounds because larger animals are hard to lift and flip, even with two people, and they won't fit on the pit design on page 231.

The actual edible meat is 40 to 50 percent of the dressed weight, after trimming fat, shrinkage during cooking, removing bones and some of the skin, and other loss. My method leaves much of the skin edible. Smaller animals have a higher bone-to-meat ratio than large animals, so the yield will be lower. A good rule of thumb is to order 2 pounds per person raw because you'll get about 1 pound of succulent, juicy meat. Most people will not eat more than ½ pound, so you'll have plenty of leftovers for guests to take home. They also freeze nicely.

Ask your butcher if the hog will arrive with head, feet, and tail. Ask if it will arrive frozen. Fresh is best if it was slaughtered within a week or 10 days. Frozen is better than "fresh" that was killed 3 weeks ago. If it is frozen, ask if your butcher will defrost it in his walk-in cooler before you pick it up.

Don't crowd your cooker. Make sure you measure the cooking surface and leave room all around before you order. If necessary, you may have to cut off the head, hocks, and feet at the elbows and knees in order to fit. Don't throw them away. Smoked hocks and trotters

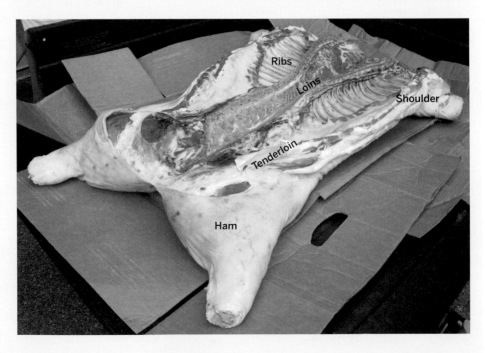

can really put split pea soup and stews over the top. And the cheeks (jowls) are a treat.

Ask your butcher to cut through the breastbone right up to the hair on its chinny chin chin so the animal can be butterflied and splayed open flat. Have him or her bust the hip sockets so the hind legs lie flat, split the spine down the middle, and remove the spinal cord so you don't have to do it. When you get it home, make sure all stray hairs are shaved with a disposable razor or burned off with a lighter.

If you aren't going to cook the pig immediately, see if your butcher will keep it cold for you until the day you plan to start cooking. Plan ahead, because many butchers are closed on Sunday. But if you plan to serve on Sunday, you need to start prep and cooking on Saturday. If your butcher cannot hold it for you, make sure you have a spare refrigerator large enough for the whole carcass or a large ice chest with plenty of ice. As a last resort, scrub and disinfect the bathtub with bleach and cover the hog with ice water.

Here's my own standard order: "I want a whole dressed hog, about 75 pounds, fresh killed within a week of delivery, never frozen, skin on, hair scalded off, and head, ears, trotters, and tail on. Please cut through the backbone and breastbone and crack the hip joints so it will lie flat. Please remove the spinal cord. Save me the liver, kidneys, tongue, and heart, on the side. And do you deliver?"

FIRE UP

I'm going to assume you don't have a big hog cooker in your backyard and that you will be building something like my design on page 231, so my instructions are for that device.

Plan on at least an hour to get the temperature dialed in on your pit. Start at least 6 chimneys full of coals in a grill or wheelbarrow or on the ground. When they are covered in a thin layer of ash, shovel them off to the side of the pit, but never under the space where the hog will lie. You want to cook this baby with indirect heat. Put a few extra coals in the four corners so the thick hams and shoulders get a bit more heat. You can use hardwood instead of charcoal, but you need to burn it down to glowing embers. Don't put raw logs on the fire because they create too much smoke.

Get the pit up to 250°F. Start with the intake vents open and put a stone under the lid so you create a chimney effect where hot air and smoke can escape and draw in oxygen. Set a probe on the cooking grate in the center and walk away for at least 30 minutes. If it is running cool, open the intake vents at the bottom and put a larger stone under the lid so the draft pulls in more oxygen. If that doesn't work, light more coals and add them. You can just throw in unlit coals, but the temperature will stabilize faster with fully engaged coals. If it is running hot, close the intake vents, but not all the way, and always leave some leaks around the lid for smoke to escape. You need draft or your fire will die and soot will coat your meat.

PREP

Cover your worktable with a plastic tablecloth. Put two more plastic tablecloths under the table to protect the ground. There will be splatters and spills. Wear old clothes and an apron.

Place the stretcher that you will use to carry the meat to the cooker on the table, and place Miss Piggy belly down on the stretcher.

As much as I like the shiny lacquered look of the competition hogs like the one by the team from The Shed, on page 222, the skin is leathery and not very good eating. I prefer the blistered, crackling, Cheeto-textured skin that Jackie Hite gets (as shown below, with mustard BBQ sauce) at his Bar-B-Q in Batesburg-Leesville, South Carolina. It ain't pretty, but my guests love munching on it, and I chop some of it up and sprinkle it on the meat.

To get that texture, wet the skin thoroughly. Don't be shy. Then take kosher salt and generously sprinkle it all over, about 2 tablespoons per square foot. Much of it will fall off during the rest of the prep and the cooking.

If your hog arrived with the rib cage connected at the chest, you can cut it open by extending the belly cut with a hatchet and hammer, a Sawzall, a handsaw, a cleaver, pruning shears, or a heavy chef's knife. Cut slightly off center. It is easier to get through the cartilage between the breastbone and the ribs than it is to split the breastbone. (Sam Jones of the Skylight Inn in Ayden, North Carolina, splits a hog's breastbone with a hatchet and hammer in the photo at right.)

Now you need to lay open the chest cavity by pushing the two sides apart. Put some weight behind the effort. To make the hog lie flat for even cooking,

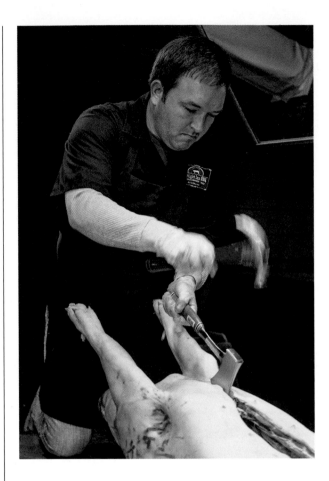

you need to use your hatchet to split the backbone right down the middle from the first rib below the shoulders all the way down to the hams.

The spinal cord will be in one or both sides of the spine bones if it hasn't already been removed by the butcher. Remove it with your fingers or a knife and discard it. Then bust the hip socket so the hind legs lie flat. The hind legs, the hams, are the thickest pieces of meat, and they determine how long the hog must cook.

Remove the skin from the thighs so you can get more rub on the hams, build bark, and speed cooking. I use a trick I learned from Sun Wah BBQ, a Chinese restaurant in Chicago. Put some cuts into the hams, about 4 inches long and 1 inch deep and about 2 inches apart, as shown opposite page, top left. This

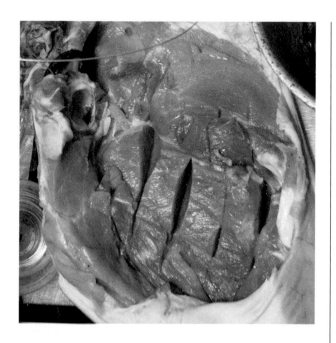

heat and seasoning. Trim jagged edges from the belly flaps. The picture below shows what a hog looks like when it is prepped by Mike Mills (note that he leaves in the whole rib cage).

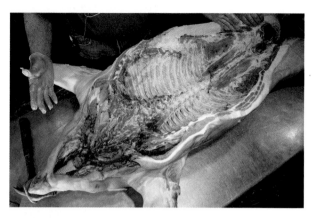

will help them cook faster, and that keeps the other parts of the animal from overcooking. It also creates more surface for seasoning and bark. (I wouldn't do this in a competition—it's too radical for the judges.)

Now you want to get in there and remove the membrane that wraps around the abdominal cavity and covers the ribs. This is the pleura, and it can be very chewy. Underneath the pleura, you want to trim off any silverskin and fat cap so there is plenty of bare meat exposed. Remove any veins, nerves, or glands (which look like marble-size white lumps). With your hands, make a gap between the three or four ribs that cover the shoulder meat. Clean out any fat and silverskin down in there so bare meat can be seen. Save the fat.

Now separate the ribs from the spine by running your knife at their junction. A Sawzall is a nice tool for this. This will help you lay the animal out flat. Cut the rib cage in half lengthwise and leave the curved baby backs, the part that was attached to the spine, in there to protect the loins, and remove the spareribs and freeze them for cooking another day. Doing so leaves the bacon and the side meat open to the

INJECTING AND RUBBING THE CAVITY

As much as I admire simplicity of the old-school Skylight Inn style, with no seasoning in the cavity, not even salt and pepper, I like to add interest by injecting a flavored brine, covering the exposed meat with a spice rub to build a crusty bark, and, just before it is finished, painting the meat with a thin coat of shiny sauce, as much for show as for flavor. I never use so much of anything that I mask the natural taste of the pork—just enough to add a few instruments to the orchestra.

The salt in the brine helps protein hold on to moisture during cooking, the liquids increase moisture and offset evaporation somewhat, and the extra flavor and sugar fight the bane of whole hogs: blandness.

Flip Babe onto her back. With a meat injector, squeeze as much brine in there as you can, poking the needle between the ribs several times to get down into the shoulders and loins, as caterer Phil Wingo is doing in the photo on page 228. Don't poke holes in the skin—inject from the inside of the cavity. Stick the needle in deep and slowly back it out,

injecting as you go. Get the hams, bacon, tenderloins, neck, even the cheeks. Some of the brine will leak out. Wipe it up with paper towels, making an effort to wipe out any bone dust, slivers, and scraps of meat and fat, too. Then dry the surface.

Sprinkle Meathead's Memphis Dust all over, lightly covering the meat. Work the rub down into the slits in the hams, the gap between the spine and the ribs, and the gap between the ribs and the shoulders.

Cover the ears and tail with foil to prevent them from burning. Finally, pop out the eyeballs with a spoon. You can leave the eyeballs in and try to sucker somebody into eating them, but if you do, expect reprisals somewhere, someday, when your back is turned.

NOW LET'S COOK THAT SUCKA

Open the pit. With your assistant, sandwich Wilbur into the stretcher, flip him skin side up, and lay him on the cooking surface. Make sure the handles of the stretcher are hanging outside the sides of the pit and that none of the flesh is directly over the coals. If some is, move him around and push the coals aside or insert a plywood heat shield, larger than the carcass, between the flesh and the flame. (The heat shield is described in detail on page 233.)

Insert a good digital meat thermometer probe into the deepest portion of one of the hams and run the cable outside the pit. Put another probe on the stretcher next to the hog to monitor the pit temperature.

Toss a fist-size chunk of dry wood on each pile of coals. Close the lid, discard the contaminated table-cloths, pull up a lawn chair, crank the tunes, and pour a drink. You have a 9- to 12-hour wait.

Keep a close eye on the proceedings. Don't leave the side of the pig for any longer than it takes to get a beer. Dripping fat can cause a grease fire that can easily engulf the whole hog and incinerate it in minutes.

If you get big flames, douse them with a squirt gun or watering can. Try to keep ash from flying onto the meat when you squirt, and try not to extinguish the coals. If the fire gets out of control, get the meat off pronto.

When the smoke starts to dwindle, toss another chunk of wood in each corner of the pit. That's it for the wood. Too much can ruin the meat.

After about an hour, or as soon as you notice the temperature starting to drop, start another bag of coals on the side, and when they're ready, shovel them in. You want to try to keep the temperature as steady as possible. That's tricky. Keep adding pre-lit coals every hour or so as necessary. Watch the meat on the underside. You want it dark golden, but not mahogany yet.

If the meat looks like it might be ready to burn, lift the hog up and insert the heat shield. There is no need to spray, spritz, or mop the hog. You want the skin to get dry and crunchy, and you want the meat to develop a nice bark. After about 4 hours, remove the foil from the ears and tail.

After about 6 hours, the temperature of the coolest part of the shoulders and hams should be getting up to 160°F or so. Push the skin on the hams. It should slide a bit and it should be hard and thump when you tap it. It is now time to flip poor Pumbaa. Get your assistant and, if you can, scrounge a few more hands to help, that would be nice. Flipping is a momentous event. Gather the troops and encourage applause. You are now on the home stretch. Have a tall boy.

About 3 hours after you flip, when the temperature in the hams and shoulders hits 185°F, the meat should be getting a nice dark crust and look a lot like pork butt or ribs when you cook them. Test the temperature in several spots. Don't worry about precision. No harm will be done if you go 10°F over. If you

APPROXIMATE TIMETABLE FOR COOKING A 75-POUNDER

A MONTH BEFORE. If you are pouring concrete, start it now so it can cure.

TWO WEEKS BEFORE. Order the hog.

SEVERAL DAYS BEFORE. Build the pit, or clean your pit if you already have one.

THE DAY BEFORE. Pick up the hog and keep it chilled. Do a mental walk-through and dry run. Light a test fire, check the temperatures, and get control over the venting.

6:00 A.M. Final dressing and cleaning of the hog. Prep, inject, and season. Fire up the pit. Aim for 250°F. Drink some strong coffee as you work.

8:00 A.M. Find an assistant/pig sitter and move the pig to the pit, skin side up. Monitor the pit temperature closely and add lit charcoal if the temperature starts declining. Have a Mimosa.

9:00 A.M.–2:00 P.M. Monitor the pit temperature closely, add lit charcoal if the temperature is declining, and check to make sure dinner isn't burning.

10:00 A.M. Remove the foil from the ears and tail.

12:01 P.M. Switch to beer.

2:00 P.M. Six hours into cooking, check the meat temperature, and with some help, flip the hog skin side down if it is ready. Have another brew.

4:00 P.M. Eight hours into cooking, check the meat temperature and paint the entire cavity with one coat of your favorite barbecue sauce. Switch to cocktails.

4:30 P.M. One more coat of sauce.

5:00 P.M. Nine hours in, check the meat temperature, remove the hog if it is ready, and serve dinner! Champagne!

wish, you can shine the meat with a glaze of sauce—just one or two layers applied 15 minutes apart. Or you can serve the meat naked and offer the sauce on the side.

Keep an eye on the skin. There's a lot of fat under it, and if it springs a leak, you could have an inferno. Don't let it burn.

When is it done? It will be done when it is done. As Mills' daughter and business partner Amy Mills says, "We're not baking a cake here." The pig is calling the shots until you've done this a few times. The exact time it takes will depend on a lot of variables: the size of the hog and its breed, age, and weight; the type and amount of charcoal; the reliability of your thermometers; the distance of the meat from the coals; the color of the inside of the pit; the size of the pit; the type of lid; wind; the outside temperature; carryover; and more.

When the pig is ready, put a layer or three of foil on the table. Don't use a plastic tablecloth, as it might melt. Move her to the table skin side down. If you left the head on, insert cherries or grapes in the eye sockets.

FINALLY, LET'S EAT!

You worked hard. You deserve a treat. Some of the choicest bits are the tenderloins, small tapered muscles nestled against the base of the spine. When nobody is looking, eat some. Make sure you sample each of the muscle groups and the skin for "educational purposes." Test the skin. Some parts will be too hard to serve, but the skin on the back and sides should be perfect, loudly crunchy, salty on the outside, and sinfully robust below.

SERVE THE MEAT TO YOUR GUESTS

You can do this in one of two ways.

1. If the skin is rubbery or leathery, don't use it. If it is crunchy and easy to chew, chop up sections of skin and scatter it inside the cavity. Simply put the hog on display and let your guests dig in with forks or tongs, a real "pig pickin.'" This way they can try different muscles and taste the differences.

2. Pull out the ribs and shred the meat with Bear Paws or chop it with cleavers. Mix all the meat together with some chopped skin and some fat from the bacon for moisture, and put it on platters. Many Carolinians insist this is the best way to serve hog because you get all the different muscle flavors and textures mixed together, the crunchy richness of the cracklins, and the last person in line isn't stuck with the lesser cuts.

THE SAUCE

When it comes to sauce, I prefer to serve it on the side in bowls with spoons so people can taste the different meats unadorned and then add sauce if they wish. This way I can also offer several sauces. You can put out buns for sandwiches if you wish or just heap the meat on plates. In many places in the southeast, barbecue sandwiches are served with a mound of sweet-and-sour coleslaw on top whether you ask for it or not. Do not let the meat sit out at room temperature for more than 2 hours. Another option is to put the serving platters on the pit to stay warm.

Be prepared: Before the guests go home, they will want to know when you plan to do it again.

THE PIT

If you want to barbecue a whole hog, you have several options:

1. Hire a pro.
2. Get a portable pit from a rental service.
3. Borrow a portable pit.
4. Buy a portable pit.
5. Build a pit.

If you rent a pit, know that gas pits are really easy to control, and you can still add wood for smoke. Charcoal and wood require nonstop vigilance.

A handful of old-timers like Skylight Inn in Ayden, North Carolina, and Jackie Hite of Bar-B-Q in Batesburg-Leesville, South Carolina, still do it old school, on concrete block pits with log embers for heat. You can do it old school, too, for very little money.

You must cook with indirect heat. Hogs drip a lot of fat. If you have hot coals underneath, you will have charhog. But you don't need anything elaborate. Jackie Hite uses old-school concrete block pits. Nothing fancy, but they make for some superb meat.

On the next page are plans for building your own no-frills pit suitable for a butterflied 75-pound hog. It is designed so it can be a temporary structure, or you can make it permanent. All together, the materials will set you back about $175, plus an extra $75 if you plan to make it a permanent structure.

(continues on page 232)

You can fit a 100-pounder or more on this rig if you cut the head and remove the trotters at the knees and elbows. But don't throw away the head and trotters. Just place them next to the torso. If you plan on cooking larger hogs, you can scale this plan up.

MATERIALS

54 concrete blocks, 16 by 8 by 8 inches (actually 15.75 by 7.75 by 7.75 inches). This will get your hog 24 inches above the embers, and you'll have a row to hold the lid.

2 sheets of ¼-inch plywood, 4- by 8-foot long.

Cut one down to about 44 by 60 inches for the lid, and the other to 20 by 36 inches for the optional heat shield. Scrap will be used to cover the intake vents.

2 rolls of heavy-duty aluminum foil

4 (48-inch) lengths of ⅜-inch rebar. You can use a sheet of expanded metal rather than rebar if you wish.

46-by-72-inch piece of at least 14-gauge non-climbable uncoated fence wire or rabbit wire. Do not use galvanized metal because it can give off noxious gases.

2 1-by-2 boards, each 6 feet long

HOG PIT

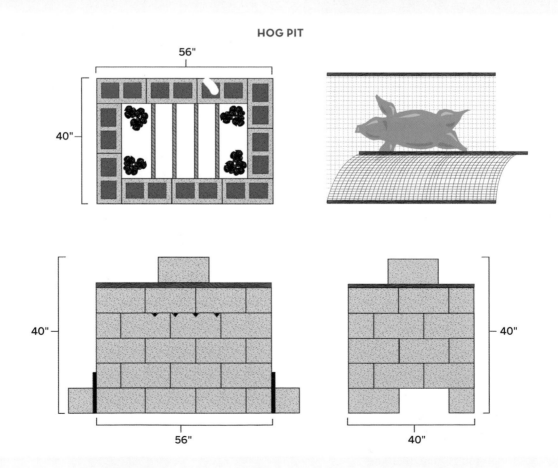

100 (6-inch) bare wire loop ties

2 pieces lightweight sheet metal, about 20 by 10 inches each, for dampers, or you can use baking sheets

OPTIONAL

More rebar to pound into the ground to prevent the blocks from shifting

Fireplace mortar to lock the blocks permanently into place

Lightweight sheet metal (not galvanized), about 44 by 60 inches, for the lid

Lightweight sheet metal (not galvanized), about 30 by 48 inches, for the heat shield

20 (40-pound) bags premixed concrete for a 3-inch-thick slab base

TOOLS

Wire cutters

Level

Hacksaw

Hammer

Chisel

Utility stapler and plenty of staples

Wheelbarrow, steel drum, or charcoal grill to start coals

Shovel

Garden hose or buckets of water or fire extinguisher

TIPS

Keep the pit at least 10 feet from buildings and overhanging trees in case of a grease fire. Keep a fire extinguisher rated for grease on hand. Fire extinguishers rated ABC can handle most everything except combustible metals. Beware: They contain a yellow powder that can damage electrical devices.

Start by clearing a 4-by-5-foot base by removing grass, and prepare an all-dirt or sand base at least 2 inches thick. For a permanent structure, pour a 3-inch-thick concrete slab. If you have a dirt base, you will need to discard some of it when you are done because fat and meat drippings will get into the dirt. If needed, you can buy sand at a hardware store. I recommend lining a dirt pit with heavy-duty aluminum foil for easy cleanup.

Make sure the ground is level. Stack the concrete blocks 4 rows high, 3 full lengths, and then turn 1 block on each course, staggering the blocks so they overlap as in the illustration opposite. Leave out a block on the head and tail side so you can add coals and wood and rake them around. Cover these holes with a board and a concrete block when they are not in use.

Make notches in the fourth course of blocks with a hammer and chisel deep enough to hold the rebar so the next course of blocks will lie flat. Put the rebar in the notches. Don't put the top course of blocks on yet.

THE HEAT SHIELD

A sheet of plywood cut down to 20 by 36 inches will serve as an optional heat shield. If you bank your coals to the sides and corners properly, you may not need it, but I recommend you have it on hand in case something starts to burn or overcook. This goes on top of the rebar and

(continues on page 234)

beneath the stretcher to shield the hog from direct heat.

This size leaves space between the shield and the inside of the pit so hot air can rise alongside the shield and bounce off the lid. You will remove it late in cooking when it is time to crisp the skin. Wrap it in aluminum foil and staple down the foil. Don't worry: It won't burn unless you have a grease fire because your pig sitter fell asleep. If the pit is to be a permanent structure, make your heat shield from sheet metal, preferably aluminum because it won't rust.

THE COVER

Cover the bottom of the plywood lid with foil. If you wish, you can use a sheet metal top instead of plywood.

THE STRETCHER

To carry the hog and hold it in place on the pit, you need to build a stretcher, with two poles for the stretcher bearers and a wire-mesh sling in between for the hog. Nonclimbable fence wire is heavier gauge and sturdier than chicken wire. You can use chicken wire, but if you do, it would be a good idea to use two layers. Make sure the wire is not galvanized or coated with plastic.

Make a sling of the wire wide enough to hang over the edges of the pit by at least 1 foot on either side. Attach two 6-foot lengths of 1-by-2-inch boards for handles with staples and reinforce them with wire loop ties.

SUCKLING PIG: SMALL ENOUGH FOR YOUR GRILL

So you don't have a place to build a pit? You can still do a pig roast and create magical meat with a young pig. Technically, suckling pigs have not been weaned, are less than 2 months old, and weigh less than 25 pounds, but butchers often call anything under 50 pounds a suckling. The muscles haven't toughened yet, and the milk-fed meat is melt-in-your-mouth tender. There is much less fat in proportion to muscle than on a grown hog. But this is important to note: The fat can taste funky to some people, somewhat reminiscent of Brie cheese, because the animal has been mostly milk-fed.

I like to serve this meal caveman style: no knives and forks—just fingers and plenty of paper towels. Flesh fest.

MAKES *10 servings*

TAKES *4 to 5 hours*

1 (25-pound) suckling pig (see Notes)
½ cup kosher salt
¼ cup Simon & Garfunkel Rub (page 168)
2 cherries, grapes, or olives, to replace the eyes
12 garlic cloves, smashed
6 onions, coarsely chopped
2 oranges, sliced
2 lemons, sliced
4 cups loosely packed fresh herbs, such as thyme, oregano, and rosemary
1 small apple, for the mouth
1 pint barbecue sauce (see Notes)

1. Prep. When you order, ask your butcher to make sure to remove all hair and to cut through the breastbone. With a butane lighter or a disposable razor, get rid of any hair or bristles. Rinse the cavity to remove any bone chips. Wet the skin thoroughly and salt both the interior of the pig and the skin. Sprinkle the Simon & Garfunkel Rub onto the bare meat in the cavity. Remove the eyes with a spoon (your butcher may have done this) and replace them with cherries, grapes, or olives.

2. Put the pig on its side and distribute the garlic, onions, citrus slices, and herbs in the cavity. Place a block of wood about the size of the apple in the pig's mouth to keep it open.

3. Fire up. Get the smoker started or set up the grill in a two-zone configuration and get the indirect zone up to about 225°F. You must cook with indirect heat or you will burn the skin and get to meet the fire department.

4. Cook. Roast at 225°F until the temperature in the deep center of the hams is 140°F. Spot-check all over. You don't need to cook it to a higher temperature because the muscles and sinew haven't gotten tough yet. Check the underside regularly to make sure it is not about to burn.

5. You should only need to flip the pig once, after about 2 hours, but if the underside is getting dark, flip more often or consider putting down a layer of foil. Rotate one side 180 degrees if the hot zone is too close to the pig. Depending on its thickness, the pig could be done in 4 hours or less. Exact timing will depend on a lot of variables you cannot control, so have plenty of appetizers and drinks on hand until the pig is ready.

6. Serve. When it is ready, move the pig to a huge platter, scoop the aromatics out of the cavity and discard them, and put the apple in its mouth. Cere-moniously carry it to the serving table still on its side. Unfold it, opening the cavity. Cut through the skin on the hams, put some serving forks or tongs on the

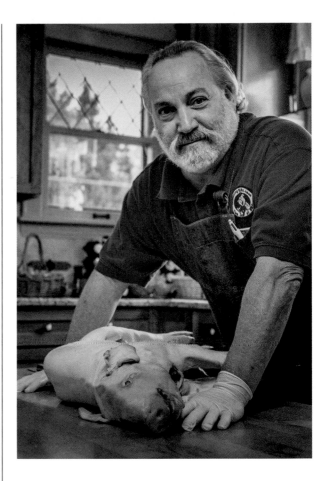

table, and give everyone a plate. Stand back or get trampled.

NOTES: You need a hacksaw with a clean blade to cut through the breastbone if your butcher doesn't do it.

About the sauce: Although I don't like covering this delicate meat with the usual sweet red barbecue sauce (page 175) some people will want it, so have a bowl on hand. My preference is a vinegary Lexington Dip (page 179) or Columbia Gold (page 177).

SUCKLING PORCHETTA

Across Italy they make some of the tastiest pork you can imagine, called *porchetta*. It features golden brown, exquisitely crispy pig skin wrapped around a tender, succulent, juicy, herbed pork loin. The fat layer under the skin melts and bastes the meat while it cooks over a hot wood fire. The concept goes back to the Roman empire, and porchetta is sold everywhere from white tablecloth restaurants to street vendors.

Each region prepares it a little differently. In many areas, porchetta is made from a huge whole hog, with the torso gutted and deboned and then stuffed with herbs, tongue, heart, liver, and kidneys. It is then stitched up and rotisseried in a wood-burning stove over a pan that collects the juices, which are used for basting. The skin is left on, encasing the meat in crunchy cracklins. That's the way it is done in Costana in Umbria, near Assisi, where they have an annual festival to celebrate the dish, the Sagra della Porchetta, in late August. Just south of Rome, the town of Ariccia is to porchetta what Kansas City is to ribs, and commercial producers there ship it all over the country.

Pictured below is a porchetta stitched like a giant football at the Trattoria Aristocampo on the edge of the famous outdoor market, Campo di Fiori, in Rome. The pig comes from a supplier in Ariccia. The skin is as hard as candy, there is a thick layer of molten fat below it, and then tenderloin meat and a stuffing. Think of it as a giant pork sausage.

That's a lot of meat and a lot of fat, so here's a similar recipe made with a 25-pound suckling pig. When you order your pig, ask your butcher to remove all hair and split the breastbone and spine. A 25-pound pig yields almost 7 pounds of porchetta plus 2 quarts of silky bone broth (see page 220).

A plastic tablecloth is a good idea to reduce cleanup. You might need a clean hacksaw blade to cut through the breastbone. A cleaver or a sturdy chef's knife comes in handy for cutting through the spine. You'll also need a thin flexible sharp filleting knife, butcher's twine or kite string, and two large bowls.

MAKES *12 to 14 servings*

TAKES *6 to 8 hours*

> 1 (25-pound) suckling pig
> Kosher salt
> 1/3 cup olive oil
> 2 large onions, coarsely chopped
> 1 pound plain crusty bread, chopped into
>   1/2-inch chunks
> 1/4 cup fresh rosemary
> 1/4 cup fresh oregano
> 2 tablespoons paprika
> 8 garlic cloves, minced or pressed
> Smoked Bone Broth (page 220; optional)

1. Prep. Lay a plastic tablecloth on your work surface. Put two large bowls on the tablecloth, one for meat and one for bones, skin, and trim.

2. Run your hand over the skin of the pig. If you feel any hair or stubble, remove it with a razor blade. You can also use a butane lighter to burn off the hair, but it will stink.

3. If it has not already been cleaved, cut through the breastbone, using a clean hacksaw blade, tin snips, or a cleaver (Picture 1). If your butcher hasn't done so, cut the ribs off the spine with a heavy knife (2). Set them aside for making broth.

4. Pull the spine out (3). Salvage any meat and put it in the meat bowl. Discard the spine. You don't want spinal cord in your broth.

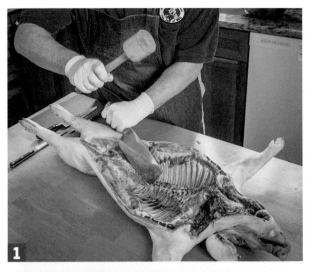

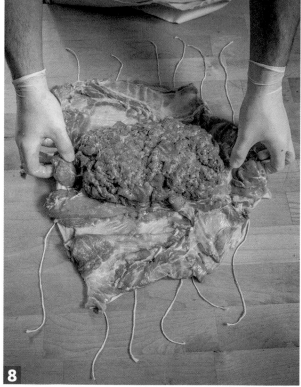

5. Remove the tenderloins. Set them aside in the meat bowl. You will use them for the stuffing.

6. Remove the shoulders, front legs, and head by cutting through the shoulder joints (4). Remove the hind legs by cutting through the hip joints. Remove the hocks by cutting off the feet at the ankles. Pull the skin off the front and hind quarters (5).

7. Put the skin, bones, and hocks in the trim bowl. Remove all the meat from the bones in the hams and shoulders and put it in the meat bowl. Skin the head and get all the meat you can off it. There's some tasty stuff in the cheeks and the tongue is good, but you have to remove the skin from it. The ears are rich in collagen, so set them aside in the trim bowl.

8. Look closely at the exposed meat on the remaining carcass. Cut out any bits of bone, veins, or glands (6).

9. Salt the interior generously. Get this done now so the salt can work its way into the meat. Chop the meat in the meat bowl into hunks 1 to 2 inches thick. Add the oil, onions, and bread. Mix in the rosemary, oregano, paprika, garlic, and about ½ teaspoon salt (7).

WASTE NOTHING

You can make good use of all the trimmings. You can freeze them for later or, if you have room in your smoker, smoke-roast them now.

Use the bones, ears, snout, skin, and the other trimmings to make Smoked Bone Broth (see page 220). The trotters can be smoked and used to amp up a split pea soup.

10. Lay down strings every 2 inches and place the center of the pig on them (8). Mound the meat mixture toward the center, roll it up, and tie it up with string. Tie off the ends.

11. Wet the skin thoroughly with a clean cloth or sponge. Soak it. Then sprinkle salt all over it, about 1 tablespoon per square foot (9). Don't worry, a lot of it will fall or melt off, but the salty water helps break down the leathery skin and turn it into crunchy cracklins.

12. Fire up and cook. Get the smoker or grill preheated to 325°F in the indirect zone. Add wood for smoke and put the porchetta into the smoker, seam side up.

13. When the porchetta reaches about 150°F in the center, sear the skin by putting it on a griddle in the smoker or, better still, move it to a hot grill and, with the lid open, sear one side, roll it 90 degrees, sear, and repeat until all sides are dark brown and crispy and the interior is 160°F. You need to cook it that high because you have essentially made a giant sausage. But don't worry, it will not be dry.

14. Serve. Snip off the strings and cut slices about ¾ inch thick. No gravy is needed, but if you happen to have a little Smoked Bone Broth, pour a little on the slices after you serve.

9

BEEF

STEAKS

How do prime steakhouses get their steaks perfect every time, with a sizzling, dark, flavorful crust, cooked edge to edge on the inside, tender and juicy with big, bold, beefy flavor?

The keys to success are the right cuts, the right grades, the seasoning, and matching the cooking temperature to the thickness of the meat. Here's how to raise your game to steakhouse level and have your guests reeling in deliria.

THE CUTS

Prime steakhouses serve the best cuts, usually from the area along the spine of the steer. They are also the most expensive: ribeyes, porterhouses, T-bones, strip steaks, and cuts from the tenderloin such as the chateaubriand and filet mignon. You can make darn tasty meals from the sirloin, round, flank, and other cuts, but these muscles are not as tender.

My preference is the ribeye. It is the best cut for flavor and tenderness combined. Some argue in favor of the strip steak, but that is the same muscle as the ribeye, the *longissimus dorsi*, so that argument is like debating which side of *Abbey Road* is better. A lot of folks prefer meat from the tenderloin because it is more tender, but tenderloins are also leaner than ribeyes, so they don't have the flavor that fat brings to the party.

THE GRADES

I refer to the best steakhouses as prime steak-houses because USDA Prime is the grade of meat they serve. USDA Prime beef has a lot of marbling—thin hairline threads of fat—and it accounts for only about 3 percent of all beef sold. You won't find USDA Prime in discount steak-houses in mall parking lots or in most grocery stores.

Wagyu is another upscale grade of beef. It comes from a special breed of cattle with roots in Japan that produces extremely marbled meat (see photo, right). It is even harder to find than Prime.

Rarest of all is genuine Japanese Kobe, which is almost *too* fatty and can cost as much as a small car. Real Kobe comes only from Japan. If the meat comes from the U.S., it is Wagyu.

The next grade down from USDA Prime is USDA Choice. Choice is common in grocery stores, but not all Choice is the same. There are actually several levels of Choice whose names never show up on the label. Don't just grab any old steak from the meat counter. Ask your butchers for help. Explain that you have a spe-cial dinner and you want the best-looking cuts they can find. They will often look in the back room for a particularly nice piece of meat or custom-cut exactly what you want.

SEASONING

Some prime steakhouses use a secret mix of herbs and spices, the most famous being Lawry's Seasoned Salt. But many prime steak-houses use only salt and pepper, and some use only salt. I've never seen a prime steakhouse marinate steak. Marinades mask the meat's

Boneless Wagyu Ribeye

natural flavors, and a wet surface creates steam and prevents crust formation.

The only prep you need to do is dry brine by salting the steaks at least an hour or two before cooking. I salt in the morning and cook in the evening. If you wish to jazz it up a bit, use my Butcher Block Seasoning (page 173). And if you can cook over wood, real smoke is a seasoning you just can't get from a jar.

MATCHING COOKING TEMPERATURE AND THICKNESS

The best temperature for cooking thick steaks is different than the recommended tempera-ture for thin steaks. This is a crucial concept. Because you want a dark but not burned crust and even doneness from top to bottom on the inside, you have to choose the right tempera-ture. The thicker the steak, the lower the cook-ing temperature. Prime steakhouses cook the same meats from the same supplier at the same thickness day in and day out, so they have their process finely tuned. Our backyard grills aren't so manageable or predictable, and they are sub-ject to weather and other variables. But there is a nifty technique that you can use for thick steakhouse steaks that will give you incredible results: the reverse sear (see page 48).

For this technique, cuts 1½ to 2 inches thick are best, but most grocery stores don't cut steaks that thick. I typically tell my butcher I want "boneless ribeyes, from the center of the roast, with the most marbling you can find, 1½ inches thick, and please try to make all steaks about the same thickness."

Plan on 12 to 16 ounces per adult for bone-in steak and 8 to 12 ounces per adult for boneless steak. There will be trim and drip loss. If there are leftovers, they can make an appearance on a sandwich or salad the next night.

As we have discussed (see page 53), medium-rare, about 130°F, is the optimum doneness for tender and juicy steaks. Sadly, many home-grilled steaks are only medium-rare in a small band in the center because the rest of the interior overcooks while we are browning the exterior. The solution is to use two cooking temperatures, one for the interior and one for the exterior, and that's the core concept in the reverse sear. You want the surface to get scorching hot so it will brown quickly without transferring heat to the center. When you cook hot and fast with the lid off and flipping often, the heat works mostly on the surface of the underside and doesn't have time to migrate deep into the meat. When you flip, the heat bleeds off into the air and doesn't overcook the meat.

The photo at the right shows the exterior of a beautifully cooked ribeye, chestnut colored all over, no grill marks.

As you reverse sear your first steak, if it is a little over- or undercooked, don't be discouraged. Adjust the procedure to accommodate your tastes. You know how to get to Carnegie Hall.

BIG, THICK STEAKHOUSE STEAKS

MAKES *2 to 4 servings*

TAKES *2 hours to dry brine and about 45 minutes to cook*

2 ribeye steaks, each about 1½ inches thick
Kosher salt (about ½ teaspoon per pound)
Coarsely ground black pepper

1. Prep. Trim most of the external fat from the steaks. Melting fat can cause flare-ups that deposit soot on the meat and burn the surface. Sprinkle with salt and dry brine in the refrigerator 1 to 2 hours before cooking. Pepper the surface of the meat to your taste and press it in. You can do this anytime. There's no need to take the meat out of the fridge early and let it come to room temperature.

2. Fire up. Set up the grill for two-zone cooking and shoot for about 225°F in the indirect zone.

3. Cook. Put the meat on the grill in the indirect zone. After about 15 minutes, start checking the interior temperature with a rapid-read thermometer. Check every 5 to 10 minutes in more than one location. At this low temperature, the exterior color should not go much beyond tan; if you add wood, it might get a ruddy glow. Flip it if one side is cooking faster than another.

4. After about 30 minutes, the temperature in the deepest part of the meat will probably hit 110°F. Open the lid and leave it open.

5. Now that the interior is getting close to target, you will sear it to get the entire surface dark. But first you have to prep your cooker.

ON A CHARCOAL GRILL: Bunch the coals together or add new fully lit hot coals so you have a pile of concentrated energy. If necessary, you can take the meat off the grill to add more coals and wait for them to get hot.

ON A KAMADO: Remove the deflector plate or move it to the direct side if you have a Divide & Conquer system that splits the deflector (right). Open the lower vent all the way and get the coals good and hot. Use a hair dryer aimed at the bottom vent to stoke the fire if needed. Lower the cooking grate as close to the coals as possible.

ON A GAS GRILL: If you have a sear burner, heat it up. If not, remove the meat and set it aside on a plate for a few minutes while you get the grill ready to sear. You might be able to remove the grates and lower them to sit right on top of the flavor bars or deflectors that protect the burners. The closer you get to the heat source, the better. Close the lid and turn all burners on high.

ON A PELLET SMOKER: Since most pellet smokers are all indirect heat all the time, you will need to preheat a heavy pan, perhaps cast iron. Take the meat off, crank up the heat all the way, and put your heavy pan on the grill and get it rip snortin' hot. Or place the meat right on top of a clean heat deflector.

6. Now we sear. Pat the meat dry and put it on the hottest part of the grill, as close to the heat source as possible. Keep the lid open and turn the meat often. All our effort is on one surface at a time. Stand by your grill! Things will move quickly because the meat's surface is already close to 212°F, and you need to be ready to react. If you have charcoal about 1 inch below the meat, each side can be done in as

little as 3 minutes. You want the surface evenly dark, with no grill marks. If a little of the edge fat blackens, that's OK, but don't blacken the muscle fibers. There may be flareups. Try to keep the meat away from direct flame.

7. When the meat hits 130°F (or your favorite temperature), get it off the flame and to the table while it is still sizzling! Err on the side of undercooking, since you can always put a steak back on the grill.

8. Serve. Don't let the meat rest and cool off and lose its crust. Some prime steakhouses, like Peter Luger in Brooklyn, slice it across the grain, and then reassemble the whole thing on the platter, as shown below. This is also a nice approach if you have huge steaks that are too big for one to a person, but the juices will soften the crust.

SKINNY STEAKS

Reverse sear works best on thicker cuts. For thin steaks and ultrathin steaks like skirt steak, you need a very different technique. As with thick steaks, the goal is the same: a dark brown exterior and a tender, juicy, medium-rare interior. For steaks 1 inch thick or less, the secret is to use very high heat and keep them moving.

MAKES *2 servings*
TAKES *10 minutes*

2 steaks, each about ¾ inch thick
Kosher salt (about ½ teaspoon per pound)
Freshly ground black pepper
Vegetable oil

1. Prep. Trim the surface fat and silverskin from the steaks if necessary. Sprinkle with salt, and dry brine in the refrigerator for 1 to 2 hours before cooking.

2. Just before you cook it, pat the meat dry with paper towels (moisture creates steam and prevents browning). Sprinkle with pepper and press it in with your hands.

3. Fire up. Get your grill screaming hot. If you are using charcoal, pile the coals just beneath the cooking surface as in the picture at the top of the opposite page. On a gas grill, drop the grate as close to the burners as possible. Leave the lid off. You won't really be using the indirect zone, but it is nice to have in case you need a safe zone away from the flames.

4. Cook. Put the meat over the hottest part of the grill. You need to stand by the grill and flip every minute so the hot surface cools, inhibiting heat buildup and preventing the interior from overcooking. Aim for a uniform dark brown without grill marks and 125 to 130°F in the middle. Things move fast, so be on your toes. You are a human rotisserie. Be the rotisserie.

PRIME RIB AND BEEF ROAST REVOLUTION

Is there anything more festive, impressive, and luxurious than a big juicy prime rib roast? Well, it's easy to make outdoors, and it definitely tastes better. This technique also works fine for other beef roasts such as strip loin and short loin, tenderloin, tri-tip, chuck eye roll, chuck roast, shoulder clod, top sirloin butt, and even tough round. The special technique? You guessed it, the reverse sear (see page 48).

If you can afford it, buy a prime rib or strip loin for the best combination of tenderness, juiciness, and tastiness. A chuck eye roast can be darn close and a lot cheaper, and top sirloin butt can be superb and cheaper still. Nothing rivals the tenderloin for tenderness, but tri-tip is close.

ORDERING YOUR RIB ROAST

The long muscle group that lies on either side of the backbone and above the curved back ribs is the most desirable part of the steer. The primary muscle running through them both is *longissimus dorsi*, the eye of the ribeye. It is tender, juicy, and woven with thin, lacy lines of fat that melt during cooking, creating deep, beefy flavor and rich, silky texture. The front half of this section is the rib roast, with 7 bones from ribs

THE AFTERBURNER METHOD FOR SKINNY STEAKS

If you have only two skinny steaks, try this: Fire up half a chimney of charcoal. When it is at peak heat, after about 15 minutes, the surface will be well over 1,000°F. Put a grate on top and cook the steak there. Flip every 30 seconds.

6 through 12. The rear is called the strip loin. If you carve the rib roast into steaks, you have ribeyes. Carve the strip loin into steaks, and you have strip steaks.

Prime rib is so named because it comes from a section called the rib primal, one of several large sections of the steer called primals. It is not necessarily USDA Prime grade, as you might think. What your grocer is probably selling is USDA Choice, and technically it should be called a "beef rib roast" rather than "prime rib." You can order USDA Prime–grade rib roast if you wish, and it's a real treat, but bring a wheelbarrow full of cash. Or simply ask your butcher for the best-looking, most marbled rib roast in the house. Or ask him to order you one. Prime rib is not something most butchers keep in stock. Order it fresh, not frozen, well in advance and take delivery 2 or 3 days before you plan to serve it. If you can get 28-day wet aged, go for it.

A typical bone-in prime rib roast weighs about 2 pounds per bone, depending on the size and age of the steer, and in recent years, that weight has gone up. Allowing for fat and bone waste and 20 percent shrinkage when cooking, you should buy at least 1 pound per person, or one bone width for two people.

BONES OFF!

A bone-in rib roast is often called a "standing rib roast" because the curved back ribs make a great stand for roasting the meat. I like to get bone-in if it is cheaper per pound. If it is the same price as boneless, you are paying the same price for bone as for meat. Ask your butcher to remove the bones for you, or remove

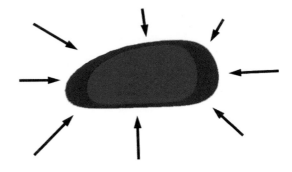

Oblong Shape Overcooks On Ends

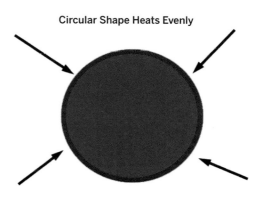

Circular Shape Heats Evenly

them yourself—they make a delicious second meal. Here's why you want the bones off:

BONES DON'T ADD FLAVOR. This myth is debunked on page 56.

BONES MAKE A ROAST OBLONG. Oblong roasts cook unevenly, with the ends and corners cooking faster because they are being attacked by heat on more sides. When you remove the bones, you can make the meat into a cylinder.

BONES GET IN THE WAY OF CRUST FORMATION. The bones keep one third of the meat surface from browning and developing that wonderful rich, seasoned crust.

BONES PREVENT EVEN COOKING. Because they have a honeycomb structure, rib bones act as an insulator, so if the meat is medium-rare in the center, it will be rare to raw near the bone.

BONES MAKE CARVING DIFFICULT. You don't want to struggle when everyone is watching, and you don't want juice all over the tablecloth.

THE HALLMARKS OF A GREAT ROAST

MAXIMUM TENDERNESS AND JUICINESS. Beef roasts are at their best when cooked to 130 to 135°F internal temperature. That's medium-rare, when they are no longer purple but deep red, and not yet pink.

EVEN COLOR. The same red color, bumper to bumper, with no overcooked meat beyond ¼ inch deep.

CRUST. A deep, dark, crunchy crust enriched by salt, herbs, and spices mixing with beef juices dried to a bark by the smoke-roasting process.

Overcooked

PRIME RIB

MAKES *6 large servings*

TAKES *1 hour to prep the meat, 24 to 48 hours to dry brine, 10 minutes to dry rub; cooking time will vary based on the thickness of the meat. To reach 130°F in the deepest part of a boneless roast, if the roast is about 4 inches thick, allow 30 minutes per inch of thickness.*

> 1 (8-pound) bone-in beef rib roast (about 3 bones wide)
> Kosher salt (about ½ teaspoon per pound)
> Mrs. O'Leary's Cow Crust (page 167)

1. Prep. Remove the rib bones from the roast and trim off all the fat cap from the top of the roast. Go ahead and trim right down to the meat. The fat will not penetrate the meat (see page 44); if you leave it on, people will trim it off at the table, and all the effects of the Maillard reaction and rub flavor will be lost. Be sure to get the silverskin, too; it can be chewy.

2. Sitting on top of the eye of the ribeye is another muscle called the rib cap (see photo, right). Shaped like a large fish fillet, it is heavily marbled. I think it is the single best muscle on the steer. It tends to go to well-done, so I like to remove it and grill it separately. You can practically peel it off with your bare hand because there is a layer of fat between the rib cap and the eye. There is also another little muscle on the opposite side of the rib cap, called the lip. There isn't much meat there and it is buried in thick layers of fat, so I remove it and grind it into hamburger.

3. Make the roast as round as possible, pressing on the sides and squishing it into a round tube. Tie

FOR THOSE WHO DON'T WANT MEDIUM-RARE

There is a high likelihood that some people at the table will want their meat cooked to medium, medium-well, or well-done. If you know there will be exactly two people who like their meat that way, then they can have the two ends. Because the ends get more heat, they will be 10 to 20°F warmer.

If there are more than two who want their meat brown, you may want to lop off a hunk of the roast just for them and essentially cook two roasts, one to medium-rare, and one to their preference. If necessary, you can put a few slices back over a hot grill for a few minutes per side and they can have well-done ribeyes.

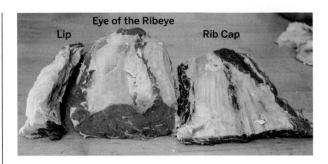
Eye of the Ribeye / Lip / Rib Cap

it with butcher's twine every inch or two to help it keep its shape. Sprinkle with salt and dry brine in the refrigerator for 24 to 48 hours.

4. An hour or two before cooking, wet the meat by patting water on it and apply the rub all over, using about 1 teaspoon of rub per 8 square inches of meat.

5. Fire up. Set up your grill for two-zone cooking and get the indirect zone to 225°F.

6. Cook. If you have a leave-in digital meat thermometer with a probe on a cable, insert it now so the tip is dead center in the thickest part of the meat. If you don't have a probe you can leave in the meat, you absolutely must have a good digital instant-read meat thermometer and you should check the roast every 30 minutes at first, and more often as the roasting progresses.

7. For a slight smokiness, add just a little bit of wood to the hot part of the fire, 2 to 4 ounces max. Don't overdo the smoke.

8. Look at the meat—if one side is getting too dark, rotate it. When the temperature in the deepest part of the interior reaches 115 to 120°F, remove the probe (it just gets in the way) and place the roast over the hottest part of the grill. If you are using charcoal, you can add more hot coals; if you are using gas, turn all burners on high; and if you have a sear burner, give 'er all she's got, Scotty. Raise the lid and stand by your grill. If you're using a pellet grill, bring the roast indoors and sear it under your broiler.

9. Get the surface of the roast a deep dark brown by leaving it on the hot part for 5 to 10 minutes. Roll it a quarter turn and repeat on all four sides. During this process, the interior temperature will rise another 10 to 15°F. Check the meat temperature again and take it off when it reaches 130 to 135°F for medium-rare, even if all sides are not browned.

10. Serve. Set the meat on a cutting board with a channel that can hold the liquid that will flow as soon as you cut into the roast, and have a platter with a lip ready to hold the carved slices. Serve your meat hot! Don't let it rest, or it will overcook by carryover (see page 5). First remove the twine and use a sharp knife to cut slices ¼ to ½ inch thick. Pour any drippings from the cutting board onto the platter holding the sliced meat and spoon it on top of the slices as they are served.

SANTA MARIA TRI-TIP: POOR MAN'S PRIME RIB

Settled by Mexican cowboys called *vaqueros,* the beautiful coastal town of Santa Maria in California's Central Coast has an international reputation for the local specialty, tri-tip steak, the unique grill invented to cook it, and the clever way it's carved to make it more tender.

The story goes that in the 1950s, a butcher named Bob Schutz was overstocked on ground beef and stew meat, so he took a triangular muscle from the bottom sirloin usually destined for chopping or grinding and put it on his store's rotisserie. He and his staff were shocked at how flavorful and tender it was. He called it tri-tip and started promoting it as a barbecue meat.

The tri-tip is from the bottom sirloin just in front of the hip. A typical tri-tip is about 8 inches long, 3 inches wide, and 3 inches thick in the center, tapers at the ends, and weighs 1½ to 2 pounds (see photo, page 252). It is available in every grocery and butcher shop in southern California, but it is hard to find elsewhere. If you don't live on the left coast, your butcher should be able to special order it. Tell him it is the *tensor fasciae latae* muscle from the bottom sirloin, number 185C in the North American Meat Processors Association (NAMP) book *The Meat Buyer's Guide* (the butcher's bible).

It has big, beefy flavor and it is very lean, so it can be on the chewy side if you don't cook and slice it properly. But cook and slice it the way they do in Santa Maria, and you can have a piece of meat almost as tender and every bit as juicy as any cut on the steer. I call it the Poor Man's Prime Rib.

The Santa Maria–style grill (see page 84)

is perfect for this cut. It has a grate that can be raised or lowered with a wheel-and-pulley system so the grillmaster can control the heat on this thick hunk o' flesh, crucial to getting it done properly without burning it to a crisp. The fuel of choice in Santa Maria is red oak logs, but you can conquer it easily with charcoal and gas.

The meat is prepped with minimal seasoning, and served without sauce, so the big, beefy flavor reigns. It is almost always taken off the grill when medium-rare and accompanied by grill-toasted bread to mop up the juices, a salsa like pico de gallo, beans, macaroni and cheese, salad, and the excellent local wines. I like to make sandwiches

BAN THE V-SHAPED RACK

Please do not use a roasting pan with a V-shaped rack for roasts or turkeys! They hamper even cooking, and they're expensive. You want to roast this meat with dry heat, not boil or braise it. If you must use a roasting pan, forgo the V-shaped rack and place a standard flat wire rack from your oven on top of the pan. On the grill, try to get the drip pan at least 2 inches below the meat.

In these illustrations you can see that when the meat is in a V-shaped rack in a roasting pan (left), the sides of the pan block hot air and the liquid in the pan cools the meat, leaving it undercooked and soggy. If we raise the meat to the top of the pan (middle), the bottom of the meat is much warmer. If we raise it at least two inches above the pan (right), warm air surrounds the meat from all sides and it cooks evenly.

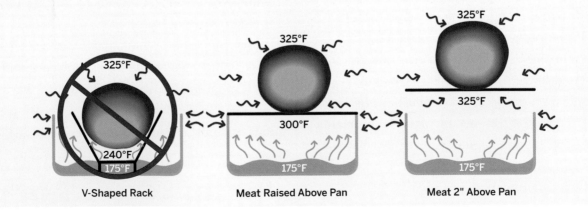

| V-Shaped Rack | Meat Raised Above Pan | Meat 2" Above Pan |

with toasted buns or use slices to top a salad.

MAKES *4 servings*

TAKES *5 minutes to prep and 45 to 90 minutes to cook, depending on how you set up your grill*

1 tri-tip steak (about 2 pounds)

Kosher salt (about ½ teaspoon per pound)

Freshly ground black pepper

Garlic powder

Sweet paprika

1. Prep. Trim off any surface fat and silverskin from the steak if necessary. Sprinkle with salt and dry brine 1 to 2 hours in the refrigerator before cooking.

2. Just before cooking, sprinkle the meat with pepper, garlic powder, and paprika in roughly equal amounts and massage them into the meat. If you have some Butcher Block Seasoning (page 173) on hand, now's the time to reach for it. Don't worry about overseasoning. The steak will be sliced very thin for serving, so each slice will have only a small lip of flavorful crust.

3. Fire up. Set up the grill in a two-zone configuration and get the indirect zone up to about 225°F.

4. Cook. In Santa Maria, where the grills have a built-in elevator, cooks raise the meat up high and flip it frequently during the cooking, which typically lasts as long as an hour. Unless you have a Santa Maria–style grill, first put the meat on the indirect-heat side of your grill with the thick end closer to the heat, close the lid, and turn the steak every 20 minutes or so until the center hits about 110°F. This can take 30 to 45 minutes.

5. Move the meat over direct high heat for about 5 minutes per side, or until it gets a nice even dark sear. Take it up to 130°F.

6. Serve. Here's the trick to carving this steak: Begin by slicing it in half through the center (see photo, bottom left).

7. Rotate each half and cut it from the tip to the cut end, across the grain, in ⅜- to ½-inch-thick slices (see photo, bottom right). Cutting across the grain ensures that the meat will be easier to chew.

8. Fan the slices on a platter, pour the juices on top, and serve.

CHATEAUBRIAND WITH COMPOUND BUTTER

A whole 5-pound beef tenderloin is a fabu-lously festive presentation, and not hard to pull off. But as you can see from the picture below, it is a little funny shaped, like a baseball bat, thick on one end, tapered on the other.

The most elegant solution is to break it down into a chateaubriand, the perfectly tubular center section of the tenderloin, for a grand, romantic, white-tablecloth dinner. It's a cinch to cook, and you can cut it with a butter knife.

A whole tenderloin will also yield a pile of trimmings for stew or stir-fry, and two tips that can be shaped and grilled as filet mignon steaks. It can often be purchased on sale in a vacuum bag at the big box stores.

To make sure it is perfectly cooked edge to edge, you'll reverse sear it and, because it is very lean, crown it with an herbed compound butter.

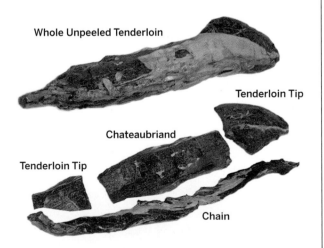

Whole Unpeeled Tenderloin

Tenderloin Tip

Chateaubriand

Tenderloin Tip

Chain

MAKES *4 servings*

TAKES *4 to 6 hours to dry brine, 5 minutes to prep, and about 60 minutes to cook*

- 1 beef tenderloin
- Kosher salt (about ½ teaspoon per pound)
- Big Bad Beef Rub (page 166) or Butcher Block Seasoning (page 173)
- Beef Butter (recipe follows)

1. Prep. If you are starting with a whole tenderloin, the goal is to cut a symmetrical log from the center. Running parallel to the main muscle is another smaller muscle called the chain. Work your thumbs into the gap between the two muscles and separate the chain from the larger piece of meat. Remove it and set it aside for stew or stir-fry.

2. Most whole tenderloins are sold "unpeeled," meaning they have a layer of tough silverskin. Get a sharp, pointed, thin knife, like a filleting knife, and remove the silverskin. Trim off large chunks of fat; you can leave small bits on.

3. You can make it symmetrical for even cooking by lopping off the ends. Another way is to remove the knob shape (butt) on one end. Now you have a long, tubular piece of meat that tapers at the other end. Because it is tapered, the "tail" will overcook. To prevent this, fold it in and tie it with butcher's twine so the roast is more uniform. The trimmed chateaubriand will be about 12 inches long and weigh about 4 pounds.

4. Once you have trimmed your chateaubriand, sprinkle it with salt and dry brine in the refrigerator for 4 to 6 hours before cooking. You can apply the rub now or wait; it doesn't matter.

5. Fire up. Set up the grill in a two-zone configuration and get the indirect zone up to about 225°F.

6. Cook. Place the meat in the indirect-heat zone. When the meat reaches 110°F, move it to direct heat to sear. Leave the lid open and roll the roast a quarter turn every 5 minutes or so. When it reaches 130°F in the center, move it to a cutting board. Slice it at least 1 inch thick and top each piece of meat with a pat of Beef Butter.

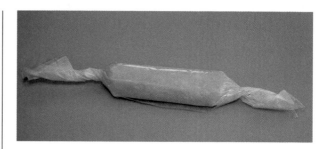

BEEF BUTTER

Beef butter is a simple compound butter that I use to top steaks occasionally. It is a mixture of butter and herbs, but it is a concept that has infinite variables. Add chipotle, ancho, brown spices, dried mushrooms, port wine, cheese, miso, or curry. Use the technique to mix butter with honey for slathering on English muffins or finishing grilled carrots or use the butter to top vegetables, potatoes, waffles, meats, and more. Let your imagination loose!

MAKES *4 ounces (1 stick) butter*
TAKES *20 minutes*

> 8 tablespoons (1 stick) salted butter
> ½ teaspoon chopped fresh rosemary
> ½ teaspoon chopped fresh parsley
> ½ teaspoon chopped fresh tarragon

Leave the butter out at room temperature for about 20 minutes, or until it is easy to spread, or microwave in short blasts of 5 seconds at a time until it is softened but not melted. Put it in a bowl and add in the rest of the ingredients. Mix well with a fork. Scoop the mixture out onto a 12-inch sheet of plastic wrap or waxed paper, and roll it up like a Tootsie Roll, about 1 inch across the middle, and twist the ends. Refrigerate overnight. It can be stored in the fridge or freezer.

BEEF RIBS: THE LONG AND THE SHORT OF THEM

Short ribs come from the lower, ventral section of the steer, usually from ribs 6 through 10. They are called short ribs not because they are short in length, but because they come from a section called the short plate. The bones are almost straight, and they have 1 to 2 inches of meat on top, depending on which end of the slab you are gnawing on. That's a cooked 2-bone slab in the top picture. The next picture is a full 4-bone slab. The meat is fastened to the bone by a thick, rubbery sheath of connective tissue that you will easily find and avoid when you eat. You can see it in the third picture.

Shorties come in many forms. You can buy slabs of shorties with 4 bones connected to each other, you can buy them cut into individual bones, you can buy riblets that are 2 to 3 inches long, you can buy steaks with cross-sections of bones, and you can even buy boneless short rib meat. The Texas way is to buy a full 4-bone "short plate," about 8 by 8 inches.

The back ribs in the bottom picture are usually cut from below the prime rib roast. Because rib roasts are so expensive, there is very little meat on the surface of the back rib bones, but there is some tasty stuff between the bones. Often back ribs can be found in slabs of 8 or more 8-inch-long bones. I prefer the meatier short ribs, but when I see a deal on back ribs, I grab them. They are quite spectacular when served in a slab.

Treat back ribs the same as short ribs. Depending on how much meat is on them and the thickness of the bones, they cook faster and can be finished in as little as 3 hours.

SHORT RIBS, TEXAS STYLE

Beef short ribs have more meat than beef back ribs, and they make an impressive presentation: A single bone with meat on top can weigh 2 pounds! But more important than looks is their taste. The muscles on top of the lower part of the rib cage near the front of the animal are hardworking and tough. Cooked low and slow for hours, the fats and collagens melt into an unctuous mouthful that lubricates the taste buds and harmonizes gloriously with the spices of the smoke-roasted rub.

MAKES *4 giant servings*

TAKES *15 minutes to prep, 4 to 6 hours to dry brine, and 8 to 10 hours to cook*

> 1 beef short plate (about 8 pounds)
> Kosher salt (about ½ teaspoon per pound)
> Big Bad Beef Rub (page 166)

1. Prep. Begin by removing all the fat and tough silverskin from the top of the meat. Don't remove the membrane from the exposed side of the bones as you do with pork ribs, because if you do, the meat will fall off. Cut slabs into 2-bone sections. You can cook them in a 4-bone slab, but it takes a lot longer, and cutting the plate in half separates the thick side from the thin side.

2. Sprinkle the ribs with salt and dry brine in the refrigerator for up to 24 hours before cooking. Any time before cooking, rub the meat with the Big Bad Beef Rub. Rub it generously into the tops and sides to coat completely.

3. Fire up. Get your smoker up to 225°F or set up the grill for two-zone cooking and shoot for about 225°F on the indirect side.

4. Cook. Put the meat over the indirect-heat zone, bone side down, and add wood to the fire. Oak is traditional in Texas, and it makes sense because it is mild, but other woods work fine. Add 2 to 4 ounces of wood on a tight cooker, double that if it leaks a lot. Cover the cooker. As the meat cooks, you will not need to add more wood and you will not need to flip the meat. The meat is done when it hits 203°F in the thickest part. Wrap it in foil and hold it for about an hour in a faux Cambro (see page 50). This last step allows it to slowly carryover cook, further melting connective tissues.

SHORT RIBS, BRAZILIAN STEAKHOUSE STYLE

Brazilian steakhouses serve beef ribs churrasco style, as a whole short plate of 4 bones, about 8 inches long and 8 inches wide, with a thick layer of meat on top. They trim it, salt it, run a sword through it, and rotisserie it over charcoal at about 400°F until the surface is dark brown. Gauchos bring it to the table and slice a thin layer of brown off it across the grain so it will be easier to chew. Beneath the surface the meat is medium-rare, and below that it is very rare, so it goes back on the rotisserie to build a new flavorful crust. It is a showy presentation, and you can do it at home. The process ensures that your guests have tender, juicy, medium-rare meat, and because it is sliced thinly, this tough cut is easy to chew. When you are done, you have some great bones to gnaw on or make into a stock.

You don't need a rotisserie—in fact, cooking

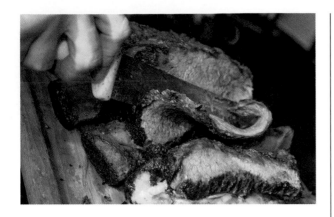

3. Cook. Grill with the meaty side down over direct heat until the exterior is dark.

4. Serve. Remove the meat from the grill, sprinkle it with Maldon-style salt and black pepper, and slice it across the grain, parallel to the surface and only about ⅛ inch deep so you get the dark surface and a thin layer of medium-rare red meat. Below this will be bright red rare meat. Put it back on the grill, meat side down, and repeat. Serve the thin slices to the guests right off the slab.

BRISKET BASICS

Briskets are the pectoral muscles of the steer, from the chest area between the forelegs. There are two per animal, and because cattle have no collarbones, these muscles bear about 60 percent of the animal's weight. They get a lot of work, so there is a lot of springy connective tissue in and around the muscle fibers. That's why they are so tough. Much of the world's brisket is simmered low and slow to break down the connective tissues and made into corned beef, pastrami, or pot roast. But it is also a fine cut for barbecue, and it is required in Kansas City Barbeque Society cooking contests.

is easier and faster with just a screaming-hot grill. After you take the first slices off the surface, enough to get three or four diners started, you have to go back to the grill and cook the meat until the surface browns, another 4 minutes or so, depending on how hot the grill is, and then bring it back to the table. But if you do it this way, I doubt your guests will complain when you finally sit down with the stubble left on the bones and hoard it for yourself. The best way to pull this off is to have the grill right by the side of the table.

You need a really sharp, thin blade to cut off the slices, and a way to hold the meat to keep it from slipping. A big carving fork will do the job.

MAKES *6 servings*

TAKES *1 hour*

> 1 beef short plate (about 8 pounds)
> Large-grain Maldon-style salt
> Freshly ground black pepper

1. Prep. Remove the fat cap from the beef, but leave the membrane on the underside of the plate or the meat will fall off the bones.

2. Fire up. Preheat the grill to warp 10 (as hot as she'll go, Scotty).

ANATOMY OF A WHOLE PACKER'S CUT BRISKET

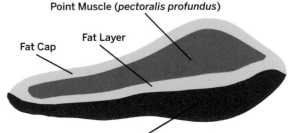

Point Muscle (*pectoralis profundus*)

Fat Layer

Fat Cap

Flat Muscle (*pectoralis superficialis*)

I cannot stress this enough: When shopping for brisket, go for the highest grade you can afford, either USDA Choice, USDA Prime, or Wagyu, and handpick the slab with the most marbling visible. If it is not labeled, chances are it is USDA Select. Avoid it!

Beware: Corned beef is brisket that has been corned, which means it has been preserved with salt, preservatives, and flavorings. *It is not suitable for this recipe!* To make Texas brisket, you need raw beef.

The whole packer brisket weighs 8 to 16 pounds and comes in an airtight Cryovac-type package. There is a fat cap on one side that can be up to 1 inch thick, and it is pretty close to fat-free on the other side.

There are two distinct muscles in a whole packer brisket: a long, flat, lean muscle that is called the flat, and a narrower, thicker, fattier, muscle called the point. The flat is pointy and the point is oval. Go figure. Your butcher probably offers three cuts of brisket, a whole packer brisket, a flat (sometimes called first cut), and a point (sometimes called second cut, or the deckle). Each cut needs to be cooked differently.

Picture 1 (right, top) shows a whole 12-pound packer brisket, untrimmed, fat side up, as it arrived from the packer. A whole packer brisket is a lot of meat! The flat is A and the point rests on top of the right side of the flat in the oval B.

Picture 2 shows the same brisket fat side down. This side is usually close to fat-free, although there may be some tough silverskin that must be removed. The flat is A and the point is B. The grain runs in the direction of the white line. Notice the fat layer that runs between the flat and the point.

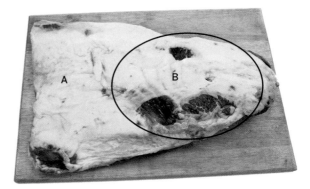

1

2

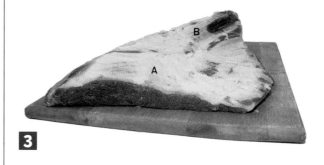

3

The side view, shown in Picture 3, looks right at the end of the flat with the point rising in the background. Notice that the flat ranges from ¼ inch thick on the right to about 1½ inches on the left, and the point is more than 4 inches thick.

Cooking a 12-pound hunk of meat is a commitment. And although the leftovers can be good, brisket is best when fresh. You might be tempted to buy a smaller cut, like a 5-pound hunk of flat or a hunk of point. If the meat case has both, choose the point. It has more marbling and will be more tender, flavorful, and a lot more juicy. Prepare and cook it the same way as a packer, but it will cook a lot faster. If you see only flats, ask the butcher if you can order points. Flats are usually tough, and it is hard to make them tender. If you get a flat, I strongly recommend you use the Texas Crutch (see page 60).

TEXAS BEEF BRISKET

Brisket is the national food of the Republic of Texas, and a whole 12-pound packer brisket is a great excuse for a party.

Brisket is a huge clod of cow that can come off the pit almost black, looking more like a meteorite than a meal. But it is not burnt, and beneath the crust is the most tender, juicy, luscious smoky meat—if you cook it right. But like a Clint Eastwood cowboy, brisket is unforgiving.

Controversy abounds in brisket cooking: what kind of rub to use, whether to inject the meat, at what temperature to cook it, whether to use a mop, whether use the Texas crutch (see page 60), whether to sauce it, and even how to slice it. I'm going to skip the controversies and give you a method and recipe that yield excellent results.

This is a long cook, so make sure you have plenty of fuel and wood. You'll also need a faux Cambro (see page 50). Don't forget a comfy chair, a book, tunes, and plenty of adult beverages.

MAKES *about 12 servings*

TAKES *about 30 minutes to trim, 2 to 24 hours to dry brine, 10 minutes to rub, and 12 to 14 hours to cook. The timing can vary significantly, depending on the size of the brisket, its moisture and fat content, the nature of your cooker, the outside air temperature, and the accuracy of your meat thermometer.*

> 1 whole packer brisket (about 12 pounds untrimmed), USDA Choice, USDA Prime, or Wagyu
> Kosher salt (about ½ teaspoon per pound)
> Big Bad Beef Rub (page 166)
> Texas Mop Sauce (page 179; optional)

1. Prep. Rinse the meat and dry it with paper towels. Trim off most of the fat cap, leaving only about ¼ inch. Until you get the hang of trimming a packer, you

might accidentally cut off some of the meat while trimming, which is OK. On the flip side, slice off any silverskin and excess fat. As discussed on page 44, melting fat does not penetrate the meat, and if you leave too much, people will cut it off at the table, along with your rub.

2. Sprinkle the meat with kosher salt, applying it more thickly where the meat is thickest.

3. Refrigerate the meat until you're ready to cook it. Chilled meat attracts more smoke. Just before cooking, dampen the meat with water and sprinkle liberally with the Big Bad Beef Rub, rubbing it in. Insert a toothpick parallel to the grain as a guide so you can carve the meat perpendicular to the grain when it is done.

4. Fire up. Get your smoker up to 225°F or set up the grill for two-zone cooking and shoot for about 225°F on the indirect side. Use a water pan if possible.

5. Cook. Put the meat on the cooker. Add about 4 ounces of wood right after the meat goes on. Add about 4 ounces more every 30 minutes for the first 2 hours. Keep an eye on the water in the pan and make sure it does not dry out. After 3 hours, turn the meat over if the color is different from top to bottom. Otherwise, leave it alone. The meat temperature will steadily climb to the stall zone (see page 59), somewhere around 150°F. Once in the stall, it will

seem to take forever to rise. The stall can last 5 hours and the temperature may not rise more than 5°F! To combat the stall employ the Texas crutch (see page 60). Wrap the meat tightly in two layers of foil so it doesn't leak. You can then insert your meat temperature probe up high so liquid doesn't escape the hole.

6. When the temperature of the meat hits 203°F, put it in a faux Cambro, close the lid, and let the hot meat sit there for at least 2 hours. If you have a tight cooler, it should hold the meat well above 160°F for hours. Holding the big thick brisket cooked almost to the boiling point allows the internal temperature to even out and the collagens to continue to melt. This carryover cooking results in more tender and juicy meat.

7. Now let's firm up the crust a bit. Unwrap the meat and put it over a hot grill or under a broiler for a few minutes on each side. Watch it closely so it doesn't burn.

8. Slice the meat at the last possible minute (see page 262). Brisket dries out quickly once it is cut. Turn the meat fat side up so the juices will run onto the meat as you slice.

9. If the meat is perfectly cooked, it should be moist and juicy. You can serve it simply sliced on a plate or as a sandwich made with Texas toast. If you wish, drizzle some Texas Mop Sauce mixed with some of the drippings from the crutch on top of the meat (taste this carefully because the drippings can be very salty).

SLICING BRISKET

THE EASY WAY

Separate the point and flat because the grains don't run in the same direction. Scrape off the fat between the two. Slice each muscle across the grain. The problem with this is that the point is juicier, so some slices are flat only and a lot drier. They may need some Texas Mop Sauce (page 179).

THE SORKIN WAY

I learned this technique from Barry Sorkin of Smoque BBQ in Chicago, renowned for some of the best brisket in the world, and the result is maximum eating pleasure.

Start by lopping off about 1 inch from the thin end of the flat. It is likely overcooked and dry. Chop and then smother it in sauce for chopped brisket sandwiches.

Look at the sides of the brisket and find the fat layer between the point and flat. Slide your knife between the two muscles and cut out that thick triangular lump of excess fat.

Find the grain of the flat and cut across the grain into lovely uniform sandwich slices about ¼ inch thick, about the thickness of a pencil, as shown in Picture 1. If the first slice falls apart, cut thicker slices. Keep cutting until you hit the place at which the point starts to overlap the flat and you see the fat layer separating the two.

Now turn the meat 45 degrees so one of the two uncut edges points away from you (2) and start slicing perpendicular to the two cut sides (3).

Sorkin then fans the slices on a bun (see opposite page, top). Notice that the sandwich he serves includes slices of both point and flat in it.

BURNT ENDS

If you separated point and flat, you can make a treat that some people consider the ultimate expression of brisket: burnt ends (below). These are dark, rich, crunchy, bite-sized nuggets that absolutely burst with delectation.

You can make them from either muscle, but most people make them from the point because its uneven shape makes it hard to get nice symmetrical slices. Plus, the extra fat makes them more lush.

I make them by cutting the meat into about ¾-inch cubes, taking them for a swim in my KC Classic Sauce (page 175), and tossing them on the grill to crisp them. Heck, I've been known to toss them in a frying pan with bacon fat or duck fat. That will get you disqualified at a competition, but not at the dinner table.

CLOSE TO KATZ'S PASTRAMI

Pastrami is Jewish barbecue, and when made properly, it is the world's best sandwich meat. It is essentially cured beef brisket, better known as corned beef, that has been smoked. My favorite pastrami in the world can be found at Katz's Delicatessen in New York City. Founded in 1888, Katz's is a timeless throwback. It has been selling smoked brisket nonstop at the same location, making it the nation's oldest barbecue joint, although I doubt many people think of it as such. It is also where Harry met Sally's fake orgasm, so when you go, be sure to sit at their table and have what she's having.

Pastrami is complex and smoky, though not in the way that other smoked meats are smoky. The smoke is not overt but blended in thoroughly. The meat is highly seasoned, but the black pepper and coriander rub is never domineering, and swimming across all your taste buds are a range of other herbs and spices.

The process starts with beef brisket (some pastrami is made from a cut called navel, but I find it too fatty). The brisket is first made into

MAKES *about 3 ½ pounds pastrami, enough for 8 big deli-style sandwiches*

TAKES *about 8 hours to soak, 25 minutes to rub, and 8 to 12 hours to smoke*

4 pounds uncooked high-quality corned beef

¼ cup coarsely ground black pepper

2 tablespoons ground coriander

1 tablespoon brown sugar

1 tablespoon paprika

2 teaspoons garlic powder

2 teaspoons onion powder

1 teaspoon mustard powder

Rye or pumpernickel bread, mustard or Thousand Island dressing, sauerkraut, and Swiss cheese for serving

1. Prep. Trim all surface fat and then put the corned beef in a nonreactive pot and cover it with cold water. Refrigerate for at least 8 hours. This removes excess salt. You need to do this or you will be gulping water all night after the meal. If you can, change the water once or twice.

2. Remove the beef from the water. Blend together the spices and apply the rub liberally, about ¼ cup per square foot of surface. Lay it on thick. Press the rub into the surface to help it adhere.

3. Fire up. Get your smoker up to 225°F or set up the grill for two-zone cooking and shoot for about 225°F on the indirect side. Add wood for smoke. If you can, use a charcoal smoker. It produces a deeper, darker crust than any other cooker.

4. Cook. Smoke the meat fat side up over indirect heat until it reaches 203°F. Add wood when the smoke dwindles. It can take 10 hours or more depending on the thickness. Don't try the Texas crutch because it can wash off a lot of rub and smoke. At this stage, you can serve it, or some folks like to steam it to make it more tender (see opposite page).

corned beef by injecting or submerging the beef in a mix of salt, spices, and curing salt (see page 33). You can corn your own beef—a tricky process that takes about a week, and if you don't do it precisely you end up throwing out the meat— or you can buy corned beef in a brine, a good one from a good butcher.

Corned beef comes in two forms: ready-to-eat and brined. Ready-to-eat corned beef is cured, then cooked, and usually packaged in slices or sliced at the deli counter. *Do not use this!* Brined corned beef is a hunk of brisket that has been cured in a salt solution and is usually packaged in a sturdy Cryovac plastic bag with some of the brine. It has not been cooked yet. That's the stuff you want. I recommend corned beef from the fatty, or point, end if you can get it.

5. Serve. Slice the pastrami across the grain just like you would a brisket (see page 262). Don't try to slice it with a machine. It will just fall apart.

6. Serve it on rye bread or pumpernickel with a schmear of mustard. Better still, toast the rye, take one slice and set it aside, and spread some Thousand Island dressing on the other slice. Pile the meat on the dressing, then top with a layer of crunchy sauerkraut from the refrigerator section of the grocery store (not the canned stuff), lay a slice of Swiss cheese on top, and stick the whole thing under the broiler to melt the cheese. Finally, put on the other slice of bread, unhinge your jaw, and enjoy the best sandwich on earth, the pastrami Reuben (Reubens are usually made with corned beef, but this is better).

7. If you have leftovers, wrap them in foil and refrigerate. You can keep them for up to a week if you wish. Bring them back to life by steaming.

STEAMING PASTRAMI

Pastrami aficionados like to steam the meat after smoking. It softens the crust, but it does make it slightly more tender. Here's how:

Do not slice the meat before steaming. If you have a bamboo or metal steamer in which the meat will fit, use that. If not, make a steamer by putting a wire rack in a baking pan and cover the rack with foil to keep the rub from washing off.

If the pan is steel, don't let the foil touch the meat. The salt, water, steel, and aluminum might interact and create electrical charges that can melt the foil, a phenomenon called the "lasagna effect."

Put the pan on a burner, add water to the bottom of the pan, turn the heat to medium-low, and steam the meat for 2 to 3 hours until heated through to 203°F. The exact time will depend on the meat's thickness and how hot the water is. Keep a close eye on it and add hot water as needed, making sure the pan never dries out. This can happen quickly and can cause a fire.

8

GROUND MEATS: BURGERS, HOT DOGS, and SAUSAGES

BURGER BASICS

Preground meat, even some ground from the better cuts of meat, such as ground chuck, may have been ground miles away and days ago. Once meat is ground, it begins to oxidize and its fat can start to get rancid. Shop at a store with a butcher in the back room who can grind meat to order for you.

Never, ever buy something labeled "hamburger" or "ground beef" for burgers. Save these for chili or sloppy Joes. Butchers toss trimmings from any cut in there, and much of the stuff in preformed patties comes from old bulls and no-longer-productive dairy cows. Those patties may also have added seasonings. You want to add your own.

You want at least 20 percent fat, not 15 percent. Many top chefs now recommend 25 to 30 percent fat, especially if you cook the meat to the USDA-recommended safe temperature of 160°F.

The easiest thing to do is pick a nice-looking USDA Choice–grade chuck steak, ask the butcher to grind it, and add more white fat if needed to get the blend up to 20 to 30 percent. Don't waste money on expensive cuts like ribeye or Wagyu beef. The grinding process will make tough cuts tender. Go for less expensive meat that has great beefy flavor, like chuck, short ribs, flank, skirt, sirloin, hanger, brisket, or a blend.

Ask for a coarse grind, using the ¼-inch holes, only once through the grinder, and ask for it to be packaged loosely. It should come out looking like thick, wavy spaghetti. Coarser grinds and looser packing make for an uneven surface plus air pockets inside, and that's good for holding juices.

If you can't get your meat ground to order, buy preground chuck, which is usually 15 to 20 percent fat. (Ground round is usually 10 to 15 percent fat; ground sirloin is only 5 to 10 percent.)

While you're at it, ask for some suet (beef fat) to freeze and mix in the next time your meat is too lean—get fresh white fat, not yellow fat. Your butcher may even grind it for you. If not, you can grind it easily in a food processor.

If you have a meat grinder, the best way to control quality is to grind the meat yourself. That way you can select the exact cut, control the fat-to-lean ratio, get the freshest meat, and reduce oxidation and the risk of microbial contamination. To further reduce risk, especially if you insist on cooking your burgers to less than 160°F, take the whole muscle steak before grinding and dip it in boiling water for 30 seconds. That will pasteurize the surface, which is where any contamination is most likely to be found. It will still grind and cook perfectly.

FLAVORING THE BURGER

A controversy rages over the wisdom of mixing ingredients into the patty. Food Network's Bobby Flay, author of the cookbook *Bobby Flay's Burgers, Fries & Shakes* and owner of several locations of Bobby's Burger Palace (among other things), once told me his patties are nothing but chuck, sprinkled with salt and pepper on the exterior just before cooking. "I don't put anything in my burgers like onion, eggs, breadcrumbs, anything. That's meatloaf."

My colleague Professor Blonder studied what happens to burger meat when salt is mixed in. Pictured below are three meatballs made from 80% lean ground beef and cooked at 325°F. As you can see, salt helped retain water so there was less weight loss during cooking, but mixing in salt also compacted the meat and it became dense and rubbery. Remember, much of the juiciness in ground meat comes from fat. The best burgers have a loose texture with pockets to hold juice. For this reason we recommend salting the exterior just before cooking or even during cooking.

As for mix-ins, I add a few seasonings such as garlic and onion powder, which would burn and get bitter if sprinkled on the surface. Avoid adding wet ingredients like wine and Worcestershire sauce, which require you to work the meat hard to mix them in. They can also retard browning.

Learn to make the same size burgers every time so you can get a sense of how long it takes to cook them properly. An ice cream scoop is a good tool for this. For steakhouse burgers, 6 to 8 ounces of meat is ideal. Make disks ½ to ¾ inch thick, packing them loosely with your hands, so there are air pockets to hold the juices.

It has become fashionable to make indentations in the centers of burgers on the theory that it will keep the burger from puffing out. I don't, because they don't puff up much and I want uniform thickness, especially in the center.

No Salt	Salt on Surface	Salt Mixed In
31% Loss	30% Loss	21% Loss

WEIGHT LOSS AND SALT

THE GREAT AMERICAN STEAKHOUSE STEAKBURGER

The succulent Steakhouse Steakburger is an elusive beast. Its natural habitat is the white tablecloth steakhouse, where it is treated like hand-carved prime rib and broiled or grilled by a flame, but the price is outlandish. It's hard to find a proper one in a restaurant and even harder to make at home.

It is a big fat fellow, about ¾ inch thick, weighing in at 8 ounces or more. It wastes no space on the bun. It has a thin, rich, salty cordovan crust and gushes juice. With each bite, it reminds us that a great burger is a gustatory delight. These are so juicy that I serve them in a bowl.

MAKES *2 servings*

TAKES *about 1 hour*

¼ teaspoon freshly ground black pepper

¼ teaspoon onion powder

¼ teaspoon garlic powder (not garlic salt)

1 pound loosely ground chuck (25% fat)

About 1 tablespoon butter

2 hamburger buns

4 thick, high-quality bacon slices

1 teaspoon kosher salt

2 tablespoons Burger Glop (page 188)

2 iceberg or romaine lettuce leaves (see Notes)

2 slices raw sweet onion, about ⅛ inch thick (see Notes)

2 slices from a large tomato

1. Prep. Mix the pepper, onion powder, and garlic powder in a small bowl. Spread the meat out on a plate and sprinkle it evenly with the mixed seasonings. Gently form the meat into two 2-inch-wide balls. Don't worry if the seasoning doesn't appear to be evenly distributed. Don't compress the meat; you want juices to collect in small air pockets and keep the burgers tender. Each one should weigh 8 ounces. If not, adjust so that they are of equal weight. Gently press the balls into disks about ¾ inch thick and 4 inches wide. Try to smooth over deep crevices, which will allow heat to penetrate to the core too quickly. Notice there is no salt on the inside of the patty.

2. Fire up. Set up the grill for two-zone cooking. The indirect side should ideally be about 225°F. No smoke yet.

3. Cook. Butter the buns and put them, buttered side down, on the direct-heat side of the grill. Do not walk away. They can go black in a hurry. When the butter has melted and the buns are lightly browned, set them aside.

4. Now get some smoke rolling by putting wood on the hot spot. Put the bacon on the indirect side. Place the burgers on the indirect side and sprinkle one side of the patties with salt. Close the lid and cook for about 10 minutes, until the bacon is the desired doneness. I like it bendable.

5. Push the tip of a rapid-read thermometer into the side of both burgers. You may discover that one is cooking faster than the other. Turn them over, sprinkle with salt, and cook for another 10 minutes. Because they are not over direct heat, you do not need to flip them often.

6. When the burgers are about 20°F below the temperature you want, get ready to move them to the direct-heat zone. If you are on a gas grill, crank it up to high. On a charcoal grill, you might want to add more pre-lit coals. If necessary, take the meat off the grill and close the lid while the hot side heats up. If you have a pellet cooker or another grill that doesn't have enough radiant heat to sear, put a cast-iron pan or griddle in there—when the griddle collects a lot of heat, it can do the job.

7. Put the burgers on the direct-heat side and leave the lid up so all the heat is concentrated on one side of the burger. If the fire flares up, move the burger to another spot—flares can deposit soot. Flip the meat every minute or so, acting like a human rotisserie, so all the energy is focused on one surface at a time. The interior will warm, but not too much. Remove the burgers when the interiors are 5°F below the desired temperature. Don't overcook them while waiting for the second side to be perfect. If one side is paler than the other, that's acceptable.

8. Serve. Set the bottom of each bun in a bowl and put some glop on it so it can help hold the burger in place. Then put the bacon on the glop. Put a burger on top of the bacon and crown it with a lettuce leaf, an onion slice, and a tomato slice. Assemble the second burger the same way. I put the big slippery stuff on top of the patties because you have eight fingers to manage the top of the bun.

9. Grasp the sandwich with both hands, and no matter what Momma told you, put both elbows on the table. Push your chair back a few inches so you are leaning forward over the bowl. The hardest part of this recipe is trying to keep the juices off your shirt.

NOTES: You want cold, crisp lettuce that crunches and squirts ice water on top of the hot meat juices. Iceberg or romaine lettuce is perfect for this.

I like a single thin slice of raw onion the same diameter as the patty. In season, I go for sweet onions like Vidalia (May through July) or Walla Walla (June through August). If they are not in season, it's red onion for me. Don't slice the onions too far in advance. Onions taste best when freshly cut. Sometimes I put the onion on top of the burger while it's on the grill to take the edge off the onion and make it less slippery. Another technique for taming onion is to soak the cut onion in cold water for about 10 minutes. If you like onion but a solid slice is too much, break the slice into rings. If you're making a cheeseburger, put the cheese on top of the onion—it will anchor the onion in place as it melts.

If you want to do some stylin', try sweet-and-sour pickle slices, pickle relish, grilled tomatoes, roasted red peppers, sautéed mushrooms, thinly sliced pears or apples, potato chips, or slaw. Many joints place a sunny-side-up egg on top for a steak-and-eggs combo.

DINER BURGERS

Diner Burgers are small, usually 4 ounces or less, the kind served at your neighborhood "grill." Chances are that "Charlie's Bar and Grill" does not really have a grill. It probably has a large, flat, thick, heavy piece of steel heated from below: a griddle. A griddle cooks by conduction. An open-flame grill cooks mostly by radiation. If you hear the waitress say, "Toss a burger on the grill, Charlie," she is really referring to a griddle, not a grill. Just don't correct her.

In George Motz's excellent guide to the best burgers in the country, *Hamburger America*, 81 of the 100 burgers he describes are cooked on a griddle, and just 13 are cooked over an open flame.

The griddle has a distinct advantage. The burger is in contact with a lot of concentrated energy, so browning happens rapidly. The method is ideal for thin burgers like quarter-pounders. But they are still easy to overcook. That's why a high fat content of the meat is so important. A burger with 20 to 30 percent fat will remain juicy even when the surface is cooked until it is GBD (Golden Brown and Delicious) and the interior is a safe 160°F.

Why put a griddle on a grill? If you try to do a proper diner burger in your kitchen, you will almost certainly make the smoke alarm cry, and then you will also be crying because you will be scrubbing spatters off the top of the range for hours.

Some special tools are needed. The ideal tool is a cast-iron or stainless-steel griddle (see page 152), or even a heavy frying pan, and a solid metal spatula (see page 109). Two spatulas are better: one to smash the raw meat, and a clean one to flip and serve.

When I make thick Steakhouse Steakburgers (page 270), I grind the meat loosely and pack it lightly, but that won't work for thin Diner Burgers. They'll fall apart on the griddle. So if you are grinding them yourself, use the smaller holes on your grinder, or grind the meat twice.

MAKES *4 quarter-pounders*

TAKES *30 minutes if you grind your own, 5 minutes if you buy ground chuck, and only 4 to 6 minutes to cook*

- ¼ teaspoon freshly ground black pepper
- ¼ teaspoon onion powder
- ¼ teaspoon garlic powder (not garlic salt)
- 1 pound finely ground chuck steak (20 to 30% fat)
- 2 tablespoons butter
- 4 hamburger buns
- 1 tablespoon beef fat, bacon fat, or vegetable oil
- ½ teaspoon kosher salt
- Burger Glop (page 188)
- Your favorite toppings

1. Prep. Mix the pepper, onion powder, and garlic powder in a small bowl. Spread the meat out on a plate and sprinkle it evenly with the mixed seasonings. Pack the meat into 4 balls about 2 inches across. A #8 ice cream scoop holds just about 4 ounces, a perfect quarter-pounder. Use a scoop or a kitchen scale or a ruler until you can make the right size balls blindfolded. Then put them in the fridge for about 20 minutes before cooking so the center is cold and does not cook as quickly.

2. Fire up. Set up the grill in two zones and preheat a cast-iron griddle or heavy frying pan over direct heat to about 350°F. This is one of the rare occasions

THE ZEN OF CHEESEBURGERS

The cheese is the last thing to go on. If you are using caramelized onions, sautéed mushrooms, or raw onion, put them on before the cheese. As the cheese melts, it will help anchor the toppings.

The prototypical American cheeseburger has a slice of bright yellow American cheese on top, but there's no reason you can't use another melting cheese, such as Asiago, Brie, Cambozola, Camembert, cheddar, chèvre, Colby, fontina, Gruyère, Havarti, Monterey Jack, mozzarella, Muenster, provolone, smoked Gouda, or Taleggio. Blue isn't melty, but a lot of folks like it. Cheese blends and spreads also work. Boursin, cheddar with port wine, cream cheese with horseradish, or pepper Jack are good choices. Pimento cheese spread is popular in the South, particularly in South Carolina and Georgia.

Slice the cheese ⅛ inch thick or grate it. Apply the cheese after one side of the burger is finished cooking and when you are close

to finishing the other side. Depending on the cheese, 2 to 3 minutes should melt it. The thicker the cheese, the longer it takes to melt, so factor that into your cooking time. You might want to move the patty off direct heat while you melt the cheese so you don't overcook the meat. Another trick is to put a metal mixing bowl over the burger; the cheese should melt in as little as 30 seconds. A coffee can or baking pan will work fine, too.

where an infrared gun thermometer (see page 97) comes in handy.

3. Cook. Melt the butter on the griddle. It will foam quickly. Spread it out evenly over the surface. Place the buns, cut side down, on the griddle, press them down with the spatula, and put a dinner plate on top so they make good contact with the surface. Cook until the bread turns golden. Yes, the tops will be smushed, but the butter will brown and get a nutty taste, and the edges of the buns should be extra crispy. Remove the buns and wipe the griddle with a paper towel.

4. Melt some beef fat on the griddle and spread it with your spatula. You want just a thin coat. (Do not use butter. It has too much water in it.) When the fat begins to smoke, add the burger balls and press down on them with a solid spatula so there is good contact between the meat and the surface and the patty has jagged edges. A slotted spatula will not do the job. You need to smash the burger soon after the patty goes on, and not again until you flip. You don't want to squeeze out hot juices. After smashing, quickly work the spatula along the edges, pressing down so they are ragged and thin and make intimate contact with the surface. We're going for brown edges here. Sprinkle the top side with the salt. Leave the lid open and back away. Don't touch the burgers for about 3 minutes. Maybe 5 minutes, depending on how hot your griddle gets.

5. It will take you a couple of tries to know exactly when to flip, so at first you may have to peek. The bottoms should be dark brown. If they are, gently work a clean spatula under the burgers, pressing on the griddle to make sure that you don't leave brown bits behind and that the burgers don't break apart. I sharpen my spatula on a grinder to make sure I don't leave anything behind. Flip the burgers and press them into maximum contact with the surface

but not so hard that you squeeze out vital fluids. No need to salt a Diner Burger on both sides. If you are making a cheeseburger, place the cheese on now and close the lid on the grill. Check the color of the bottom after 2 minutes. Don't take them off until the surface is right, even if you fear the interior is overcooking. If you got meat with 20 to 30 percent fat and you didn't cook too hot, they'll be juicy.

6. Serve. When they are brown, serve them immediately. Use the glop as a base to anchor the burgers to the buns and top them with onion, lettuce, pickle slices, whatever.

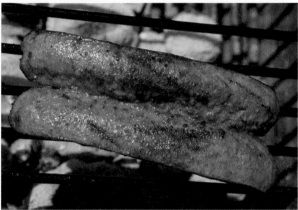

HOT DOGS

Everybody can cook hot dogs, but I might be able to teach an old dog like you a new trick or two. First, turn down the heat! Set up the grill in a two-zone configuration and get the direct zone up to about 325°F. You'll cook over the direct heat, but the hot dogs won't split open, and you'll be able to brown them evenly on all sides. Use that indirect zone as a safe zone to hold them when they are done.

Here's a trick I learned from Gold Coast Dogs in Chicago: Cut an X in the ends of the dog. When they cook, the ends will curl up and get extra crispy. Another trick for more crispy surfaces is to split them lengthwise. Or spiral cut them, a technique sure to start a conversation.

If the franks are curved, bend them gently in order to straighten them out a bit. Then place them in the gap between the grates, not across the grates. This way you can roll them about a quarter turn at a time by rolling into the next gap. Yes, pinstripes look weird, but you'll have a more evenly cooked frank. Cook the dogs over direct heat until the skin darkens a nice golden brown all around.

Meanwhile, toast the buns so they have some crunch.

Serve hot dogs hot. Don't let them sit around and shrivel.

Have a variety of toppings for guests to try: yellow mustard, Dijon mustard, Columbia Gold (page 177), pickle relish, chopped onions, caramelized or grilled onions, pickled peppers, celery salt, sauerkraut, slaw, chopped tomato, and Yankee chili (ground meat, canned beans, sweet peppers, and brown spices in a tomato sauce).

REGIONAL DOGS

Many cities have a signature method for dressing their frankfurters. I love throwing parties with a hot dog road trip as the theme. Here are some of the most iconic styles.

THE CHICAGO DOG is a juicy, crunchy, sloppy combo that leaves your fingers fragrant for hours. It starts with a garlicky all-beef frankfurter with a snappy natural casing, simmered in water laden with flavor from other dogs. This "dirty water" method is standard, but there are a few renegades like me who grill or griddle them. They are served on a bun studded with poppy seeds and topped with seven ingredients, no more, no less, no variation allowed: solar-yellow mustard, kryptonite-green sweet pickle relish, chopped raw onion, juicy tomato slices, spicy hot "sport" peppers, a crunchy salty kosher pickle spear, and a sprinkle of that magic dust, celery salt. Ketchup is strictly forbidden. The result is a sandwich with so much vegetation that it is called a "garden on a bun."

THE CONEY ISLAND HOT DOG, found all over New York City, is an all-beef frank wrapped with a natural casing, cooked on a griddle or simmered, and most often dressed with spicy brown mustard, sauerkraut, and griddled onions. Sometimes those onions have been mixed with a sweet mustard sauce. That's all. No relish, chili, and especially no ketchup. A purist orders only mustard, kraut, and onions.

THE WEST VIRGINIA SLAW DOG is a tasty but improbable construct of frank, bun, beanless ground beef sauce sometimes forming a bed beneath the frank (they insist it is a "meat sauce" and not to be called chili), yellow mustard, and finely chopped creamy coleslaw crowning it.

THE CINCINNATI CHEESE CONEY is a pork-and-beef frank with a natural casing topped with mustard, then chili, then chopped onions, and finally an ungodly amount of shredded cheddar mounded on top.

THE DETROIT CONEY DOG is a skinless beef frank loaded with mustard, then a chili made mostly from beef hearts, no beans allowed, and crowned with chopped onions. It is served all around the state in restaurants called Coney Islands.

And then there's the **TEXAS WIENER** served in Connecticut, the **NEW YORK SYSTEM HOT WIENERS** in Rhode Island, the **NORTH JERSEY ITALIAN DOG**, the **ROCHESTER GARBAGE PLATE**, the **MONTANA TATER-PIG**, the **SONORAN HOT DOG**, the **SEATTLE CREAM CHEESE DOG**, the **HAWAIIAN PUKA DOG**, the **FENWAY FRANK**, and the **DODGER DOG**. Ironically, there is no such regionality with hamburgers—maybe because there are so many huge burger chains that have globalized the genre. Let's hope the same fate never befalls hot dogs!

A BETTER ITALIAN SAUSAGE SANDWICH

In Italy there are hundreds of regional salsiccia. In the U.S., the term *Italian sausage* has a specific flavor profile. It is a thick tube of coarsely ground pork sausage in natural pork casings, with a distinctive flavor from fennel seed. It is sold raw by butchers, and it can be bought in links, in coiled ropes, or loose like burger meat. It usually comes in three flavors: sweet, mild, and hot. The main difference is the amount of hot pepper added, although some sweet blends include basil, and the heat and

COOKING SAUSAGES

Some sausages are precooked, but most are sold raw, so you need to read the label. The average sausage is probably 25 percent fat. Be sure to use a two-zone setup and keep the heat in the direct zone down. You will cook over direct heat most of the time, but you need that indirect zone as a safe zone or to hold them when they are finished.

As with hot dogs, I recommend that you try to get the bend out so they lie flat and are easier to turn, and I also recommend that you line them up parallel to the grates so you can roll them from gap to gap and get the allover tan of a Hollywood movie star.

Unlike frankfurters, raw sausages should not be cut into or they will fall apart. The other key is to be sure to use your instant-read

thermometer. You need to take it to 140°F for precooked, 160°F for uncooked. Most of the sausages you've cooked in the past have been drier than necessary because you overcooked them. You will be amazed how much juicier your sausages are if you use a thermometer. Rather than puncture the casing, stick the thermometer in through one end. And don't let them split like this one.

other seasonings vary significantly from butcher to butcher. If you can't find a butcher selling good sausage near you, try the Italian sausage recipe on AmazingRibs.com.

A versatile ingredient, Italian sausage commonly shows up on pizza, in red sauce for pasta, in bean soups, and in bread-based stuffings. But its greatest glory is in a bun. The classic Italian sausage sandwich is grilled and topped with griddle-fried onions and sweet peppers, and often anointed with giardiniera, a spicy-hot blend of chopped hot peppers, carrots, cauliflower, celery, olives, herbs, salt, and black pepper, all packed in oil and/or vinegar. Some places offer sausage sandwiches with a marinara sauce and melted mozzarella. The trick is to grill the sausages over medium heat so the casings don't split.

MAKES *4 sandwiches*

TAKES *about 50 minutes*

- 4 (6-inch-long) slices Italian bread, from a long skinny loaf, or 4 oblong Italian bread rolls, split (see Notes)
- 4 tablespoons olive oil (see Notes)
- 2 green bell peppers, halved lengthwise and cut into ¼-inch-wide strips
- 2 red bell peppers, halved lengthwise and cut into ¼-inch-wide strips
- 2 large onions, halved through the root and sliced into half-moons
- 4 fresh Italian sausage links

1. Prep. Let the sausages sit at room temperature for about 15 minutes so the skins warm a bit. This helps keep them from splitting, spilling their guts, and dumping oil on the fire.

2. Fire up. Set up the grill for two-zone cooking and shoot for about 325°F on the indirect side.

3. Cook. Toast the bread over direct heat, if you like.

4. Put an 8- to 12-inch oven-proof frying pan on the heat. Pour in the olive oil and swirl the pan to coat the bottom in the oil. Add the peppers and onions and stir to coat with oil. Stir the peppers and onions and cook until wilted and slightly browned, but not burned. A scorch mark or two is OK. Take them off when they are done and let them sit at room temperature. You can cook the peppers and onions a day in advance, even indoors if you wish, and just warm them before serving.

5. If the sausages are curved, bend them gently to straighten them slightly. Lay them on the direct-heat side between the gaps of the grate. Cook with the lid open so you can watch them to prevent burning. Do not poke them to drain the fat! This dries them out and causes flare-ups and soot. They must cook until they are 160°F in the center to be safe. Usually they are properly cooked after two or three of the sides have browned. Don't burn them and don't overcook them and dry them out.

6. Nestle the sausage in the bread and top liberally with peppers and onions, making sure plenty of flavorful oil gets into the bread, and serve.

NOTES: Italian bread is a spongy, high-gluten loaf with a medium-hard crust.

The amount of olive oil listed is about twice as much as you may think you need, but it's the way it's done. You can grill the peppers and onions on a grill topper (see page 103) if you wish, although it is not exactly traditional and you don't get the richness of the olive oil.

TOUCHDOWN TAILGATE BRAT TUB

Bratwurst (BRAHT-vurst), better known as brats, are the perfect tailgate food. Madison, Wisconsin, calls itself the "Brat Capital of the World" and is home of the giant annual Brat Fest over Memorial Day weekend, where more than two hundred thousand brats are served. Only slightly more modest, Sheboygan, an hour south of Green Bay, calls itself the "Bratwurst Capital of America." Near Madison, in Middleton, is the Mustard Museum (a must visit, pun intended).

Bratwurst contains coarsely ground pork and/or veal, pepper, garlic, mustard, ginger, savory, mace, and milk, all stuffed into natural pork casings. For this recipe, buy plain brats, not cheese-filled aberrations. Brats are not pre-cooked, so they must be heated to at least 160°F in the center to be safe.

The beauty of this recipe is that you can make the sauce at home, chill everything, and then finish it at the game. You will need a 9-x-13-inch disposable aluminum pan about for the brat tub.

MAKES *6 sandwiches*

TAKES *about 1 hour*

  6 nice buns (see Notes)
  2 (12-ounce) bottles cheap American lager, nothing bitter
  6 bratwursts
  2 medium onions, halved through the root and sliced into half rings
  ½ cup KC Classic (page 175)
  ¼ cup Dijon-style mustard
  ¼ teaspoon your favorite hot sauce (see Notes)
  ¼ teaspoon liquid smoke (optional)

1. Fire up. Set up the grill for two-zone cooking and get the indirect-heat zone to about 325°F.

2. Cook. Open the buns and place them, cut sides down, on the direct side of the grill to warm and toast slightly. (Butter them first if you like. I like.)

3. Dump the beer into a pan and bring it to a simmer.

4. Most brats are curved. Bend and flex them so they are close to straight. They are easier to turn on the grill and they fit the buns better when they are straight, allowing more room for the sauce. Add the brats to the beer and simmer for about 15 minutes to absorb flavor. Roll the brats around if they are not covered in beer and simmer for about 15 minutes longer.

5. Push the brat tub to the side, remove the brats, and grill over direct heat just long enough to get some snap and brown onto the skin, 1 to 3 minutes on each side. They should read at least 160°F in the center on a good digital thermometer when they are done.

6. While the brats are grilling, add the onions, barbecue sauce, mustard, hot sauce, and liquid smoke (if using) to the hot tub and stir.

7. When the brats are the right shade of brown, move the hot tub onto the direct-heat side of the grill. Slip the brats into the tub, coat them with the sauce, and

DOES THE BEER PENETRATE?

I asked Professor Blonder to run some tests to see if the beer actually gets into the brat, or if you need to puncture the casing for it to penetrate. He mixed beer with a green dye that is heat stable and moves through meat in a manner similar to salt. He punctured some brats with a fork, and even cut the ends of a few to see if the beer entered more quickly. When he removed them and sliced them open, the dye had clearly penetrated 1 to 2 mm, but surprisingly, the depth of penetration did not increase much whether they were simmered for 15 minutes, 30 minutes, or 45 minutes.

Also, the beer did not penetrate bare meat on the cut end or through punctures any more than through the intact casing.

The conclusions: Simmering in beer actually does add flavor to a thin band of meat under the casing; puncturing with a fork does not accelerate the penetration (but does cause the brats to shrink a bit); and simmering for 15 minutes is nearly as effective as simmering for 45 minutes.

BRATS SIMMERED IN DYED BEER

| Raw | 15 Minutes | 30 Minutes | 45 Minutes | Cut End |

cook down until it is gloppy. This will take 20 to 30 minutes.

8. Nestle the brats on the buns with the onions and the sauce. Not too much sauce—you want to taste the brats. Put extra brats back in the sauce on the indirect part of the grill to hold for when people want seconds.

NOTES: In Wisconsin the brats go on "sausage rolls" or "sausage buns," which are thicker, firmer, and have a more substantial crust than a hot dog bun. They make a difference.

I usually use Tabasco Chipotle Sauce. Add more if you wish.

9
LAMB

If I were placed midway between a perfectly cooked lamb ribeye and a perfectly cooked beef ribeye, I would starve to death trying to pick which to eat. If you love red meat and don't love lamb, then you've never had it cooked properly. I'm talking to you, steak lover who was turned off lamb as a child because it was mutton and cooked to death and served with mint jelly. Well, I am here to conduct a culinary conversion.

WOOD-GRILLED RACK OF LAMB

A rack of lamb is essentially the same thing as a beef prime rib roast: the muscle attached to the back ribs. But on a lamb it is smaller and more tender. So when you get a full 8-bone rack of lamb, it is only enough to feed two hungry people. I'll bet you could eat one all by yourself if you'd just try it.

MAKES *2 servings*

TAKES *about 2 hours*

1 (8-bone) rack of lamb (about 2 pounds), chine bone removed

2 teaspoons kosher salt

3 tablespoons Dolly's Lamb Rub (page 169)

1. Prep. Trim as much fat as you can. Otherwise, it will melt and cause huge flare-ups. Even if you sacrifice a little meat in the trimming, get rid of the fat and the silverskin beneath it. Sprinkle the lamb with salt and dry brine for about 2 hours before cooking. Rub the spice rub over the meat at any time.

2. Fire up. Start a wood fire as described on page 148. This can be done in a wheelbarrow, a fire pit, or an extra charcoal grill. Once you have a good glowing bed of hot coals, move them to your grill and set up a two-zone configuration and get the indirect-heat zone to 225°F.

3. Cook. Place the meat over indirect heat and close the lid. Monitor the temperature with a rapid-read thermometer and flip the meat after it reaches about 80°F. When it hits about 100°F, move the roast over direct heat to begin searing. Turn and rotate the meat frequently until there is even color on all the surfaces and the internal temperature is about 130°F.

4. Serve. Cut the rack at every other bone for 4 double-wide chops. You can serve the meat as is or with a simple Board Sauce (see page 188).

HERBED LAMB LOLLIPOPS

You can cook a whole rack of lamb or break it down into individual ribeyes, which give you more brown surfaces. Cutting it into single-bone sections leaves you with chops that are too thin to brown on the outside without overcooking the inside, plus it is tricky to get all 8 chops the same thickness. So I prefer double-wide chops. I call these lollipops because the knob of meat, perhaps 2 inches in diameter and 1½ inches thick, can easily be eaten without the aid of knife and fork in about six bites.

MAKES *2 servings*

TAKES *20 minutes to trim, 1 to 2 hours to dry brine, and 30 minutes to cook*

- 1 (8-bone) rack of lamb (about 2 pounds), chine bone removed
- Kosher salt
- 4 garlic cloves, minced or pressed
- 3 tablespoons finely chopped fresh rosemary, or 2 teaspoons dried
- ½ teaspoon coarsely ground black pepper

1. Prep. Trim the fat and the tough silverskin beneath it. Yes, this is a lot of waste. Work carefully so you

don't waste any of the expensive meat. Cut the rack into 4 fat, double-wide chops by slicing between every second bone. Try to make all four the same thickness so they will cook at the same rate. Sprinkle the meat with salt and dry brine in the fridge 1 to 2 hours before cooking.

2. Mix the garlic, rosemary, and pepper together, sprinkle the mixture over the meat and rub it in at any time after dry brining. Much of it will fall off during cooking, which is why you need so much to begin with.

3. Fire up. Set up the grill for two-zone cooking with the direct-heat side as hot as you can get it.

4. Cook. Warm the meat gently on the indirect side with the lid down for about 5 minutes per side until the meat hits about 115°F. Move the chops to the direct side to sear the exterior. Leave the lid open. The bones will char badly, so if you want to prevent this, wrap them with foil or let them hang over the

edge of the grill. Otherwise, let 'em char. When you turn the meat, try not to drag it across the grates and scrape off the rub, but turn the chops often, about every minute. When the meat hits 130°F, make sure everyone is in their seats. Serve immediately.

MARINATED LAMB LOIN CHOPS

L amb loin chops are the porterhouse steaks of the lamb, with a T-bone separating the strip steak on one side and the filet mignon on the other. But they are a lot smaller than beef porterhouses and are typically 1 inch thick, no bigger than a child's fist, and under 6 ounces including the bone. Choose thick ones, at least 1 inch thick.

This marinade is great on all cuts of lamb, including rack, leg, and kebabs. The result is amazingly flavorful, tender, and juicy. But it is strong, so don't overdo it and cover over the meat flavor.

MAKES *2 servings*

TAKES *40 minutes for the marinade to come together, 20 minutes to marinate, and 20 minutes to cook*

> 6 lamb loin chops, at least 1 inch thick
> ½ teaspoon kosher salt
> ¼ cup red wine vinegar
> ¼ cup balsamic vinegar
> ¼ cup olive oil
> 3 tablespoons toasted sesame oil
> 3 tablespoons chopped fresh rosemary leaves or 1 teaspoon dried (see Note)
> 6 garlic cloves, minced or pressed

1. Prep. Trim the fat from the meat, taking care to get as much of the surface fat as you can—it will melt and cause flare-ups if left on the chops. Sprinkle with salt and dry brine in the refrigerator 1 to 2 hours before cooking.

2. Meanwhile, whisk together the vinegars, olive oil, sesame oil, rosemary, and garlic. Pour the marinade into a nonreactive pan large enough to hold the chops comfortably but snugly. Let the marinade sit for 40 minutes so the flavors marry while the meat dry brines.

3. Arrange the chops in the pan—you can crowd them in, but they should not overlap. Turn them to coat all sides with marinade and let them sit for 10 minutes per side at room temperature. Do not marinate for any longer than 20 minutes.

4. Fire up. Set up the grill for two-zone cooking with the direct-heat side at warp 10 (as hot as you can get it).

5. Cook. Because the chops are usually thin and small, you will not need to reverse sear. Grill the chops on the hot side with the lid up so all the energy is pumped into one side while the other side cools. Turn the chops frequently, until the meat is 130°F in the center. It's OK if they get really dark—that's the

balsamic talking—but don't let them burn, and for heaven's sake, do not overcook!

6. Monitor each chop's temperature individually; they each have a mind of their own. Use the cool side of the grill to hold the chops as they finish cooking. If the exteriors are really dark and the interiors are not done, stand them on end, flat side of the T-bone down, for about 5 minutes.

NOTE: If you have fresh rosemary, strip the spindly leaves from the stem and chop them up so the herb will ooze its deliciousness into the marinade. If you use dried rosemary, crush it lightly with a mortar and pestle or crush it between your palms.

LEG O' LAMB

Leg of lamb is thick at the hip end and tapers to the ankle end like a ham, yielding enough meat to feed eight or more. It's a complex bundle of muscles with layers of fat and connective tissue throughout. This huge mass of meat is an impressive sight and is certain to get your guests salivating.

MAKES *8 to 10 servings*

TAKES *up to 24 hours to dry brine and about 2 hours to cook*

> 1 bone-in leg of lamb, about 9 pounds before trimming (see Note, page 289)
> Kosher salt
> 1 recipe Dolly's Lamb Rub (page 169)
> 3 recipes Board Sauce (page 188), heavy on mint or rosemary

1. Prep. Remove as much as possible of the thick fat cap on the surface of the lamb and all the silverskin underneath. Remove the aitchbone (see page 288) if you didn't have it removed at the store. If you wish, gash the surface so it can get crunchy and to create more surface area for the rub (see page 227).

2. Dry brine. Sprinkle less salt over thin parts of the meat and a little more on the thicker parts. If there are loose flaps of meat, tie the leg with butcher's twine so the flaps lie flat against the rest of the leg.

3. Wet your hands and pat the surface of the meat so it is moist and the rub will stick. Pat the rub all over the meat and massage it deep into the gashes.

4. Prep the Board Sauce in a coffee cup.

5. Fire up. Set up the grill for two-zone cooking so the indirect side is about 225°F. This cut of lamb performs

CHOOSING A LEG O' LAMB

There are four ways to prepare a big ol' leg o' lamb: bone-in, boneless, butterflied, or cut apart into cubes for spiedies (opposite).

BONE-IN With a bone-in leg (below), the thick end can be cooked to a perfect medium-rare, while the narrow end will be closer to well-done. There's always someone who doesn't like red or pink meat, so this may suit your guests.

If you are going to cook a bone-in leg, have your butcher remove the shank, shown in the picture below. The bone is hard to cut through at home, but it can be done with a shiny new hacksaw blade. The shank is the end that tapers to the ankle; it is tough, laden with leathery tendons, and always cooks well-done because it is so narrow. Save a few in the freezer and use them to make stew.

Also ask your butcher to remove the aitch-bone, the part of the pelvic bone that has the

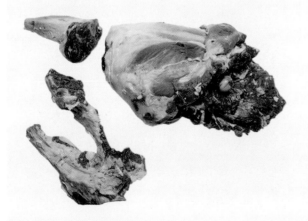

socket into which the ball of the thighbone fits. In the photo below left, you can see the aitchbone in the lower left, the ball of the femur (thighbone) peeking out of the thigh, and the tibia and fibula (shank) in the upper left. Getting it out makes carving the finished meat a lot easier and unless you know what you are doing, it can be a real pain to remove at home.

BONELESS ROAST You can buy boneless legs, and that's what I usually do. A boneless leg comes rolled and tied into a more symmetrical shape, so it cooks more evenly and is easier to carve with no bones in the way. You can do it yourself, but it is tedious. Make sure you ask the butcher to remove the ugly-tasting gland located in the triangle of fat near the knee.

You can even cut the string, open the leg, and stuff the leg with dried fruits and/or seasoned bread crumbs, and then tie it up again. Prunes are a classic stuffing.

BUTTERFLIED Another great way to cook leg of lamb is to bone it but not roll it up. When you are done, you'll have a big flap of meat, perhaps 2 by 2 feet and 1 to 4 inches thick. The exterior will be fairly even and smooth, but the inside will be irregular and have mountains and valleys from the deboning effort. These nooks and crannies are perfect places to hide the flavors of Dolly's Lamb Rub (page 169), but they make it hard to cook it evenly. If you reverse sear it, you'll get more even cooking and lots of great crispy brown surface.

much better at low temperatures. If you'd like a little smoke flavor, add a small amount of dry wood now.

6. Cook. Roast on the indirect-heat side with the lid down until the meat's internal temperature hits about 120°F. Move the meat to the direct-heat side and sear it until it is dark on all four sides and the temperature in the center reaches 130°F. As you can see in the picture below, I used a pair of preheated foil-wrapped bricks to hold the roast on edge and get an all-over sear.

7. Serve. Pour the Board Sauce on the cutting board, plop the meat on top of it, and start carving. Slice the lamb across the grain into ¼-inch-thick slices, get plenty of the sauce on them and let the meat juices mingle with the sauce.

NOTE: A typical bone-in leg of lamb will usually be in the 8- to 9-pound range, perhaps smaller in the spring. After it is trimmed and has the aitchbone removed, it will weigh about 6 pounds. The same boned leg will yield about 5 pounds of meat.

BINGHAMTON SPIEDIE SANDWICHES

Spiedies were probably created by Augustine Iacovelli, who immigrated from Abruzzi, Italy, and settled near Binghamton, New York, where he opened a restaurant named Augies. His *spiedini*, which in his homeland meant, roughly, "little roasted things," were marinated and heavily seasoned lamb chunks served on Italian bread to hungry laborers who dubbed them "spiedies."

They are like kebabs but better. It's nearly impossible to get the exterior of kebabs crisp while keeping the interior red or pink because the cubes are too small. The solution is to cut larger cubes that can be rolled around without a skewer. They get dark and crispy on the outside and still don't overcook in the center.

The meat is served rare to medium, and the brinerade flavor is almost as strong as the meat flavor. Spiedies are usually served on rolls, but they are just fine rolling around loose on your plate or on top of a pile of rice or couscous or bulgur wheat. Although this recipe is for lamb, you can use the same technique with cubes of pork, beef, or even chicken. For the life of me, I cannot understand why spiedies have not spread beyond upstate New York.

MAKES *4 large sandwiches*

TAKES *20 minutes to make the brinerade, 8 to 24 hours to marinate, 20 to 30 minutes to cook*

¾ cup Basic Brinerade (page 161)

¼ cup dry red wine

4 garlic cloves, crushed

1 teaspoon kosher salt

2 pounds boneless lamb leg or shoulder meat, cut into 1½- to 2-inch cubes

4 (6-inch-long) Italian bread rolls, split lengthwise

2 red, yellow, or green bell peppers, or a mix, seeded, quartered

2 large onions, cut into ½-inch-thick disks and separated into rings

1. Prep. Put the brinerade, wine, garlic, and salt in a large zipper-top bag or a bowl and mix thoroughly. Remove and reserve ¼ cup for later use.

2. Add the lamb cubes to the brinerade, mix well, and refrigerate for at least 8 hours and up to 24 hours, the longer the better.

3. Fire up. Set up the grill for two-zone cooking but don't get the hot side all the way up to warp 10 (high). You'll cook these chunks mostly in the direct zone, lid up, and reserve the indirect zone for holding pieces when they finish.

4. Cook. Toast the rolls on the cut side. Watch carefully so they don't burn; they can be done in as little as 1 minute. If they blacken a bit, scrape off the char and the bread will be fine. Set aside on a serving platter at room temperature.

5. Grill the peppers on the hot side until they soften but are not limp. Set aside in a serving bowl at room temperature.

6. Put the onion rings into a bowl with the reserved ¼ cup marinade and toss until the rings are well coated. Grill the rings until they are slightly soft. I like them a bit undercooked and crunchy, but if you prefer them softer, cook them longer. Transfer to the bowl with the peppers.

7. Put a colander or strainer in the sink and dump the meat and brinerade into it. Let the meat drain for a few minutes so the liquid will not drip onto the fire when you cook it. Move the meat to the direct-heat side of the grill and separate the chunks so they are not touching. Grill on one side with the lid up. Let the pieces sit untouched so they get grill marks. With small pieces of meat, grill marks are a good thing since the lamb will overcook if you try to get it dark brown all over. Turn the meat over with tongs and cook some more. Test by biting into one. A thermometer won't be much help because the cubes are small. Don't overcook.

8. Serve. Put the meat on the rolls and top it with the peppers and onions. Have plenty of napkins on hand.

SUNLITE KENTUCKY MUTTON OR LAMB

In and around Owensboro, in western Kentucky, mutton is the local specialty. When a one-year-old sheep is no longer producing enough wool, it is slaughtered and the meat is called mutton. It has a gamier taste than younger, more succulent lamb. As with so many other barbecue meats such as pork ribs and beef brisket, mutton shoulder and leg found their way to the low, slow smoker because they can be tough, full of connective tissue, and less marketable than lamb.

Barbecued mutton is prepared in a similar fashion to pulled pork, but it is usually sliced, not shredded. It is then doused with a thin vinegar-and-Worcestershire-based sauce that enters all the openings it can find. The most famous barbeque restaurant in Owensboro is the Moonlite Bar-B-Q Inn, and I have modeled my sauce after theirs.

The funny thing is, it is hard to find mutton, so this recipe calls for lamb. All the better.

MAKES *6 to 8 servings*

TAKES *6 to 8 hours*

> 1 (4-pound) lamb shoulder
> 2 teaspoons kosher salt
> 1 recipe (about ⅓ cup) Dolly's Lamb Rub (page 169)
> 1 recipe Sunlite Kentucky Black Sauce (page 182)

1. Prep. Remove all the surface fat from the lamb and the tough silverskin hiding under it. Sprinkle the lamb with salt and dry brine in the refrigerator for 6 to 12 hours, if possible.

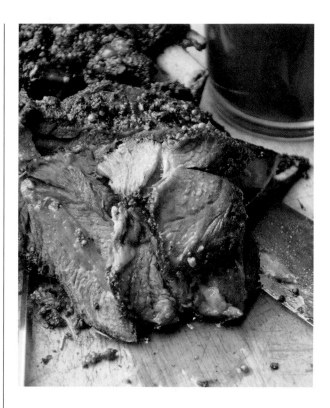

2. Just before cooking, mix the rub with a little water, about 2 to 3 tablespoons, to make a thick paste and coat the meat with the paste.

3. Set aside 1 cup of the sauce for serving and use the remainder for basting. Keep warm.

4. Fire up. Get your smoker up to 225°F or set up the grill for two-zone cooking and shoot for about 225°F on the indirect side.

5. Cook. Warm the lamb for about 30 minutes in smoky indirect heat. Paint it with the sauce, brushing it on every 15 minutes or so, and cook until the internal temperature reaches about 203°F. This could take up to 8 hours. Start early and have a faux Cambro (see page 50) on hand in case it finishes earlier than expected. If it is moving too slow through the stall, use the Texas crutch (see page 60).

6. Serve. Cut the meat off the bone in ⅛- to ¼-inch-thick slices. Arrange the slices on a serving platter and douse with warm sauce just before serving.

10

CHICKEN
and TURKEY

TIPS ON COOKING POULTRY

In general, the goal is to have crispy golden skin on top of tender, moist meat, and to not mask the natural meat flavors.

REVERSE SEAR. The best cooking technique for poultry is the reverse sear. Set up a two-zone configuration on your grill. Slowly warm the bird at low to moderate temperatures (225 to 325°F) in the indirect zone with the lid down until it is not quite done (about 145°F). This helps render fat and prevents flare-ups and burning the volatile skin. Then hit it with high direct radiant heat, lid up, to brown and crisp the skin and meaty side.

BREAK DOWN THE BIRD. When you grill chicken parts, the meat can brown on all sides (remember, brown is flavor), and you can remove each piece when it hits the optimum temperature. Some cooks worry that more cut surfaces mean more moisture loss, but cut parts cook a whole lot faster than a whole bird, and the longer the bird is on the heat, the more it dries out.

You can save money by purchasing a whole bird and cutting it up yourself. Use kitchen shears to remove the backbone and save it for making chicken stock. Chicken stock is one of those ingredients that has endless uses, and homemade is always better than store-bought. Trim off excess fat and skin and the tips of the wings and throw them in with the back for stock. Add the neck and giblets. Save the liver in the freezer and when you get enough you can grill them or make a pâté.

Snip the thin meat that connects the thigh to the breast. If you wish, you can cut the drumstick off the thigh and you can cut the wing off the breast.

HALVING THE BIRD. Cutting the bird in half is also a good technique. The fat drains easily through the cut skin, and you can brown both sides. The problem is that the thighs easily tear off when you move the meat around, since there is little other than skin holding them to the breasts, and the wings are on top of the breast, so they cook at a much different rate than everything else.

SPATCHCOCK (BUTTERFLY) THE BIRD. Take out the backbone and flatten the bird. Cook the bird skin up on the indirect side, then flip it skin down on the direct side for a few minutes. This browns all sides, but you have to be careful that the legs don't fall off when you flip.

ROASTING IT WHOLE. You can roast a whole bird easily on the grill. The problem is that all the heat still comes from the outside, so the outside tends to overcook while the inside remains colorless and sometimes undercooked. Because breasts are much thicker than other parts, and they are not very forgiving, cooking whole birds usually ends up with something over- or undercooked.

ROTISSERIE CHICKEN. Season the interior and exterior of a whole bird, and the juices from the rotating bird will roll around on the surface and fewer juices will fall into the fire compared to when it is sitting still on the grill.

VERTICAL ROAST. If you must cook whole birds, I recommend vertical wire roasting frames, which allow air to enter the cavity and cook the meat on the inside. Vertical roasting over indirect heat uniformly cooks the meat and crisps the skin. The legs are closer to the heat so they get close to optimal temperature, while the breasts lag just the right amount behind. As long as you monitor the temperature the meat will be moist and tender. But the inside still doesn't brown because the air gets trapped in there, and convection flow browns better. If you use a wire roasting frame, I recommend that you insert a knife down into the neck cavity from above and open a "chimney" connecting to the abdominal cavity, so hot air can travel through.

MYTH Beer can chicken is the best way to cook a bird.

BUSTED! Yes, I know your BCC tastes wonderful. Yes, I know your neighbors and family think it is absolutely, positively fabulous. That's because it is a roast chicken, and what's not to love about roast chicken?

But beer can chicken is a waste of good beer and an inferior cooking technique.

The popular procedure is to use room-temperature beer, drink half the can, and punch holes in the top. Some folks put herbs and spices in the can and use a nice flavorful rub. Insert the can in the cavity of the bird and place it on the grill.

Believers think the beer moisturizes the meat. But there's no way the beer can escape the can and contact the flesh because the can blocks sideways movement of the beer and the beer never gets hot enough to steam and come out the top. We have measured it.

Here's why: The chicken is a thick, wet insulation blanket wrapped around the beer. It is, in effect, a chicken beer koozie, so the beer warms at about the same rate as the meat. Remember, the meat is 70 percent water and the beer is more than 92 percent water. The beer and chicken become a single thermal mass. If you cook the chicken to 160°F, the beer will not rise above 150°F, 62°F below the boiling point of water. In all my tests, the weight of the can was the same before and after cooking, and in some cases, because fat had dripped into the can, it weighed more! With a fat layer on top, metal can all around, and a temperature below boiling, there is no way the beer can escape the can and moisten or flavor the meat.

Believers also say the beer adds flavor. According to Scott Bruslind, laboratory manager at Analysis Laboratory, on average, 92 percent of beer is flavorless water and 5 percent is flavorless alcohol. If you want to add flavor to the inside of the bird, throw herbs and spices in there!

BCC is also a health risk. Since the center of the bird is cooled by the beer can, the risk of undercooking is high. And wiggling that can out of the cavity can cause a nasty burn.

The final proof: Many fine dining restaurants serve roast chicken, but you've never seen a white-tablecloth restaurant serve beer can chicken, have you? That's because professional chefs know there are many better ways to roast a chicken. And they hate wasting beer.

PROPER MEAT TEMPERATURE. Remember, you cannot tell when chicken is safe by wiggling the drumstick, or watching for the juices to run clear, or looking at the color of the flesh. There is only one way: a modern digital thermometer (see page 96). Place your instant-read food thermometer probe in the thickest part of each piece, but don't touch the bones. The wings will finish much faster than the other parts, so put them on late and be prepared to remove them early.

Dark meat has about 10 percent fat, so it tastes and feels best at about 170°F. Since white meat has only about 6 percent fat, and it dries out quickly if it is overcooked, it has its best texture and juiciness at about 155°F, but that's 10°F below the USDA recommendation and the risk is too great at that temperature. I recommend cooking it to 160°F and letting the temperature rise to 165°F from carryover while it moves from the cooker to the carving board.

COOKING TEMPERATURE. Chicken and turkey don't have a lot of tough connective tissue, so they don't have to be cooked as low and slow as things like pork ribs. You can reverse sear parts and halves starting at 325°F on the indirect side in order to render more fat from the skin and get it crispier. If you have a smoker or grill that doesn't get to 325°F in the indirect zone, you will need to cook the bird longer. Don't sweat it. The skin will still brown because the Maillard reaction can take place at lower temperatures, though at a much slower pace. Besides, the smoke is going to darken the skin, too. If the skin isn't crisp by the time the meat hits 145°F, move the bird over direct heat or put it in an indoor oven or on a grill at 350 to 400°F.

GOING SKINLESS. I know the skin tastes great, and there is a lot of moisture and flavor in the fat just under the skin, but if you take it off, you can save enough calories to have ice cream for dessert. Surprisingly, you can get a nice crispiness on skinless chicken during the searing part of the reverse sear. Add the right rub and you get a bark.

SMOKING POULTRY. Go easy on smoke. It is really easy to oversmoke poultry. It likes smoke, but not too much.

SIMON & GARFUNKEL CHICKEN

Simon & Garfunkel Rub is an herb-based rub that is great on chicken. It allows the natural flavors to shine. This is my favorite weeknight chicken recipe, and I never get tired of it.

MAKES *3 or 4 servings*

TAKES *1 or 2 hours to dry brine and 30 to 40 minutes to cook*

1 (3- to 4-pound) chicken

1½ teaspoons kosher salt

2 tablespoons Simon & Garfunkel Rub (page 168)

1. Prep. Buy cut-up chicken or cut it up yourself. Cut the backbone out of the chicken and then cut the bird into six parts: breasts, wings, and drum-with-thigh combo. Sprinkle the chicken with salt and dry brine in the fridge for 1 to 2 hours. Then dampen the chicken parts with a little water and gently work the rub into the meat.

2. Fire up. Set up the grill for two-zone cooking and shoot for about 325°F on the indirect side.

3. Cook. Place the chicken parts on the indirect side, skin side up, and close the lid. Let them get nice and brown on the bottoms, but check to make sure they're not burning. You probably won't need to flip them. When the meat hits about 145°F, move them over high direct heat, skin down, with the lid up. Flip every minute or two so both sides get good and dark, but don't allow them to burn. As the white meat pieces hit 160°F and the dark meat pieces hit 165°F, move them back to the indirect heat side to wait for the others to finish.

CORNELL CHICKEN

If you like grilled chicken with golden, crispy skin, say thank you to Bob Baker. Baker was a professor of food science and poultry science at Cornell University who helped invent chicken nuggets, turkey ham, and poultry hot dogs. He died in 2006, but his memory will live on for a long time in western New York state. In Ithaca, New York, where Cornell is located, he is famous for Cornell Chicken, a recipe that has

become so popular that it is practically required at parties and fund-raisers.

Baker's recipe called for cutting the birds in half, but I think it is better to quarter them, since breasts and thighs cook at different rates. His marinade is very close to a mayonnaise; because there is raw egg involved, cooking it to 160°F is essential.

Here is my slightly modernized version of Dr. Baker's original recipe. He recommends cooking the chicken over an open flame without a cover, but I find it works much better if you reverse sear.

MAKES *3 or 4 servings*

TAKES *15 minutes to make the marinade, 3 to 24 hours for the meat to swim in it, and about 45 minutes to cook*

1 large egg

¼ cup vegetable oil

½ cup apple cider vinegar

1 teaspoon table salt

1 teaspoon Simon & Garfunkel Rub (page 168)

¼ teaspoon freshly ground black pepper

1 (3- to 4-pound) chicken, cut into quarters

1. **Prep.** In a large bowl, whisk the egg. Add the oil and whisk until the mixture is thick, homogeneous, and bright yellow, about 2 minutes. Whisk in the vinegar, salt, rub, and pepper. Pour the marinade into a large zipper-top bag or a bowl and add the chicken pieces. Make sure the pieces are coated with the marinade. Leave it in the fridge for 3 to 24 hours. Turn the meat occasionally so all surfaces get well coated.

2. **Fire up.** Set up the grill for two-zone cooking and shoot for about 325°F on the indirect side.

3. **Cook.** Place the chicken over the indirect zone and close the lid. Turn the pieces every 5 minutes or so, and baste the chicken with the marinade. Cook for about 45 minutes, until the internal temperature of each piece reaches 145°F. At this point, stop basting, discard the contaminated marinade, and don't touch the meat again with the brush. Lift the lid and move the pieces over the direct-heat side of the grill, skin side down. Flip every few minutes. When the skin is crisp and the internal temperature reaches 160°F, take the meat off and serve.

HAWAIIAN HULI-HULI TERIYAKI CHICKEN

As popular as this dish is in Hawaii, it is surprising that it hasn't become more known on the mainland. Let's change that! Huli-huli sauce is like teriyaki sauce and contains salty soy sauce, so it works like a brinerade. It also makes a nice glaze when basted on during cooking.

MAKES *3 or 4 servings*

TAKES *about 30 minutes to prep, 3 to 24 hours to marinate, and about 30 minutes to cook*

1 cup Hawaiian Huli-Huli Teriyaki Sauce and Marinade (page 183)
1 (3- to 4-pound) chicken, cut into 4 to 8 parts

1. **Prep.** Pour the marinade into a large zipper-top bag or a bowl. Add the chicken and marinate for 3 to 24 hours in the refrigerator. Every hour or so, turn the meat a bit so all surfaces get well coated.

2. **Fire up.** Set up the grill for two-zone cooking. Try to get the indirect side in the 325°F range.

3. **Cook.** Lift the chicken pieces from the marinade, place them on the indirect side of the grill, and close the lid. Baste with the marinade periodically. Watch so the sugar doesn't blacken. Take the meat's temperature, and as it approaches 145°F, stop basting and discard the contaminated marinade.

4. Move the chicken to the direct-heat side of the grill and cook skin side down to crisp the skin. Flip it every 1 to 2 minutes to make sure it is not burning. When the white meat is 160°F, you're ready for your luau.

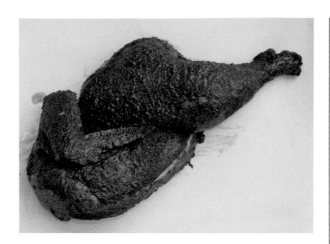

SWEET GEORGIA BROWN SMOKED YARD BIRD

Smoked chicken, Georgia style, is big, bold, and assertive, but the skin, although it is packed with flavor, is not crisp. I can show you how to fix this.

MAKES *3 or 4 servings*

TAKES *1 to 3 hours to dry brine, 60 to 90 minutes to cook*

> 1 (3- to 4-pound) chicken
> 1½ teaspoons kosher salt
> ¼ cup Meathead's Memphis Dust (page 167)

1. Prep. Split the chicken in half or cut it into 8 parts, sprinkle the pieces with salt, and dry brine in the fridge for 1 to 3 hours. Dust both sides thoroughly with the rub.

2. Fire up. Get your smoker up to 225°F or set up the grill for two-zone cooking and shoot for about 225°F on the indirect side.

3. Cook. Put the meat on the indirect side of the grill and add wood. Add less wood than you normally do. Chicken doesn't need much smoke. After you've tasted the finished product, you can decide if you want to use more wood the next time you cook it. Smoke for 60 to 90 minutes, or until the temperature in the thickest part of the meat (without touching bone) is 145°F. Now fire up your grill as hot as you can get it, lid open, and move the chicken there, skin side down, and sear it until the internal temperature is 160°F and the skin is crispy.

PULLED CHICKEN

All the fun of pulled pork with a fraction of the fat. And a pulled chicken sandwich takes a lot less time. If you make cracklins from the skin, you can make a noisier sandwich, too.

MAKES *3 or 4 servings*

TAKES *1 to 3 hours to dry brine, 60 to 90 minutes to cook*

> 1 (3- to 4-pound) chicken
> 1½ teaspoons kosher salt
> ¼ cup Meathead's Memphis Dust (page 167)

1. Prep. Remove the chicken skin, but try to keep it in big pieces. Split the chicken in half or cut it into 8 parts. Sprinkle the pieces with salt and dry brine in the fridge for 1 to 3 hours. Dust both sides thoroughly with the rub.

2. Fire up. Get your smoker up to 225°F or set up the grill for two-zone cooking and shoot for about 225°F on the indirect side.

3. Cook. Put the meat and the skins on the indirect side of the grill and add wood. Stretch the skin out, outer side up, as much as possible so it is not bunched up. Smoke for 60 to 90 minutes, or until the temperature in the thickest part of the meat (without touching bone) is 145°F. The skins should come out crunchy. If not, you can finish them on the direct side of the grill or in a hot pan. Move the chicken pieces to the hot side, lid open, and sear them until the internal temperature is 160°F.

4. Serve. Pull the chicken off the bones and shred it. Put the shredded meat on a bun with just a dollop of your favorite sauce, sprinkle the cracklins on top, and serve.

BIG BOB GIBSON'S CHICKEN IN 'BAMA WHITE SAUCE

At Big Bob Gibson Bar-B-Q in Decatur, Alabama, they smoke chickens and dip them in a bucket of white barbecue sauce. It is not like any barbecue sauce you have ever tasted, and it has become a major thang in Alabama.

MAKES *3 or 4 servings*

TAKES *10 minutes to prep, about 45 minutes to cook*

> 1 (3- to 4-pound) chicken
> Kosher salt and freshly ground black pepper
> 1½ cups Alabama White Sauce (page 181)

1. Prep. Cut the chickens into 6 parts: 2 drumstick and thigh combos, 2 breasts, and 2 wings. Sprinkle

the pieces liberally with salt and pepper on both sides. Let the salt soak into the meat in the fridge for a couple of hours.

2. Fire up. Get your smoker up to 225°F or set up the grill for two-zone cooking and shoot for about 225°F on the indirect side. Get some smoke rolling.

3. Cook. Place the chicken skin side up on the indirect side of the grill. Check the temperature of each piece independently because they will cook at different rates. When all parts hit about 145°F, move the pieces to the hot side of the grill, skin side down. When they reach 160°F, paint them generously on all sides with the sauce. Serve immediately.

PIRI PIRI CHICKEN

Piri piri (sometimes called peri peri) is a chicken recipe popular in Mozambique and other African nations. The bird is marinated in a hot pepper sauce made from pili pili (or African bird's-eye) chile peppers. If you want, you can use it as a finishing sauce as well. It is not for the faint of tongue, so I have toned it down. Since pili pili chiles are hard to find, I've

suggested that you use your favorite hot sauce. If you want it four-alarm hot, make the recipe, taste it, and add more heat. If you prefer, you can simply get fresh hot peppers, perhaps Thai bird peppers, remove the stems and seeds, and puree them in a food processor or blender and add them to the rest of the ingredients.

MAKES *3 or 4 servings*

TAKES *20 minutes to make the marinade, overnight or longer to marinate, and 40 to 60 minutes to cook*

- Zest and juice of 1 lemon
- Zest and juice of 1 lime
- ¼ cup of your favorite hot sauce, or more, depending on your taste (see headnote)
- ¼ cup chopped red bell pepper
- 3 tablespoons vegetable oil
- 3 garlic cloves, minced or pressed
- 3 tablespoons sweet paprika
- 2 tablespoons dried oregano
- 1 tablespoon grated fresh ginger
- 1 teaspoon kosher salt
- 1 (3- to 4-pound) chicken, cut into 4 to 8 parts

1. Prep. In a blender, combine the lemon zest and juice, lime zest and juice, hot sauce, bell pepper, oil, garlic, paprika, oregano, ginger, and salt. Puree until smooth. Put a third of the marinade into a lidded jar and refrigerate to use later as a dipping sauce. Divide the rest of the marinade between two gallon-size zipper-top bags.

2. Divide the chicken parts between the bags and squish it around to coat with the marinade. Seal the bags, put them in a bowl, and refrigerate for 12 to 24 hours. Every couple of hours, squish the bags a bit to make sure the chicken is well coated.

3. Fire up. Set up the grill for two-zone cooking. Try to get the indirect side in the 325°F range.

4. Cook. Place the chicken in the indirect zone and close the lid. Cook until the meat hits about 145°F, then move it to the direct-heat side and turn frequently until the surface darkens to brown, but not black, and the interior temperature hits 160°F.

5. Serve. Warm the reserved sauce and serve it alongside the meat for dipping.

BLASPHEMY BUFFALO CHICKEN WINGS

Wings are a hugely popular dish made from a part of the chicken that once upon a time was considered scrap. Heck, even chickens can't use chicken wings. Buffalo wings were invented in Buffalo, New York, at the fabled Anchor Bar, which can still be found at 1047 Main Street, although its ownership has changed. The new owners tell this tale: Late on a Friday night in 1964, Dominic Bellissimo, son of owners Frank and Theresa, was working at the Anchor when some of his buddies showed up with the munchies. Theresa was shutting

down the kitchen, so she looked for something quick and easy. She had a box of wings to use for making soup, and, thinking on her feet, she tossed them into the deep fryer, which was still hot. When they emerged, she sprinkled them with hot sauce and some melted margarine, and to make sure the boys had a well-rounded meal, she added a side of celery and blue cheese dressing to dunk the celery into. The boys dipped both the celery and the saucy wings in the blue cheese dressing, and an international sensation was born.

True Buffalo wings are deep-fried, but I love the flavor and convenience of cooking them on the grill. Sometimes I smoke them first. Blasphemy, I know. But tasty blasphemy.

MAKES *4 to 6 appetizer servings*

TAKES *45 minutes to prep and 30 minutes to cook*

BLUE CHEESE DIP (SEE NOTES)

3 ounces cream cheese, at room temperature

3 ounces blue cheese, crumbled, at room temperature

½ teaspoon Simon & Garfunkel Rub (page 168)

½ cup half-and-half

¼ cup sour cream

CLASSIC BUFFALO HOT SAUCE

8 tablespoons (1 stick) salted butter

2 garlic cloves, minced or pressed

½ cup Frank's RedHot sauce (see Notes)

THE REST

24 whole chicken wings (about 4 pounds)

Kosher salt and freshly ground black pepper

6 celery stalks, cut into 4-inch lengths

1. Prep. To make the blue cheese dip, in a medium bowl, stir together the cream cheese, blue cheese, and Simon & Garfunkel Rub. Mix in the half-and-half and sour cream. Cover and refrigerate until ready to use. (The dip can be made and refrigerated a day or two ahead.)

2. To make the Buffalo hot sauce, melt the butter in a saucepan over low heat. Add the garlic and let the mixture simmer for about 1 minute. Don't let the garlic brown. Add the hot sauce and let it get to know the butter mixture for 3 to 4 minutes.

3. For the rest, cut the wings into 3 parts (see page 304) and freeze the tips for making stock. Season with salt and pepper.

4. Fire up. You can start the wings on a smoker if you wish, but I usually grill them. Set up the grill for two-zone cooking. Try to get the indirect side in the 325°F range. If you wish, add wood to the fire to create smoke.

5. Cook. Place the wings on the grill in the indirect zone, close the lid, and cook until the skins are golden, 7 to 10 minutes per side. By then they are pretty close to done. You are shooting for about 140°F, but because they are so thin, it is really hard to get a good read. The good news is that wings are hard to overcook.

6. Get the direct-heat side as hot as possible. Add more lit coals or turn the dial to 11. Open the lid, move the wings onto the direct-heat side, and stand there, turning the wings frequently, until the skin is dark golden to brown but not burned. Keep a close eye on the skinnier pieces, moving them to the indirect zone when they are done.

7. Put the hot sauce in a big bowl or pot and put it on the grill to warm it. Stir or whisk well. When the wings are done, chuck them in with the sauce and toss or stir until they are well coated.

8. Serve. Slide the wings onto a serving platter. Put the celery sticks next to them, and serve with the blue cheese dip on the side.

NOTES: When I'm feeling lazy, I just use Marie's Blue Cheese salad dressing, which you can find in the refrigerator section of the supermarket.

Frank's RedHot is the classic base for Buffalo wing sauce, and its charm is its fresh red pepper flavor. But if you want more heat, try Sriracha. For a change of pace I will often forgo the hot sauce and use D.C. Mumbo Sauce (page 195) or KC Classic (page 175). Not authentic, but mighty tasty.

ANATOMY OF A CHICKEN WING

There are 3 distinct pieces of the wing, each with different thicknesses and ratios of skin to meat: the tips; the wingettes (or flats) in the center; and the drumettes on the end that attach to the shoulders. These pieces cook at different rates and finish at different times. The best thing to do is separate them into their component parts. I serve only the drumettes and wingettes and freeze the tips for use in making stock.

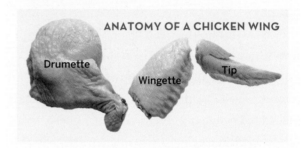

ANATOMY OF A CHICKEN WING

Drumette · Wingette · Tip

ROTISSERIE CHICKEN PROVENÇAL

Traditional oven-roasted chicken is the ultimate comfort food one-pan meal: herbed chicken sitting on a bed of potatoes and vegetables, embellished with garlic, white wine, and olive oil.

To pull off this variation on the classic, you need a rotisserie. Most gas grills have them, or you can buy one to attach to them. The Weber Kettle and a few other charcoal grills sell rotisserie attachments as well.

On a rotating spit, you can get the bird golden and crisp on all sides, not just the top, give it a wisp of smoke, and keep it juicy as it self-bastes. Drippings collect in a pan below that holds the veggies. They simmer at first in the wine, and when it boils off, they will fry in the oil. Start with whatever vegetables you love and whatever are fresh. Firm foods work best: potatoes, squash, Brussels sprouts, carrots. Cut everything to about the same size so they will cook at about the same rate, and don't crowd the pan.

MAKES *4 servings*

TAKES *about 3 hours to dry brine, about 30 minutes to prep, and up to an hour to cook*

- 1 (3- to 4-pound) whole chicken, with a giblet pouch
- 12 Brussels sprouts
- 4 carrots, peeled
- 4 large potatoes, peeled
- 2 white or yellow onions
- 1 fennel bulb, cored
- 6 garlic cloves
- ¼ cup olive oil
- 1 cup dry white wine (see Notes)
- 1¾ teaspoons kosher salt
- 3 tablespoons herbes de Provence (see Notes)
- 12 pitted Kalamata olives
- 2 tablespoons honey
- ¼ teaspoon freshly ground black pepper
- 2 tablespoons chopped fresh flat-leaf parsley or chives, for garnish

1. Prep. Before dry brining, pour any juices from the cavity of the bird into a 9-by-13-inch baking pan. If you have a dark pan, use it (see sidebar, page 306). Open the pouch, remove the liver, and freeze it for another use. Toss the rest of the giblets and the neck in the pan. Snip off the wing tips from the chicken and toss them in the pan with the giblets. Chop the Brussels sprouts, carrots, potatoes, onions, and fennel into bite-size chunks. Toss them in. Coarsely chop the garlic and throw it in, too. Pour in the oil and toss the veggies to coat them. Make sure there is a thin layer of oil in the pan. Add the wine. If needed, add enough water so that the liquid in the pan is about ¼ inch deep. Place the pan in the refrigerator to chill.

2. Sprinkle the chicken with salt and the herbes de Provence. Dry brine the chicken in the fridge for 1 to 3 hours. Tie the drumsticks together with butcher's twine so they don't flop around and fall off as they cook. Cover the wings with foil so they don't burn because they will be closest to the heat. Refrigerate until ready to cook.

3. Fire up. Preheat the grill. Shoot for a temperature of about 325°F near the bird. On a gas grill, if you have a rotisserie burner, fire it up and put the lower burners on as low as possible. Mount the bird on the spit and if there is a counterweight, set it to offset the wobble of the bird. Turn on the motor. Place the drip pan holding the veggies under the chicken. If you wish, put some wood near a hot burner for a kiss of smoke.

On a charcoal grill, push most of the coals to the left and right sides of the bird, but leave a few under the drip pan. Place the chicken on the spit over the pan with the veggies and turn it on. Make sure the top vent is open and the bottom is at least half open.

4. Cook. Close the lid and, as the water evaporates, keep an eye on the veggies. Once the water is gone, depending on how hot the grill is and where the heat is coming from, they can go from brown to black in a hurry. When the vegetables brown on one side, toss and turn them with a spatula or tongs. They're done when they are fork-tender. If they're done and the chicken needs more time, add a little water. You want the water to evaporate and the veggies to fry just before you serve them.

THE COLOR OF THE PAN MATTERS

A black pan browns better than a light-colored pan because it absorbs and transmits more heat instead of reflecting it. I always roast in a black enamel pan if I want good browning. And who doesn't love that crunchy crust on a pan-roasted potato?

Stainless Steel Pan

Black Enamel Pan

5. Just before removing the veggies from the heat, throw in the olives, drizzle in the honey, and stir. Taste, and season with salt and pepper as needed.

6. Serve. When the breast meat hits 160°F, remove the spit with gloves on both hands and carefully remove the bird from the spit. Cut the chicken into quarters. Spoon the veggies onto serving plates and top each serving with a chicken quarter. Garnish with the parsley.

NOTES: You can substitute chicken stock or water for the wine and the dish will still be wonderful.

Herbes de Provence is a traditional seasoning blend from the south of France. Usually it's a mixture of dried rosemary, thyme, oregano, savory, marjoram, and sometimes lavender. If you can't find it, you can use Simon & Garfunkel Rub (page 168).

MARINATED CORNISH GAME HENS

My sister, Ann, has used her favorite marinade on Cornish game hens for years. It was inspired by a 1981 recipe she found in the *New York Times* that she tweaked, but, since she's my kid sister, I couldn't run it unadulterated, and I had to tweak it further.

This recipe calls for Cornish game hens, which are not game birds or even a different breed. They are immature chickens younger than five weeks, of either sex, weighing two pounds or less. You can double the recipe and use a whole chicken, but the younger birds absorb the marinade better. If you wish, you can also cook this recipe on a rotisserie.

MAKES *2 servings*

TAKES *15 minutes to prep, 12 hours to marinate, and about 45 minutes to cook*

½ cup apple cider vinegar

2 teaspoons kosher salt

2 teaspoons chili powder

½ teaspoon garlic powder

½ teaspoon ground bay leaf (see Note)

½ teaspoon sugar

½ teaspoon dry mustard

½ teaspoon sweet paprika

1 teaspoon freshly ground black pepper

¼ teaspoon ground cumin

1 Cornish game hen, cut in half

1. Prep. Combine all the ingredients except the hen in a zipper-top bag and shake until the salt and sugar have dissolved. Put the hen in the bag and turn several times to coat. Put the bag in a bowl to catch drips and refrigerate for 12 hours or overnight.

2. Fire up. Set up the grill for two-zone cooking. Try to get the indirect side to 325°F.

3. Cook. Lift the hen from the marinade and set the pieces skin side up on the indirect-heat side of the grill. When the internal temperature of the breasts hits 145°F, place them over direct heat, skin side down, to crisp the skin. Flip them often, and when the internal temperature hits 160°F, bring them in.

NOTE: If you can't find ground bay leaves in your local grocery store, you can order them online or grind whole bay leaves yourself in a coffee grinder, mortar and pestle, or blender.

THE ULTIMATE SMOKED TURKEY

This is no ordinary turkey preparation, pilgrims. Say good-bye to dry, stringy turkey—this will be the best turkey you've ever tasted. In fact, hundreds of readers have written to tell me just that. The result will be a magnificent-looking, dark mahogany avian, with incredibly tender and juicy flesh, delicately and elegantly flavored with savory herbs and seductive smoke, and anointed with a gravy that eclipses all others.

CHOOSING YOUR TURKEY

As a rule of thumb, 1 pound raw weight per person will be more than enough. When you subtract bones, giblets, and shrinkage, you will have about ½ pound per person—still more than enough and folks can take home leftovers.

If you need a lot of turkey, it is better to cook two small birds than one giant one. They will cook faster and be more tender and juicy. The bigger the bird, the thicker the breasts and the longer it takes to cook the center of the breasts to proper doneness. By the time they are done, thinner parts are overcooked, and the outer parts of the breasts are dry.

Turkeys that say "basted" or "self-basted" or "enhanced" have been injected with a salt solution and possibly flavor enhancers and tenderizers. Processors are allowed to inject up to 8 percent of the weight of the bird. Even if a bird has had salt and water injected, the law still allows it to be labeled "natural" or "organic."

"Kosher" birds have been salted on the outside and inside the cavity. You do not want to brine these birds—they will be too salty.

Finding a bird in the supermarket that has not been salted is almost mission impossible. To get one that is not pumped, you may need to special order it, go to a specialty store like Whole Foods, or buy it directly from a farmer.

Surprisingly, fresh turkey may not be the best choice. "Fresh" means, according to USDA, that the bird has not been taken below 26°F by the processor. At that point it can be as hard as a bowling ball. The USDA is allowing marketers to deceive the public.

Sometimes you can buy a truly fresh turkey from a farmer or specialty butcher. Buy a truly fresh turkey only if you are certain it has been killed within a week of the date you will consume it. I would rather have a bird that was flash frozen right after slaughter than an unfrozen bird that has been sitting around in the fridge for a couple of weeks. Proper cooking is far more important than having a "fresh" bird. To thaw a frozen turkey, allow 24 hours in the fridge for every 4 pounds.

COOKING *THE PERFECT* TURKEY

DO NOT TAKE RISKS WITH THANKSGIVING DINNER. If you have doubts, practice before the big day. You're allowed to eat turkey in August or October.

LET THE TURKEY FLAVOR SHINE. Don't go crazy with powerful injections and rubs that hide the natural flavor of the bird.

DO NOT TRUST THE POP-UP THERMOMETER. The key to turkey success is to avoid overcooking or undercooking it even the slightest bit. A good digital thermometer is never more important. Remove the turkey from the heat when the breasts hit 160°F—not 170 to 180°F, as many recipes recommend.

DO NOT PUT ANYTHING IN THE CAVITY. When you stuff the bird, heat takes far longer to travel to the center of the stuffing, and in the process, the exterior gets way too hot and the meat becomes overcooked. When you leave the cavity empty, the heat and smoke flavors can enter the cavity, cooking the bird much faster and more evenly. Onions and oranges in the cavity do very little to enhance flavor and just block airflow. To bring flavor, sprinkle the cavity with spices and herbs.

DRY BRINE. If your turkey has not been salted by the processor, use a dry brine. Don't waste money making a big bucket of wet brine loaded with apple juice, sugar, and spices that can't penetrate muscle. But the proper amount of salt is a game changer.

NEVER PUT THE TURKEY IN A ROASTING PAN. Roasting pans block airflow, and the underside of the bird doesn't cook properly.

Instead, place the turkey above a roasting pan so air can flow all around it, cooking and browning it properly on the underside. (See the illustration on page 252.) On a grill or smoker, putting the drip pan under the grate is perfect.

DO NOT TRUSS THE LEGS. If you cook the bird whole, do not truss or tie the bird. Let the entire surface brown, even the armpits and crotch, because nobody wants to eat rubbery skin. This will help the thighs and drumsticks cook faster because they need to be cooked to a higher temperature than the breasts.

COOK IT AT THE RIGHT TEMPERATURE. Roast the bird as close to 325°F as your cooker will let you. This crisps the skin.

DO NOT BASTE DURING COOKING. Putting drippings on the skin just makes it soft.

DO NOT REST OR TENT WITH FOIL. Many recipes tell you to cover the bird with foil when you bring it in. Steam trapped under the foil softens the skin. Resting to redistribute juices is not necessary (see page 7).

PREVENT CARRYOVER COOKING. Remember, meat keeps cooking after you take it out of the heat. Take the bird off and start carving immediately.

CONSIDER BUTTERFLYING (AKA SPATCHCOCKING) the bird (as shown on page 295) or cutting it in pieces. This guarantees more delicious brown surfaces and cooks it much faster, producing moister meat. Yes, a Norman Rockwell whole turkey looks cool, but it really isn't the best way to cook it.

There is an added benefit to cooking the bird outdoors: You not only get great flavor, but you also free up the indoor oven for sweet potatoes, stuffing, green beans, and pie. Try it and you'll be cooking turkey on the grill all year-round.

MAKES *1 turkey, any size*

TAKES *1 week to thaw if you have a frozen bird, 12 to 24 hours to dry brine, and 20 minutes to prep. Cooking time depends on the thickness of the thickest piece of meat, the breast, and if it is thoroughly defrosted. Here is a rough guide for how long it will take to get a whole bird to 160°F.*

Pounds	Hours at 325°F
12 to 14	2 to 2½
14 to 18	2½ to 3
18 to 20	3 to 3½
20 to 24	3½ to 4
24 to 30	4 to 5

1 turkey (any size), whole

Kosher salt

3 quarts water or chicken broth

1 cup apple juice

2 onions, skin on, ends removed, quartered

2 carrots, cut into 2-inch lengths

1 celery stalk, leaves and all, cut into 2-inch lengths

1 tablespoon dried sage leaves, crumbled

1 tablespoon dried thyme

2 bay leaves

About ¼ cup Simon & Garfunkel Rub (page 168)

Cooking oil

1. Prep. The day before cooking, open the bag the bird came in and pour the juices into a pot or large zipper-top bag. If there is a plastic pop-up indicator stuck in the bird, remove and discard it. If the tops of the drumsticks are tied together, cut the tie.

Pull the neck and giblets out of the bird. Put everything except the liver in the bag. Freeze the liver for another use—it will not be used for the gravy. Remove the tail and trim the excess skin and fat from around both cavities, front and rear, and put the trimmings in the bag. Lop off the wing tips at the first joint and toss them in the bag. Refrigerate the bag of trimmings.

2. If the turkey has not been salted, sprinkle it with salt, using ½ teaspoon kosher salt per pound of meat, and dry brine it in the refrigerator. Brine for 12 to 24 hours if possible. The salt can go right on the skin. Surprisingly, Professor Blonder's tests have shown that it will penetrate and get into the meat.

3. The day you plan to cook, get out a rectangular pan with at least 3½-quart capacity, preferably stainless steel, ceramic, or CorningWare. It must be large enough to fit under the entire bird and catch the drippings. The pan will get smoky and need serious scrubbing. Don't use copper because it can react with the salts and acids in the gravy. Beware! A disposable aluminum pan will not hold the rack and a bird on top without collapsing, so if you use a disposable pan, it must go under the grill grate and the bird must go on top of the grate. Put the turkey juices and trimmings, the water, apple juice, onions, carrots, celery, sage, thyme, and bay leaves in the pan.

4. Carefully push the rub under the skin covering the turkey breasts. Spread it out and work it as far down to the thighs and legs as possible. Spread some rub on top of the skin and in the cavity. If there is extra, add it to the gravy pan. Take four pieces of foil about 6 by 6 inches, coat one side of each with oil, and cover the wing tips and the ends of the drumsticks to keep them from burning.

5. Fire up. About 5 hours before your guests are ready to sit down, heat up the smoker or set up the grill for two-zone cooking and try to get the indirect side in the 325°F range.

6. Place the gravy pan below where the bird will go. You can put it under the cooking grates, but make sure they are clean on both sides—you don't want grease in the gravy. Ideally the grate should sit a few inches above the gravy pan so heat and smoke can travel between them.

7. Put just a little wood on the heat source, perhaps 4 ounces. On a charcoal grill or smoker, you may not need any wood at all. The charcoal will probably give you all the smoke flavor you need.

8. Cook. Place the bird on the grate over the pan and close the lid. If you have a digital leave-in thermometer, insert it in the breast a little past dead center. If the level of the liquid in the drip pan gets below 2 inches, add a quart of boiling water (don't add cold water, which would cool the cooking chamber). Do not let the solids burn or stick to the pan.

9. As the meat temperature approaches 150°F in the center of the breast, tilt the bird and drain the liquid in the cavity into the gravy. When the meat hits 150°F,

remove the bird and set aside for a minute while you carefully remove the gravy pan. Place the bird back on and the dry heat will finish crisping the underside.

10. Strain the gravy through a sieve into a large pot. Discard the solids. Taste it. It should be rich and flavorful. If is thin, bring it to a boil and let it cook down a little to concentrate the flavors while the bird finishes. When it is the concentration you want (rich), use a fat separator (above), large spoon, or basting bulb to remove most of the fat from the surface of the gravy. Add salt to taste. Resist the temptation to thicken this gravy with flour or cornstarch, since the thin gravy will soak into the meat and add more flavor. A thick, starchy gravy sits on top of the meat and doesn't penetrate.

11. Serve. To lift the hot turkey from the cooker, use Bear Paws (see page 109), or use two spatulas or wooden spoons—just stick the handle of each into the front and rear cavity and lift. Serve your turkey hot and crispy. Don't tent it and let it rest, so carryover cooking dries it out. Place the bird on a cutting board with channels that can hold the copious juices. Carve, following the instructions on page 312. Place the carved meat on a platter with a lip to contain the juices.

HOW TO CARVE A TURKEY

Go ahead and parade the whole bird around the room and take a few bows, but do the carving in the kitchen, not at the dining table. It can be messy. You will need a sharp knife (not serrated), a cutting board with gutters to catch the ample juices, and a serving platter.

Start with the dark meat. Take a paper towel and grab the top of a drumstick and bend it until the joint between it and the thigh is visible. Flex it back and forth until you have a good clear shot at the knee from behind. Sever the meat around the joint and then cut between the ball and socket to remove the leg (Picture 1).

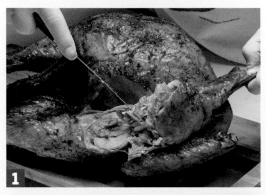

You can serve the drumstick whole for cavemen like me, or you can stand it on the meaty end and slice downward, removing the meat (2).

Now pull out those pieces of stiff tendon with your fingers (3).

Hold the thigh and bend it back to find the hip. Cut through the ball joint, removing the thigh (4).

You can serve the thigh whole, but then the choicest pieces of dark meat will go to only two guests. If you have more people who want thigh meat, you need to remove the bone so you can slice the meat. To do this, flip the thigh skin side down and run the knife around the bone and under it until you can lift it out. Then turn the thigh skin side up and cut it into slices across the grain.

Grab a wing, bend it back to locate the shoulder joint, and cut through the tendons holding together the ball and socket (5).

Now for the breasts. Don't slice them while they are still on the bird. That is cutting with the grain and makes the meat stringy when you chew. Instead, remove each breast lobe and slice it across the grain. Here's how: In the middle of the two lobes is the breastbone, sometimes called the keel bone. Cut down along one side of the breastbone with long strokes until the knife hits the rib cage (6).

Tilt the knife and work along the rib cage with long strokes. Toward the front, the knife will slide along the wishbone. Slice until the breast falls away in one teardrop-shaped hunk.

Lay each breast skin side up on a cutting board and slice it across the grain in slices at least ¼ inch thick (7). I like thicker slices, especially if the meat is tender. If you're not careful, the skin will slip and you won't get neat slices with skin on each slice of meat. Place the knife on the center of the breast near its handle. Place the thumb and forefinger of your free hand on either side of the knife, pressing down on the skin gently. In one gentle, steady stroke, with slight downward pressure, draw the knife toward yourself across the skin, cutting down through it and into the meat. Don't use a sawing motion, or the skin will move around. When you have the meat cut, reassemble it into a breast in order to keep it warm and wet.

Flip the carcass over so the backbone is facing up. Run your fingers along the sides of the backbone. Near the joints where the wings were attached, right under each shoulder blade, you'll find a tender, juicy blob of meat, about the size and shape of the meat from an oyster, hence the nickname, turkey oysters. Pop them out with your fingers. They are some of the best meat on the bird. Give yourself a reward.

Now pour a little gravy over the meat on the platter, enough to moisten but not drown it, and serve.

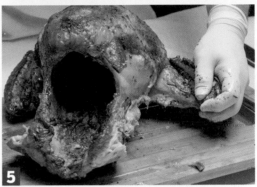

TURKEY BREAST TERIYAKI

You can serve this boneless turkey breast warm or cold on sandwiches with a little sesame mayo.

MAKES *4 to 6 servings*

TAKES *12 to 48 hours to marinate, 60 to 90 minutes to cook*

- 1 (2- to 3-pound) boneless turkey breast lobe (see Notes)
- 2 cups Hawaiian Huli-Huli Teriyaki Sauce and Marinade (page 183)

1. Prep. Use a sharp fillet knife to remove the tendon from the tenderloin.

2. Put the turkey breast in a 1-gallon zipper-top bag. Pour the sauce over it and squish it around. Try to get as much air out of the bag as you can before you seal it. Put the bag in a large bowl in case it leaks and refrigerate for 12 to 48 hours. Every few hours, squish it around and flip it so all parts get wet.

3. Fire up. Set up your grill for indirect cooking or crank up your smoker. Preheat to 225°F. Toss a few ounces of wood on the heat source.

4. Cook. Roast on the indirect side until the breast hits 160°F. (No need to reverse sear because the skin is sliced thin and the heat will just dry out this cut.)

5. Serve. Slice the turkey across the grain. Slice only as much as you need. It dries out quickly.

NOTES: A turkey lobe is a boned half of the breast. There are 2 lobes per turkey. A lobe typically weighs 2 to 3 pounds, although some push the 4-pound mark.

MYTH If you cook a turkey breast side down, the juices will flow into the breast meat and make it moister.

BUSTED! Juices simply can't travel very far through muscle fibers that confine them. The muscles are not pipes. And where would the juices come from? Visualize an upside-down turkey. What is directly above the breast? The cavity! No juices there! If you cook breast down, you smush the breasts and put marks on the skin. Ugly.

I like to make turkey sandwiches with leftovers. I mix about ¼ cup mayonnaise with 4 drips of toasted sesame oil. Taste and add more if you wish, but not much is needed. Spread the mayo on bread and make your sandwich.

GRILLED DUCK BREASTS IN CHERRY-PORT SAUCE

There is not a lot of meat on a duck. You can smoke or grill the whole bird, but when you get down to it, most of it is waste. So the best strategy for duck is to remove the legs and breasts, make cracklins from the remaining skin, render the fat by frying, make stock from the carcass, smoke the legs, and grill the breasts.

The breasts are special, a unique cut and a delicacy prized by those in the know. Duck breasts are a lot like beef or lamb, but there is one spectacular difference: They are covered on one side by a fat layer under the skin. The skin is so delectable that you shouldn't waste it. Long ago, chefs developed a technique for dealing with the subcutaneous fat layer. They gash the skin right down to the muscle and sear the breast in a frying pan so the fat will melt and run into the pan and fry the skin crisp. Then they flip it and sear the back side and serve the meat medium-rare to medium, in the 135°F range. This can make a real mess of the kitchen with spattering and smoke. So here's how to do it outdoors where you don't worry about smoke and spattering.

MAKES *2 servings*

TAKES *3 hours to dry brine, 20 minutes to prepare the breasts, 40 minutes to cook them*

    2 plump duck breast lobes
    Kosher salt
    1 teaspoon Simon & Garfunkel Rub (page 168)
    4 tablespoons (½ stick) unsalted butter
    2 shallots, diced
    ½ cup chicken broth
    ¼ cup ruby port
    ¼ cup balsamic vinegar (see Notes)
    8 ounces dried cherries (see Notes)

1. Prep. With the breasts skin side up, gently draw the knife across the skin of each one, cutting through the fat (see page 317). Make parallel cuts every ¾ to 1 inch. Make similar perpendicular cuts so you have squares of skin still attached to the breast. These will act as drains to allow the fat to run off during cooking. Salt both sides of the breasts and then sprinkle the rub on both sides. Dry brine the breasts in the fridge for about 3 hours.

2. Fire up. Set up your grill for two-zone cooking. Although you will probably not need the indirect zone, it's nice to have a safe zone. Put a heavy pan, a griddle, or a big skillet with ovenproof handles over the direct-heat side and close the lid (do not use

TIPS FOR COOKING DUCK

Before you start cooking, it is a good idea to understand the properties of this wonderful meat. Simply roasting or smoking a whole duck will likely produce greasy meat and rubbery skin. Grilling it over direct heat will result in flames emanating from all orifices of your grill. But if you know how to cook the bird, duck skins can be crisp and glow like burnished bronze.

THE SKIN. Duck skin is thicker than chicken and turkey skin, and there is a layer of fat underneath that can be ¼ inch or more deep. That's because waterfowl were designed to swim in icy cold waters and forage in frozen fields so they need the fat for insulation, energy storage, and flotation. This alone is a good reason to cook duck outdoors, unless you have a very high-volume exhaust fan, because the dripping fat can set off fire alarms.

THE MEAT. Because ducks fly vigorously, unlike chickens, duck breasts are slow-twitch muscles. They are a rich purple color when raw, loaded with darkly pigmented myoglobin like beef or lamb, and when cooked to medium-rare they can be juicy and have all the luxe richness and succulence of a fine steak.

THE FAT. Duck fat is in a league with bacon fat as a frying medium, rich and silky. It can keep for months in the fridge and you can even freeze it for a year or more. Use it as you would any other oil: to deep-fry potatoes, shallow-fry potato pancakes, roast potatoes, make caramelized onions, stir-fry veggies, and so forth.

Add the shallots and cook until limp. Add the broth, port, vinegar, and cherries. Cook over high heat until the volume has reduced by half. Move the pan to indirect heat and keep the sauce warm until you are ready to serve.

5. Serve. Just before serving, add the remaining 2 tablespoons butter to the sauce and whisk it in. This is called mounting with butter, a classic French technique that thickens and enriches the sauce at the last minute. Slice the breasts at an angle across the grain—just a little more than ⅛ inch thick—and keep the slices bunched in order. Spoon some sauce onto each of two plates, fan the slices out on top of the sauce, and drizzle a little more on top of the meat.

NOTES: Raspberry vinegar is very nice with this as a substitute for balsamic.

Dried cranberries or even raisins can be substituted for the cherries.

nonstick pans over high heat; fumes from the coating can be hazardous). Preheat the pan for at least 10 minutes, until it's rip-snorting hot.

3. Cook. Place the duck breasts in the hot pan, skin side down. They will pop and sizzle and a lot of fat will render. When the skin is dark brown, flip the breasts over so some of the rendered fat will get on the meat side and sear for about 3 minutes to brown it. Move the meat to the grill grates on the indirect-heat side. When the interior temperature of the breasts is 135°F, medium-rare, about 30 minutes, take them off the heat.

4. While the duck is grilling, pour off the burned duck fat and discard it. Wipe the pan with a paper towel, place it on the indirect side, and melt 2 tablespoons of the butter in the pan over medium heat.

11

SEAFOOD

BUYING FISH

There is one overriding secret to cooking great fish: Buy fresh fish. Fish quality deteriorates rapidly after it dies, more rapidly than any other meat. There is a noticeable quality difference in a fish caught today and a fish caught three days ago. Freshness often trumps the type of fish. I would rather have fresh farm-raised salmon than week-old wild grouper. If you live along the coasts, you have a distinct advantage. But even if you live in the center of the country, it's possible to get good fish, but it isn't easy and you need to be prepared to pay more.

Fish remain freshest when covered in ice. The flesh needs to be as cold as possible without freezing. Freezing can create ice shards that rupture the cells, which in turn causes juice to purge and creates a mushy texture. The surface of the fish should remain moist. There is no substitute for fish in direct contact with ice. Stores that lay the fish on trays or plastic on top of ice are just trying to save money on ice.

That doesn't mean you should avoid all frozen fish. Fishing boats are often at sea for weeks, and many have flash-freezing equipment. These chillers are extremely cold and freeze the fish so quickly that large ice crystals can't form. A flash-frozen fish is far superior to a never-frozen fish that has been in a ship's hold for a few days, then shipped to a warehouse, and finally to your store.

Buy from a store that sells a lot of fish. Specialty fish stores that buy directly from the docks or seafood distributors are the best sources. Get to know your fishmonger. When you go in, ask for him or her by name and inquire what is fresh today. Find out when your favorite species are in season and what regions produce the best. Cold-water varieties tend to be fattier, and it's the fat that carries flavor and moisture. Sword-fish from the northern hemisphere, for example, is best in late summer. Line-caught Alaskan salmon is at its prime in spring.

A good source of information is the seafood guides section of FishChoice.com. It also tells you which species are endangered and should be avoided.

Fish is often labeled with the catch date, but there are several indicators of freshness if you don't have the catch date. Your nose is the best judge: Fresh fish should smell more like the ocean or seaweed than fish. Its eyes should be clear. Sometimes eyes get bruised in han-dling, but cloudy eyes are one indicator that the fish may be older. Gills should be bright red. Gills mix blood and oxygen; if they are turning brown, it is a good sign the fish has been dead a while.

The cut matters a lot, too. You can get fish whole (usually gutted and scaled), filleted (each side is removed from the spine, backbones, and ribs), or as steaks (cut across the body). Each cut requires a different approach to cooking.

COOKING FISH

Most fish is white fleshed, lower in myo-globin, higher in water content, and lower in fat than other meat. This poses some problems for the grillmaster, but they are easily overcome.

The good news is that fish absorbs mari-nades and salt better, so you can flavor it more

easily—30 to 60 minutes of dry or wet brining improves its flavor and moisture significantly. The bad news is that it cooks quickly, is delicate, and can fall apart unless you handle it carefully. Fish loves the grill so much that it sometimes just won't let go. I discuss how to deal with this problem on page 107.

TO FILLET A WHOLE FISH

Snip off the fins with kitchen shears. Be very careful because they can stab you and you can get a nasty infection. You can leave the tail on or remove it (it tends to burn on the grill).

If necessary, scrape off the scales. Do this in the sink, because scales tend to fly everywhere. Special fish scalers make easy work of them, but a serrated knife or another small knife can do the job.

Practically all fish in stores have been gutted, but if this is a fresh catch, you will need to remove the intestines. Get a sharp, pointed knife and insert it just in front of the anal fin and cut forward to the collar. You can use scissors for this, too. Reach in and pull out all the entrails. Rinse the fish, especially the cavity. If there is still a vein or

FISH ANATOMY

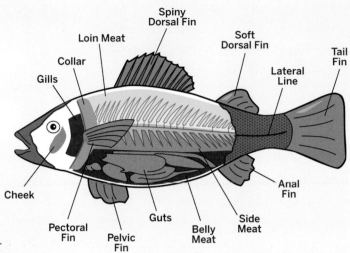

blood in the cavity, try to get it out. If you can't, don't worry, because it is right along the spine and you likely won't be eating there.

As for the head, there is a nugget of delight in the cheeks. But some people just don't like eating something that's watching them, so you may want to remove the head. Lift the gill cover and cut through. Behind the gill slot is a bone called the collar, and there is good meat on it. (Here's a tip: Toss the head in a zipper-top freezer bag and freeze it. Anytime you prep a fish, add the head to the bag, and when you get half a dozen or so, simmer them to make fish stock that can be used as a soup base or for cooking couscous or rice.)

You can now cook the fish whole, cut it perpendicular to the spine to make steaks, or fillet

CHEF BONNER'S FISH FILLETS WITH BRIONI BROTH

it. To fillet it, run your knife along the spine. Make a shallow cut.

Keep working the tip down farther and farther, scraping along the top of the bones.

After the fillet is removed from the skeleton, run your hands along it to feel for pin bones. There are often rib bones around the belly cavity left behind. Pull them straight out with clean needle-nose pliers.

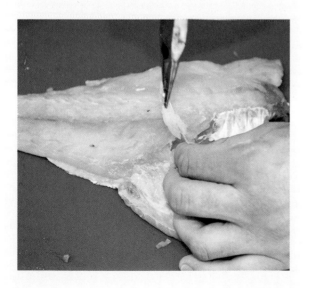

Chef Mychael Bonner is co-owner of my favorite seafood restaurant, The Reel Club in Oak Brook, Illinois. He serves a wide range of perfectly cooked seasonal fish without masking the beauty of the leading character. He has several tricks under his toque.

1. When grilling fillets, which tend to be thin, he cooks them on one side only, a technique he calls "unilateral cooking." Unilateral also can make crunchy, potato chip–like skin, although Chef Bonner warns that the skins of catfish and other fish without scales aren't very good.

2. He uses mayonnaise on the skin. Mayo is about 60 percent oil, so it prevents sticking and adds flavor. Don't use light mayonnaise or mayonnaise substitutes. If your fish still sticks, next time use a metal grill topper like the Weber Stainless Steel Grill Pan (see page 103).

3. A perfectly grilled fillet needs no sauce, but Bonner sometimes serves his with a thin buttery sauce he calls a Brioni Broth (named after a chef friend) that never challenges even the most delicate fish for center stage. You shouldn't need it, but it is a sterling accompaniment.

Here's my interpretation of one of his dishes. My recipe calls for fresh branzino, a type of sea bass from the Mediterranean. This fish is one of Chef Bonner's favorites, but it is hard to find. You can use this technique to grill just about any fresh fillet, such as sea bass, snapper, salmon, grouper, or trout.

MAKES *4 servings*

TAKES *1 hour to dry brine, 5 minutes to prep, and 15 minutes to cook*

FISH

¼ teaspoon kosher salt

4 fresh branzino fillets (see headnote), about 6 ounces each

1 teaspoon Marietta's Fish Rub (page 169)

Mayonnaise

BRIONI BROTH

3 tablespoons unsalted butter

¼ cup diced white onion

FISH OILS PERMEATE EVERYTHING

Fish oils can get into the walls of your smoker, so it is a good idea to give it a thorough washing after smoking fish. If you do a lot of fish, it might be worthwhile to have a separate smoker just for fish.

1 teaspoon fresh thyme leaves

½ cup dry white wine

2 cups low-sodium chicken broth

⅛ teaspoon white pepper

Salt to taste

Carrot sticks (optional)

1. Prep. To make the fish, salt the fillets on both sides and dry brine for about 1 hour. Just before cooking, pat the fish totally dry with paper towels, sprinkle both sides with Marietta's Fish Rub, and lightly coat the skin side with mayonnaise to help keep it from sticking to the grill.

2. To make the broth, melt 1 tablespoon of the butter in a saucepan over medium heat and add the onion and thyme. Sauté until the onion is limp and a very light color (not golden). Add the wine, turn up the heat, and boil until it is almost gone. Add the chicken broth and bring to a boil. Turn the heat back down and simmer for 5 minutes. Strain to remove the onion and thyme solids. Whisk in the remaining 2 tablespoons butter over low heat until it is melted and blended in. Keep warm until the fish is done.

3. Fire up. Set up the grill for two-zone cooking and shoot for about 450°F on the direct-heat side.

4. Cook. Put the fillets on the grates over direct heat, skin side down, close the lid, and leave them alone until they get dark grill marks. As the fish cooks, rotate it 45 degrees to make crosshatches and to prevent burning, but don't flip it. If the fish won't let go of the grates, just leave it alone for now. When it hits 120°F in the center, remove it from the grill. If it is close to burning but not warmed through, move it to the indirect zone and close the lid until it hits the mark. Don't risk breaking it up by flipping it.

5. Serve. Divide the sauce among the plates and place the fish in the center, skin side facing up. If the skin has charred or torn, plate it skin side down.

Bonner floats his on a raft of carrot sticks to keep the skin crisp.

SMOKED TROUT, FLORIDA MULLET STYLE

If you go looking for the origin of American barbecue, the path will lead you to smoked mullet. Long before the conquistadors arrived with hogs and cattle, Native Americans in the Caribbean and Florida were slow smoking fish on an open-air wooden grate called a barbacoa. That tradition continues today, but few people know about it, and fewer still recognize smoked mullet as the mother of American barbecue.

Mullet is netted in the Gulf of Mexico. It is oily, and its flavor is not as refined as that of most other fish from the Gulf, so it is best heavily seasoned and smoked.

The mecca for smoked mullet is Ted Peters Famous Smoked Fish, a landmark destination in South St. Petersburg, Florida, since 1945. Most of the tables are outdoors, and across the parking lot is a smokehouse with handmade wooden drawers for the fish. You can eat at the restaurant or just walk into the smokehouse and order takeout.

Since mullet is next to impossible to find far from the Florida Gulf Coast, I have replicated the process with trout. Most trout is farm raised, easy to find, and about the same size as mullet. Although it doesn't have exactly the same flavor, it is mighty good when smoked like mullet. Some might even say it is better. You can also

use bluefish, which, like mullet, is oily.

This recipe uses whole fish, but you can also use fillets.

MAKES *1 serving*

TAKES *5 minutes to prep, 30 minutes to cook*

1 (1-pound) trout, boned
¼ teaspoon kosher salt
1 tablespoon Meathead's Memphis Dust (page 167)
Lemon wedges or Tartar Sauce (page 184)

1. Prep. Scale and gut the fish (see page 322). Remove the head and tail, open the fish so it lies flat, and sprinkle it with the salt and Memphis Dust. Refrigerate for about 30 minutes.

2. Fire up. Get your smoker up to 225°F or set up the grill for two-zone cooking and shoot for about 225°F on the indirect side. Get some dense smoke rolling.

3. Cook. Put the fish in the smoke, splayed open, skin side down. The target temperature is 130°F and it won't take long to get there—30 to 45 minutes, depending on the thickness of the fish.

4. Serve. Mullet is often served right out of the smoker or cold, with a wedge of lemon or tartar sauce. If you flake the flesh off the skin with a fork, you can use it for a fish salad (see page 330), or mixed with eggs, pasta, or potatoes.

SCHMANCY HOT-SMOKED SALMON

No fish is more grill- and smoker-friendly than salmon. Long before Europeans set foot in North America, Native Americans and Aboriginal Canadians on the Pacific coast practically subsisted on this fish.

To preserve their catch in the days before refrigeration, they would cut huge meaty fillets, coat them with salt to cure them, attach the fillets to alder planks, and jam the planks into the ground around a smoky campfire, gently cooking and smoking them for hours. Sometimes they would simply drape the fillets over a pole above a smoldering fire. They even built smokehouses with walls made of animal hides. This recipe modernizes the ancient technique. It produces a delicate, moist fish that you can take in either the sweet or savory direction by the way you season it.

I serve it as a room-temperature appetizer on a platter so people can help themselves and flake it onto crackers, rye toast, apple slices, or cheese slices. You can make a variation on bagels and lox by serving it on bagel chips with cream cheese and chives. This salmon is also wonderful on small boiled potato halves, topped with sour cream. Try it on a toast point with a dollop of horseradish cream sauce or minced hard-boiled egg. Or mix it into scrambled eggs, an omelet, or risotto. It also makes a fine sandwich. Put it in a bowl and flake it with a fork, add a very tiny splash of sesame oil and a bit of mayo, and serve on rye. Or make the canapés on page 329.

Occasionally I have some left over. If it is tightly packaged in plastic wrap and then aluminum foil, it can be refrigerated for up to a week or frozen for a month or so.

MAKES *4 main-course servings, 8 or more appetizer servings*

TAKES *20 minutes to prep, 1 to 2 hours to brine, and about 1 hour to cook*

- 2 pounds skin-on salmon fillets of similar thickness, scales removed
- ¼ pound salt
- 1 teaspoon garlic powder
- 1 teaspoon freshly ground black pepper
- 8 tablespoons brown sugar, maple syrup, or honey (optional)

1. Prep. Run your fingers over the flesh of the fish and make sure all the pin bones are gone. If not, drape the fish over the edge of a bowl so the bones stick out and yank them out with clean tweezers or needle-nose pliers. Don't worry if there are a few scales left on the skin. You will be removing it. If the lining of the belly of the fish has a milky membrane on it, remove it with a sharp filleting knife (otherwise it will get leathery when cooked). Cut the meat into strips about 3 inches wide.

2. You can make the brine days in advance and keep it chilled, if you wish. Start by putting ½ cup hot water in a 1-cup measuring cup. Pour in salt until the water line reaches ¾ cup. The water will swallow up almost exactly ¼ pound of salt, regardless of whether you use table salt, kosher salt, pickling salt, or sea salt. The volume of these salts may differ, but their water displacement will be the same. Pour the mixture into a container large enough to hold the salmon and 2 quarts of cold water, which you can add now. Choose a very clean food-grade nonreactive brining container; plastic zipper-top bags work fine. For large quantities, get turkey brining bags or Ziploc

ABOUT OTHER RECIPES

Some popular recipes call for adding sugar and spices to the brine, but as I have explained, they don't penetrate more than a fraction of an inch, especially in such a short time. Sprinkling on sugar and spices after brining is far more effective.

There is also a common misconception that the cured fish must be dried until a coating of proteins, known as a pellicle, forms on the surface. I've tasted the two methods side by side blind and waiting for a tacky pellicle is not necessary.

There are also many recipes that call for you to cold-smoke fish at temperatures well below 200°F. This is a very high-risk technique best left to commercial smokehouses. Please don't cook at temperatures below 200°F. The penalty for a mistake can be death.

XL or XXL bags. If you brine in a zipper-top bag, place the bag in a pan to catch leaks.

3. Submerge the fish in the brine, skin side up, and refrigerate. Make sure the meaty part is thoroughly submerged. Occasionally gently stir the brine or squish the bag around to make sure all parts of the fish come into contact with the brine. The length of brining will vary depending on how thick the fillets are. Brine 2-inch-thick fillets for about 2 hours, 1-inch-thick fillets for 1 hour.

4. Cut pieces of paper bag or plain white paper about the same size as each hunk of fish. Drain the fish and discard the brine. Rinse the fish to remove excess surface salt, pat dry with paper towels, and place the fish on the paper, skin side down. The fish will stick to the paper and when you remove the paper, the skin will come right off with it. Don't use aluminum foil or parchment paper—the fish won't stick to either. If the paper is a lot larger than the fish, trim it down so air can flow between the chunks of fish on the grates.

5. Sprinkle the tops of the fish with the garlic powder and black pepper. Now you need to make a decision: sweet, savory, or both. For appetizers I like a sweet glaze. For entrees, unglazed. You can glaze some pieces with the brown sugar and leave the others unglazed to see which you like best. If you decide to glaze the fish, coat the flesh side of each fillet with the brown sugar (you can use maple syrup or honey if you wish).

6. Fire up. Get your smoker up to 225°F or set up the grill for two-zone cooking and shoot for about 225°F on the indirect side. Add wood. Alder is traditional, but any mild wood works.

7. Cook. Place the fish, paper side down, on the grates in the indirect zone. The pieces of fish should not touch one another and if you can, leave air gaps between the pieces of paper so smoke can get between the pieces.

8. Start spot-checking the salmon's temperature after about 30 minutes. Droplets of milky liquid may rise to the surface. This is a protein called albumin, which comes from the fibers in the muscles (see page 58). If you don't like the look of it, you can get rid of it with a wet brush. You can remove the fish when its internal temperature is about 130°F. However, if you plan to leave it out as an appetizer at room temperature, you must cook it to 160°F. The total cooking time will be about 60 minutes, depending on the actual temperature of your cooker and the thickness of the meat.

9. Remove the fillets and let them cool for about 15 minutes, or until you can handle them. Peel off the paper; the skins should come right off. If there is any dark brown flesh on the skin side of the salmon, scrape it off with a serrated knife and discard it. It can taste muddy.

SMOKED SALMON MOUSSE CANAPÉS

Smoked salmon contrasts beautifully with the crisp coolness of the cucumber.

MAKES *about 1 ½ pounds, enough for 50 canapés*

TAKES *2 hours*

MOUSSE

    8 ounces Schmancy Hot-Smoked Salmon (page 326; about ¼ recipe)

    Grated zest and juice of ¼ lemon

    2 ounces cream cheese

    ¼ cup sour cream

    ½ tablespoon prepared white horseradish

    1 teaspoon minced fresh dill or chives

    ¼ teaspoon freshly ground white pepper

    ½ teaspoon kosher salt

CANAPÉS

    1 seedless cucumber

    1 loaf cocktail rye or pumpernickel bread (see Note)

    4 or 5 long, thin chives

1. To make the mousse, make sure all the bones have been removed from the salmon and put it in a food processor or blender. Add the lemon zest, lemon juice, cream cheese, sour cream, horseradish, dill, white pepper, and salt. Puree. Taste and adjust the flavor by adding a little more of any of the ingredients.

2. Spoon the mousse into a piping bag fitted with a small star tip and stash it in the fridge until well chilled. If you don't have a piping bag, spoon the mousse into a plastic bag, and when you're ready to pipe it, cut off one corner. Or you can just use a spoon.

3. To make the canapés, use a vegetable peeler to cut long ribbons of skin from tip to tip of the cucumber, making stripes. Leaving some skin on will give it a bit more crunch and texture. Cut the ends from the cuke and slice it into ⅛-inch-thick slices. (If you have a mandoline, now's the time to trot it out.)

4. Cut the bread into small, round slices just a little larger than the cucumber slices. Use a small, round cookie cutter or cut around the lip of a glass with a sharp knife. Toast the bread rounds on the grill or under the broiler until they are golden brown on one side. Watch closely; they can burn in a hurry.

5. Use kitchen scissors to snip the chives into 1-inch lengths.

6. To assemble the canapés, pipe a dab of the mousse on each slice of bread to act as glue. Stick a slice of cucumber to the dab. Pipe a nice-sized mound of the mousse on top of the cucumber, garnish with pieces of chive, and serve.

NOTE: You can use crackers or toast points if you prefer.

SMOKED SALMON QUICHE

The recipe for this time-honored Sunday brunch dish calls for smoked salmon, but you can substitute other smoked fish such as trout, mullet, or even swordfish. It's a great way to repurpose leftover smoked fish.

MAKES *1 (9-inch) pie (6 servings)*

TAKES *30 minutes to prepare if you have the smoked fish and piecrust ready, 40 to 50 minutes to bake*

1 (9-inch) piecrust, store-bought or
   homemade
1 cup fresh spinach leaves
¼ red onion, thinly sliced
6 ounces Schmancy Hot-Smoked Salmon
   (page 326)
5 large eggs
½ cup whole or 2% milk
¼ teaspoon kosher salt
⅛ teaspoon freshly ground black pepper

1. Prep. Preheat the oven to 325°F. Fit the crust into a pie pan, prick the bottom of the crust with a fork about 6 times. Add pie weights or dried beans and bake for about 20 minutes, until the dough starts to turn light brown. Remove from the oven (leave the oven on), remove the pie weights, and let the crust cool on a rack for 10 minutes.

2. Spread the spinach over the piecrust and top with the sliced onion. Make sure there are no bones in the salmon, then flake it and spread it over the onion.

3. In a bowl, whisk together the eggs, milk, salt, and pepper until well blended. Pour the egg mixture over the ingredients in the piecrust. Give the pie pan a little shake to be sure everything settles and any air gaps are filled by the egg mixture.

4. Cook. Bake for 40 to 50 minutes, until the internal temperature of the quiche reaches 180 to 185°F, the egg is set throughout, and the crust is a nice golden brown.

5. Serve. Let the quiche cool on a rack for at least 15 minutes, then slice and serve. It is equally good hot or at room temperature. In fact, it's pretty good cold.

SMOKED HALIBUT SALAD

This is similar to classic tuna salad, but the smoked halibut amps it up to 11. Feel free to substitute salmon, trout, or another fish. Spread it on crackers for an appetizer or on bread for a sandwich.

MAKES *about 2 servings*

TAKES *20 minutes*

8 ounces fresh halibut fillets
⅛ teaspoon kosher salt
⅛ teaspoon freshly ground black pepper
½ cup mayonnaise
Juice of 1 lemon
1 celery stalk, minced
1½ tablespoons minced onion

1 tablespoon minced sweet pickle or pickle
   relish
2 pinches of curry powder
2 hard-boiled large eggs

1. Prep. Season the fish with the salt and pepper.

2. Fire up. Get your smoker up to 225°F or set up the grill for two-zone cooking and shoot for about 225°F on the indirect side. Add a mild wood for smoke.

3. Cook. Put the fish in the smoke. If you will eat the fish within 1 day, smoke it until its internal temperature hits 140 to 145°F. If it will be in the fridge for a few days, cook it to 160°F. Remove the halibut from the smoker and refrigerate until cold.

4. Serve. In a bowl, whisk together the mayonnaise, lemon juice, celery, onion, pickle, and curry powder. Flake the chilled fish into bite-size chunks, making sure there are no bones. Using an egg slicer or a knife, chop the eggs into small pieces. Gently fold the fish and eggs into the mayonnaise dressing. Taste, adjust the seasonings if necessary, then serve.

BUTTER-POACHED FILLETS

It was a cold late-autumn day in the 1980s when my wife and I pushed our canoe into Treman Lake above Buttermilk Falls in Ithaca, New York. The valleys between the steep hills were filled with cold, clear water. I cast out toward a small stand of submerged trees. Almost instantly, my lure was swallowed by a five-pound largemouth bass.

When I got home, I improvised a cooking method. It was so good I've done it again and again with a wide variety of fish, but delicate white-fleshed fillets like bass or even tilapia work best. Serve with crusty bread to mop up the garlicky brown butter.

MAKES *4 servings*
TAKES *about 40 minutes*

4 pounds fresh white-fleshed fish, such as
    bass or tilapia, filleted (see page 322)

2 teaspoons kosher salt

8 tablespoons (1 stick) unsalted butter

3 tablespoons olive oil

3 tablespoons chopped fresh tarragon (see
    Note)

3 garlic cloves, crushed

1. Prep. Sprinkle the fish with salt and dry brine it for an hour. Find a baking pan or oven-safe frying pan not much bigger than the fish but large enough so the fillets lie flat and don't overlap. Melt the butter in the pan over medium-low heat. Add the oil. There should be enough fat to cover the bottom of the pan to a depth of ⅛ inch. If necessary, increase the quantities. Stir the tarragon and garlic into the butter mixture and cook gently for about 5 minutes to give the garlic and tarragon time to flavor the butter.

2. Fire up. Set up the grill for two-zone cooking and shoot for about 225°F on the indirect side or get your smoker up to 225°F. Put a lot of smoke in the air by placing a pan with sawdust, wood chips, dried herbs, or even tea right over the flames.

3. Cook. Put the fish in the pan and spoon some of the butter over it. Place it in the indirect-heat zone and close the lid. The butter will probably brown— that's OK. Brown butter has a nutty flavor that loves holding hands with fish. Just don't let the butter blacken. When the flesh in the center of the fish hits 120°F, transfer it to a serving platter and spoon some brown butter over the top.

NOTE: Fresh tarragon is best, but if you can't find it, use 2 tablespoons dried.

BAJA FISH TACOS

The fish taco is to Baja, California, as the cheese steak is to Philly or the deep-dish pizza is to Chicago. They are sold in taquerias, restaurants, bars, and by street vendors everywhere. This is truly a signature regional dish whose popularity has spread to all corners of the United States.

Cabbage, pico de gallo, and avocado are the classic toppings, but I've had wonderful riffs on the theme with chopped mango, pineapple, tomato, cilantro, pickled cabbage, red pepper, cucumber, scallions, raw onion, pickled onion, grilled onion, minced jalapeño, shredded cheese, and more. Purists may object, but your taste buds will not.

The original is deep-fried, but grilling really lets fresh fish shine. Heck, you can even smoke the fish if you wish.

MAKES *2 servings*

TAKES *45 minutes*

1 pound skinless mild white-fleshed fish
   fillets, such as snapper, mahi-mahi,
   grouper, or tilapia

Kosher salt

1 tablespoon ancho chile powder

1 tablespoon freshly ground black pepper

½ cup sour cream

1 tablespoon mayonnaise, plus more for
   coating the fish

2½ teaspoons finely chopped chipotle in
   adobo sauce

4 fresh corn tortillas (see Note)

1 ripe avocado

2 limes, quartered

¼ small head cabbage, shredded

Pico de gallo or red salsa

1. Prep. Put the fish fillets on a plate. Sprinkle them with about ½ teaspoon salt, and dust them liberally with the ancho chile powder and black pepper.

2. In a small bowl, mix together the sour cream, 1 tablespoon mayonnaise, and the chipotle in adobo. Season with a pinch of salt. Refrigerate.

3. Fire up. Set up a grill in a two-zone configuration. (The indirect zone is the safe zone.) Preheat the grill and a metal grill topper (see page 103) to medium-high heat in the direct zone.

4. Cook. Coat the fish with a thin layer of mayonnaise and place it on the hot grill topper. Cook the fish with the lid up until you get some nice golden color on one side. Turn the fish over and cook until the internal temperature is about 125°F. It shouldn't need more than 5 minutes per side. Don't worry if the fish starts to break apart. Transfer the fish to a warm bowl and break it into large chunks.

5. Meanwhile, to cook the tortillas, warm an empty skillet that is just larger than the tortillas. Lightly toast them by tossing them on the hot grill for about 30 seconds per side, until they get a few dark spots.

Be careful not to dry them out, as they need to be flexible. Put them in the skillet and cover it to keep them warm. If they are a little stiff when you open the pan to use them, moisten two paper towels, squeeze out most of the water, sandwich the tortillas between them, and heat in the microwave for just a few seconds or in the oven until pliable.

6. While the fish and tortillas are cooking, halve the avocado, remove the pit, and carefully scoop out the flesh. Lay it curved side up on a cutting board and cut it into ¼-inch-thick slices. Put them in a bowl and drizzle with some lime juice to keep them from browning. Put the cabbage and pico de gallo in separate bowls with spoons so people can assemble their own tacos at the table.

7. Serve. Divide the fish among the tortillas. Top with the sour cream mixture and any toppings you like. Serve with the lime wedges.

NOTE: The classic fish taco is made with corn tortillas, but flour tortillas work just fine. You can get fresh tortillas at a Mexican market; otherwise, supermarket tortillas will work. If the tortillas are thin, double them up.

GRILLED CALAMARI LADOLEMONO

T he key to grilling squid is not to overcook it or it will turn into rubber bands. It is best when salted lightly, grilled quickly, and then sauced after grilling. If you marinate or sauce it before grilling, it will steam, and you won't get that grill flavor.

MAKES *2 servings*

TAKES *30 minutes*

- 3 pounds whole squid (about 2 pounds cleaned)
- ½ teaspoon kosher salt
- 1 large onion, quartered and separated into layers
- 3 tablespoons high-quality extra-virgin olive oil
- Greek Ladolemono for Seafood (page 192)
- Finely chopped fresh parsley, for garnish (optional)
- 1 loaf crusty bread

1. Prep. Clean the squid as described on the opposite page. Pat it dry with a paper towel. Salt it.

2. Add the squid and onion slices to a bowl with the oil and toss to lightly coat so they don't stick to the grill.

3. Fire up. Set up a grill in a two-zone configuration. Get the hot zone pretty hot and preheat a grill topper (see page 103) on it to prevent the smaller pieces from dropping to their doom.

4. Cook. Use a slotted spoon to move the squid and onions to the grill topper. Drain off the excess oil, or it will cause flare-ups and soot. Grill everything for about 1 minute, or until it gets some brown spots, stir it around, cook for another minute, and repeat, 3 to

4 minutes total. The squid should be tender but firm and not at all rubbery. The tentacles will shrink quite a bit and be done at about the same time as the bodies. Nibble one to be sure it's done. That's why being the cook is fun!

5. Serve. Transfer the squid and onions to a serving bowl, pour on the sauce, and garnish with fresh parsley if you wish. Serve in a bowl with crusty bread to soak up juices and make impromptu sandwiches.

CLAMS, OYSTERS, AND MUSSELS

BUYING AND HANDLING BIVALVES

The most important thing is to get live clams, mussels, and oysters in their shell—size isn't crucial. By law, they will be labeled with the harvest date and location; you can also ask your fishmonger where they come from. They all have slightly different flavors depending on where they were harvested. Shoot for two days old, but anything less than one week old is OK. After that their death rate could be high. As long as they are alive, they are fine.

Store fresh live bivalves in the refrigerator in a bowl covered by a few layers of wet paper towel or with a bag of ice. Do not submerge them in water, or they will drown. They need air, and they will rapidly deplete the air in the water. In the wild, they are often above water at low tide, so they can handle being out of the water.

When it is time to cook them, sniff each and every one of them. They should smell like the ocean. Discard any that smell funky. Any that rattle or are too heavy are probably dead and filled with sand. Some people advise pressing the shells closed if they are open a bit and

CHOOSING AND CLEANING SQUID

FRESH SQUID. If you get fresh or uncleaned squid, try to find small ones, about 7 inches long or less. Avoid pink, yellow, or purple squid, which are probably not fresh. Chop off the tentacles just below the eyes. Remove the hard beak from the center of the tentacles; it should pop right out. Reach up into the tube and pull out the head with the eyes, the innards, and the thin, clear, hard piece of cartilage (this is called the feather). Grasp the fins near the pointy end of the tube and pull them off. Some of the skin will come along; that's good. Go back and get the rest of the skin off the body—scraping with a knife works pretty well. You can now slice open the tube and clean the inside under running water, or if you want rings, cut off a tiny bit of the pointy end and hold the tube open under cold running water. Rinse the fins and tentacles, too. Pat them dry with paper towels.

FROZEN WHOLE SQUID. Unless you live near the shore and can get really fresh squid, you should buy frozen. If you get whole frozen squid, they must be defrosted and cleaned like fresh squid.

FROZEN CLEANED SQUID. Frozen cleaned squid may cost a bit more, but the bag contains ready-to-cook whole tubes and whole tentacles. Just check to make sure the tubes have had the feather removed.

SQUID ANATOMY

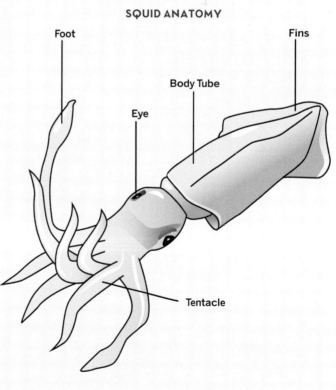

Foot

Eye

Body Tube

Fins

Tentacle

discarding them if they don't stay closed. Don't bother. Sometimes they pop open again, yet they are still alive and fresh. Despite what you may have read, you do not have to discard the ones that are slightly open, as long as they smell fresh. If the two shells slide horizontally, the clam is probably dead. If it resists, the adductor muscles are probably still alive and working. *The rule is: When in doubt, throw it out.*

Wild bivalves often live in the sand or mud, while cultured bivalves grow on ropes hung above the bottom. Scrub the shells well under cold running water, especially when working with wild bivalves, because dirt, mud, and sand can ruin the eating experience.

The next step is to get them to spit their sand out. Soak them in a bowl of salted water for several hours, or up to 24 hours. They will open a bit, suck in the saltwater, and spit out the sand. Old salts call this "purging." The best way to purge is with a bucket of ocean water. If you are lucky enough to dig the clams yourself, bring them home in buckets of seawater. If you bought them in a store, make your own approximation. The oceans vary in salinity, but on average seawater is about 3.5 percent salt. The Simple Blonder Wet Brine (page 160) is 6.3 percent, so make a batch and dilute it by almost doubling the water. Try to keep the temperature of the water similar to the temperature of the clams. If you dug them in summer, leave them at room temperature. If you bought them in the store, purge them in the fridge. Use lots of brine or try to change the water every 2 to 4 hours to make sure they don't deplete the oxygen supply.

OPENING CLAMS

Some people say that putting clams in the freezer for about 15 minutes makes opening them a bit easier. That has never worked for me. What does work is the opposite. Put them in some hot water—not boiling water, just hot from the tap—for about 10 minutes. This hot water trick also works on oysters.

If you plan to shuck them yourself, you should buy a clam-shucking knife so you don't ruin your paring knife. While you're at it, get some protective gloves.

I prefer to open clams from the lip side, oysters from the hinge side. Hold the clam in the upturned palm of your hand, with the pointed hinge facing the heel of your palm and the lip facing your fingers. Hold your hand over a large bowl to catch the drippings. That juice, called the liquor, is full of flavor, and it makes a fine pasta sauce and poaching liquid.

Insert the blade of your knife, not the point, between the thin lips. Wiggle it in a bit and slide it all around the exterior almost to the hinge on both sides. Do not push the knife in very far, or you will cut the meat in half. Now twist the knife so the opening is large enough to pry it open with your fingers. If the shell breaks, don't sweat it. Pull open the top shell, twist it off, drain the clam into the bowl, and discard the shell.

Cut the two upper adductor muscles that hold the clam to the shell on both sides. This is good meat. Don't lose it. You can see the adductor muscles in the photo below.

Dump all the meat and liquor into the bowl and discard the bottom shell. After the clams are all shucked, pour everything through a fine-mesh strainer to separate the liquor.

OPENING OYSTERS

The method for opening oysters is different than the method for opening clams. Make sure the oyster is stable and flat side down. If it slips, you can do serious damage to your hand. Start at the pointed hinge and insert the tip of a sturdy pointy knife.

Once you break the hinge, flip the shell over so the flat side is up, wiggle the knifepoint in, and twist the blade to pop open the shell.

Work the blade around the perimeter of the shell with the tip pointing up, scraping along the inside to cut the adductor muscles that hold it to the shell.

The oyster and liquor should all be in the cup-shaped bottom shell. Run the blade along the shell to cut it free.

QUICK-SMOKED CLAMS, MUSSELS, OR OYSTERS

Clams, mussels, and oysters taste different, but can be cooked similarly. You can remove one of their shells when raw for cooking, but that's a lot of work. They are a lot easier to shuck when cooked. They're great with smoke, but they cook in a hurry, and when their shells pop open, they are pretty close to done. There isn't much time for smoke to flavor their meat, so you have to crank up the smoke to get it into the little crack between the lips of their shells. I usually do them on my gas grill and generate copious quantities of smoke with hardwood sawdust, old dried herbs, and even clean, dry hay.

MAKES *1 dozen oysters, clams, or mussels*

TAKES *2 hours or more to purge the sand and 25 minutes to prep and cook*

- 4 tablespoons (½ stick) butter
- Zest of ½ lemon or lime
- 1 dozen oysters, clams, or mussels, cleaned and purged (see page 336)
- Bottled horseradish, for garnish (optional)
- Hot sauce, for garnish (optional)
- 1 loaf fresh crusty bread or plenty of crostini (page 350)

1. Prep. Melt the butter in a saucepan and add the zest. Remove from the heat and cover to keep warm.

2. Find a pan that fits below the grill grates and will sit on top of the heat source. I use a disposable pan. Toss in three or four handfuls of hardwood sawdust, wood chips, pellets, old dried herbs, or clean, dry hay.

3. Fire up. Get the grill up to warp 10 (maximum) and place the pan directly over the heat source to get things smoking. Place the grate over the pan.

4. Cook. Place the shellfish on the grate, arranging them hump side down to hold in the juices. Make sure the seams are level so when they pop open, their juices will not spill out. Work with long tongs and work fast, because the sawdust can burst into flames.

5. Place a second pan on top of the bivalves to trap the smoke so it has a better chance of infiltrating them as they open. Close the lid. Check after 5 minutes. They are ready when the shells open slightly and you can see some steam escaping. They will not open all the way. Do not overcook them or they will become tough and chewy.

MYTH You can purge bivalves with cornmeal and water.

BUSTED! Purging requires a long soak in saltwater as described on page 336. Plain tap water or tap water with cornmeal is ineffective and could kill them.

6. Carefully remove them by grasping the lip of the lower shell with tongs or pick them up with an insulated glove. When they're cool enough to handle, remove the top shells. Do this over a bowl to capture any spilled liquor.

7. Serve. Put the bivalves on a platter and spoon a little melted butter over them and then drizzle with the captured liquor. If you wish, add a dash of horseradish or hot sauce to each shell. Serve with plenty of bread to sop up the juices.

CLAMBAKE WITH GRILLED CROSTINI

A traditional New England clambake involves digging holes in the sand and burying clams, lobsters, corn, seaweed, burlap, and hot rocks. Here is a simpler version that can be done anytime—even in the winter, when clams are at their plumpest and juiciest—and you don't need a shovel. This method is special because the clams and the shells get smoky, and the sauce absorbs that smoke. The sauce and the clam juice beg to be sopped up by grilled crostini. Even if you have a smoker, do this on the grill because you want high heat and lots of thick smoke in a hurry. This is messy finger food, so make sure you have a roll of paper towels on the table when you serve it.

MAKES *2 dinner servings or 4 appetizer servings*
TAKES *about 40 minutes*

> 1 slice good-quality bacon
> 4 tablespoons (½ stick) butter
> ¼ cup minced shallot or onion
> 2 teaspoons fresh tarragon or 1 teaspoon dried
> 2 garlic cloves, minced or pressed
> ¼ teaspoon freshly ground black pepper
> ½ cup dry white wine
> 2 dozen clams, cleaned and purged (see page 336)
> 2 tablespoons fresh lemon juice
> ¼ cup chopped fresh chives
> 1 loaf crusty bread or crostini (page 350)

1. Prep. In a skillet on the grill, the side burner, or indoors, cook the bacon to your favorite degree of doneness. Drain it on paper towels, let cool, then finely chop it. Leave the bacon fat in the skillet.

2. Add the butter, shallot, tarragon, garlic, and pepper to the bacon fat and cook over low heat, stirring occasionally, for about 5 minutes. Add the white wine and bring to a boil. Cook for about 5 minutes to cook off the alcohol. Don't skip the boiling—the alcohol can mess up the taste. Remove from the heat.

3. Fire up. Get the grill up to warp 10 (maximum). Place a disposable pan below the grill grates and on top of the heat source. Add three or four handfuls of hardwood sawdust, wood chips, pellets, old dried herbs, or clean, dry hay.

4. Cook. Prepare the clams as described in Quick-Smoked Clams on page 338.

5. Serve. Put the clams in a serving bowl big enough to hold them all. Pour the sauce over the clams. Add the lemon juice, chives, and chopped bacon. Give everyone a bowl and scoop some clams and juice into each bowl. Use the bread or crostini to make open-face sandwiches and soak up the juices.

GRILLED OYSTERS WITH WHITE WINE SAUCE

This simple prep was inspired by a similar method used at the original Wintzell's Oyster House on Dauphin Street in Mobile, Alabama, a landmark since 1938. You can sit at the oyster bar and try to eat oysters faster than the shucker can open them (you can't), or relax in one of their tiled dining rooms and enjoy the best catch from the Gulf of Mexico, as fresh as it gets.

MAKES *3 dozen oysters (6 appetizer servings)*
TAKES *about 1 hour*

- 2 tablespoons high-quality extra-virgin olive oil
- 2 tablespoons minced shallot
- 2 tablespoons sliced scallion
- 1 tablespoon minced garlic
- 1½ tablespoons sliced fresh lemongrass
- 1 tablespoon grated lemon zest
- 1 cup dry white wine
- ¼ cup fish stock or chicken stock
- 1 tablespoon chopped fresh flat-leaf parsley
- 2 pinches of kosher salt, plus more as needed
- 2 pinches of freshly ground black pepper, plus more as needed
- 3 dozen fresh oysters, cleaned and purged (see page 336)
- 2 baguettes or 3 dozen crostini (page 350)

1. Prep. In a medium saucepan, heat the oil over medium heat. When it is hot, add the shallot, scallion, garlic, lemongrass, and lemon zest. Cook for 2 minutes. Add the white wine and stock, turn up the heat, and boil for 20 minutes to cook off some of the alcohol and reduce the liquid by about two thirds. Remove from the heat.

2. Add the parsley, salt, and pepper to the sauce. Taste and season with more salt and pepper as needed.

3. Get two sheet pans and place a kitchen towel on each. Remove the flat shell from the oysters, but leave the meat in the cupped half. Sit the shells on the towel and bunch it around them if necessary to keep them from falling over and spilling.

4. Fire up. Get your grill up to warp 10 (high heat).

5. Cook. Place the saucepan on the grill to get the sauce hot. Place the oysters right on the grill grates and try to get them level. Spoon some of the sauce over them. If the juice runneth over, so be it. As they flame up, the smoke will ever so slightly tinge the oysters. Close the lid. After the liquid in the shells has bubbled for about 4 minutes, they should be done.

6. Serve. Put the oysters on serving plates, hit them with some more sauce, and serve, with extra sauce on the table and bread to mop up after you.

SMOKED OYSTERS

These are so much better than the smoked oysters in cans. They are super snacks with beer or white wine. Serve them on crostini (page 350), crackers, or toast with cream cheese, or in chowder. They beg for pasta. We have even wrapped them in puffed pastry.

MAKES *1 dozen smoked oysters*

TAKES *about 40 minutes*

> 1 dozen fresh oysters, cleaned and purged (see page 336)

1. Prep. Open the oysters with an oyster knife (see page 337). Discard the shells. Save and freeze the liquor for use in chowder or a pasta dish.

2. Fire up. Set up the grill in a two-zone configuration and get the indirect zone up to about 225°F, or get the smoker started and pegged at 225°F. The meat can easily slip through the grates, so set a grill topper over the indirect zone if you are on a grill. If you don't have one, use a sheet of foil on top of the grates and poke a lot of holes in it.

3. Cook. Get a lot of smoke rolling. On a grill you might even place a pan of sawdust over the direct

heat. Close the lid and smoke the oysters with indirect heat for about 20 minutes, or until the oysters have a mahogany tint and have firmed up a bit.

4. Serve. Remove from the fire and serve warm or at room temperature, use as an ingredient, or chill until you are ready to eat.

SHRIMP

CHOOSING AND PREPPING SHRIMP

Today most shrimp are farm raised in Asia, and in recent years there have been some unpleasant revelations about conditions there, for both people and shrimp. If you can get wild shrimp from the Gulf of Mexico, you should.

As with so much seafood, flash-frozen shrimp will usually be of high quality; just defrost it in the fridge. So-called "fresh" shrimp has often been frozen and then thawed or traveled a long distance, and is not really fresh.

SHRIMP ANATOMY

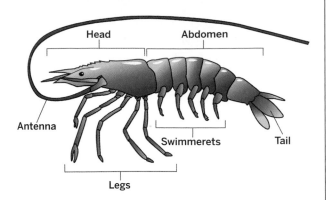

Shrimp are sold by the pound, and headless shrimp are measured by the number of shrimp per pound. Shrimp labeled "31/35" come 31 to 35 per pound and should be called medium, though they are sometimes called large. The size names can vary from merchant to merchant. Those labeled "16/20" are called jumbos, but I consider them large. U-12 and U-10 (meaning under 12 or under 10 per pound), are called colossal or super colossal.

Small shrimp can be tedious to clean, fall through the grates, and often get cooked through before they become dark on the outside. Large shrimp are easier to prep, easier to cook properly, and benefit from dark grill marks. I recommend 16/20 or larger for grilling.

Shrimp shells protect the delicate meat from overcooking, and because they contain chitin (pronounced KITE-in), which is rich in sugars, the shells contribute flavor to the meat. Shrimp absorbs more marinade than almost any other meat, but if you marinate with the shell on, the shell blocks much of the marinade from reaching the abdomen meat. If there are a lot of spices, herbs, or marinade on the outside of the shells, however, they get on your fingers and then on the meat as you eat. Your fingers become like brushes, acting as part of the seasoning process.

Some people even eat the shells, swimmerets, and tails if they are soft enough. They are tasty, covered with seasonings and smoke from the grill, and laden with nutrients. If you are a shell eater, snip off the point between the tail fins before cooking so it won't lodge in your throat and interrupt dinner with a trip to the emergency room.

If you have whole shrimp, clean them by breaking off the heads at the point where the large solid shell, called the carapace, meets the smaller segmented shell sections of the abdomen. Then rip off the legs.

REMOVING THE VEIN

I recommend cooking shrimp with the shell on, but this is problematic because the digestive tract, called the vein, sometimes contains grit. The best of all worlds is to leave the shell on and still remove the vein, thus exposing more meat to seasoning or marinade.

The vein runs along the convex side, the back of the abdomen. Sometimes it is hard to see, especially if the shrimp didn't eat much before being killed. When filled, it is often black. To remove the vein but leave the shell on, cut the shell with scissors along the center of the back all the way to the tail. Using a sharp paring knife, cut through the flesh until you see the vein (do not cut all the way through the shrimp—you don't want shrimp halves). When the vein is exposed, slip the tip of your knife or fingernail

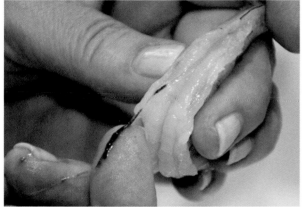

under it and gently lift. It should all come out in one piece. If it breaks, repeat the action.

Some recipes call for butterflied shrimp. After you remove the vein, just extend the cut you made a little deeper—but not all the way through—and spread the two halves open.

When you're done, rinse the shrimp to remove any sand or shell, pat them dry, and wash your hands thoroughly.

BRINING SHRIMP

Before you grill, plump shrimp with a quick swim in a brine. They really soak it up, and the extra moisture counteracts the drying effect of the grill.

For each pound of shrimp, add ¼ cup kosher salt to 1 cup warm water in a bowl and stir until it has dissolved. Pour in 2 cups cold water and then add the shrimp. Let it soak for about 20 minutes—but no longer. Drain and pat dry before grilling.

JOE'S FIREPROOF GRILLED SHRIMP

Joe Parajecki is a butcher I admire in Madison, Wisconsin. He's the operation manager of the Kettle Range Meat Company, but he also knows seafood. He cuts his shrimp shells down the back with scissors and removes the vein, leaving the shells on. He says, "Burnt shells, nobody cares. Burnt shrimp, everybody cares. The shells also keep moisture in. As you eat them, when you peel the shrimp, the smoky, garlicky oil gets on your fingers and then onto the shrimp."

MAKES *2 servings as a main dish*

TAKES *50 to 60 minutes*

1 pound shell-on large (at least 16/20 count) wild Gulf shrimp, split down the back and deveined (see page 342)

3 tablespoons olive oil

3 garlic cloves, crushed or minced

¼ teaspoon kosher salt

¼ teaspoon freshly ground black pepper

Minced fresh flat-leaf parsley, thyme, or cilantro, for garnish (optional)

1. Prep. Put the shrimp in a zipper-top bag and add the olive oil, garlic, salt, and pepper. Smoosh everything around to mix and coat the shrimp. Put the bag in the refrigerator to marinate for 15 or 20 minutes.

2. Fire up. Set up the grill in a two-zone configuration and get the direct zone up to medium-high. If your shrimp are small, you might want to use a grill topper.

3. Cook. Place the shrimp on the direct-heat side and cook for 2 to 3 minutes per side, until the meat is pearly white and opaque. If the grill flares up from dripping oil, move the shrimp to the indirect side for a few minutes.

4. Serve. Put the shrimp in a large bowl and garnish with the herbs, if desired. Serve immediately and let everyone peel their own.

CHAMPIONSHIP BACON-WRAPPED STUFFED SHRIMP

Melissa Cookston is one of the world's best competition barbecue cooks. Her team, Yazoo's Delta Q, based in Nesbitt, Missouri, has

won practically every major competition, including the Kingsford Invitational and Memphis in May, where she triumphed in the whole hog category for an unbelievable third year in a row. This recipe is inspired by her winning entry in the Kingsford Invitational the year I judged it.

MAKES *20 appetizer servings*

TAKES *about 1 hour*

20 shell-on large (16/20 count) shrimp, preferably wild Gulf shrimp

Kosher salt

3 jalapeños

20 bacon slices, preferably pepper crusted

1 (8-ounce) package cream cheese

Thai sweet chili sauce, such as Maggi Taste of Asia Mild Sweet Chili Sauce

Finely chopped fresh chives or flat-leaf parsley for garnish (optional)

1. Prep. Peel and devein the shrimp as described on page 342, but leave the tails on. Brine as described on page 343. Cut the tops off the jalapeños, split them in half, remove the seeds and veins, and slice each half into 4 strips.

2. Fire up. Set up the grill for two-zone cooking and shoot for about 325°F on the indirect side.

3. Cook. Roast the bacon right on the grates on the indirect side, lid closed, until it is about halfway done, perhaps 4 minutes. Don't overcook it. It must remain flexible. Remove from the grill and set aside on paper towels to drain until cool enough to handle.

4. Place a ¼-inch strip of cream cheese on each shrimp's back where the vein was. Top with a strip of jalapeño, wrap the whole thing with a strip of bacon, and hold it in place with 1 or 2 toothpicks.

5. Grill the bacon-wrapped shrimp on the indirect side of the grill with the lid closed until the shrimp are pink throughout and the bacon is done the way you like it.

6. Serve. Remove the shrimp, brush generously with Thai sweet chili sauce, garnish with some herbs if you wish, and serve.

LOBSTER

CHOOSING AND PREPARING LOBSTER

The lobsters sold in the United States are either cold-water lobsters or warm-water lobsters, and, although they taste similar, there is a big difference. Cold-water lobsters, sometimes known as Maine lobsters, are dark, usually black or brown but sometimes greenish, and have two large front claws. Many come from Maine, but some come from the cool waters farther down the coast.

Warm-water lobsters, sometimes called Florida lobsters, spiny lobsters, or rock lobsters,

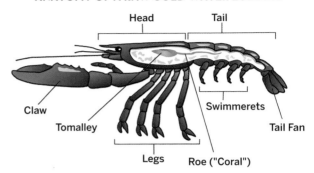

ANATOMY OF A RAW COLD-WATER LOBSTER

Head · Tail · Claw · Tomalley · Legs · Roe ("Coral") · Swimmerets · Tail Fan

usually come from the Caribbean or the Gulf of Mexico. Spiny lobsters don't have the big meaty claws of the cold-water specimens, and they tend to be tan or orange. They look more like humongous shrimp with really thick antennae. Use warm-water lobsters when you only need tails.

You want a cold-water lobster for this recipe because you want the toothsome claw meat.

Cold-water lobsters usually weigh 1½ to 2 pounds. A typical 1½-pound lobster will have less than 1 pound of raw tail and claw meat. Pick an animal that is lively—walking or swimming. A listless specimen with a curled tail and meat visible between the tail and the upper thoracic carapace is a bad choice. Don't worry if there is a little green algae in the lobster tank.

Live cold-water lobsters will have rubber bands on the large front claws. Leave them on until after the animals are dead unless you type with only two fingers like me. Always grasp a lobster from above by the solid shell on the upper half, never by the tail. There are some sharp edges on that tail that can gash you, even when the lobster is dead.

You should cook a live lobster the same day you get it, although it will stay alive and fresh in the fridge for 2 to 3 days if it has been handled well. Never submerge a saltwater lobster in fresh water. This will kill it. If you have to keep it a day or two, put it in a pot so it does not crawl around in the fridge, put about ¼ inch of water in the bottom to keep it moist, and cover it with a damp cloth or newspapers. Lobsters can breathe air, so they will be fine. *Do not cover with ice.*

GREG'S GRILLED LOBSTER

L obster is at its apex fresh from the grill. Yes, the dry heat makes it just a bit chewy but it is still plenty tender, and the concentrated flavors, undiluted by boiling water, are well worth

it. Best of all, grilled lobster is never mushy, as boiled lobster can be.

Leftover lobster meat is great on a sandwich with mayo, and it is especially good mixed into mac and cheese. Here's how Professor Blonder cooks his lobsters.

MAKES *2 servings*

TAKES *30 minutes*

3 tablespoons unsalted butter (see Note)
½ tablespoon olive oil
1 tablespoon minced fresh flat-leaf parsley
1 teaspoon chopped fresh tarragon or
   ½ teaspoon dried
1 teaspoon chopped fresh chives
¼ teaspoon kosher salt (see Note)
Freshly cracked black pepper
2 live Maine lobsters, each about 1½ pounds
2 lemon wedges (optional)

1. Prep. In a small saucepan, melt the butter over medium heat. Stir in the olive oil, parsley, tarragon, chives, salt, and pepper to taste. Let the flavors blend for a bit over low heat but be careful not to let the butter turn brown. Remove from the heat and cover to keep warm.

2. Kill the lobsters quickly and painlessly: Put a lobster in a baking pan or sheet pan facing you. Place the tip of a sharp, heavy chef's knife between the lobster's eyes about 1/2 inch behind them, with the sharp edge of the knife facing you. Plunge the knife all the way through the lobster's head and slice down, cutting the head right between the eyes, severing all major nerves. The lobster may twitch afterward, but it is dead, and because you've cut the nerves, it feels no pain. Flip it over with its legs in the air and cut the lobster in half along the midsection. Hold the lobster firmly so it doesn't slip on the work surface. Save any juices that emerge in the pan and mix them into the basting sauce. Repeat with the second lobster.

3. Remove the rubber bands from the claws. Scoop out any roe and tomalley from the head area. Roe, sometimes called coral, is a sac of eggs in female lobsters. It is dark green or black when fresh and turns reddish or orange when cooked. You may even find some in the tail if the female was laying. You can add them to the butter. The pale green tomalley is part of the digestive system. In 2008 the USDA issued a warning against eating it because it filters pollutants, including bacteria, from the water in which the lobster lived. Until our waters are cleaner, you should discard it.

4. Fire up. Preheat the grill for two-zone cooking with the direct-heat side on warp 10 (maximum). You'll be cooking with direct heat, and the indirect zone is your safe zone.

5. Cook. Place the lobsters, shell sides down, over direct heat. Position the shells between two rungs in the cooking grate to prevent the lobsters from rolling. You may have to manipulate the large claw or place two halves side by side to keep them from rolling. Some folks start them meat side down for a few minutes to get a bit more smoke flavor and some grill marks, but that tends to dry them out. Baste the meat with the butter sauce, close the lid, and baste once again after 3 to 4 minutes. When the meat in the thickest part of the tails is a minimum of 145°F and has changed from translucent to pearly white, perhaps 6 to 10 minutes, the lobsters are done. Baste one last time and remove them.

6. Serve. Crack open the claws with a wooden mallet, rolling pin, meat tenderizer, hammer, or kitchen shears. Serve them with any leftover butter for dunking, and squeeze the lemon wedges on the meat, if you wish. You can suck on the feathery gills and the small legs, or freeze them for making lobster bisque.

NOTE: If you use salted butter, cut the amount of salt in half. Remember, you can always add salt, but you can't take it away.

12
SIDES

or a tomato in half and rub it all over the surface before grilling. Sprinkle with salt and pepper.

2. Fire up. Heat the grill to medium-high.

3. Cook. Toast the bread slices on their oiled sides only, keeping the lid open and checking often. They can burn in a hurry. Sprinkle with some Parmigiano-Reggiano cheese if you like.

4. Serve. Transfer to a platter. Crostini are best warm, but still mighty good at room temperature.

SIMPLE GRILLED CROSTINI

Crostini make a dandy side for pastas and all manner of barbecue, and they especially shine with clams, oysters, and mussels, where they soak up the cooking liquid like a delectable sponge. Quality ingredients are essential.

MAKES *1 baguette*

TAKES *20 minutes*

- 1 fresh baguette or another loaf of crusty bread, cut into slices about ¾ inch thick
- High-quality extra-virgin olive oil
- Halved garlic clove or tomato, for rubbing (optional)
- Large-grain salt, such as Maldon
- Coarsely ground black pepper
- Parmigiano-Reggiano cheese, grated (optional)

1. Prep. Paint each slice of bread with olive oil. Be generous. Make sure you get it all the way to the edges or they will burn. Alternatively, you can pour oil in a plate and dip the cut side of the bread in it. If you want to amp up the crostini a bit, slice a garlic clove

GRILLED ASPARAGUS

Grilled asparagus develops rich flavors and a crunch you can't get from boiling or steaming. Asparagus is freshest, sweetest, and crispiest in spring. Look for spears with firm, closed tips (flowers) and select bunches with spears that are about the same diameter so they cook uniformly. Watch out for soft, mushy tips. Some folks think that skinny spears are best, but I've had fabulous fat asparagus, and the Michigan Asparagus Advisory Board says, "Larger diameter spears are more tender." So there. You can cook this dish ahead, as it is excellent at room temperature.

- 16 fresh asparagus stalks
- 1 tablespoon extra-virgin olive oil
- 1¼ teaspoons Simon & Garfunkel Rub (page 168)
- ¼ teaspoon kosher salt
- 4 ounces Parmigiano-Reggiano cheese
- 1 tablespoon balsamico condimento or balsamic reduction (see below)

1. Prep. If you have balsamico tradizionale or condimento, you can use it straight. If you have inexpensive salad-grade balsamic, then make a reduction as described in the sidebar below.

2. Chop off the woody bottoms of the asparagus spears, 1 to 3 inches. Lay the spears on a platter or in a pan, pour the oil over them, and roll them around until they are lightly covered. Sprinkle with the rub and the salt. Shave the cheese on the long shaving side of a box grater so you have wide ribbons and set it aside.

3. Fire up. Set up your grill for two-zone cooking and get it up to about 325°F on the indirect side.

ABOUT BALSAMIC

Remember about ten years ago when nobody had heard of balsamic vinegar? And now the grocery has scores of brands. Well, that's the problem. A lot of them are simply wine vinegar with sugar and caramel coloring. As a result, there's a good chance you've never tasted the real thing, which is hard to make, barrel-aged, and expensive. The real stuff comes only from Modena, Italy. The top of the line, *Aceto Balsamico Tradizionale Extra Vecchio,* is a blend and might average twenty-five years old. A 100 ml bottle (less than ½ cup) sells for about $150. *Aceto Balsamico Tradizionale Affinato* might average twelve years old and it sells for about $100. *Aceto Balsamico Condimento* is the best value at about $40 for 250 ml (about 1 cup). If you can afford it, get it.

The rest, *Balsamic Vinegar di Modena,* sell for about $1 an ounce and are labeled inconsistently and often fraudulently. For lack of a better name, let's call them salad-grade balsamic, although marinating-grade might be a better sobriquet. The first thing to know is that if it states an age on the bottle, it is a lie. It's against the law. And there is no such thing as white balsamico, raspberry balsamico, or any other flavor (although I must confess an affection for raspberry, no matter what is in there).

I recommend you go to your grocery and buy several varieties and taste them either on a spoon or on bread. Then take the ones you liked least and make a balsamic reduction by simmering it over a low burner until it reduces in half and you have a thick, sweet syrup. Be careful not to boil it or it can form a taffy-like candy. The syrup is very nice on salads and dishes like Grilled Asparagus (opposite). I keep a bottle on hand at all times.

4. Cook. Place the asparagus spears over direct heat. If you have a grill topper (see page 103), this is a good time to use it, otherwise arrange the spears at a right angle to the grill grates so they don't fall through. Cook the asparagus, lid on, until they get some brown spots on one side, about 5 minutes, roll them, and cook for only 2 to 3 minutes on the second side. A few char marks are OK, but don't blacken them. Stand by your grill. Bite into one near the base to make sure the doneness is the way you like it (I like it with a bit of crunch). Skinnier spears will finish first, so yank them off as soon as they bend when lifted by tongs.

5. Serve. Arrange the spears on a platter so they are all pointing in the same direction. Let them cool for about 5 minutes. Drizzle with the balsamic and top with the shaved cheese.

GRILLED CAULIFLOWER

Cauliflower doesn't get the respect it deserves. Most of us just steam or boil it. But I do it several ways: grill it as steaks, grill it as florets, even grill it and then puree it into a sauce or soup.

Grilled cauliflower is just fine on its own, but it adapts well to a variety of sauces. The fan-shaped grilled caulilflower steak shown above is lounging in a drizzle of my best olive oil. It also loves walnut oil, which brings out its nuttiness, and sometimes, for a treat, chopped hazelnuts. You can also top it with hollandaise sauce.

I have served chopped florets on pasta and in risotto. In the picture shown on the opposite page, florets accompany a grilled filet mignon topped with mashed potatoes and a rich roasted red pepper sauce.

MAKES *2 to 4 servings*

TAKES *40 minutes*

> 1 head cauliflower
> Kosher salt and freshly ground black pepper
> Olive oil
> Butter (optional)

1. Prep. Here's how to make the steaks: Because they need the stem to remain intact, you'll probably only get 2 to 4 steaks from a head. We'll use the rest for florets, discussed in a minute. Remove all leaves, and with a sharp knife, shave off any brown spots. Cut off the lower 1/8 inch of the stem. Stand the head stem side up and, with a long, sharp knife, cut straight down through the stem, making 2 to 4 fan-shaped steaks, 1/4 to 1/2 inch thick. Put them on a plate, salt and pepper them, and sprinkle them with oil.

2. With your hands, break the remainder of the head into florets. Put them in a bowl, salt and pepper them, and sprinkle with oil.

3. Fire up. Set up your grill for two-zone cooking and get it to about 325°F on the indirect side. Put a grill topper (see page 103) over the indirect side.

4. Cook. When the topper has warmed up, drizzle or spray some more oil on to prevent sticking and spread the florets onto the topper in one layer. Close the lid and cook until they are almost the desired tenderness, about 20 minutes. Then scoot the grill topper, florets and all, onto the direct side and finish them there for about 5 minutes, giving them some color, until they are the desired tenderness.

5. While the florets are cooking on the indirect side, place the cauliflower steaks on the direct side. Cook until they get some dark marks, perhaps 4 minutes, flip, and keep flipping until they are tender enough that a fork slides in easily.

6. Serve. You can simply serve the steaks or florets right off the grill, or top them with a drizzle of oil or melted butter.

THE ULTIMATE GRILLED CORN ON THE COB

The great bard Garrison Keillor said, "Sex is good, but not as good as fresh sweet corn," and in August, it is hard to disagree.

The best way to cook corn is on the grill. I'm not talking about the popular method of soaking the corn, husk and all, in water and then grilling it in the husk. Or wrapping it in foil. That is steamed corn, not grilled. Grilling corn does leave it a bit chewier than steaming, microwaving, or boiling it, but if you remove the husks, the sugars can caramelize, adding a depth of flavor no other method can produce.

While the corn is grilling, I paint it with tarragon butter for a hint of an exotic sweetness. Some of it gets between the kernels, but most of the butter drips off so the corn isn't the least bit greasy; it is buttery and so flavorful you won't want to put anything on it at tableside. This technique is really best on a gas grill, but you can use a charcoal grill if you control the heat.

I usually grill more corn than I can eat. I cool the leftover corn, cut the kernels off the cob with a sharp knife, and put it in the freezer. Grilled corn livens up a tomato salsa or cornbread, and it makes restaurant-grade corn soup. I like to mix grilled corn with chopped tomatoes, minced jalapeño, fresh tarragon, and thinly sliced red onion, then drizzle it with my best olive oil. It's a perfect August lunch.

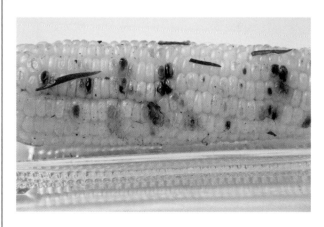

MAKES *4 ears*

TAKES *25 minutes to prepare and 20 minutes to cook*

- 4 ears very fresh sweet corn (Mirai is my current favorite)
- 4 tablespoons (½ stick) butter
- ¼ cup loosely packed fresh tarragon, minced (see Note)

1. Prep. Remove the husks from the corn and pull off all the silky threads. Wash the ears in cold water.

2. Melt the butter in a small saucepan over medium-low heat. Add the tarragon to the butter. Reduce the heat to very low and let the tarragon infuse the butter for at least 15 minutes.

3. Fire up. Set up your grill for two-zone cooking and get the direct-heat side to medium-hot.

4. Cook. Put the corn on the direct-heat side of the grill. Rest the ears between the bars of the grates so you can roll them from groove to groove. Paint them lightly on the top with the tarragon butter, making sure to get some bits of tarragon on the corn. Try not to let too much butter drip onto the fire or it will cause flare-ups, which will coat the corn in soot. If there is a flare-up, move the corn away. Close the lid and grill until some of the kernels get toasty golden to brown, about 5 minutes per side. Roll the ears a couple of grooves, about a quarter turn, and paint them again. Keep browning, turning, and painting until you have done all four quarters.

5. Serve. You can put butter and salt on the table, but urge your guests to taste their corn unadulterated first. Chances are, they won't use any more butter or salt.

NOTE: You can use other herbs such as thyme, oregano, rosemary, or basil, but tarragon is by far my favorite. And yes, you can use dried herbs. Remember, they are more concentrated, so use about half the amount of fresh.

CHIPOTLE-LIME CORN ON THE COB

Toward the end of summer, as corn goes past its peak, or if I find some ears in the back of the fridge that have been there for a week, I like to give them some help.

MAKES *2 ears*

TAKES *30 minutes*

- ½ lime
- 2 tablespoons unsalted butter
- 1 teaspoon adobo sauce from a can of chipotle in adobo
- ¼ teaspoon kosher salt
- 2 ears corn, husked

1. Prep. Scrub the lime thoroughly. Zest it into a small bowl. In a small saucepan, melt the butter over medium heat. Stir in the adobo sauce, lime zest, and salt and simmer on low for about 3 minutes. Turn off the heat.

2. Fire up. Set up your grill for two-zone cooking and get it medium-hot on the direct-heat side.

3. Cook. Place the corn over direct heat, close the lid, and check the corn in about 2 minutes. As the kernels begin to darken, roll the corn a quarter turn

and repeat until all sides are golden with a few brown spots. Move the corn to the indirect side and paint it all over with the chipotle butter. Don't paint it over direct heat or there could be flare-ups and soot. It should only take about 5 minutes per side, depending on how hot your grill is.

4. Serve. Transfer the corn to a platter for serving. Put the remaining chipotle butter in a cup on the table so people can add more if they wish.

GRILLED ROMAINE SALAD

Yep. You can grill your salad. And when you do, you get the same effect as when you grill most anything else: You amp up the flavors. Romaine is perfect for the job because when you cut the heads in half, the stems are tenacious enough to hold each half together, but the leaves are loosely packed so the dressing can get in between them.

MAKES *4 servings*

TAKES *30 minutes*

LEMON-BASIL DRESSING

> ¾ cup olive oil
>
> ¼ cup red wine vinegar
>
> 24 fresh medium basil leaves
>
> Zest and juice of 1 lemon
>
> ½ teaspoon sugar
>
> Kosher salt and freshly ground black pepper

SALAD

> 12–16 cherry tomatoes, halved
>
> Kosher salt and freshly ground black pepper

> 2 heads romaine lettuce, cut in half lengthwise, rinsed and patted dry
>
> 4 ounces blue cheese, crumbled
>
> ½ cup candied or roasted pecans (see Note)

1. Prep. To make the dressing, add all the ingredients except the salt and pepper to a blender or food processor and puree. Season with salt and pepper.

2. To make the salad, season the tomato halves with salt and pepper and set aside. Paint the outsides of the romaine halves with some of the dressing. Set the remaining dressing aside for serving.

3. Fire up. Set up your grill for two-zone cooking and get the direct side to medium-hot.

4. Cook. Put the romaine halves on the direct-heat side of the grill and cook, lid up, until the edges of the leaves get dark. Turn the halves as they cook to brown both sides.

5. Serve. Place each romaine half on a plate. Divide the blue cheese, pecans, and tomatoes between the plates and finish with a generous drizzle of the dressing.

NOTE: If you can't get candied nuts, toast some walnuts in a dry skillet over medium heat until they start to darken and get fragrant, about 5 minutes.

3 tablespoons tahini (see Notes)
3 tablespoons fresh lemon juice
1 teaspoon kosher salt
Sweet paprika, for garnish (optional)
Finely chopped fresh cilantro or flat-leaf
    parsley, for garnish (optional)

1. Prep. Peel the eggplants completely and remove the stems. Halve them lengthwise and then cut them into thick half-moons. In a bowl, toss the pieces of eggplant with ¼ cup of the olive oil.

2. Fire up. Set up your grill for two-zone cooking. Get the direct-heat side medium-hot. You will cook with direct heat, and the indirect zone is your safe zone.

3. Cook. Place the eggplant pieces over direct heat and cook, lid down, until they get some brown spots and grill marks. Flip and cook the other side. The interior should be soft and custardlike. As each piece is finished, transfer it to a platter.

4. Toss the pitas right on the grill grates and toast them up until they're nice and crispy, then remove them from the grill and cut them into wedges.

5. In a small skillet, combine 2 tablespoons of the olive oil, the garlic, harissa powder, and garam masala and cook over low heat for 2 to 3 minutes. Transfer to a blender or food processor, add the grilled eggplant, tahini, lemon juice, and salt and puree until smooth. Taste and adjust the seasonings.

6. Serve. Spoon the dip into your favorite serving bowl, garnish with paprika and fresh herbs, if desired, and serve with the toasted pita wedges.

NOTES: Harissa is a blend of chile peppers, garlic, coriander, and other spices, sometimes sold as a powder and sometimes as a paste. It is available in better grocery stores or in Middle Eastern stores. In a pinch, you can substitute American chili powder.

Garam masala is a popular spice blend from India, typically made with peppercorns, cumin,

FIRE-ROASTED EGGPLANT BABA GHANOUSH

Baba ghanoush is a classic Middle Eastern dip made from roasted eggplant. It belongs at your next party. Intensify the flavors by roasting the eggplant on the grill. This version is lighter and fluffier than most. Fresh pita wedges make a classic accompaniment, or serve with chunks of fresh vegetables like carrots, celery, broccoli, or Grilled Cauliflower (page 352).

MAKES *1 ½ to 2 cups*

TAKES *45 minutes*

   1½ pounds eggplant
   6 tablespoons olive oil
   6 (8-inch) pitas
   3 garlic cloves, minced or pressed
   ½ teaspoon harissa powder (see Notes)
   ½ teaspoon garam masala (see Notes)

cinnamon, clove, nutmeg, bay leaf, and cardamom.

Tahini is a paste of crushed sesame seeds and is available in most grocery stores (check the international foods aisle) or Middle Eastern stores.

SMOKED POTATO SALAD

Yes, there are a bazillion ways to make potato salad, but this recipe ups the ante by smoking the potatoes. You can also use your favorite potato salad recipe and replace those plain ol' boring boiled potatoes with these smoked potatoes.

MAKES *8 servings*

TAKES *1 ½ hours*

POTATOES

10 small red potatoes, peels left on, chopped into bite-size pieces

Kosher salt

3 tablespoons cooking oil

DRESSING

¼ cup finely chopped onion

2 celery stalks, finely chopped

2 tablespoons sweet pickle relish

1 cup mayonnaise

2 tablespoons Dijon mustard

¼ cup chopped fresh flat-leaf parsley

¼ teaspoon dried dill

Zest and juice of ½ lemon

½ teaspoon sugar

½ teaspoon garlic powder

½ teaspoon kosher salt

¼ teaspoon coarsely ground black pepper

1. Prep. To make the potatoes, place them in a saucepan and add cold water to cover them by at least ½

inch. Add 2 pinches of salt. Fill a large bowl with ice and water and set it nearby. Bring the water in the saucepan to a boil and cook the potatoes until they hit about 150°F in the center. You do not want to cook them all the way through. Test more than one chunk. Drain and cool them immediately in the ice water. Drain them again after they've cooled for about 15 minutes, then transfer to a bowl and coat them lightly with the oil.

2. Fire up. Get your smoker up to 225°F or set up the grill for two-zone cooking and shoot for about 225°F on the indirect side. Place a grill topper (see page 103) in the indirect zone and lightly oil it. Add wood and get some smoke rolling.

3. Cook. Gently slide the potatoes onto the topper and space them out so they do not overlap. Close the lid and smoke the potatoes for about 45 minutes, then transfer them to a platter and let cool to room temperature. You can smoke them a day ahead.

4. To make the dressing, in a serving bowl, whisk together the dressing ingredients. Fold in the potatoes, trying not to smush them. Taste and adjust the seasonings. Stash the salad in your fridge for a couple of hours before serving to let the flavors meld; overnight is even better.

5. Serve. Remove the salad from the fridge 30 minutes before serving to let it warm slightly.

BAKED POTATOES ARE BEST ON THE GRILL

When baking a potato, we are faced with a food whose center and surface need separate treatment, just like meat. We want a soft, moist, fluffy inside and a dry, crisp skin. Once again, a two-zone setup and reverse sear are the solutions.

Amazingly, I have never seen a website or cookbook that tells you what doneness temperature is optimal for a baked potato. Here's a guide: 205°F for al dente, a bit crunchy; 208°F for crumbly; and 212°F for fluffy.

MAKES *2 servings*

TAKES *1 hour 45 minutes*

  1 russet Burbank potato (¾ to 1 pound; see Note, page 360)
  2 teaspoons kosher salt
  2 teaspoons Meathead's Memphis Dust (page 167)
  4 tablespoons (½ stick) butter, melted

1. Prep. With a brush or scrub sponge devoid of soap, scrub the potato skin to remove all dirt, but not so hard as to remove the skin. Cut out any bad spots. Slice the potato in half lengthwise. Sniff it carefully. Nothing is worse than a musty potato.

2. While the potato is wet, generously sprinkle salt all over and press it in. Then sprinkle on the spice rub. Let sit at room temperature for 15 to 30 minutes, so the salt will dissolve and begin migrating toward the center.

HOW TO GUSSY UP THE HUMBLE SPUD

Purists use only butter or sour cream, with salt and pepper and perhaps a sprinkling of chopped fresh chives or green onions. Or you can go the cheese route, with a few dollops of Boursin, pimento cheese spread, fresh chèvre, crumbled blue cheese, or shredded cheddar.

The more adventurous will use Mexican crema, crème fraîche, or horseradish sauce. Some will add broccoli florets, fresh thyme, fresh dill, fresh basil, candied jalapeños, bacon, lobster, shrimp, pulled pork, chopped brisket, hot dog chili, Genovese pesto, tomato salsa, caramelized onions, or chopped hard-boiled eggs with chopped onions. Caviar and hard-boiled eggs are another classic. Go crazy!

Here's one of my all-time favorites: splashes of malt vinegar. That's right, just plain malt vinegar, no dairy. Tons of flavor, zero calories. If you've ever been to England, you've tasted fish and chips with malt vinegar. Balsamic or sherry vinegar work, too, but not nearly as well as malt.

3. Fire up. Set up your grill for two-zone cooking and shoot for 325°F in the indirect zone.

4. Cook. Put the potato halves on the indirect-heat side of the grill and let them bake, cut side up, lid down, for about 90 minutes, until the temperature in the center is 10 to 15°F below your target. The edges, which are thinner, will be a little hotter. If you are in a hurry, you can precook them in the microwave for 5 minutes on high. Cooking on the grill will take as little as 30 minutes after microwaving.

5. Paint the potatoes all over with melted butter. Move them to the direct-heat side, cut side down, and let the cut sides toast, lid down, for about 3 minutes until they start to get golden. Don't continue painting them if you want crispy skins. Roll them over and brown the skin sides.

6. Serve. Remove the potato halves from the grill, mash the insides with a fork, and gussy them up if you like (see sidebar, opposite).

TWICE-BAKED POTATOES

Mashed potatoes enrobed in melted cheese lounging in a gondola of chewy potato skins? Why hasn't the inventor of this dish gotten the Nobel Prize? The only way to improve on it is to smoke the potatoes!

MAKES *6 servings (½ potato each)*

TAKES *90 minutes*

　　3 russet Burbank potatoes (each ¾ to
　　　　1 pound) (see Note)
　　1 teaspoon kosher salt
　　1 teaspoon Simon & Garfunkel Rub (page 168)
　　½ cup sour cream
　　¼ cup shredded cheddar cheese

Paprika or ground chipotle and chopped fresh chives, for garnish

1. Prep. Scrub the potatoes clean enough to eat. I like to use a scrub sponge that has absolutely no soap in it. While the skins are wet, sprinkle them with the salt. Let them sit at room temperature for about 15 minutes so the salt can dissolve and move into the skin and beyond.

2. Fire up. Set up your grill for two-zone cooking and get the indirect side up to about 325°F. Throw a small amount of wood on the flames, about a handful, for smoke.

3. Cook. Bake the potatoes until they are 208 to 212°F, about 90 minutes. You can cut the baking time down to about 30 minutes if you microwave the potatoes for about 5 minutes on high before grilling them.

4. Wearing a heavy glove, grip each potato and cut it in half lengthwise. Scoop out the innards, leaving at least ¼ inch of flesh all around to reinforce the skin. Place the potato flesh in a bowl, add the rub and sour cream, and mix with a fork, leaving it a little lumpy. Don't use a blender or you will end up with a plasticky paste. Spoon the mixture back into the potato skins or, if you want to be fancy, use a piping bag.

5. Sprinkle the filling with cheese and put the potato halves back on the grill, filled side up, over direct heat and close the lid. Grill until the skin begins to darken and the cheese melts.

6. Serve. Sprinkle with the paprika and chives and serve immediately.

NOTE: Burbanks are the standard baking potato. If you pile the filling high when you put it back into the skins, you might have a couple of skins left. You can eat them straight, or they can be frozen and later filled with chili, bacon and cheese, or pulled pork (page 202).

GRILLED POLENTA

In Italy, they call their grits "polenta," a gluten-free grainy corn porridge that is served with breakfast, lunch, and supper. Although there are minor differences, you can buy either grits or polenta and use them interchangeably. Both are made from dried corn, ground into tiny nuggets. Purists prefer stone-ground, but you can use quick-cooking polenta or grits for this recipe if you wish.

Grits/polenta contain a small amount of

natural corn oil, so they should be used when fresh or stored in the refrigerator, or else they can go rancid.

If you wish, add 2 teaspoons of fresh herbs about 1 minute before you turn off the heat. (I like thyme, rosemary, or sage.) If you use dried herbs, use only 1 teaspoon and add them 15 minutes before turning off the heat. You can also add chopped chiles or bell peppers, or kernels of grilled corn. New York City chef Mario Batali likes to top his with sautéed spinach and cheese. Or serve polenta the way they serve hush puppies in central Florida, with a trail of honey.

Start this recipe the day before.

MAKES *4 servings*

TAKES *1 hour and 20 minutes to make the polenta, 6 hours to chill, 20 minutes to grill*

- 1 cup polenta or grits, preferably stone-ground
- 4 tablespoons (½ stick) unsalted butter, plus more for grilling the polenta and serving
- ¼ teaspoon kosher salt, plus more for serving
- ½ cup finely grated Parmigiano-Reggiano cheese (see Note)
- Olive oil
- Freshly ground black pepper

1. Prep. Bring 4 cups water to a rolling boil on the stove top. Use a nonstick pot if you have one. Add the polenta slowly, stirring all the while. Turn the heat down to medium. Let the polenta bubble and gurgle for about 10 minutes. Turn the heat to the lowest setting, add the butter, and cook for 1 hour, stirring occasionally to make sure it doesn't stick to the bottom. Add the salt and cheese and stir well to combine. When the polenta is done (taste it—it should be tender and not crunchy), remove from the heat and let cool slightly.

2. Meanwhile, grease the inside of an 8-inch square pan with olive oil. When the polenta has cooled a bit, scrape it into the pan. Refrigerate the polenta for 6 hours or overnight, uncovered, so it can dry and get firm. The next day, cut the chilled polenta into rectangles.

3. Fire up. Set up your grill for two-zone cooking and get the direct-heat side moderately hot.

4. Cook. Paint the polenta rectangles with a light coating of olive oil or melted butter and warm them over indirect heat for about 10 minutes, then move them to the direct-heat side, lid open, and grill them until golden.

5. Serve. Sprinkle the polenta rectangles with salt and pepper at the table and dress them with a pat of butter.

NOTE: Please use real Parmigiano-Reggiano from Italy. It is so much better than the American versions.

BOSTON BARBECUE BEANS

They don't call it Beantown for naught, for it was in Boston that the notion of mixing beans with molasses was probably conceived, and this practice still reaches the peak of perfection there.

The original Boston baked beans were baked in an earthenware pot. They were sweetened with molasses, but the beans were not as sweet as you might expect them to be. Your kids probably would not like the traditional recipe, because the dominant taste is, well, beans. So I have kicked things up a bit to make it Boston Barbecue Beans. The secret is to cook them underneath a slab of ribs or pork butt so they catch the flavorful rub-laden drippings. The kids as well as Gramps will love these.

MAKES *4 servings*

TAKES *3 to 4 hours to cook*

> 2 slabs baby back ribs
>
> 6 thick bacon slices or ¼ pound pork fatback
>
> 1 large onion, coarsely chopped
>
> 2 (15-ounce) cans navy or pea beans, rinsed and drained
>
> ¼ cup dark molasses
>
> ¼ cup KC Classic (page 175), plus more for the ribs
>
> 1 tablespoon Dijon mustard
>
> 1 bay leaf
>
> ½ teaspoon kosher salt
>
> ¼ teaspoon freshly ground black pepper
>
> 1 teaspoon fresh lemon juice (optional)
>
> Diced fresh jalapeños (optional)

1. Prep. Prepare the baby backs as directed for Last-Meal Ribs (page 206). Remove the membrane, trim, salt, and rub them.

2. Fire up. Get your smoker up to 225°F or set up the grill for two-zone cooking and shoot for about 225°F on the indirect side. Warm a 9-by-13-inch pan on the direct-heat side.

3. Cook. Put the bacon in the pan and cook until browned on both sides. Remove the bacon before it is hard and crunchy and set aside. When it cools, chop it into ½-inch chunks. Pour off all but 1 tablespoon of the fat from the pan and save it in the fridge for another day.

4. Add the onion to the fat remaining in the pan and cook until it is limp but not brown. Add 2 cups hot water and then the beans, molasses, barbecue sauce, mustard, bay leaf, salt, pepper, and the cooked bacon. Stir thoroughly and scrape up any browned bits from the bottom of the pan.

5. Move the pan of beans to the indirect side and put the ribs on a rack above them. Start the smoke rolling by adding wood, close the lid, and let the beans catch the drippings while the meat cooks.

6. Stir the beans occasionally, scraping the bottom of the pan to prevent things from sticking and burning. If one side is overcooking, turn the pan. Cooking time will be 3 to 4 hours, depending on the ribs, the temperature of your grill, and the weather. If the beans begin to dry out, add some water. Just before serving, taste them and add salt and pepper to taste, barbecue sauce, water, or more molasses. Stir in the lemon juice and/or the jalapeños, if desired.

7. Serve. Finish the ribs by painting them with barbecue sauce and sizzling them on the direct-heat side. Serve with the beans and other sides of your choice.

SWEET-SOUR SLAW

There are two kinds of slaw, and the rivalry is as savage as Auburn vs Alabama. Sweet-sour is vinegar and sugar based. Creamy is mayo or sour cream or buttermilk based (or a blend). This sweet-sour is simple and quick. If you prefer creamy, check out page 364.

MAKES *8 small servings*
TAKES *30 minutes*

DRESSING
- 2 tablespoons brown sugar
- 1 tablespoon granulated sugar
- 1 teaspoon mustard powder
- ½ teaspoon kosher salt
- ½ teaspoon freshly ground black pepper
- ½ teaspoon celery seeds
- ¼ cup distilled white vinegar
- 2 tablespoons vegetable oil

SLAW
- 1 pound green cabbage (about ½ medium cabbage)
- 1 large carrot, peeled
- 1 small white onion
- ½ bell pepper (any color)
- Radishes or a small jalapeño, if you like a jab of heat (optional)

1. To make the dressing, in a bowl large enough for the whole shootin' match, whisk together all the dressing ingredients. Be sure to whisk out all the lumps.

2. To make the slaw, chop the cabbage, carrot, onion, pepper, and radishes (see sidebar below). Add the vegetables to the bowl with the dressing and mix. Taste and add more of the seasonings to your preference. When you serve the slaw, mix thoroughly and scoop from the bottom so the veggies have dressing on them.

PREPPING CABBAGE FOR SLAW

The first step is to decide how you want to cut the cabbage, carrots, pepper, and onions: chopped, grated, or hashed. Whichever method, I like to serve the slaw soon after preparation, before the cabbage starts to release its water. Yes, I know *Cook's Illustrated* recommends salting the ingredients and letting them sit a while in a strainer to draw out the water, but I don't want to throw out all that juice. Plus, the salting technique can result in salty slaw.

CHOPPED (AKA COUNTRY-STYLE). This is hand cutting, my favorite method. Chopping produces an uneven slice that is larger and crunchier than with the other methods and lets the cabbage flavor come through. It also releases less water because there are fewer cut surfaces. Cut the head in half or quarters, lay it cut side down on a cutting board, and cut it into ⅛-inch-thick slices, working from one end to the other. Then cut across the slices once or twice (see photo).

GRATED (AKA SHREDDED). This method produces pieces that are more uniform in size and texture. Use the large holes on a box grater (watch your knuckles) or the shredding attachment on a food processor. The picture accompanying the recipe for Sweet-Sour Slaw on the opposite page shows a grated slaw.

HASHED (AKA CONFETTI). Hashing is mincing the slaw finely into ⅛-inch shards, usually with the shredding blade of a food processor, although you can get there with a box grater or knives or cleavers. This method is very popular in the southeast, especially in places where the slaw is served on top of pulled pork sandwiches and hot dogs. I'm not a fan of hashing because the leaves lose a lot of liquid and the results can be runny. The picture accompanying the recipe for Classic Deli Slaw with Sour Cream and Mayo on page 364 shows a hash.

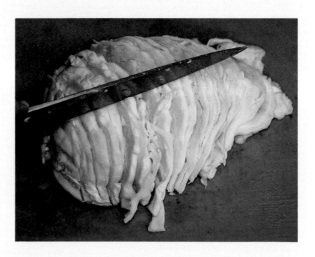

CLASSIC DELI SLAW WITH SOUR CREAM AND MAYO

This is the slaw you get at delis and diners: usually hashed, creamy, slightly sweet and sour, wet but not too runny. The secret to the best is using both sour cream and mayo. The slaw is a great accompaniment that will put out the fire of hot barbecue sauces. A fine counterpoint to vinegar-based sauces, it makes the perfect topping for vinegary East Carolina–type pulled pork sandwiches.

You can also add two tart apples, like Granny Smith. This gives a hidden flavor dimension that people will appreciate but have trouble identifying. In Florida some places add 1 cup chopped (pea-size) fresh (not canned) pineapple. Or substitute about 3 tablespoons concentrated apple juice for the sugar. I also like to add a fennel bulb. A minced jalapeño gives a nice contrast, and horseradish, just a tablespoon in the background, is a surprisingly good addition.

MAKES *8 small servings*

TAKES *30 minutes to prepare, 1 hour or more to chill*

DRESSING

- ¼ cup sour cream
- ¼ cup mayonnaise
- 3 tablespoons sweet pickle relish
- 1 tablespoon sugar
- 1 tablespoon distilled white vinegar
- ¼ teaspoon mustard powder
- ¼ teaspoon white pepper
- ½ teaspoon celery seed
- ¼ teaspoon kosher salt

SLAW

- 1 pound green cabbage (about ½ medium cabbage)
- 1 large carrot, peeled
- ½ bell pepper, green, red, yellow, or orange, (your choice), cored and stemmed
- ½ small onion

1. To make the dressing, in a large bowl, whisk together all the dressing ingredients.

2. To make the slaw, cut the vegetables so you can feed them into your food processor. Shred them using the fine grating disk or grate them on the small holes of a box grater to create a fine hash.

3. Add the vegetables to the bowl with the dressing and mix thoroughly. Adjust the seasonings to your taste. Chill for at least 1 hour and serve.

SPECIAL THANKS

I have been very lucky, and much of that luck is due to the help of some really talented people to whom thanks is an inadequate word.

PROFESSOR GREG BLONDER, PH.D. Greg is an amazing polymath and the science advisor to this book and AmazingRibs.com. Greg attended MIT as an undergraduate and has a Ph.D. in physics from Harvard. He has served as chief technical advisor at AT&T's legendary Bell Labs, he holds more than eighty patents, and he is currently a professor of design and manufacturing at Boston University. His love of food, especially barbecue, brought him to culinary science research, some of which appears in this book. His kitchen-science research and more can be found at genuineideas.com.

SALLY EKUS, Agent Extraordinaire, The Lisa Ekus Group. Sally is my negotiator, taskmistress, consultant, shrink, and favorite jalapeño. What an honor to be invited to join her family of distinguished authors and work with the effective and efficient LEG staff.

JERRY GOLDWYN, Inspiration. Dad grilled and he let me watch. He was also a serial entrepreneur, with a degree in food technology, so in more ways than one, I am a chip off the old block.

NORMA GOLDWYN. One of the fringe benefits of having a retired schoolteacher for a mom is that she will gladly underline all the spelling and grammar errors in red and tell you how wrong you are.

MAX GOOD, Director of Equipment Reviews and Keeper of the Flame, AmazingRibs.com. Max is the man in charge of finding the best products for the huge equipment reviews section on AmazingRibs.com, and he keeps me informed on the latest grills and smokers.

DAVID JOACHIM, Editor of my first draft. David is the author or co-author of many cookbooks, among them *Fire It Up: More Than 400 Recipes for Grilling Everything* by Andrew Schloss and David Joachim. He tightened, focused, and helped make this book flow.

LISA KOLEK, Illustrator. How lucky can a writer get? My neighbor is an accomplished artist, and she is responsible for the polished illustrations that explain the concepts in these pages.

SARAHLYNN PABLO, Assistant Editor, AmazingRibs.com. When the load got heavy, she carried more than her share.

CHEF RYAN UDVETT, Test Kitchen Director. Ryan is my closest collaborator and a great coworker. He is excellent at fixing problems in my recipes. Several of these recipes began as his formulations.

RUX MARTIN, Editor at Houghton Mifflin Harcourt, and her team. Rux has welcomed me to her prestigious stable of cookbook authors, including such luminaries as Jacques Pépin, Dorie Greenspan, Bruce Aidells, and Mollie

Katzen. She really worked hard to make this a better book.

REBECCA SPRINGER, HMH Managing Editor. Her knowledge, patience, effort, and care were indispensable to this book. She was assisted by Allison Rottman and Jacinta Monniere.

MELISSA LOTFY, HMH Art Director, and **JILL LAZER**, HMH Production VP. They saw this book through from the beginning to the end.

ENDPAPER STUDIO. They are responsible for the bold and polished look of my book.

INSPIRATIONS

ALTON BROWN, my paragon and inspiration. When I grow up, I want to be like him.

MELISSA CLARK of the *New York Times* often inspires me. She has such a love of food and cooking it right.

J. KENJI LÓPEZ-ALT of SeriousEats.com and author of *The Food Lab: Better Home Cooking Through Science*. He thinks about food the same way I do, never accepting conventional wisdom without testing it first.

HAROLD MCGEE, PH.D., food scientist and author whose seminal volume *On Food and Cooking: The Science and Lore of the Kitchen* made me hunger for the whys and hows that led to this volume.

JERRY N. UELSMANN and **JOHN PAUL CAPONIGRO**, my mentors, muses, and guides to the worlds of art, photography, and creativity.

OTHERS TO WHOM I AM INDEBTED

I have benefitted from the help of scores of people more knowledgeable than me, and I could fill pages naming them all. Here are a few: Sterling Ball, Brigit Binns, Ardie "Remus Powers" Davis, Stephen Gerike, Paul Huntsberger, James Maivald, Antonio Mata, Chef Etienne Merle, Marietta Sims, Barry Sorkin, and Carolyn Wells.

THE HELPFUL LIBRARIANS I have met at the many libraries I have visited over the years. They are uniformly the most helpful, friendly professionals you can imagine.

THE MANY CHEFS who have let me pick their brains.

DOCTORS BRADLEY CLIFFORD, JEFFREY SCHWARTZ, LOWELL STEEN JR., and their teams at Loyola University Health System. I am alive because of them.

YOU. I am especially indebted to the readers of AmazingRibs.com who have questioned, commented, spell-checked, and criticized. They have helped me fill the gaps in my writing with their questions. As Dad said, "Praise is cheap, but criticism is priceless."

AND SPECIAL THANKS to the gods of grape, grain, and fire who have watched over me so far.

Index